W9-BEZ-745

European competitiveness report
2004

Commission staff working document

SEC(2004)1397

European
Commission

*Europe Direct is a service to help you find answers
to your questions about the European Union*

Freephone number:

00 800 6 7 8 9 10 11

This publication has been prepared by Unit B2, Competitiveness and Economic Reforms, DG Enterprise and Industry. For further information contact entr-competit-benchmarkg@cec.eu.int

A great deal of additional information on the European Union is available on the Internet.
It can be accessed through the Europa server (http://europa.eu.int).

Cataloguing data can be found at the end of this publication.

Luxembourg: Office for Official Publications of the European Communities, 2004

ISBN 92-894-8227-3

Table of Contents

Chapter 3:

Performance in the EU Health Sector 113

Chapter 4:

Chapter 5:

The Challenge to the EU of a Rising Chinese Economy 235

Executive Summary

This is the eighth edition of the Commission's Report on European Competitiveness since the 1994 Industry Council Resolution that established the basis for the Competitiveness Report. As in recent editions, competitiveness in this Report is understood to mean a sustained rise in the standards of living of a nation and as low a level of involuntary unemployment possible.

The special theme of this Report concerns the impact of public policies on economic performance. Both because of its size and of its involvement in economic life the public sector exerts an important influence on economic performance. The first three Chapters of the Report review the impact of the public sector on productivity growth, the role of public sector funding in research and development and the performance of the health sector, a key component of the public sector. The following, Chapter 4, reviews recent developments in the European automotive sector, a key sector in Europe's industrial structure, where government regulation is significant and where competitiveness improvements have been realized in recent years. The final, Chapter 5, discusses the growing integration of China in the world economy and its implications for the European economy. These implications are most pronounced in the case of the new Member States which are increasingly competing with Chinese exports.

Productivity Growth and the Public Sector

Public policies play a key role in shaping competitiveness and growth in an economy. The effects of public policies on productivity come about both via productivity growth in the public sector and via the effects of public policies – taxation, public spending and regulations – on the private sector. Chapter 1 discusses the effects of public policies on productivity mainly by means of a literature review.

Public sector activities carry a large weight in the overall output of an economy: public employment accounts for between 10 % (Germany) and 30 % (Sweden) of all jobs in EU-15 Member States. Labour productivity within the public sector is thus a major determinant of average labour productivity at the national level.

Difficulties in the measurement if public sector output as well as the lack of internationally harmonised data often inhibit comparisons of public sector productivity across countries. Available studies suggest that there is scope for further improvements in *public sector efficiency* in the EU, and that the current public sector output could be achieved at a significantly smaller cost. There is also some evidence suggesting that smaller governments are more efficient, pointing to the existence of declining marginal products of public spending beyond a given size of government.

Reforms in the public sector are often a response to pressures to curb public spending, seek to raise economic growth or aim at introducing innovations which are already in use in the private sector, such as information technology. Chapter 1 identifies three types of reforms that have been applied by many EU countries in order to enhance the efficiency in the public sector: (i) management reforms; (ii) introduction of information technology; and (iii) privatisation and outsourcing. Empirical research suggests that privatisation is usually associated with increased efficiency, profitability and capital investment spending.

Taxation is necessary in order to finance governments. Empirical research on the relationship between the overall tax ratio (total taxes to GDP) and GDP growth has not yielded conclusive results. However, there is plenty of empirical evidence on the distortive effects of specific taxes. High taxes on labour are found to affect labour market participation as well the willingness to acquire skills and human capital. High taxation also acts as a brake on entrepreneurship, although some authors argue that the incentive effects may not be very large. International differences in taxation affect foreign direct investment flows and may affect productivity growth in catch-up countries which rely on foreign investors to acquire new technologies and modern management methods.

Government spending on areas such as education, research and development or infrastructure, affects the production possibilities and costs of private enterprises. Government spending is thus a determinant of competitiveness and affects the location decisions of international enterprises. Available empirical evidence suggests that government spending has generally a positive impact on economic performance; however, evidence on the net effect of government spending on the economy remains inconclusive suggesting that there may be cases where the resources would have been in a more productive use in the private sector.

Cross-country studies investigating the role of public capital in explaining productivity growth differentials provide no clear conclusions: while many studies find a positive impact, the effect is often not significant. Recent studies on the impact of public infrastructures on productivity find either no significant impact or a small positive impact for the US, while the estimated impact is higher and mostly significant for European countries. Moreover, some studies point to decreasing marginal returns of public infrastructures, but no such evidence is found for European countries.

Research has established a link between human capital and productivity. However, the results are more ambiguous as to the extent to which governments should subsidise the educational system. For both education and research and development (R&D), the case for government involvement is often based on the existence of externalities: such investments have larger benefits to society than an individual or enterprise can appropriate, thus leaving private investments at a sub-optimal level.

There is econometric evidence suggesting that research performed by governments and universities could have a stronger impact on productivity growth than business R&D, but by far the largest productivity effect comes from the absorption of the results of foreign R&D. The extent to which

public research can strengthen productivity growth depends also on the exploitation of the results in the business sector. Finally, some studies conclude that public R&D has to some extent taken the place of private research rather than adding to it; however, most available studies do not find such substitution effects.

Regulations may promote objectives such as social goals, consumer protection or the quality of environment. At the same time, regulations limit the choices which individuals and enterprises can make; and compliance with regulations usually involves costs. The productivity effects of regulations come as a by-product and are often hard to measure in quantitative terms.

A significant part of research focuses on the role of product market regulation, market entry and competition policies. Regulations which inhibit competition are found to have a negative effect on productivity mainly because they slow down the technological catch-up. On the other hand, regulations adopted at EU level can have the beneficial effect of creating a level playing field for all participants in the market. The largest productivity effects of liberalisation measures have been found in services which have traditionally been most heavily regulated, in particular network industries such as telecommunications, postal services, electricity, gas, railways and air transport. The EU, in particular in comparison to the US, is seen to place a relatively heavy regulatory burden on enterprises. It has been suggested that an increase in competition in product and labour markets to US levels could raise euro area GDP by even as much as 12 %.

A large number of studies have identified negative productivity effects linked to environmental regulations. The results are however disputed by others who argue that adjustment to environmental regulations can lead enterprises to discover more cost-effective production methods, with the cost savings offsetting the initial compliance cost of the regulations. Finally, sector- or industry-specific regulations may play an important role in influencing productivity growth in individual industries, but a closer analysis of their impacts falls outside the scope of this Report.

European Productivity, Innovation and Public Sector R&D

This chapter analyses empirically the influence of public support of R&D on output and industrial innovations in the EU. It investigates two sets of questions: a) whether publicly financed R&D acts as complement to industry financed R&D and b) whether R&D performed in the public sector has a positive impact on growth and on innovation output as measured by patents or other proxies for scientific output. Under the first set of questions - dealing with the relation between publicly- and industry-financed R&D - the impact of direct R&D funding in the form of subsidies and of R&D tax credits on R&D conducted by the business sector is analysed as is the relationship between R&D performed in the public sector – both in public research institutions and in the higher education sector – and R&D performed in the business sector.

Using industry-level data for EU countries for the period 1987-1999, estimation results suggest that government-financed R&D expenditures complement domestic industry-financed expenditures on R&D. Furthermore, using economy-wide data for a panel of OECD/EU countries for the period 1981-2002, the results suggest that both direct funding of business R&D and tax incentives for R&D have a significant and positive impact on business R&D spending in OECD and EU countries. However, the majority of the increase in the average R&D intensity cannot be explained by tax credits or direct funding. Other factors such as the shift to R&D intensive industries seem to be more important than direct support for R&D in explaining the change in the R&D intensity in the business sector across EU countries. To the extent that reallocation of production factors towards high-technology industries is being hampered by lack of flexibility in product or factor markets, structural reforms aimed at rendering markets more flexible will play an important role in increasing the level of business R&D across the EU. Another result is the importance of R&D performed in the public sector for productivity and spillover effects in the private R&D sector. Expenditures on R&D performed by universities and public research organisations are significantly positively related to business enterprise sector expenditures on R&D, indicating that public sector R&D and private sector R&D are complements. Furthermore, econometric results using data on OECD/EU countries suggest that expenditures on R&D in the higher education sector significantly stimulate growth of GDP per capita. Finally, public sector R&D spending as a percentage of GDP has a positive and significant impact on EPO patent applications per capita, even after private R&D spending and country specificities have been controlled for.

The effectiveness of public support to R&D and innovation is also analysed using firm-level data from the latest Community Innovation Survey (CIS). Firms from three Member States are studied: Germany, Finland and Austria. The first country case study compares the propensity to patent in German and in Finnish firms and how this propensity depends on receiving government support and on participation in innovation cooperation. The second country case estimates the effect of government funding for innovation on R&D and on the share of innovative sales among Austrian firms.

Both studies conclude that the public sector has an important role to play in innovation by giving financial support and/or by stimulating R&D cooperation. The largest impact is achieved when collaboration among firms and public funding are present simultaneously. In Germany, public funding has no additional impact once firms cooperate already, but it does have an impact in Finland. In Austria, central government support increases the companies' share in total sales of both products new to the firm and of products new to the market. The relevance of collaboration in fostering innovative performance reflects the importance of the interconnections between public and private agents in driving innovation. It is precisely in this area that the EU tends to score low relative to the US where public and higher education research institutions have developed a far more effective system of linkages with the world of innovation.

These results have some implications for public policy. Given the significant and positive impact of tax incentives on R&D spending, increasing the generosity of R&D subsidies may become instrumental in increasing business R&D to levels closer to those of other main world leaders in this area. This is likely to be particularly true for countries with little or no tax-based support schemes (e.g. the new EU Member States and some large EU countries, notably Germany and Italy for large firms). Firm-level results suggest that collaboration in R&D activities accelerate technological diffusion via patents. Policies should improve the collaboration of public research organisations with firms and foster technology transfer through funding and specific programs. There is also a need to improve the infrastructure for commercialisation of research findings such as technology transfer offices and providers of risk capital.

The analysis also suggests that governments should provide appropriate funding for R&D conducted by public institutions, in particular research and development in the higher education sector. The role of higher education research in fostering R&D output and economic growth reinforces the need to integrate education policy reforms in the EU efforts to foster research and innovation throughout the economy. Government research institutions should demonstrate the relevance of their work by making more evident their contribution to economic performance. However, the decline in funding for government research organisations in the EU implies that restructuring will have to be accomplished through reallocation of existing resources. This creates increasing pressure on public sector organisations to engage in the systematic evaluation of their programs and, clearly, such evaluation should include researchers and programs as well as institutions.

Performance in the EU Health Sector

Governments intervene both directly through the provision of funding and indirectly through regulation, in the health sector. Moreover, policies must balance efficiency concerns with equity a conflict that can have serious implications for the health sector's performance. Chapter 3 discusses issues related to the performance of the EU health sector.

The health sector accounts for a significant share in national income and has potentially important implications for the economy's competitiveness. These implications relate not just to the health sector's contribution to the well-being of the citizens but also to its more direct contribution to measured national productivity. An inefficient health sector using resources wastefully can be a serious burden to the public sector and to an economy. The performance of the health sector has implications for labour mobility and labour market flexibility as, for example, in occupational insurance schemes.

In general, the health sector is characterized by a number of market imperfections, including moral hazard, adverse selection and the presence of externalities. The literature on health economics emphasises the unique nature of this sector so that, unlike other service industries, it is necessary to analyse its performance in a wider than otherwise contextual framework. Its unique features range from its historical development, with its original concentration on equity rather than efficiency goals, to a high degree of government intervention and regulation and to the important role played by technological change in determining both expenditure developments and input use. Information asymmetries make it difficult to distinguish between activities and outputs, whereas final outcomes are highly influenced by extraneous influences such as lifestyle. Thus, performance is difficult to measure as is drawing conclusions about the relative efficiency of systems of health services provision and their impact on competitiveness.

There are considerable differences in the structure of the health care system in the EU. Current health care systems are characterized by diversity in both the funding and delivery of health care. Efficiency and equity considerations, but also in order to promote productivity growth, have led recently many Member States to embark upon reforms of their systems of health care provision. Although rapid advances in technology have been responsible for much of the increase in health expenditure, this must be weighed against the considerable benefits that they produce in terms of improvements in health outcomes.

Both aggregate and micro studies reveal some weak evidence linking increased expenditure on health care to better outcomes, with the evidence somewhat stronger in the case of microeconomic studies. There is mixed evidence on the relationship between health expenditure and outcomes based on macro aggregate indicators. Health sector productivity may well be affected by changes to the system of health care provision, with supply-side incentives influencing the use of treatments and technology diffusion. However, it is important to note that much of the observed improvements in health outcomes appear not to be a result of the health care system itself but other outside factors which exert a much greater influence. The evidence to date, even from microeconomic studies, reveals a considerable diversity across countries in outcomes, resource use and adoption of technological changes. Thus, it is difficult to draw concrete conclusions. Demand-side incentives, such as cost-sharing, may also influence health system efficiency, although there is little by way of concrete evidence on the impact of such policies.

Currently many EU countries are engaged in a process of reform with emphasis on efficiency objectives. Despite the paucity of evidence at the country level, there is general agreement that the rise in expenditures in health care provision world-wide requires more consideration of efficiency than has hitherto been the case. But the pace of reform will be determined by the historical evolution of systems of provision and preferences regarding equity. It is unlikely that there are easy solutions to these issues. In private market services, for example, a commonly employed argument is that less competition and excess regulation in the EU may hinder productivity growth. To date there is little hard evidence to support this thesis but proponents at least can point to considerably higher productivity in the past decade in the US, probably the most competitive and least regulated industrial economy. In the health care sector, in contrast, the US experience is not supportive of unfettered competition and deregulation. Although there is a general recognition that providing greater incentives may enhance efficiency, there are few academics and certainly fewer policy makers who would advocate that EU economies should imitate the US system of health provision. In particular when equity considerations are given a significant weight the weaknesses of the US health care sector become more apparent.

On the input side, there appears to be some scope for better use of resources, in particular labour. Thus oversupply of physicians in some EU countries coincide with shortages in others and in many there is also scope to improve the mix between general and specialist physicians and nurses. Better and more co-ordinated training programs may be a policy change that is worth exploring. Expenditure on pharmaceuticals has been rising and therefore subject to numerous cost containment reforms. At the same time, pharmaceuticals contribute enormously to improvements in health outcomes. A balance therefore ought to be achieved between cost containment and ensuring sufficient incentives for continued innovation. However, far less systematic evidence is available to compare the role of capital across countries, in both quantity and quality terms.

Organisational changes play an important role in economic performance. Recent literature suggests that productivity improvements can arise from the use of organizational capital complementing other investments in traditional capital and in ICT. Many organizational changes in the health sector reflect reforms by which Member States seek to find the appropriate mix of decentralisation and centralisation in delivery matching individual choice with efficiency. The extent of patient choice varies among EU countries. Many have chosen to increase choice in order to improve health outcomes, as well as the quality of care and patient satisfaction. However, the literature suggests that the success of such reforms is dependent on the information available to individuals. Improving the efficiency of the health sector, securing benefits from advanced technology at reasonable cost and ensuring equity are major challenges facing the EU.

Reforms of the health sector are likely to improve the efficiency of the public sector and to ultimately contribute to the productivity performance of the Member States. A principal challenge facing the EU in coming years concerns a reconciliation of realising efficiency improvements, securing benefits from advanced technology at reasonable cost and ensuring fair access to quality health services for all citizens.

The European Automotive Sector

This chapter presents a broad picture of the European automotive industry and seeks to determine how competitive it is internationally and which are the sources of its competitiveness. Competitiveness is defined as the ability of an industrial sector to defend and/or gain market share in open, international markets by relying on price and/or quality of goods. This ability is affected by a wide range of factors, including framework conditions ranging from production costs to technological and organisational innovation, from the regulatory framework to macro-economic conditions. Given this variety, drawing a definitive conclusion about the future of the sector is not possible. Instead, a systematic analysis of strengths, weaknesses, opportunities and threats (SWOT) draws together the possible implications of the various elements identified in the Report as relevant to the competitiveness of the industry.

The automotive industry is one of Europe's major industries. It contributes about 6 % to total European manufacturing employment and 7 % to total manufacturing output. Almost 20 % of all R&D in manufacturing is undertaken by car manufacturers. The importance of the automotive industry derives to a large degree from linkages within the domestic and international economy. There is evidence for upstream inputs of about up to two times the volume of value added that the industry produces.

The EU automotive industry is highly concentrated, with Germany alone accounting for close to half of total value added. Besides Sweden, Germany and France, a specialisation in auto manufacturing is clear in the Czech Republic, Slovakia and Hungary.

The EU automotive industry has been able to maintain its international position both in terms of exports (where its share has increased considerably) and in terms of global sales, i.e. worldwide sales, including the home market, exports and sales to foreign markets through subsidiaries. This could only be done by establishing and maintaining a substantial presence in foreign markets through which European companies can gather customer feedback and market information.

A large and sophisticated home market, in which European brands dominate, constitutes a first and decisive competitive advantage for the European automotive industry. This market presents a wide variety of consumer demands; it permits the early commercialisation of innovations as well as strategies of product differentiation. However, this market is to a large extent mature, most sales are for replacement of existing cars. Therefore, perspectives for further growth are rather limited.

The EU automotive industry still lags behind the US and Japan in terms of productivity. The catching-up process of the EU automotive industry has slowed down in the last decade despite steep increases in some Member States. Another increasingly serious problem is the level of labour costs in some Member States. Relatively high labour costs and their negative impact on price competitiveness are a special threat in light of structural overcapacity in the global automotive industry.

Enlargement has been a very important development to the European automotive industry. First, the new Member States are developing a very dynamic manufacturing cluster with high output and export potential. Second, investment there reinforces the European value chain by adding to it lower cost locations and permitting more options in combining existing components and intermediary parts. Third, the European home market is extended too to include a high-growth potential customer base which displays a variety of preferences in comparison to the EU-15 Member States. On the other hand, increased capacity in the new Member States - be it from European or overseas owned plants - will exacerbate competition and price pressures for existing locations.

The combination of mass production with the complexity of specific goods such as cars and other transport equipment makes the risks of failure related to radical innovations very high. Therefore, processes and products are developed incrementally. In-house R&D activities and product engineering are the main sources of technical progress. Additionally, the work of specialised suppliers – sometimes research facilities – is integrated into the value chain.

EU firms have increased their investments in new products, new processes and new technologies considerably in the 1990s. Compared to the US and Japan, the EU has improved its position in terms of R&D investment. The technological competitiveness of the European automotive industry rests not only on the presence of leading car makers but also on widespread innovation activities within the supplier part of the industry.

The impact of a new regulation on the automotive industry is complex. It can vary with the time horizon and introduce dynamic effects that are difficult to assess accurately. Measures like new pollution standards can have a negative effect on the performance and cost structure of carmakers, challenging the competitive strength of the industry. At the same time, dealing with the measures can be the first step towards new markets and achieving technology or quality leadership.

World-wide demands to make vehicles safer and more environment-friendly will continue. These demands will drive research and innovation; it is of crucial importance to identify and implement innovative technical solutions that will become global, thus giving European industry a first mover advantage.

The key technological problem facing the automobile industry today is the complexity of demands emanating from society. The need to address several issues at the same time can make the development of technical solutions more demanding as the underlying physical and technical characteristics can give rise to trade-offs.

On the other hand, measures that manage to reduce the wide differences in tax systems should have a positive impact on the ability of the car industry - and European consumers - to reap the benefits of operating within a Single Market. Car market fragmentation prevents industry from exploiting economies of scale, or to produce motor vehicles for the entire Internal Market, applying the same specifications and contributes to significant variations of pre-tax prices within the internal market.

Clearly, the competitiveness of the automotive industry depends on a coherent and cost-effective regulatory framework. To achieve this, the Commission is using increasingly the tools of 'Better regulation' such as *Impact Assessment* techniques. Progress is still to be made, however, in reducing regulatory complexity and in designing regulations so as to meet their goals while taking into account possible conflicts between regulations, their cumulative impact and their external aspects. These concerns are of particular importance to the automobile industry.

The Challenge to the EU by a Rising Chinese Economy

China's economic transformation during the last 25 years has been dramatic. Industry has been growing at an annual rate of 10.9 % between 1979 and

2002 while GDP by an annual average of 9.0 % during the same period. These economic trends were triggered off primarily by the reforms introduced by Deng Xiaoping in 1978. Since then, China has moved from isolation to a gradual integration in the world economy.

In recent years China has emerged as an important supplier of goods in international trade following a path which will undoubtedly lead it to greater prominence. China is competing with other nations on the basis of labour abundance but also on the basis of goods embodying skills and technology. Chinese exports to the EU include technology-intensive and knowledge-based products as well as capital intensive manufactured products and labour intensive manufactured products. The vast, inexpensive work force, combined with the development of a knowledge economy provides an excellent basis for the establishment of offshore centres for the manufacture of a broad range of products and services. Western direct investment intended primarily to serve a large and expanding domestic market but also to supply products internationally, has led to concerns that jobs in the industrial world but also in other nations competing with China are being delocalized and lost. Thus, the opening up of China poses an important competitiveness challenge to the advanced industrial nations including the EU. Among those most vulnerable to this competitiveness challenge are the new Member States.

Competition from lower-wage locations is nothing new for EU industries which have been adapting to a changing world trade environment, exploiting 'soft factors' such as time, customisation, service and reliability to improve productivity and make up for labour costs disadvantages. But although the challenge of China may not be entirely unfamiliar, the combination of low labour costs and rapidly developing high technical and research capacities is less familiar. For EU firms to remain profitable and compete in segments of the value chain, it is necessary to continue exploiting advantages other than labour costs. It is necessary to maintain the productivity advantage by opening up to new areas and products. Concentrating on products in which old comparative advantage was held is not sustainable. But creating high value added jobs requires a dynamic framework where innovation can spur productivity and job growth. This will require, among others, to strengthen R&D efforts and stimulate innovation as well as exploit advantages in organization, coordination, marketing, logistics, etc. Currently, institutional conditions for implementing innovations are better in the EU-15, and also in the

new Member States, compared to China. Yet, the emergence of China will inevitably lead to a change in the international division of labour and the place of the EU in it.

The greatest challenge of the emergence of China as a prominent trading partner concerns the new Member States. The new Member States and the candidate countries have so far offered more attractive nearshore centres and have provided opportunities for specialization across segments of the value chain, reflecting their integration into the European economy since the early 1990s. The metal industries in particular have entered in a mutually beneficial division of labour between the EU-15 and new Member States. Despite the promise that enlargement offers for the division of labour and the location of production across the wider Europe, it is not certain that these will be adequate to respond effectively to China's challenge. Chinese exports to the new Member States have been growing at rates much higher than to the EU-15 for all of the industries reviewed in the Report - total exports to new Member States have also grown at a higher rate – reflecting the fact that their integration into the global division of labour has progressed significantly since the mid-1990s. Some employment losses have also occurred from relocation of activities to China, notably in the Hungarian electronics industry, indicating that even manufacturing of high-tech, imitation-based, products has been challenged by China's low-cost locations.

China's emergence as a supplier of high-tech products is a reflection of a more general concept undertaken to upgrade the Chinese economy through a clear industrial policy the basis of which is to transform knowledge into economic success for domestic companies. The transition to a market economy has been accompanied by a regulatory system and administrative guidance to ensure the development of internationally viable national companies with the potential to compete with the top global players in their markets. Chinese companies are already playing a crucial role as original equipment manufacturers (OEM) for the world's leading brands and retail labels. However, the greatest challenge to established Western multinationals and brand owners will ultimately arise from Chinese brand name producers whose growth established patterns of international trade have so far concealed. Europe's advanced industrial economies – France, Germany, Italy, and the UK – will likely be those to experience most notably this challenge especially as Chinese brands become entrenched in European markets and outbound Chinese foreign direct investment rises. In this context, European corporations will see a decline in their competitive edge in new global economic structures.

The opening up of China provides many opportunities for European companies and certainly more than those which emerged with the integration of Japan or Korea into the world economy. China has already dismantled many of the barriers to market access during to process of market reforms and with China's access to the WTO new steps towards market opening will be undertaken. China has clearly a fundamental interest in developing framework conditions that are supportive of strengthening inward foreign direct investment.

Clearly, the Chinese market offers strong long-term growth opportunities especially for those industries that are dominated by global multinationals. Foreign enterprises are establishing themselves in China to take advantage of growth opportunities and the prospects for rising real incomes. All the international brands of the automotive industry and OEM manufacturers have established local production facilities and are in strong competition with each other to sustain and improve market shares. Indigenous Chinese enterprises are virtually absent

from these markets and play no independent role. Success in this market will not only contribute to raising economic growth but will also make possible the exploitation of economies of scale that will confer a strategic advantage to large players to protect their position against their competitors. Similar remarks apply to the chemical industry and also other industries characterized by large-batch production or the processing of commodities; production facilities in China will be necessary in order to protect market shares against competitors and to sustain their competitive edge.

Some years ago concerns that Japan would become an economic superpower to sweep away older industrial economies simply did not materialize. In retrospect, Japan's rise and integration in the world economy contributed, through the exchange of goods and services and through international capital flows, not only to economic growth in the developing world but also to enriching consumers and producers in the industrial economies. China offers similar possibilities today. Europe should design a strategy based on strengthening its productivity, innovation and competitiveness to meet China's challenge and take advantage of the emerging growth opportunities.

Introduction

This is the eighth edition of the Commission's European Competitiveness Report since the 1994 Industry Council Resolution that established its basis. Competitiveness in this Report is understood to mean a sustained rise in the standards of living of a nation and as low a level of involuntary unemployment as possible.

Recent Competitiveness Reports have reviewed the diverging growth patterns within Europe and between Europe and the United States. In the 1990s, the EU and OECD countries have seen widening disparities in output and productivity growth. Economic growth patterns in the second half of the 1990s have diverged from earlier trends in both Europe and the United States. In the period since the World War II, Europe registered higher productivity growth than the US reflecting a catching up process. Since 1995 this has been reversed: US productivity growth has been 1 percentage point higher than Europe's while unemployment has been at a historical low in the US and stagnating at a high level in Europe.

A theme of this year's Report concerns the role of the public sector in the competitiveness of the European economies. Measuring productivity growth in the service sector is notoriously difficult and, especially so, in the public sector. Since the presence (however measured) of the public sector is quite substantial not just in the EU but in other industrialized nations, it is possible that public sector inefficiencies will ultimately show up in such measures of economic performance as productivity growth. Although direct measures of the importance of the public sector, such as the share of government expenditure or of revenues in GDP are indicative of the extent of its involvement in economic activity, another crucial area that might have a direct impact on incentives to

engage in economic activity is the web of rules and regulations that delineate the framework conditions within which economic activity is taking place. Despite indirect and conjectural evidence, especially the effect of these is not easy to identify empirically. The hypothesis is that the public sector matters in productivity growth and, therefore, it is important to consider the influence of its structure, size, strategy, quality and the efficiency of its activities that impinge upon decision to produce, work, modernize and innovate in the EU. A large part of this edition of the Competitiveness Report is concerned with these issues.

The Report comprises five chapters. Chapter 1 reviews the general issues related the role of the public sector in economic activity. The material considers issues of taxation, spending and incentives. Measured by the share of public expenditure in GDP, the EU stands out as having the largest public sector among the triad nations. Notwithstanding the fact that the size of the public sector varies considerably across the Member States, the EU has a significantly larger share of expenditures for social protection and general public services than its international competitors. The evidence on the influence of public sector activities in aggregate productivity growth is fragmentary, inconclusive and incomplete. With the advent of monetary unification in Europe, the need for fiscal consolidation but, also importantly, recognition that the involvement of the pubic sector in many aspects of economic life may be harmful to performance, has led to a reform process undertaken across the Member States. Clearly, public sector reforms are central issues in the Lisbon agenda.

Chapter 2 examines issues related to the impact of public support of R&D on innovation output and growth. Spending on R&D has drawn significant

17

attention in recent years. The chapter takes an empirical view, examining the influence of public sector R&D on output and industrial innovations in the EU at the firm, industry and country level. The results confirm that both tax incentives for R&D and direct funding of business R&D have a significant and positive impact on business R&D spending. However, the majority of the increase in the average R&D intensity cannot be explained by tax credits or direct funding. Other factors, such as the shift towards R&D intensive industries, appear to be more important than direct support in explaining the change in R&D intensity in the business sector across EU countries. Expenditures on R&D performed by universities and public research organisations are also found to be significantly positively related to business sector expenditures on R&D, indicating that public sector R&D and private sector R&D are complements and suggesting the presence of spillover effects from academic research. Results also suggest that expenditure on R&D in the higher education sector contributes significantly to growth of GDP per capita, and that the ratio of public sector R&D to GDP is an important predictor of EPO patent applications per capita. Community Innovation Survey (CIS) evidence at firm level for Austria, Germany and Finland confirm that the public sector contributes importantly to innovation through financial support and/or through stimulating cooperation. The largest impact on innovation occurs when R&D collaboration and public funding are conducted simultaneously.

Chapter 3 reviews the performance of the health sector. The efficiency of this large sector undoubtedly has implications for measured productivity growth essentially because it affects resource allocation in the face of idiosyncratic circumstances – market imperfections including moral hazard, adverse selection and the presence of externalities, are notorious in this sector. Rapid advances in technology are one reason for increase in health expenditure but they also produce improvements in health outcomes. The evidence that increased expenditure on health care leads to better outcomes is generally weak but stronger in the case of specific disease-based studies.

Efficiency considerations are receiving greater attention than has hitherto been the case and reforms are under way in many Member States. On the input side, there appears to be some scope for better use of resources, in particular labour – physicians and nurses. Furthermore, as pharmaceuticals contribute enormously to improvements in health outcomes, it is necessary to find a balance between cost containment and incentives provision for continued innovation. Finally, the role of organisa-

tional change is also important. Realising efficiency gains, securing benefits from advanced technology at reasonable cost and ensuring fair access for all citizens is one of the major challenges facing the EU in the coming decades.

Chapter 4 examines the competitive position and recent developments in the European automotive sector as well as regulation issues impinging on the sector's performance. Europe has a strong position in automotive production and trade and European companies have established leading international positions both as exporters and as investors. This success rests on the large and sophisticated European market which is dominated by local brands.

The industry is under permanent change as globalisation, consolidation and restructuring of the value chain occurs; one such development was the upgrading of the role of the supplier industry. At the same time, the European automotive industry seems to have fully grasped the opportunities of the recent enlargement of the EU.

The importance of the car in the economy and in everyday life places it necessarily at the centre of many, sometimes divergent, regulatory requirements. The industry has an interest in the continuation and fruition of the efforts to better regulate. Of crucial importance will be to identify and implement innovative solutions that will become global, thus giving European industry a competitive advantage.

Chapter 5 mainly discusses the challenges the rising economy of China is posing for the competitiveness of the EU. The specific economic structures and factor endowments of the new Member States and of the candidate countries make them more susceptible to competitive pressure arising from China that is rapidly integrating in the global economy; the EU-15 economies, which are significantly more industrialized, are les vulnerable.

The chapter discusses, first, the driving forces of China's recent advance in the global economy as well as the downside risks inherent in China's recent economic and social development; secondly, China's role in the global division of labour and Chinese-European economic relations including trade patterns and foreign direct investment flows; and, third, the impact a rising Chinese economy might have on various industries in the EU and especially those in the new Member States.

China's economic transformation during the last 25 years has been dramatic. Industry has been growing at an annual rate of 10.9 % between 1979 and 2002 and GDP by 9.0 % during the same period. China's exports to Europe include a surprisingly high share of technology-intensive and knowledge-based products as well as capital intensive manufactured goods. China's growing importance as producer of high-tech products is a reflection of a clear industrial policy. The opening up of China, given its market potential and appetite for strategic-sector and government-driven foreign companies engagement, provides substantial trading and investment opportunities for European companies; however, the greatest challenge to established multinationals and to brand owners in the industrial world will arise from Chinese brand name producers whose growth has been concealed in the traditional patterns of the international labour division.

Chapter 1:
Productivity and the Public Sector

1.1 Introduction

Public policies play an essential role in shaping competitiveness and growth in an economy. This Chapter discusses the effects of public policies on productivity. The public sector affects overall labour productivity in an economy in two ways:

First, the public sector itself has a large weight in the overall economy. In Sweden, which has the highest share of government employment in EU-15, one out of three jobs is in the government sector (Table 1.1). The Netherlands has the smallest share of government employment, one tenth of all jobs. Due to the size of government activity, labour productivity *in the*

public sector is an important determinant of average labour productivity at the national level.

Secondly, the organisation and functioning of governments affects productivity *in the private sector*. This Chapter considers three main channels through which government action can have an impact on productivity:

- *Taxation* is needed in order to finance governments. However, taxes distort relative prices in the economy and thus influence economic incentives such as the willingness to work, to invest or to engage in entrepreneurial activities;

- *Government spending* on areas such as education, research and development or infrastructure

Table 1.1: Government employment in EU Member States, US and Japan in 2003, % of total employment

Country	Government employment % of total
Sweden	31.7
Denmark	30.4
Finland	25.6
France	23.0
Hungary	17.8
Slovak Republic	21.1
United Kingdom	18.8
Belgium	18.3
Portugal	17.9
Poland	17.4
Czech Republic	16.2
Italy	16.0
Luxembourg	15.4
Spain	15.0
Austria	12.9
Greece	12.5
Ireland	12.0
Germany	11.1
Netherlands	11.0
EU-15	16.7
United States	15.7
Japan	8.7

Source: OECD (2003a).

influences the development of economic activity. For example, the development of high-tech production is often linked to research activity and depends on the availability of high-skilled labour;

- *Regulations* exist in order to correct distortions, guarantee the basic economic rights and to promote objectives such as consumer protection or the quality of environment. At the same time, regulations limit the choices which individuals and enterprises can make, and compliance with regulations usually involves costs.

This Chapter starts with a discussion of productivity within the public sector in Section 1.2. Some recent studies on public sector efficiency are reviewed, followed by a brief description of recent reforms. The remainder of the Chapter is devoted to the effects of public sector involvement on productivity in the private sector. Sections 1.3, 1.4 and 1.5 respectively discuss the effects of taxation, public spending and regulations on private sector productivity. Section 1.6 concludes. Significant omissions from the analysis include institutional factors; industry- or sector-specific regulations; and regulations on labour markets.

1.2 Productivity in the provision of public services

1.2.1 International comparisons of public sector efficiency

Most empirical studies on public sector performance assess either the relative performance of specific producing units (e.g. hospitals) against each other, frequently using frontier analysis, or broad sector aggregates (e.g. health, education, or administration), assessing performance over time or across countries. Measurement of public sector output is more difficult than the valuation of private sector output, as public services are often provided at a subsidised price to the customer and no market prices are available to valuate them. Box 1.1 discusses methodological issues in the measurement of productivity in the public sector.

Lack of internationally harmonised data often prevents cross-country comparisons of public sector productivity across countries. Cross-country studies on public sector efficiency frequently rely on indicators such as the educational achievement of school pupils at a given age; infant mortality or life expectancy; survey results on how managers

perceive the functioning of justice and the extent of corruption in a given country;[1] or macroeconomic indicators such as GDP per head, economic growth, or income distribution. Two recent studies which use such indicators are discussed next.

Afonso, Schuknecht and Tanzi (2003) compute indicators of public sector *performance* (which describes the outcomes of public sector activity) and public sector *efficiency* (which relates the outcomes to resource use i.e. public spending) for a sample of 23 OECD countries in 2000. To establish indicators of overall public sector performance, they use selected socioeconomic indicators for public administration, education, health, infrastructure, income distribution, economic stability and economic performance.

In general, the *performance* differences across countries are rather small. Countries with small public sectors (government spending less than 40 % of GDP) on average report the highest scores in particular for administrative and economic performance. Countries with large public sectors show more equal income distribution.[2] Of the individual countries, the highest performance scores were reported for Luxembourg, Japan, Norway, Austria and the Netherlands; the lowest for Greece, Portugal and Italy. It is worth noting that within the group of 23 OECD countries, the overall performance score for EU-15[3] is clearly below the average (0.94 against a normalised average of 1.00) and below the scores of the US and Japan (1.02 and 1.14 respectively).

Afonso et al. (op cit.) subsequently compute indicators of public sector *efficiency* which relate the above mentioned performance measures to inputs. Inputs are proxied by government spending on each type of activity. While cross-country differences were rather limited in terms of the performance indicators, the efficiency scores suggest rather large differences between individual countries. Countries with small public sectors report significantly higher efficiency indicators than countries with medium-sized or large public sectors. Overall efficiency is highest in Japan, Luxembourg, Australia, US and Switzerland. At the other end of the range, Italy, Sweden, France and Belgium report the weakest scores. EU-15 ranks below the sample average of 1.04 with a score of 0.94; this compares to 1.26 in the US and 1.38 for Japan.

---

[1] Examples of data sources include the OECD Programme for International Student Assessment (PISA), World Economic Forum (2003), or IMD (2004).
[2] On the link between government size and productivity, see also Section 1.4 below.
[3] Weighted average using GDP weights.

Box 1.1: Measurement of public sector productivity

The most important issues in the measurement of the efficiency in the production of public services are:

- how to *define output* (output vs. outcome, gross output vs. value added, number of activities vs. deflated expenditures);

- how to define *aggregate* output over a range of different products;

- how to incorporate *exogenous conditions* (such as the general health condition of a patient) in the valuation of efficiency.

Conventional productivity measurement relates outputs to inputs. The intrinsic problem in the measurement of public sector productivity is the lack of information on the market value of the output. As public services are often provided to the user at no cost or at a subsidised price, there are no market prices that reflect the value of the services.

When market prices are not available for the output of public sector activity, the value of output is usually derived from input data.[4] Inputs are to a large extent provided through the market, and it is therefore easier to value them. As with private sector activities, inputs can be approximated (a) for labour inputs: by the number of employees involved or by hours worked, and (b) for capital inputs: by investment outlays.

The construction of an output measure for a particular field of government activity would involve a number of steps (Baxter 2000): (i) set up a list of all relevant activities in that field; (ii) find a volume measure to describe how the amount of work in that field is changing over time; and (iii) use weights that are proportional to nominal expenditure on the activities in a base year to produce an aggregate measure for the whole field.

Efforts are being made at national and international level to improve the measurement of public sector output. The current version of the European System of National Accounts (ESA95) recommends the use of output indicator methods. Eurostat, the statistical office of the EU, attempts to improve price and volume measures of non-market output, concentrating on the health, education and general administration branches of public services.[5] At the OECD, the Statistics Directorate and the Public Management Directorate (PUMA) consider ways to advance on public sector output and productivity measurement (OECD, 1999).

National measurement methods have been developed in individual countries. In the UK, the Office for National Statistics (ONS) has developed genuine output measures for education, health and social security and more recently for courts, prisons, agricultural intervention, fire, social services and the probation service (Pritchard, 2002).

Since 1994, the productivity of all general government agencies except Ministries in Finland has been measured by the output indicator method. A questionnaire, sent annually to those units that provide services to external customers, collects information on the quantities of final products, their shares in terms of cost, income or working time, as well as on the quantity of labour input and gross expenditures (Lehtoranta and Niemi, 1997).

The Dutch authorities implemented the 'modified deflator method' in 1992 to quantify the volume of government output in the national accounts. This method avoids the estimation of output. Alternative methods, such as the output indicator approach and the structural determinants method, though they yielded similar results, were rejected.

---

[4] The *value of non-market output* is traditionally approximated by summing up the production costs at current prices. To arrive at *non-market output in real terms*, the current year cost components (such as labour inputs) are deflated using the relevant inflation rate (e.g. wage inflation).
[5] See also the Eurostat Handbook on Price and Volume Measures.

Graph 1.1 compares public sector performance with the efficiency at which the results are achieved in the 23 OECD countries:

- Luxembourg, Japan, Switzerland, Australia and the US report high performance at a low cost in terms of public spending;

- The Netherlands, Denmark, Sweden and Iceland report above-average performance in the public sector, but this is achieved at a disproportionately high cost in terms of public expenditure;

- The countries close to the average efficiency line combine low public spending with low performance (Greece, Portugal, Spain and the UK), or higher performance with above-average spending levels (Norway, Austria, Ireland, Canada and Finland);

- Italy, France and Belgium, and to a lesser extent New Zealand and Germany, appear as relatively inefficient in their use of public resources, while they also score badly in terms of performance.

Afonso, Schuknecht and Tanzi (2003) conclude that the higher performance and efficiency scores of small governments may suggest that the size of government could be too large in many industrialised countries, leading to the prevalence of declining marginal products. In interpreting the results, it is important to keep in mind that the rankings depend on choices such as the selection of indicators to measure performance.[6]

Afonso et al. (2003) also conduct a Free Disposable Hull (FDH) analysis[7] to measure the efficiency of public spending across the sample of 23 OECD

---

[6] Other methodological choices include the decision to give equal weights to all indicators in the computation of performance scores by area and the overall performance score (the authors maintain that the results are relatively robust to moderate changes in weighting), and the choice of spending relative to GDP as a measure of inputs (the latter assumes that production costs of public services are proportional to GDP per capita – this may be a good approximation for labour intensive services such as education, but less so for items such as infrastructure).

[7] FDH is a deterministic production frontier technique to estimate the extent of slack in government expenditure. In contrast to the related Data Envelopment Analysis (DEA), it does not require a convex production frontier. *Input efficiency scores* indicate how much less input a country could use to achieve the same level of output. *Output efficiency scores* show how much more output a country would be able to produce with the same inputs as currently employed.

Graph 1.1: Indicators of public sector performance and efficiency

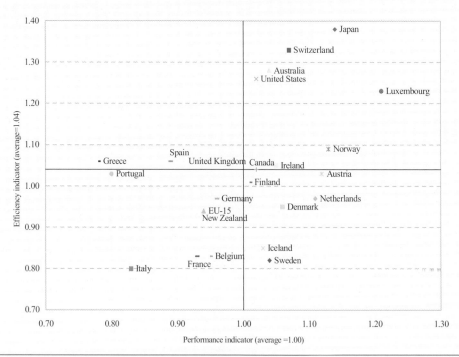

Notes: The performance indicator is an unweighted average of performance scores in seven areas of government activity: public administration, education, health, infrastructure, income distribution, economic stability and economic performance. Indicator values have been normalised with the average set as 1.00.

The efficiency indicator is computed as the ratio of the performance indicator to public spending on the relevant items (the spending indicator is expressed as % of GDP, and normalised with the average set as 1.00).

Source: Afonso et al. (2003).

countries. Public sector outputs are approximated by the performance indicators which were described above, and inputs are measured by public spending as a percentage of GDP in 2000. The US, Japan and Luxembourg are identified as the most efficient countries in the sample, followed by Australia, Ireland and Switzerland.

Most of the EU countries lie well inside the production possibility frontier, suggesting that the same results could be achieved with fewer inputs. For EU-15, the average input efficiency is estimated at 0.73, meaning that the same level of output could be attained by using 73 % of the inputs which are currently used.

In a sectoral analysis of education and health activities of the public sector in selected OECD countries, Afonso and St. Aubyn (2004) estimate efficiency frontiers and compare the results of Free Disposable Hull (FDH) and Data Envelopment Analysis (DEA).[8] In their analysis of *education,* they use (i) financial inputs: annual expenditure on secondary education per student in 1999 (in purchasing power parities), and (ii) physical inputs, such as hours of instruction per year and per school in 2000, or the number of teachers per 100 students in 2000. PISA (the OECD Programme for International Student Assessment) survey data on the performance of 15-year-olds are used as output indicators.

For education, Afonso and St. Aubyn (op cit.) estimate average input efficiencies in terms of output for all countries considered as ranging between 0.52 and 0.89, depending on the estimation method used. This means that on average the same output could be achieved by using 11 % to 48 % fewer inputs than are currently employed. The country by country results differ considerably according to whether inputs are measured in terms of financial resources or in physical terms. Sweden and Finland appear as efficient when inputs are measured in physical terms, but not in terms of expenditure, which may reflect the relatively high price of inputs in these two countries. Hungary, where inputs are rather inexpensive, appears efficient when inputs are measured in financial terms, but no longer qualifies as efficient when inputs are measured in physical terms. Mexico, Japan and Korea are efficient no matter which method is used.

Similar results are obtained for the provision of *health care* services. Using as inputs alternatively (i) per capita health expenditures in purchasing power

parities and (ii) the number of doctors, nurses and beds; and as output indicator either the infant survival rate or life expectancy, the estimated input efficiency in terms of output varies between 0.74 and 0.96 across countries. Sweden is positioned on the efficiency frontier only when inputs are physically measured, reflecting comparatively high input prices. In contrast, owing to their relatively inexpensive inputs, the Czech Republic and Poland are efficient in financial terms, but not efficient in physical terms. As was the case for education, Mexico, Japan and Korea are identified as efficient independently of the method employed. The authors note that the estimated efficiency scores in both education and health care may be partly attributable to cross-country differences in population density, the composition of population as well as the mix of public and private funding.

1.2.2 Recent reforms in the public sector

Comprehensive reforms of public administration in many countries during the 1970s and 1980s have given way to more targeted reforms. Recent reforms in the public sector have often been carried out as a response to pressures to limit public spending, to strengthen economic performance or to keep up with the innovations introduced in the private sector, such as the introduction of information technologies. Country-specific forces are usually at the root of public sector reforms (Knox, 2002).

This section will briefly discuss three types of reforms to enhance efficiency in the public sector:

- Management reforms;

- Introduction of information technology; and

- Privatisation and outsourcing.

Human resources management – wage differentiation, hiring and firing practices, promotion – in the public sector often differs substantially from that in the private sector. Improvements in the incentive structure are seen as a central device to enhance the performance of the public sector. Measures such as explicitly defined objectives, incentive mechanisms to encourage results-oriented management, and evaluations of the outcomes have been introduced in many OECD countries. Reliable output and performance indicators are a critical factor for the success of such mechanisms.

Public administration has traditionally operated in a non-profit environment, and reforms in public

---

[8]   See footnote 7.

management have frequently involved the introduction of commercial management practices, aiming at enhanced performance and customer orientation of public administration. Prominent examples are New Public Management and Total Quality Management. The term New Public Management originated in New Zealand in the 1980s and aims at creating a management culture that focuses on citizens and involves accountability for results. It promotes well-defined targets, contract-like arrangements to provide performance incentives, and decentralised budget control through cost centres.

Total Quality Management was first developed for application in business enterprises, but was later on introduced also in the production of public services. It is a 'person-focused management system with the main target of continuously increasing customer satisfaction at the lowest possible cost' (Lindsay and Petrick 1997, 20).

Since the 1990s, the *introduction of information and communication technologies* has been a major tool to improve the performance of the public sector. The introduction of information and communication technologies, together with the associated changes in working methods ('e-Government') offers the potential for improvements in the quality of information, time savings, and increased speed of response in interaction with citizens and businesses; it promotes the establishment of common standards across public agencies, and encourages the elimination of redundant systems.

*e*Europe 2005 Action Plan and the subsequent e-Government policy[9] put forward measures to speed up the development of e-Government in the EU. One of the aims is to connect the public administrations of Member States to broadband by 2005. The Action Plan proposes i.a. the following: (a) access to public services for all via multiple platforms (PC, TV, and mobile terminals); (b) new services via broadband development; (c) three-year action plan on electronic public procurement by 2004; (d) development of pan-European services; (e) one-stop shop for e-Government related activities of the EU. European Commission (2003a) identifies Sweden and Ireland as leading countries in the introduction of e-Government, while Germany and Belgium are found to lag behind.

The US Government launched a large-scale programme in 2002 to facilitate the use of information technology in the public sector. It includes facilities for disaster management, access to federal and state level benefit programmes, participation in the rulemaking processes concerning small business, e-training courses, a job search engine, and electronic tax filing services.

Privatisation and outsourcing to private service providers have been seen as solutions to the incentive problems in public sector production. Mukherjee and Wilkins (1999) report on outsourcing via the extensive creation of arms-length agencies and on some of the problems in achieving the desired goals. Batley (1999) concludes that the effects of outsourcing have not been exclusively positive. Particularly in developing countries, radical outsourcing of service delivery agencies has resulted in transaction costs that outweigh the efficiency gains of unbundling. In general, reforms that attempt to separate purchasers from providers may reduce accountability.

Empirical research on the effects of privatisation[10] suggests that privatisation is usually associated with increased efficiency, profitability and capital investment spending. On the other hand, in the short run privatisation often leads to employment reductions, which are linked with increased labour productivity (see Meggison and Netter, 2001, for a survey). Nicoletti and Scarpetta (2003) find that a gradual move over some ten years towards the OECD average share of state-owned enterprises in total value added boosts annual multi-factor productivity growth by 0.7 percentage points in those EU countries where government ownership of industries is high, notably in Austria, France, Greece, Italy and Portugal.

Public-private partnerships are an alternative to outright privatisations. The involvement of the private sector can yield benefits by bringing the projects closer to the market in terms of risk-sharing, management skills and the quality of public services.

The remainder of the Chapter discusses the effects of government policies on *productivity in the private sector*. Three channels of influence are considered: Section 1.3 examines questions of taxation, Section 1.4 deals with government spending and, finally, Section 1.5 provides a brief overview of the effects of regulations.

---

[9] See European Commission (2003a).

[10] See Bennett et al. (2004), Claessens and Djankov (2002), Djankov and Murrell (2002), Frydman et al. (1999), Gonenc et al. (2000), La Porta and López-de-Silanes (1999), Nicoletti and Scarpetta (2003), Van den Noord (2002), and Vickers and Yarrow (1988).

Graph 1.2: Total taxes in EU-15, the US and Japan in 1980-2002, % of GDP

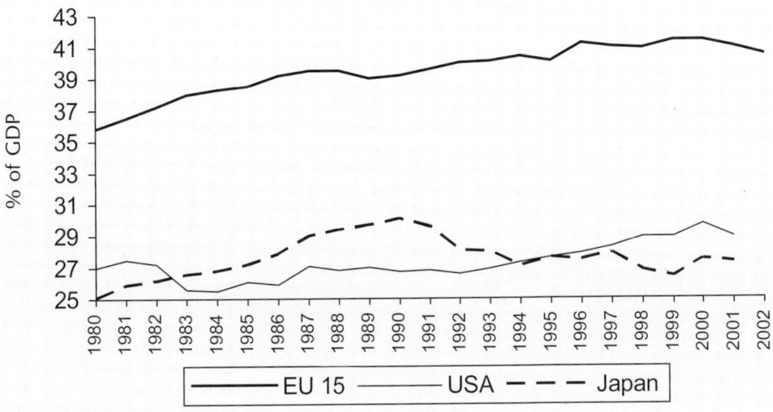

Notes: Data for the US and Japan only available until 2001; taxes include social security contributions.

Source: OECD (2003b).

1.3 Taxation

1.3.1 Introduction

Graph 1.2 shows the evolution of the ratio of total taxes to GDP in EU-15, the US and Japan. The average tax ratio in EU-15 increased trendwise until the mid-1990 and has declined slightly in the recent years. In 2002, total taxes in EU-15 amounted to 40.5 % of GDP. In the US and Japan, the tax ratios remain below 30 % of GDP.

Graph 1.3 illustrates the large differences in the tax burden across the EU-25 member states. In Sweden and Denmark, the sum of taxes and social security contributions equals half the value of GDP. At the lower end of the range, Ireland and Lithuania have tax ratios just below 30 per cent. The average tax ratio in EU-25 is 40 per cent, the same level as in the mid-1990s.

Empirical research on the relationship between the overall tax ratio (total taxes to GDP) and GDP growth has not yielded conclusive results. Barro (1991) analyses the relation between the growth rate of GDP per capita and the tax ratio. His findings suggest that the tax burden has a negative impact on a country's growth performance. This result has been contested by subsequent studies that show a slightly positive or insignificant correlation (e.g. Easterly and Rebelo, 1993).

Not only the overall tax burden, but also the composition of the tax mix is considered as relevant for the growth performance, as the size of the incentive effects varies from one type of tax to another. Easterly and Rebelo (1993) suggest that there is a relationship between the level of national income and the composition of overall taxes. Kneller, Bleaney and Gemmell (1999) find a growth-reducing impact of distortionary taxes. In contrast, Mendoza, Milesi-Ferretti and Asea (1997) show that the growth effects of changes in the tax structure (implicit tax rates on capital, labour and consumption) are negligible.

In the following, two types of taxes are discussed: (i) taxes on labour; and (ii) taxes which affect entrepreneurship and innovation.

1.3.2 Labour taxation

The taxation of labour exerts an influence on overall labour productivity in the economy via two main channels:

- First, taxes affect the *incentives to work*;

- Secondly, taxes on labour have an impact on the *incentives for human capital formation*.

High taxation can induce more individuals to stay outside the labour market, or make them work

Graph 1.3: Tax ratios by EU-25 Member State in 2002

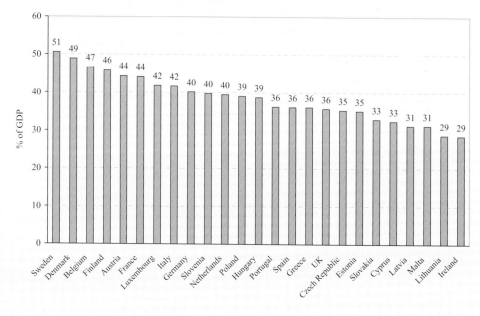

Note: Total taxes including social security contributions.

Source: European Commission (2004).

shorter hours in exchange for more leisure time.[11] Empirical studies suggest that labour taxation influences the decision to participate in the labour market, in particular for low-income earners, married women and single parents. In contrast, labour supply of males and those in the high-wage segment of the labour market appears to be quite insensitive to labour taxation.

Prescott (2004) observes that the lower labour supply in Europe, and not so much the lower hourly productivity of labour, accounts for the difference in living standards against the US. In studying the G-7 countries, he finds that tax rates alone account for most of the cross-country differences in labour supply.[12] In the early 1970s, Europeans worked more than Americans, while the opposite is true at present. Prescott argues that changes in tax rates since the early 1970s account for most of the changes in labour supply; significant increases in

taxation in the EU G-7 members after the early 1970s coincide with a relatively large decline in labour supply.

Within the neoclassical framework, lower employment should lead to higher average labour productivity, as the workers with below-average productivity are the first to exit from the labour market. However, there are other factors that may work in the opposite direction. Spill-over effects from increased employment can enhance the productivity of skilled workers and of capital, as suggested in some models of endogenous growth (e.g. Barro and Sala-i-Martin, 2003). Moreover, when individuals are outside the labour market, their skills deteriorate which reduces the potential for future productivity growth.

Several empirical studies have found significant positive correlation between measures of *human capital* and a country's growth performance (e.g. Romer, 1990, Mankiw, Romer and Weil, 1992), although the magnitude of this effect is disputed (Barro and Lee, 1992). Human capital affects productivity both directly and indirectly:

- First, an increase in human capital directly improves the *quality of labour* and therefore its productivity (Harberger 1996);

---

[11] In the standard neoclassical textbook labour-leisure model (see Zagler and Duernecker, 2003), at a given gross wage, labour taxes affect individual labour supply decisions through an income effect (higher taxes reduce the net incomes, and an individual has to work more to maintain the same income level) and a substitution effect (an increase in taxation reduces the net income from an hour worked and, at the margin, makes leisure time more attractive). As these effects work in opposite directions, the total effect on labour supply is indeterminate.

[12] Labour supply is measured as hours worked per person aged 15 to 64. The study abstracts from a number of other possible factors that may explain labour supply, such as the number of wage earners in a household.

- Secondly, as the literature on economic growth suggests, additional human capital is associated with *positive spill-overs* which affect indirectly the productivity of labour and capital. In the activities of high-skilled workers (production, research), individual productivity also depends on co-workers' productivity (Lucas, 1988). Therefore a higher level of individual human capital should not only enhance individual earning capacities but also promote overall productivity growth in the economy (Caucutt, Imrohoroglu and Kumar, 2003).

Tax rates and the design of income tax systems have been found to affect human capital formation. The primary economic incentive for individuals to invest in human capital is the expectation of higher lifetime earnings and future wages (Zagler and Duernecker, 2003). As higher tax wedges on labour are associated with lower future net earnings, they reduce the incentives to acquire skills.

Moreover, a more progressive tax schedule is associated with higher disincentive effects, as the future returns on investments in human capital are taxed at a higher tax rate than the lower earnings without additional schooling that would be foregone when engaging in the acquisition of additional knowledge (Poterba, 2002; Gentry and Hubbard, 2002). However, Heckman, Lochner and Taber (1998) show that replacing the progressive U.S. income tax by a proportional tax can be expected to have only small effects on skill formation. On the basis of a simulation study, Trostel (1993) shows that a one percentage point decrease in the marginal tax rate induces a long-term increase in human capital of 0.97 %.

1.3.3 Taxation of enterprises

Productivity-enhancing innovations are often introduced to the market by new enterprises. OECD (2003c), on the basis of data from a firm-level database, shows that new firms in general contribute positively to industry productivity growth in European countries, and their contribution is higher than in the US. However, most of the observed productivity growth at the aggregate industry level is due to incumbent firms. Moreover, cross-country differences with regard to the contribution of new firms to productivity growth are considerable.

This section focuses on the enterprise sector and discusses two potential channels via which taxation can influence productivity growth:

- First, taxation affects the incentives to start an enterprise;

- Secondly, taxation influences enterprises' investment behaviour and, at the international level, may influence foreign direct investment flows.

Robson, Wren (1999) show that higher marginal tax rates lead to a decline in self-employment rates as they reduce the return to effort and therefore discourage *entrepreneurial activity*. Gentry, Hubbard (2000) point at the role of the progression of the tax schedule: a more progressive taxation of business incomes disproportionately reduces the after-tax return of successful entrepreneurs and thus lowers average returns, hence reducing the incentives for entrepreneurial activity. For the US, they show that the probability of entry into self-employment is negatively correlated with the progression of the tax schedule.

On the other hand, Long (1982) and Blau (1987), using time series regressions to explore the relationship between marginal federal tax rates and the rates of self-employment in the U.S., find a positive correlation. The explanation offered for this result is that high tax rates induce workers to shift from paid employment to self-employment where taxes can be evaded more easily. A number of more recent studies (e.g. Fairlie and Meyer, 2000; Briscoe, Dainty and Millett, 2000) conclude that the correlation between tax rates and self-employment is in general weak and of a limited size. Gordon (1998) and Cullen and Gordon (2003) point to the importance of the tax treatment of losses in influencing the incentives for entrepreneurship.

Several authors stress the importance of capital gains taxation under imperfect capital markets (Gordon, 1998; Fuest and Huber, 2003). They argue that taxes on capital gains realised by venture capitalists who provide capital to start-ups can lead to a sub-optimal supply of venture capital and therefore dampen innovation and entrepreneurship. Anand (1996) shows that the taxation of capital gains has a significant influence on the supply of venture capital in the telecommunication industry. In contrast, Poterba (1989) argues that cuts in capital gains taxes are not an effective instrument to spur innovative activities, as venture capital only accounts for a small share in investors' total capital income.

International tax differentials may distort the *international allocation of capital*, impeding the equalization of the marginal productivity of capital across countries. This implies that overall (global) productivity could be increased by a re-allocation of capital from low-tax to high-tax Member States. Foreign direct investment (FDI) is also an important channel for the transfer of productivity-enhancing technologies and management methods. Several empirical contributions focusing on the US and the UK find that foreign-owned firms show higher labour productivity than domestically-owned firms (e.g. Doms and Jensen, 1998; Griffith, 2003).[13]

Empirical studies show that FDI displays some sensitivity to international tax differentials, although the magnitude of the correlation is disputed (for a review of empirical contributions see Hines, 1999 and de Mooij and Ederveen, 2003). In an empirical analysis of the sensitivity of the operations of multinational corporations to host country taxation, Mutti and Grubert (2004) show that the location decisions of US majority-owned foreign affiliates oriented to export markets are considerably and increasingly influenced by host country taxation.

In a recent study including the EU Member States, Gorter and Parikh (2003) find that a one percentage point reduction in the effective corporate income tax rate relative to the European mean in an EU Member State induces investors from the other Member States to increase their FDI position by about 4 %. In their meta analysis, covering 25 empirical studies on the impact of corporate taxes on the allocation of FDI, de Mooij and Ederveen (2003) find that the median value of the tax rate elasticity of FDI is about -3.3, i.e. a one percentage point reduction in the host-country tax rate increases FDI in that country by 3.3 %.

The case for international harmonisation or co-ordination of corporate taxation remains disputed.[14] The evidence for the past quarter of century in the EU points to a downward convergence of statutory corporate income tax rates and effective corporate tax rates.[15]

1.4 Public spending

1.4.1 Introduction

Pressures to increase the efficiency of public spending come from many directions: in many countries, there is a need to reduce the high levels of public debt or to cut taxation; simultaneously, population ageing is leading to an increase in pension and health expenditures. EU Member States outline their medium-term budgetary discipline strategies in their Stability or Convergence Programmes. These often target also the procedural side of government spending by the use of fiscal rules (tax, expenditure, budget balance or debt ceilings); extension of the planning horizon; reduction in the fragmentation of the budget (into extra-budgetary funds and contingent liabilities).[16] In general, there is an increasing emphasis on the outcomes of public spending.

In 2003, overall government spending amounted to 49 % of GDP in EU-15. Differences in expenditure levels across the Member States are large, with the Czech Republic, Sweden, Denmark and France displaying the highest public expenditures and the Baltic States and Ireland the lowest (Graph 1.4). In most EU-15 Member States, the share of public spending in GDP has declined since the early 1990s.

Over the last 40 years, economists have profoundly changed the way they seek to quantify the impact of public expenditures on economic performance. They have abandoned the traditional Keynesian and neoclassical macroeconomic frameworks in favour of an empirically-oriented approach. Current economic analysis, instead of considering the multiplier effects of the overall size of government spending, distinguishes between the impacts of different types of government spending. While the available empirical studies suggest that government spending has some positive effects on economic performance, the *net* effect of the government activities on the economy often remains ambiguous.

At an aggregated level, Afonso, Schuknecht and Tanzi (2003; see also section 1.2) analyse the performance of public sectors in 23 OECD countries. They find that countries with small governments (public spending below 40 % of GDP in 2000) in general performed better than countries with medium-sized or large governments. The higher public sector efficiency in countries with small governments points to diminishing marginal products in public spending.

The results of Afonso et al. (op cit.) stand in contrast to those of La Porta et al. (1999). The latter carry out a correlation analysis and report that (a) high taxes are not necessarily a sign of an inferior

---

[13] Chapter 4 in European Commission (2003b) discusses the role of foreign direct investment in boosting productivity growth in the Central and East European new Member States and candidate countries.

[14] For a discussion of the initiatives on company tax harmonisation currently contemplated on the EU level see e.g. Cnossen (2003), Devereux (2004), Sorensen (2004) or Zodrow (2003).

[15] For the development of nominal corporate income tax rates in the OECD, see KPMG (2004); for a survey of a number of recent studies on effective tax rates based on different methodologies, see Schratzenstaller (2003).

[16] See also Joumard et al. (2004).

Graph 1.4: General government expenditure in EU Member States in 2003, % of GDP

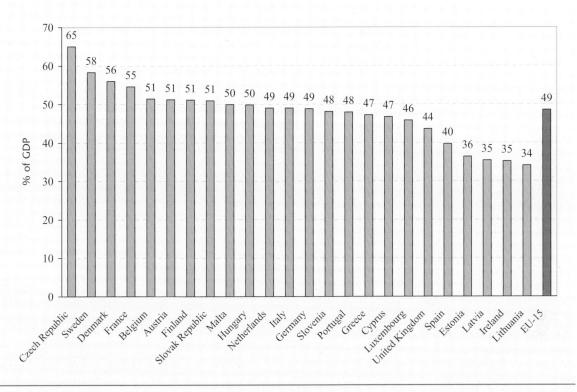

Notes: No data available for Poland; data for Slovakia and Slovenia are for 2002.

Source: Eurostat New Cronos.

government; (b) the quality of public goods is high in countries with efficient governments; (c) countries with larger governments are less corrupt, have fewer bureaucratic delays, better provision of public goods, but also higher tax rates; and (d) freer governments are larger, more efficient, they intervene less and provide better public goods. In the study by La Porta et al., larger governments on average perform better with respect to performance indicators such as the quality of business regulation, bureaucratic delays and infrastructure quality. The conflicting results of Afonso et al. and La Porta et al. may partly be explained by the differences in the country samples: Afonso et al. consider OECD countries only, while La Porta et al. include many developing countries in their sample.

Graph 1.5 compares the size of government and labour productivity in the total economy across the Member States. At such an aggregated level, it is difficult to detect any link between productivity and government size. Ireland stands out with its high productivity and low level of government spending. Also Luxembourg combines a very high level of productivity with below-average government size. The three Member States with the highest level of

government spending – Czech Republic, Sweden and Denmark – display productivity levels below or close to the EU average. The three Baltic States are characterised by very low levels of both productivity and government spending.

The structure of public expenditures in EU-15 is illustrated in Graph 1.6. By far the largest part of overall public spending goes to social protection which amounts to almost 19 % of GDP and is a major instrument of redistribution. The next two largest spending items in EU-15 are health and general public services.[17] The high spending on social protection is the most important single feature which distinguishes the EU from the US and Japan (where public spending on social protection accounts for 7 % and 10 % of GDP respectively). On health, EU-15 governments spend slightly more than the US, while the GDP share of education spending in EU-15 is slightly below that of the US.

---

[17] General public services are composed of expenditures for executive and legislative organs, financial and fiscal affairs, external affairs; foreign economic aid; general services; basic research; R&D, general public services; public debt transactions; and transfers of a general character between different levels of government. A detailed classification is provided at: http://unstats.un.org/unsd/cr/registry/regcst.asp?Cl=4&Lg=1.

Graph 1.5: Government expenditures and labour productivity in EU Member States in 2003

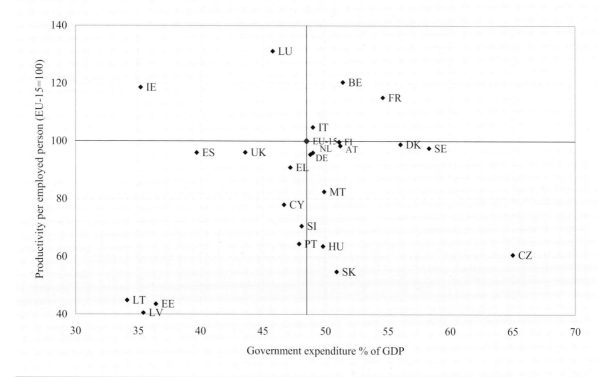

Notes: Labour productivity refers to the total (public and private) economy. Poland is not included due to lack of data on government expenditure; government expenditures in Slovakia and Slovenia refer to 2002.

Source: Eurostat New Cronos.

Graph 1.6: Public expenditures by category in EU-15 in 2001, % of GDP

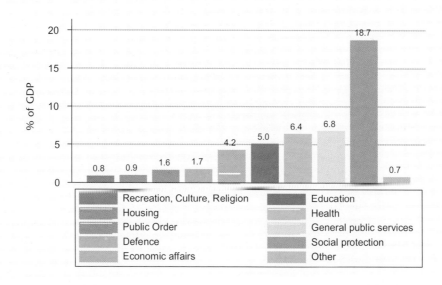

Note: The categories of expenditure are following COFOG (classification of the functions of government).

Source: Eurostat New Cronos.

On defence, EU-15 Member States spend on average 1.7 % of GDP, less than half of the US defence spending.

The remainder of this section reviews recent literature on the productivity effects of government outlays by type of spending. Outlays on public infrastructure, education, research and development are reviewed in turn.

1.4.2 Physical infrastructure

Physical infrastructure can be seen as a public good, which should be provided collectively – consumers and firms can usually not be excluded from consumption, and one person's consumption does not reduce the amount available to others. In empirical studies, infrastructures provided by the public sector are usually defined as comprising roads and motorways, water and sewer system, dwellings and sometimes public research and development capital. Most studies show that public infrastructures (i) decrease the costs of firms and contribute to their production possibilities, and (ii) are an important factor for attracting firms and start-ups.

European Commission (2003c) provides a survey of recent studies on the effect of investments in public capital. The majority of existing work suggests that public capital has a positive impact on output, productivity or growth. However, in most studies the positive impact is not strong, and there are cases where the impact is insignificant or even negative. The weak results may reflect the fact that a large part of public investments only have an indirect influence on productivity (for example, provision of public housing, or water and sewers).

There is considerably more empirical work available for the USA than for other economic regions (see Table 1.2). A number of contributions estimate the impact of public capital on production and rely on panel data for the 48 states of continental USA over the period from 1970 to the end of the 1980s. Stephan (1997) provides a survey of 15 studies using such data. Early investigations concluded that public capital had a positive impact on production, with an estimated output elasticity with respect to public capital included between 0.05 and 0.30. However, more recent studies have not been able to confirm these findings. Holtz-Eakin (1994), for instance, argues that an apparent impact of public capital on value added could be due to neglecting individual heterogeneity in panel data analysis.

Zegeye (2000) uses very detailed data for a sample of 1,514 U.S. counties covering the years 1982, 1987 and 1992 and concludes that public capital significantly increases productivity. The elasticity of output to capital he finds is relatively small (between 0.022 and 0.133), but statistically significant. Fernald (1999) considers a longer time period (1953-1989) for 29 U.S. sectors and finds that roads had an important impact on productivity in the sub-period 1953-1973; thereafter, the productivity impact gradually declined to a very low level. The detailed data Fernald uses, containing information on vehicles used for production, allow him to conclude that 'correlation between productivity and public capital primarily reflects causation from public capital to productivity'.

Most contributions for European and Japanese regions report a positive impact of public infrastructure on production. Regional data are available for France, Germany, Italy, Spain and Japan, yielding estimates for the output elasticity with respect to public capital which lie between 0.08 and 0.65 (see Stephan 1997, 2003). Also national-level data have

Table 1.2: Estimates of the impact of infrastructure on production

Surveys	Data	Results
15 contributions reviewed by Stephan (1997)	Panel of 48 U.S. states for the period 1970 to end of the1980s	$\varepsilon(y;g)=0.15$ on average in studies prior to 1994. This elasticity is not significant in post 1994 studies
9 papers reviewed by Stephan (1997 and 2003) and Picci (1999)	Panel of regions for different European countries	$\varepsilon(y;g)=0.20$ on average and almost always significantly different from zero
7 studies reviewed by Stephan (1997)	Panel of OECD or G7 countries	$\varepsilon(y;g)$ is only significant in 3 out of 7 studies, in which case $\varepsilon(y;g)=0.30$ on average
9 studies reviewed by Stephan (1997)	Time series for economy wide or sector level, different countries	$\varepsilon(y;g)=0.30$ on average and often significant

been used to investigate the impact of variations in the level of public capital on productivity growth differentials between countries. However, no clear conclusions arise from such cross-country comparisons; in four of the seven studies, the impact is insignificant.

Instead of relying on data for different geographic areas, time series data for a country or for different industries within a country have been used to relate temporal variations in the level of the public capital stock to variations in the level of production (see Stephan, 1997). Empirical studies using such data find a positive impact of public capital on productivity growth. The mean value of the production elasticity with respect to public capital is about 0.30 and mostly significant. However, two caveats are worth mentioning: (i) time series variables are often non-stationary, and (ii) in this framework, it is difficult to deal with reverse causation from productivity to public investment.

Finally, instead of estimating the impact of public capital on the level of output, many studies assess the effects of public capital on the (private) cost of production. It can be shown that any production-enhancing public infrastructure also decreases the private costs of production. Since cost and input demand functions are related, this framework allows one to derive directly the impact of public infrastructure on private input demands. Musolesi (2002) reviews 22 papers, published during the last 15 years, using the cost function approach. The empirical estimates of the cost saving impact of public infrastructure are in line with those obtained from the production function approach: on average, one percent additional public capital reduces private costs of production by 0.16 percent.

The empirical findings lead to two concluding observations. First, the outcomes are different for the US and Europe. Whereas recent studies for the US find either no significant, or a small positive, impact of public infrastructure on productivity, the estimated impact is higher and mostly significant for European countries. Secondly, some studies point to decreasing marginal returns in public infrastructure. This could explain the variety of empirical results for US regions. Decreasing returns in public infrastructure may be relevant also for European countries, but there is no evidence of them yet.

1.4.3 Education

The economic rationale for government involvement in education rests on the existence of externalities, economies of scale and other market failures, as well as distributional motives (Hanushek, 2002). If the social rate of return on human capital is, due to externalities, higher than the private rate of return, individuals' investment in human capital may be sub-optimal. Also capital market imperfections (difficulty to finance studies) may impede a socially optimal investment in human capital. Public expenditures, such as the costless provision of education, or subsidies to higher education, can be justified on these grounds.

A vast theoretical literature stresses the importance of education and human capital for economic growth: a skilled workforce is more likely to develop and adopt new technologies, thereby shifting potential output and productivity upwards. However, there is no consensual evidence as to whether the education system is under- or over-financed by the public sector.

Following Barro (1991), many empirical contributions report positive correlation between schooling and growth. This literature, however, is subject to three important qualifications:

• The strong correlation between schooling and growth may be a consequence of the omission of other relevant variables from the analysis;

• Anticipated economic growth may induce more people to stay longer at schools. Bils and Klenow (2000) provide empirical evidence of this. As a consequence, a part of the observed correlation between schooling and growth is explained by the fact that expected growth implies more schooling, not by the fact that schooling leads to economic growth.

• Acemoglu and Angrist (2000) are unable to find significant evidence for the presence of externalities in schooling. This is in line with Hanushek (2002, p. 2066) who concludes that: 'little evidence exists that distinguishes externalities in economic growth from simply the impact of better workers and more human capital'.

The thrust of empirical work that fails to establish a firm positive relationship between the level of education and income growth is based on endogenous growth models which treat human capital not as an input of the production function, but as a determinant of innovation. In such a setting, Benhabib and Spiegel (1994) were not able to find a positive contribution of changes in years of schooling in their growth regressions. In another strand of the literature, based on an extended version of the neoclassical growth model in the tradition of Mankiw, Romer and Weil (1992), human capital is regarded as a factor of production. Soto (2002) applies this model to empirical estimation and concludes that years of schooling fit well in a neoclassical production function.

While most contributions consider the relationship between the quantity of schooling (such as the number of years spent in education) and growth, Hanushek and Kimko (2000) analyse the quality of schooling. To measure quality, they use the cognitive performance of students in various international tests. They find that differences in the quality of schooling contribute significantly to explaining differences in economic performance. Although Barro (2001) reports similar results, the robustness of his findings has not yet been confirmed. Coulombe et al. (2004) analyse panel data of cross-country growth in 14 OECD countries. Their results suggest that human capital indicators based on literacy scores have a positive and significant effect on the long run levels of GDP per capita and labour productivity. Neri (2003) includes life expectancy as an indicator for health in the model, which not only has a significant impact on growth, but also lowers the impact of schooling quality.

1.4.4 Research and development[18]

When the commercial exploitation of an innovation cannot be confined to the firm which conducted the relevant research, also competitors will share in the benefits of the research activity. As a consequence, each individual firm will innovate less than would be optimal from a social point of view. This has frequently been used as a justification of government spending on research and development (R&D) for sustaining an innovative economy.

Whereas the lack of incentives for carrying out R&D projects was identified by Arrow (1962), first empirical studies trying to measure the rate of return of R&D appeared soon afterwards. Estimations of the difference between private and the social rate of return of R&D were surveyed by Griliches (1992) and by Griffith (2000). The empirical framework used to evaluate the impact of public infrastructures on private productivity is easily extended to analyse the effects of R&D on productivity. The result that the social rate of return to R&D is about twice as high as the private rate of return appears to be a robust – but not always significant – finding.

Public involvement in research and development activity can take two forms: (i) government research at universities or in government laboratories; and (ii) indirect involvement through financing or subsidising R&D in the business sector. Some studies have sought to find out whether public spending on R&D simply replaces private research (substitution) or whether the public funds lead to an increase in overall R&D (additionality). David, Hall and Toole (2000) review the available econometric evidence accumulated over more than 35 years on possible crowding out of private R&D. They conclude that one third of the 33 studies considered, conducted on all levels of aggregation, report some kind of substitution, while two thirds do not.

A number of empirical studies attempt to distinguish the growth effects of (i) business R&D, (ii) government R&D and (iii) foreign R&D. Guellec and van Pottelsberghe (2001) estimate regressions for 16 OECD countries covering the period 1980-1998, explaining total factor productivity by the various R&D aggregates. They find a long-term elasticity of government and university performed research on productivity of 0.17, which compares to 0.13 for business R&D and 0.45 to 0.50 for foreign R&D.

Part of the impact of public research on overall productivity is indirect and depends on the exploitation of the results in the business sector. Established strong links between public and private research should enhance this effect. The provision of high quality scientific, technical and managerial education is essential to the successful dissemination of innovation. The result of foreign R&D having a higher impact on productivity growth than domestic R&D points to the importance of the capacity to absorb foreign technology.

1.5 Regulatory framework

1.5.1 Introduction

A basic function of government is to safeguard public order and safety. In industrialised economies, the regulatory system seeks to promote many other goals as well, including public health and safety, social objectives or the protection of the environment. The quality of the regulatory system, as well as the efficiency of public administration, affect the production costs of firms and the ways in which production is organised. An efficient regulatory system promotes efficiency and innovation while excessively bureaucratic procedures or outdated technical regulations can harm productivity and competitiveness.

---

[18]   See also Chapter 2 of the present Report.

Since productivity growth is usually not the primary objective of regulations, the effects on productivity come as a by-product and are often hard to measure in quantitative terms. A significant part of research on regulations and productivity growth focuses on the role of product market regulation, market entry and competition policies. These will be discussed briefly below. A short review of recent analysis on the role of environmental regulations closes the section. In many cases, sector- or industry-specific regulations are particularly important for firm productivity but a discussion of sector-specific rules is outside the scope of this Chapter.

1.5.2 Competition

Competition can be expected to provide incentives for improved efficiency via three channels (see Armstrong, Cowan and Vickers, 1994):

- First, *allocative efficiency*. Competition leads to an efficient allocation of resources across markets, equalizing the marginal rate of transformation to the marginal rate of substitution. A large body of literature highlights the importance of market entry for productivity performance (see for example Caves, 1998; Geroski, 1995);

- Secondly, *efficient organisation of production* within firms. Competition provides managerial incentives for the reduction of organisational slack and X-inefficiency (Leibenstein, 1966). A series of studies in the tradition of principal-agent theory show that competition induces firms to be more efficient by reducing their agency problems (Hart, 1983; Nalebuff and Stiglitz, 1983; Mookherjee, 1984; Willig, 1987; Hermalin, 1992);

- Thirdly, competition may lead to *increased innovative activity*. Empirical support for the assumption that competition forces firms to innovate is quite broad (e.g. Nickell, 1996; Blundell et al., 1995; Geroski, 1990; 1995; Porter, 2000). A number of economists believe that the relationship between competition and innovation has the shape of an inverted U: introduction of competition into monopolistic markets enhances innovation until a given level of market de-concentration. Beyond that point, higher intensity of competition would reduce the rents on innovation: atomistic competition would not necessarily spur innovation.[19]

Bayoumi et al. (2004) note that the US has a lower regulatory burden than other countries, which is reflected in more competitive markets and lower markups. They use a general equilibrium model to assess the macroeconomic effects of increased competition in Europe. Bayoumi et al. (op cit.) estimate that an increase in competition in labour and product markets to US levels could boost GDP in the euro area by more than 12 %, as both investment and hours worked would rise markedly (over 20 % and 10 %, respectively). This is an important empirical finding and suggests that incompletely competitive markets in the EU are leading to sub-optimal economic performance.

Scarpetta et al. (2002) find firm-level evidence suggesting that a stringent regulatory setting in product markets has a negative effect on productivity and on market access by (mainly small- and medium-sized) firms.

Djankov et al. (2000) note that entry regulation may be acceptable if it leads to higher consumer welfare in terms of factors such as product quality, water pollution, death from accidental poisoning or the size of the unofficial economy. However, the authors conclude that the opposite seems to hold: their empirical 'results are broadly consistent with the public choice theory that sees regulation as a mechanism to create rents for politicians and the firms they support'.

Nicoletti and Scarpetta (2003) estimate the impact of regulations on multi-factor productivity using indicators of regulation as developed in Nicoletti et al. (1999). They note that overall regulations have been substantially reduced since the 1970s. In manufacturing, regulatory reforms mostly concerned administrative simplification and trade liberalisation. However, reform has been deepest in non-manufacturing where, partly due to strong economies of scale and pervasive market failure, markets were most restricted by regulations on entry, prices and supply.

Nicoletti and Scarpetta (op cit.) conclude that economy-wide product market regulations that curb competition and private governance have a negative effect on productivity, mainly by slowing down technological catch-up. This effect is strongest for countries which are further behind the technological frontier. They estimate that entry liberalisation in services should boost annual multi-factor productivity growth in the overall business sector by about 0.1–0.2 percentage points in countries like Portugal, Greece and Italy.

Within the services sector, major efforts of market liberalisation have been made in particular in

---

[19] Empirical evidence for the 'inverted-U' is quite strong (e.g. Scherer, 1967; Scott, 1984; Levin et al., 1985; Caves and Barton, 1990; Green and Mayes, 1991; Caves et al., 1992; Aghion et al., 2002).

network industries: telecommunications, postal services, electricity, gas, railways and air transport. In telecommunications, EU legislation imposed full competition as from January 1998: although market concentration remains high, prices declined by about 23 % between 1996 and 2000 (ECB, 2001).[20] Liberalisation in the energy sector proceeded at a slower pace.

Bains, Dierx, Pichelmann and Roeger (2002) estimate that the liberalisation of energy and telecommunications markets resulted in a reduction of some $^1/_2$ percentage point in the aggregate economy-wide mark-up. Evidence for individual countries suggests generally positive effects of liberalisation (see Gagnepain and Marin, 2004, for aviation; Friebel et al., 2004, for the railroad sector; Arocena and Price, 2002, for electricity generators in Spain).

1.5.3 Environmental regulations

Environmental regulations set standards or incentives which induce enterprises to behave in environmentally responsible ways. They may require enterprises to change their production methods and hence involve compliance costs. The effects on competitiveness and productivity depend on issues such as the degree of competition on the market and the method of financing the compliance costs (productivity may be affected if environmental improvements are financed e.g. by cutting research expenditures). In a survey of several empirical studies on the impact of environmental regulation on productivity growth, Jaffe et al. (1995) conclude that 'empirical analyses of these productivity effects have found modest adverse impacts of environmental regulation'.

Gollop and Roberts (1983) report that regulating the emission of electric utilities lowered total factor productivity by 0.59 percentage points. Gray (1987) finds that health, safety and environmental regulations caused total factor productivity in US manufacturing industries to decrease by 0.44 percentage points on average (that is, 30 % of the productivity growth). Conrad and Wastl (1995) find a smaller but growing negative impact of environmental regulations on total factor productivity in German manufacturing industries. Gray and Shadbegian (1998) show that regulation crowds out more productive investments in other areas.

Porter (1990) and Porter and van der Linden (1995) challenge the conventional view of the exclusively negative productivity impact of environmental regulations. Porter and van der Linden (op cit.) maintain that strict regulations, if properly designed, can stimulate firms to discover cost-effective ways of complying with environmental regulation. The revenues from such innovations can outweigh the compliance costs. Furthermore, firms may gain first-mover advantages through the development of environmental technology which can be beneficial later on when also other countries introduce stricter environmental legislation. Porter and van der Linden (op cit.) present case study evidence in support of their hypothesis.

Porter and van Linden's (op cit.) work has triggered a huge body of literature (see for example Haq et al. 2001; Xepapadeas and de Zeeuw, 1999; Köppl and Pichl, 1997; and Palmer, Oates and Portney, 1995). Critiques of the 'Porter hypothesis' – regulations stimulate firms to become more innovative – argue that within rational economic modelling, it cannot be explained why firms would not see the opportunities for cost-reducing innovations by themselves in the absence of regulation. Palmer, Oates and Portney (1995) point out that the message of cost-less regulation in Porter and van der Linden (op cit.) distracts attention from the cost-benefit-analysis which should be at the core of policy decisions.

An increasing number of contributions lend support to the 'Porter Hypothesis'. OECD (2001, 9), in reviewing the environmental achievements of its member countries, notes that 'environmental policies have often provided positive incentives for economic restructuring and technological innovation.' According to Lanoie, Patry and Lajeunesse (2001), while current environmental regulation lowers total factor productivity growth, past regulations have a positive impact on productivity. Esty and Porter (2001) find a relationship between environmental regulation and competitiveness at country level. Using an international database on environmental performance, environmental regulatory regimes, economic and legal framework and economic competitiveness, they find 'no evidence that improving environmental quality compromises economic progress'. On the contrary, strong environmental performance appears to be positively correlated with competitiveness.

1.6 Concluding remarks

This Chapter has discussed various ways in which government interventions affect productivity and economic growth. The importance of a high-quality public service for national competitiveness is widely

---

[20]   See also European Commission (2003d).

recognised: it reaches from the role of the public sector as an efficient producer of public services to the effects of modern infrastructure, education and public research, to taxation and the regulatory system.

In many cases, the productivity effects of government action come as a by-product of policies which primarily target other goals. Productivity effects may be positive or negative; where trade-offs are unavoidable, awareness of the costs and benefits helps policy makers in making their choices.

Over the last ten years, most EU Member States have been under pressure to curb public spending. Monetary Union and the Stability and Growth Pact have set norms on public debt and deficits; international tax competition makes it difficult to maintain tax rates significantly above those of other countries; and the persistently high unemployment rate has created pressures to reduce taxes on labour which are likely adversely to affect work incentives. Moreover, population ageing has forced governments to take measures to consolidate public finances in anticipation of the increasing financing burden of public pensions.

The pressures on financing the public sector call for a careful assessment of the justification for each type of public spending. Two conclusions from the review of empirical studies in this Chapter are worth recalling. First, there is some cross-country evidence suggesting that, despite the reforms which have been carried out in the public sector in recent years, many countries should be able to provide the same public services as today at a significantly lower budgetary cost by enhancing the efficiency in their provision. Productivity improvements in the provision of public services would free resources for other uses.

Secondly, many types of public spending – such as education, infrastructure, or research – are identified as having positive effects on the productivity of private enterprises. However, there is much more ambiguity surrounding the estimates of the optimal extent of government spending on each item: while an increase in government spending may have a further favourable effect on growth, in some cases the additional resources might have been in a more productive use in the private sector. There is some evidence suggesting that smaller governments are more efficient than larger ones, which points to the existence of diminishing marginal products of public spending.

Governments that wish to increase public spending are faced with the need to increase taxes or to raise debt. As a regulator, governments are less directly confronted with the economic costs of the regulations, as these tend to fall on producers or consumers. Nevertheless, regulatory reforms are high on the agenda in many countries as well as the EU where the European Commission has adopted an action plan for Better Regulation.

This Chapter has omitted the discussion of the links between productivity and the general institutional and legal framework. Institutions may have a role in determining productivity performance, but are outside the scope of the present Report, as are industry-specific regulations and the regulation of labour markets.

References

Acemoglu, D. and Angrist, J. (2000): 'How large are human-capital externalities? Evidence from compulsory schooling laws', in: Bernanke, B. S. and Rogoff, K., *NBER Macroeconomics Annual*, Cambridge, MIT Press.

Afonso, A., Schuknecht, L. and Tanzi, V. (2003): 'Public sector efficiency: An international comparison', European Central Bank, Working Paper 242, July.

Afonso, A. and St.Aubyn, M. (2004): 'Non-parametric approaches to education and health expenditure efficiency in OECD countries', Technical University of Lisbon, Economics Working Paper 1/2004, January.

Aghion, P., Bloom, N., Blundell, R., Griffithe, R. and Howitt, P. (2002): 'Competition and innovation: An inverted U relationship', The Institute of Fiscal Studies, WP02/04.

Anand, B.N. (1996): 'Tax effects on venture capital', mimeo, Yale.

Armstrong, M., Cowan, S. and Vickers, J. (1994): 'Regulatory reform – Economic analysis and British experience', Cambridge, MIT Press.

Arocena, P. and Price, C.W. (2002): 'Generating efficiency: Economic and environmental regulation of public and private electricity generators in Spain', International Journal of Industrial Organization 20, pp. 41-69.

Arrow, K. (1962): 'Economic welfare and the allocation of resources for inventions', in: Nelson, R. (ed.): *The rate and direction of inventive activity*, Princeton University Press, Princeton, pp. 609-625.

Bains, M., Dierx, A., Pichelmann, K. and Roeger, W. (2002): 'Structural reforms in labour and product markets and macroeconomic performance in the EU', Chapter 2, The EU Economy, 2002 Review.

Barro, R. (1991): 'Economic growth in a cross-section of countries', Quarterly Journal of Economics, 106, pp. 407-443.

Barro, R. (2001): 'Human capital and growth', American Economic Review, 91, pp. 12-17.

Barro, R.J. and Lee, J.W. (1992): 'International comparisons of educational attainment, 1960-1985', mimeo, Harvard.

Barro, R.J. and Sala-i-Martin, X. (2003): 'Economic growth', 2nd ed., New York et al.

Batley, R. (1999): 'The role of government in adjusting economies: an overview of findings', International Development Department, University of Birmingham, Birmingham, Alabama.

Baxter, M. (2000): 'Developments in the measurement of general government output', Economic Trends 562, pp. 3-5, September.

Bayoumi, T., Laxton, D. and Pesenti, P. (2004): 'Benefits and Spillovers of Greater Competition in Europe: A Macroeconomic Assessment', International Finance Discussion Papers No. 803, Board of Governors of the Federal Reserve System, April.

Benhabib, J. and Spiegel, M. (1994): 'The role of human capital in economic development: evidence from aggregate cross-country data', Journal of Monetary Economics, 34, pp. 143-173.

Bennett, J., Estrin, S., Maw, J. and Urga, G. (2004): 'Privatization methods and economic growth in transition economies', Centre for Economic Policy Research, Discussion Paper No. 4291, March.

Bils, M., and Klenow, P. (2000): 'Does schooling cause growth?', American Economic Review 90, pp. 1160-1183, December.

Blau, D.M. (1987): 'A time-series analysis of self-employment in the United States', Journal of Political Economy, 95, pp. 445-467.

Blundell, R., Griffiths, R. and Reenen, J.V. (1995): 'Dynamic count data model of technological innovations', Economic Journal 105, pp. 333-344.

Briscoe, G., Dainty, A. and Millett, S. (2000): 'The impact of the tax system on self-employment in the British construction industry', International Journal of Manpower, 21, pp. 596-613.

Caucutt, E.M., Imrohoroglu, S. and Kumar, K.B. (2003): 'Growth and welfare analysis of tax progressivity in a heterogeneous-agent model', Review of Economic Dynamics, 6, pp. 546-577.

Caves, R.E. (1998): 'Industrial organization and new findings on the turnover and mobility of firms', Journal of Economic Literature, 36, pp. 1947-82.

Caves, R.E. et al. (1992): 'Industrial efficiency in six nations', Cambridge, Mass., MIT Press.

Caves, R.E. and Barton, D.R. (1990): 'Efficiency in US manufacturing Industries', Cambridge, Mass., MIT Press.

Claessens, S. and Djankov, S. (2002): 'Privatization benefits in Eastern Europe', Journal of Public Economics 83, pp. 307-324.

Cnossen, S. (2003): 'How Much Tax Coordination in the European Union?', International Tax and Public Finance, 10, pp. 625-649.

Conrad, K. and Wastl, D. (1995): 'The Impact of Environmental Regulation on Productivity in German Industries', Empirical Economics, 20, pp. 615-633.

Coulombe, S., Tremblay, J.-F. and Marchand, S. (2004): 'Literacy scores, human capital and growth across fourteen OECD countries', Statistics Canada International Adult Literacy Survey, June.

Cullen, J.B. and Gordon, R.H. (2002): 'Taxes and Entrepreneurial Activity: Theory and Evidence for the U.S.', NBER Working Paper 9015.

David, P.A., Hall, B.H. and Toole, A.A. (2000): 'Is public R&D a complement or substitute for private R&D? A review of the econometric evidence', Research Policy 29(4-5), pp. 497-529, April.

De Mooij, R. and Ederveen, S. (2003): 'Taxation and Foreign Direct Investment: A Synthesis of Empirical Research', International Tax and Public Finance, 10, pp. 673-693.

Devereux, M.P. (2004): 'Debating Proposed Reforms of the Taxation of Corporate Income in the

European Union', International Tax and Public Finance, 11, pp. 71-89.

Djankov, S. and La Porta, R., López-de-Silanes, F. and Shleifer, A. (2002): 'The regulation of entry', Quarterly Journal of Economics, February.

Djankov, S. and Murrell, P. (2002): 'Enterprise restructuring in transition: A quantitative survey', Department of Economics, University of Maryland, mimeo (http://papers.ssrn.com/sol3/delivery.cfm/SSRN_ID 238716_code001031600.pdf?abstractid=238716).

Doms, M. and Jensen, B. (1998): 'Comparing Wages, Skills, and Productivity between Domestically- and Foreign-Owned Manufacturing Establishments in the United States', in: Lipsey, R.E., Baldwin, R.E., and Richardson, J.D. (eds.), Geography and Ownership as Bases for Economic Accounting, Chicago, pp. 235-258.

Easterly, W. and Rebelo, S. (1993): 'Fiscal policy and economic growth: An empirical investigation', Journal of Monetary Economics, 32, pp. 417-458.

ECB (2001): 'Price effects of regulatory reform in selected network industries', March.

Esty, D. and Porter, M.E. (2001): 'Ranking national environmental regulation and performance: A leading indicator of future competitiveness', The Global Competitiveness Report 2001-2002, New York, Oxford University Press.

European Commission (2004): 'Structures of the taxation systems in the European Union', 2004 edition, data 1995-2002, Eurostat.

European Commission (2003a): 'The role of eGovernment for Europe's future', COM(2003)567, 29 September.

European Commission (2003b): 'European Competitiveness Report 2003', SEC(2003)1299.

European Commission (2003c): 'Public finances in EMU 2003', European Economy No. 3.

European Commission (2003d): 'European Electronic Communications Regulation and Markets 2003 - Report on the Implementation of the EU Electronic Communications Regulatory Package', COM(2003)715 final.

Fairlie, R.W. and Meyer, B.D. (2000): 'Trends in Self-Employment Among White and Black Men: 1910-1990', Journal of Human Resources, 35, pp. 643-669.

Fernald, J. (1999): 'Roads to Prosperity? Assessing the Link Between Public Capital and Productivity', American Economic Review, 89, pp. 619-638.

Friebel, G., Ivaldi, M. and Vibes, C. (2004): 'Railway (de)regulation: A European efficiency comparison', Centre for Economic Policy Research (CEPR), Discussion Paper No. 4319, March.

Frydman, R., Gray, C., Hessel, M. and Rapaczynski, A. (1999): 'When does privatization work? The impact of private ownership on corporate performance in the transition economies', The Quarterly Journal of Economics, pp. 1153-1191, November.

Fuest, C. and Huber, B. (2003): 'Capital Gains Taxes, Venture Capitalists, and Entrepreneurship', mimeo, Cologne.

Gagnepain, P. and Marín, P.L. (2004): 'Regulation and incentives in European aviation', Centre for Economic Policy Research (CEPR), Discussion Paper No. 4318, March.

Gentry, W.M. and Hubbard, R.G. (2000): 'Tax Policy and Entrepreneurial Entry', American Economic Review, 90, pp. 283-287.

Gentry, W.M. and Hubbard, R.G. (2002): 'The Effect of Progressive Income Taxation on Job Turnover', NBER Working Paper 9226.

Geroski, P.A. (1995): 'Market structure, corporate performance and innovative activity', Oxford, Oxford University Press.

Gollop, F.M. and Roberts, M.J. (1983): 'Environmental Regulations and Productivity Growth: The case of Fossil-fueled Electric Power Generation', Journal of Political Economic, 91, pp. 654-674.

Gonenc, R., Maher, M. and Nicoletti, G. (2000): 'The implementation and the effects of regulatory reform: past experience and current issues', OECD Economics Department Working Papers, No. 251, June.

Gordon, R.H. (1998): 'Can High Personal Tax Rates Encourage Entrepreneurial Activity?', IMF Staff Papers, 45, pp. 49-80.

Gorter, J. and Parikh, A. (2003): 'How Sensitive is FDI to Differences in Corporate Income Taxation within the EU?', De Economist, 151(2), pp. 193-204.

Gray, W. (1987): 'The Cost of Regulation: OSHA, EPA and the Productivity Slowdown', American Economic Review, 77, pp. 998-1006.

Gray, W.B. and Shadbegian, R.J. (1998): 'Environmental Regulation, Investment Timing and Technology Choice', The Journal of Industrial Economics, 46, pp. 235-256.

Green, A. and Mayes, D.G. (1991): 'Technological inefficiency in manufacturing industries', Economic Journal 101, pp. 523-538.

Griffith, R. (2000): 'How important is business R&D for economic growth and should the government subsidise it?', Institute of Fiscal Studies, Briefing Notes No. 12, London.

Griffith, R. (2003): 'Characteristics of Foreign-Owned Firms in British Manufacturing', NBER Working Paper 9573.

Griliches, Z. (1992): 'The search for R&D spillovers', Scandinavian Journal of Economics, 94, pp. 29-47.

Guellec, D. and van Pottelsberghe de la Potterie, B. (2001): 'R&D and productivity growth: Panel data analysis of 16 OECD countries', OECD, STI Working Paper 2001/3, June.

Hanushek, E.A. (2002): 'Publicly Provided Education', in: Auerbach, A.J. and Feldstein, M. (eds.), Handbook of Public Economics, 4, North-Holland.

Hanushek, E.A. and Kimko, D.D. (2000): 'Schooling, labor force quality, and the growth of nations', American Economic Review, 90, pp. 1184-1208.

Haq, G. et al. (2001): 'Determining the costs to industry of environmental regulation', European Environment, 11.

Harberger (1998): 'A vision of the growth process', American Economic Review, 88, pp. 1-32.

Hart, O.D. (1983): 'The Market mechanism as an incentive scheme', Bell Journal of Economics, 14, pp. 366-82.

Heckman, J.J., Lochner, L. and Taber, Ch. (1998): 'Tax policy and human capital formation', NBER Working Paper 6462.

Hermalin, B.E. (1992): 'The effects of competition on executive behavior', Rand Journal of Economics, 23, pp. 350-65.

Hines, J.R. (1999): 'Lessons from Behavioral Responses to International Taxation', National Tax Journal, 52, pp. 305-322.

Holtz-Eakin, D. (1994): 'Public-Sector Capital and the Productivity Puzzle', Review of Economics and Statistics, 76, pp. 12-21.

IMD (2004): 'World Competitiveness Yearbook'.

Jaffe, A. B., Peterson, S.R., Portney, P.R. and Stavins, R.N. (1995): 'Environmental Regulation and the Competitiveness of U.S Manufacturing: What Does the Evidence Tell Us?', Journal of Economic Literature, 33, pp. 132-163.

Joumard, I., Kongsrud, P.M., Nam, Y.S. and Price, R. (2004): 'Enhancing the effectiveness of public spending: experience in OECD countries', OECD, Economics Department Working Papers, No. 380, 12 February, Paris.

Kneller, R., Bleaney, M.F. and Gemmell, N. (1999): 'Fiscal policy and economic growth: Evidence from OECD countries', Journal of Public Economics, 74, pp. 171-90.

Knox, C. (2002): 'Public service reform, Northern Ireland Executive', Review of Public Administration, Briefing Paper, 26 September (http://www.rpani.gov.uk/reform.pdf).

Köppl, A. and Pichl, C. (1997): 'Wettbewerbsvorteile durch umweltorientierte Innovationen, Überprüfung der First-Mover-These', Austrian Institute of Economic Research (WIFO).

KPMG (2004): Corporate tax rates survey – January, www.kpmg.com.

La Porta, R. and López-de-Silanes, F. (1999): 'The benefits of privatization: Evidence from Mexico', The Quarterly Journal of Economics, pp. 1193-1242, November.

La Porta, R., López-de-Silanes, F., Shleifer, A. and Vishny, R. (1999): 'The quality of government', Journal of Law Economics and Organizations, 15(1), pp. 222-279, Spring.

Lanoie, P., Patry, M. and Lajeunesse R. (2001): 'Environmental Regulation and Productivity: New Findings on the Porter Analysis', Cirano Working Paper 2001s-53, Montréal.

Lehtoranta, O. and Niemi, M. (1997): 'Measuring public sector productivity in Finland: progress report', Statistics Finland, March.

Leibenstein, H. (1966): 'Allocative efficiency versus X-efficiency', American Economic Review, 56, pp. 392-415.

Levin, R.C., Cohen, W.M. and Mowery D.C. (1985): 'R&D Appropriability, Opportunity, and Market Structure: New Evidence on Some Schumpeterian Hypotheses,' American Economic Review, 75, pp. 20-24.

Long, J.E. (1982): 'The Income Tax and Self-Employment', National Tax Journal, 35, pp. 31-42.

Lucas, R.E. (1988): 'On the mechanics of economic development', Journal of Monetary Economics, 22, pp. 3-42.

Mankiw, N.G., Romer, D. and Weil, D.N. (1992): 'A Contribution to the Empirics of Economic Growth', Quarterly Journal of Economics, 107(2), pp. 407-438.

Megginson, W.L. and Netter, J.M. (2001): 'From state to market: A survey of empirical studies on privatization', Journal of Economic Literature, 39(2), pp. 321-389, June.

Mendoza, E.G., Milesi-Ferretti G.M. and Asea, P. (1997): 'On the ineffectiveness of tax policy in altering long-run growth: Harberger's superneutrality conjecture', Journal of Public Economics, 66, pp. 99-126.

Mookherjee, D. (1984): 'Optimal incentive schemes with many agents', Review of Economic Studies, 51, pp. 433-46.

Mukherjee, R. and Wilkins, J.K. (1999): 'Unbundling Bureaucracy through Agency Creation', adjudicated paper presented at the IPAC National Conference, August 30, New Brunswick, Canada.

Musolesi, A. (2002): 'The Public Capital Hypothesis: A Review of Estimation Results', Dynamis-Quaderni, Discussion Paper No. 4/02.

Mutti, J. and Grubert, H. (2004): 'Empirical Asymmetries in Foreign Direct Investment and Taxation', Journal of International Economics, 62, pp. 337-358.

Nalebuff, B.J. and Stiglitz, J.E. (1983): 'Prizes and incentives: towards a general theory of compensation and competition', Bell Journal of Economics, 14, pp. 21-43.

Neri, F. (2003): 'Schooling, Labour Force Quality and the Growth of Nations: Comment', Working Paper 03-04, Department of Economics, University of Wollongong.

Nickell, S.J. (1996): 'Competition and corporate performance,' Journal of Political Economy, 104, pp. 724-766.

Nicoletti, G. and Scarpetta, S. (2003): 'Regulation, productivity and growth: OECD evidence', OECD, Economics Department Working Papers, No. 347, 13 January (World Bank Policy Research Working Paper 2944, Washington DC).

Nicoletti, G., Scarpetta, S. and Boylaud, O. (1999): 'Summary indicators of product market regulation with an extension to employment protection legislation', OECD, Economics Department Working Papers, No. 226.

OECD (1999): 'Productivity measurement in the general government sector', PUMA/HRM/M(99)1, Public Management Committee, April, OECD, Paris.

OECD (2003a): 'Economic Outlook', No. 74, OECD, Paris.

OECD (2003b): 'Revenue Statistics', OECD, Paris.

OECD (2003c): 'The sources of economic growth in OECD countries', OECD, Paris.

OECD (2001): 'Environmental performance reviews. Achievements in OECD countries', OECD, Paris.

Palmer, K., Oates, W.E. and Portney, P.R. (1995): 'Tightening environmental standards: The benefit-cost or the no-cost paradigm?' Journal of Economic Perspectives, 9(4), pp. 119-32.

Picci, L. (1999): 'Productivity and infrastructure in the Italian regions', Giornale degli Economisti e Annali di Economia, December.

Porter, M.E. (1990): 'The competitive advantage of nations', Free Press, New York.

Porter, M.E. (2000): 'The current competitiveness index: measuring the economic foundations of prosperity', in: The Global Competitiveness Report 2000, Geneva, World Economic Forum.

Porter, M. and Van der Linden, C. (1995): 'Green and competitive: breaking the stalemate', Harvard Business Review.

Poterba, J.M. (1989): 'Venture capital and capital gains taxation', in: Summers, L. (ed.), *Tax policy and the economy*, vol. 3, pp. 47-68, Cambridge.

Poterba, J.M. (2002): 'Taxation, Risk-Taking, and Household Portfolio Behavior', in: Auerbach, A.J. and Feldstein, M. (eds.), *Handbook of Public Economics*, Amsterdam.

Prescott, E.C. (2004): 'Why do Americans work so much more than Europeans?', NBER Working Paper 10316, February.

Pritchard, A. (2002): 'Measuring productivity change in the provision of public service', paper for the NIESR Conference on Productivity and Performance in the Provision of Public Services, 19 November, London.

Robson, M.T. and Wren, C. (1999): 'Marginal and Average Tax Rates and the Incentive for Self-Employment', Southern Economic Journal, 65, pp. 757-773.

Romer, P.M. (1990): 'Human capital and growth: Theory and evidence', Carnegie-Rochester Conference Series on Public Policy, 32, pp. 251-286.

Scarpetta, S., Hemmings, P., Tressel, T. and Woo, J. (2002): 'The role of policy and institutions for productivity and firm dynamics: Evidence from micro and industry data', OECD, Economics Department Working Papers, No. 329, Paris.

Scherer, F.M. (1967): 'Market structure and the employment of scientists and engineers', American Economic Review, 57, pp. 524-531.

Schratzenstaller, M. (2003): 'Zur Steuerreform 2005', WIFO Monatsbericht, 76, pp. 879-900.

Scott, J.T. (1984): 'Firm versus industry variability in R&D intensity', in: Griliches, Z. (ed.), *R&D, Patents and productivity*, Chicago, University of Chicago Press.

Sorensen, P.B. (2004): 'Company Tax Reform in the European Union', International Tax and Public Finance, 11, pp. 91-115.

Soto, M. (2002): 'Rediscovering education in growth regressions', OECD Development Centre, Technical Paper No. 202, November.

Stephan, A. (1997): 'The Impact of Transportation Infrastructure on Productivity and Growth: Some Preliminary Results for the German Manufacturing Sector', WZB discussion paper, FS IV 97-47.

Stephan, A. (2003): 'Assessing the Contribution of Public Capital to Private Production: Evidence from the German Manufacturing Sector', International Review of Applied Economics, 17, pp. 399-418.

Trostel, P.A. (1993): 'The Effect of Taxation on Human Capital', Journal of Political Economy, 101, pp. 327-350.

Van den Noord, P. (2002): 'Managing public expenditure: The UK approach', OECD, Economics Department Working Papers, No. 341, ECO/WKP(2002)27.

Vickers, J. and Yarrow, G. (1988): 'Privatisation: An Economic Analysis', MIT Press.

Willig, R.D. (1987): 'Corporate governance and market structure', in: Razin, A. and Sadka, E. (eds.), *Economic Policy in Theory and Practice,* pp. 481-494, London: Macmillan.

World Economic Forum (2003): Global Competitiveness Report 2003-2004.

Xepapadeas, A. and de Zeeuw, A. (1999): 'Environmental policy and competitiveness: The Porter hypothesis and the composition of capital', Journal of Environmental Economics and Management.

Zagler, M. and Duernecker, G. (2003): 'Fiscal policy and economic growth', Journal of Economic Surveys, 17, pp. 397-418.

Zegeye, A.A. (2000): 'U.S. public infrastructure and its contribution to private sector productivity', Working Paper 329, U.S. Bureau of Labor Statistics.

Zodrow, G.R. (2003): 'Tax Competition and Tax Coordination in the European Union', International Tax and Public Finance, 10, pp. 651-671.

Chapter 2:
European Productivity, Innovation and Public Sector R&D

2.1 Introduction

Public scientific research plays a key role in technological change and consequently in economic growth. Industrial innovation increasingly draws on scientific research, in particular in information technology and biotechnology (OECD, 2001).[21]

In recent years, a number of trends have emerged, heightening interest in the economic effects of public research both in policy and academic circles. Firstly, budget constraints are leading policymakers to re-evaluate public spending for R&D. Secondly, public academic research is being asked to contribute directly to industrial innovations and economic performance. However, economic returns are not the primary purpose of scientific research (OTA, 1986); specific mission goals such as national security, public health and the exploration of space are essential parts of public research spending.[22]

Faced with slower growth in overall public funding and pressure to generate more economic benefits, some universities have become more entrepreneurial in seeking new sources of funding (Mowery and Sampat, 2002; OECD, 2002). In addition, a number of EU countries have implemented or consider implementing policies to strengthen the linkages between universities and industry in order to enhance the contributions of university-based research to innovation and economic performance. These policies include encouraging the formation of science parks located nearby universities, spin-offs based on university research in science and tech-

nology, as well as policies which attempt to stimulate university patenting and licensing activities (OECD, 2002, Mowery, Sampat, 2002).

Furthermore, the public sector is not only a performer of R&D, but also an important source of R&D funding in the business sector. In the Barcelona European Council 2002, the Member States decided to intensify their efforts to increase investment in research and technology development and close the growing gap between Europe and its main competitors. Expenditures on business sector R&D as a percentage of GDP in the European Union (EU-15: 1.30 % in 2002) lag significantly behind the US (1.86 % in 2002) and Japan (2.26 % in 2001) whereas there is virtually no gap in public sector expenditures on R&D (including the government and higher education sector). The gap in private research investment between the EU and the US has alarming consequences for the long-term potential for innovation, growth and the creation of employment in Europe. For this reason, the European Council decided to strive to increase gross expenditures on R&D from 1.9 % to 3.0 % of GDP in the European Union by 2010 with industry contributing two-thirds of the total amount of R&D expenditures (European Commission, 2003a; 2003d).

A significant range of public goods is necessary in a knowledge-driven economy to create the competitive advantage European countries need to compete successfully with the most dynamic industrial economies in the world. These public goods include an effective science and technology base, incentives for knowledge transfer and business R&D, the support of conditions fostering innovation, and improvements in human capital endowments both through formal education and long-life training. To achieve these aims European governments use different mixes of indirect and direct

---

[21] University researchers have significantly contributed to the development of ATM switches, digital subscriber lines (DSL) technology, search engines, medical devices such as magnetic resonance imaging machines and lasers for a broad medical applications, financial services and logistic services (e.g. portfolio theory, linear programming and derivative pricing theory). Often, spin-off companies have commercialized much of these developments (National Academy of Engineering, 2003).

[22] For instance, the outcomes and social benefits of public research in health include longer lives, better health and lower costs of illness.

measures to stimulate technological activity. Direct policies include the funding of government R&D labs, universities or businesses, the investment in human capital formation as well as the extension of patent protection and fiscal incentives for R&D (EC 2003a; Griffith, 2000). Other policies not directly targeted at R&D may also have a positive impact on the level of R&D expenditure. These measures include competition policy and regulation in several sectors, including pharmaceuticals and telecommunications (Griffith, 2000).

The aim of this chapter is to empirically analyse the influence that public support in the area of research and innovation might exert on growth and research output. There are two important features of public R&D support. Firstly, the public sector is a performer of R&D conducted in public institutions such as universities and government laboratories. Secondly, the public sector is a source of funding for research activities performed in the private sector. The first step in the analysis is to test whether R&D performed in public institutions such as universities and government laboratories acts as stimulus to private investment in R&D or whether it crowds out, or substitutes for, private activity. Another aim of this chapter is to investigate whether both direct subsidies and tax incentives are an effective means of stimulating private investment in R&D. This will be investigated econometrically using panel data on EU/OECD countries and industries.

Guellec and van Pottelsberghe (2001) suggest that considerable caution is needed in drawing policy conclusions from empirical analysis at the aggregate level. Therefore, the study will also analyse the impact of public support for R&D using firm level data.

The Chapter is divided into five sections. Section 2 presents a brief overview of the literature on the impact of public sector research and government support for R&D on private R&D spending, on industrial innovation and on overall productivity growth. Section 3 describes some recent trends in government support for R&D and in public sector R&D spending in the European Union. This section also provides a detailed empirical analysis of the impact of public sector research and government support for R&D. This section's starting point is the relationship between industry and government funding of R&D at the industry and country level followed by an investigation of the impact of R&D performed in public institutions on growth and research output. Section 4 contains two case studies; the first investigates to what extent public subsidies and R&D collaboration are effective in leading to patent applications based on firm level

data for Finland and Germany. The second case study concentrates on the experience of Austria and compares various measures of public support for innovation. It analyses to what extent the sources of public support account for higher shares in the sales of innovative products. Section 5 concludes.

2.2 Theoretical background and literature review

2.2.1 Justification for public intervention in R&D and instruments

Innovative activities of private companies are a key contributor to wealth creation in economies. The social benefits of R&D are larger than the private benefits because some of the generated knowledge can be used not only by the inventing company but also by its competitors. Therefore, R&D activity creates **externalities** which give rise to **spill-over effects**. One can speak of externalities when the action of one party affects the welfare of another party in ways that do not require payment according to the existing definition of property rights. In the case of R&D, the companies benefiting from the general increase in the knowledge stock do not need to pay for it. While the costs are fully borne by the inventing company, others can build on this additional knowledge. Since externalities of R&D activities are positive, firms tend to under-invest in R&D – they spend less than the social optimum (cf. Nelson, 1959; Arrow, 1962). Companies have some leeway to exclude competitors from research results, for example through patents or secrecy. However, in these cases research efforts may be wastefully duplicated.

The market failure manifest in the under-provision of R&D provides a rationale for government intervention whose aim is to raise R&D expenditure closer to the socially optimal level by making use of appropriate instruments. Other than R&D directly performed by the government sector there are two instruments commonly employed in order to achieve this social optimum: tax incentives and grants. Both of these instruments are market-compatible in the sense that they aim to induce a change in behaviour rather than trying to command it. This aim is achieved by altering relative prices. The input for production that should be used more heavily, in our case R&D, is made cheaper. **Tax incentives** reduce the cost of the R&D activity and therefore encourage companies to invest more in R&D. More specifically, it is possible to allow an immediate write-off of R&D-related

expenses, to give R&D tax credits or to allow an accelerated depreciation of R&D-related investment. Tax incentives do not discriminate between R&D projects – they are available for any R&D activity. This is in contrast with the other important instrument, **grants**. Grants usually match private R&D expenditures at a certain percentage with public money (matching grants). The government can select specific projects, for example those from which it expects large spill-over effects. Grants allow the government to influence the investment behaviour of companies in a more specific way. It can therefore be an efficient instrument to achieve specific objectives.

There are important questions that need be asked about the efficacy of any government intervention. Since the aim of government intervention when using these instruments is the *increase* of private R&D expenditure, it is necessary to investigate whether the public money is really spent on *additional* R&D activities (also referred to as input additionality): does this funding motivate companies to undertake R&D projects that would otherwise not be pursued? The danger is that instead of undertaking additional R&D, companies reduce their own contribution to R&D as they receive the subsidy. Government intervention can only be deemed successful if companies previously not engaged in R&D activities start to innovate or if existing innovators increase their R&D budget.

Even if R&D subsidies are successful in increasing R&D activity, it is still not certain whether it is actually socially beneficial to intervene. In addition to input additionality, it is of importance that public money leads to an increase in R&D output (output additionality). It is not sufficient that the money is being spent, there also needs to be a 'return' on this money. The 'return' on R&D subsidies could, for example, be the development of an improved or cheaper product. In other words, public funding should stimulate innovations that are valued by society.

A first task is therefore to investigate whether public subsidies increase private R&D spending; or, in other words, whether public subsidies are a complement or a substitute for private R&D expenditure. It is useful to differentiate between total and net R&D spending at the company level. *Total* R&D spending is the sum of private R&D spending (financed exclusively by the company) and public R&D subsidies. *Net* R&D spending concerns only the privately financed part of total R&D spending. Thus, if a public subsidy increases net R&D spending, then a relationship of **complementarity** is found, indicating that new R&D projects have been undertaken or that existing R&D

projects have been enlarged. On the contrary, if a public subsidy reduces net R&D spending, then a relationship of **substitutability** is established (see David et al., 2000). This indicates that companies reduce their own contribution to R&D as a response to the subsidy.[23]

Economic policy analysis needs to go a step further. To foster economic growth it is not enough that resources be spent on innovative activities, it is also crucial that the innovative activities be successful. Only in the case of successful innovation activities will there be a welfare-enhancing effect. An important task is therefore the measurement of R&D output achieved by public subsidies. The research area of testing the efficacy of public subsidies by measuring R&D output at the company level is quite unexplored. Yet it is a necessity if governments wish to be accountable to taxpayers in the way they spend their money.

2.2.2 Measuring public intervention in R&D activity and its impact

Public activity in the area of R&D can be discussed from two angles. First, it is possible to describe the actions of the public sector, i.e. to measure the degree of public intervention. This includes a discussion of direct R&D expenditures by the public sector (for example expenditures for higher education or civilian and non-civilian R&D) as well as government instruments aimed at raising the economy-wide degree of R&D activity (for example tax subsidies, tax credits and matching grants). Secondly, it is equally important to assess the impact (or effects) of public R&D. These impacts concern both the additional R&D activity induced in the private sector and the impact of public R&D efforts on outcomes such as patents, new products and labour productivity.[24]

---

[23] It is not always possible to differentiate between complementarity and substitutability in empirical studies due to lack of information on the *size* of the subsidy. Often the available information concerns only total R&D spending and whether a company receives a subsidy or not. If it is found that public money increases *total* R&D spending, it can only be concluded that there is **no total crowding out**: a direct (one for one) substitution of public for private money. When the size of the subsidy is available, complementarity at the company level can be tested in two ways. In a regression with total R&D spending as the dependent variable (total R&D = $\alpha + \beta$ R&D subsidy + ε) one tests for $\beta > 1$ whereas in a regression with net R&D spending as the dependent variable (net R&D = $\alpha + \beta$ R&D subsidy + ε) one tests for $\beta > 0$.

[24] A main challenge in microeconomic studies measuring the impact of public innovation intervention is the **endogeneity** of a company's decision to participate in government support programmes. Neither the decision to apply for a grant nor the probability of receiving a grant is independent of company characteristics. For example, it is more likely that companies with outstanding research ideas apply for funding or that the government selects companies undertaking R&D projects with limited risk and a high success probability. Another important problem lies in the **heterogeneity** of companies. One would expect that companies differ in their reaction to R&D subsidies. For example, the size of the company can be influential. Also, the technological possibilities differ according to the sector of the company. The impact of government intervention can also differ according to the general economic situation: private R&D activity may depend on the economic cycle.

(A) Measurement of public/government research and innovation interventions

(a) Government research organisations

The two main public sector R&D performers comprise higher education and government research organisations. Government-owned R&D centres are usually involved in missions in areas such as nuclear power, agriculture, construction, health and defence (European Commission 2003b). In recent years, the environment of government-owned laboratory centres has changed considerably. These changes can be seen in the increasing pressure to generate commercial income and technology transfer (Bozeman, 1994; OECD, 2002), in the privatisation or the shift to private management schemes (Boden et al, 2001), in the introduction of new business practices and in reactions to budget constraints imposed by governments (European Commission, 2003b). In this chapter, the level of R&D activity performed in the government sector as a proportion of GDP is used as an indicator of government R&D (GOVERD).

(b) R&D performed by the higher education sector

Universities and other higher education institutions are key elements in the science system in all EU countries. They perform research and train researchers and other skilled personnel. The role of universities and scientific research in the innovation system has broadened in recent years. For example, according to the OECD, there is a 'growing demand for economic relevance' of research, and 'universities are under pressure to contribute more directly to the innovation systems of their national economies' (OECD, 1998). In particular, universities are becoming more dependent on output and performance criteria and academic research is increasingly mission-oriented as well as contract-based (European Commission 2003c; OECD, 1998). At the same time, universities have established closer links with business through cooperative research, networks and exchange of information (European Commission, 2003c). The other principal indicator of public sector R&D used in this chapter is expenditures on R&D in the higher education sector (or HERD).

When measuring R&D performance in the higher education and government sector and their evolution, it should be noted that a large part of the data for this sector is estimates by national authorities and that evaluation methods are periodically revised (see Box 2.2 in section 2.3.1). Furthermore, certain national characteristics may strongly influence the performance of R&D by government and higher education. For example in France, CRNS (Centre National de la Recherche Scientifique) is classified as part of the higher education sector, whereas in Italy, similar research organisations are treated as part of the government sector (see OECD 2003, Annex 2).

(c) Civilian and non-civilian R&D

The benefits of defence R&D spending have been the subject of an ongoing controversy (Adams, 2004). Supporters of defence R&D have traditionally argued that defence R&D has produced important technology spin-offs to the civilian economy. The Global Positioning System (GPS) is claimed as a direct result of defence funding. Generations of jet engines and transport aircraft have been the product of the concurrent development of military and civilian applications of common, defence-funded technologies (Adams, 2004). In this chapter, a distinction will be made between civilian and non-civilian R&D government outlays for R&D.

(d) Tax Incentives for R&D

Tax incentives are typically used to provide support to a broad range of sectors. With tax incentives, firms decide which R&D projects will be undertaken. Tax incentives can be more effective in encouraging long-term expenditures in R&D than other measures such as R&D subsidies. Furthermore, tax incentives can be less costly and less burdensome than direct R&D subsidies. Fiscal incentives for R&D may take various forms. Some EU countries provide R&D tax credits (European Commission, 2003a). These are deducted from the corporate income tax and are applicable either to the level of R&D expenditures or to the increase in these expenditures with respect to a given base. In addition, some countries allow for the accelerated depreciation of investment in machinery, equipment, and buildings devoted to R&D activities. The generosity of R&D tax incentives can be measured by the B-index (Warda, 1996, 2002).[25] This is a composite index computed as the present value of income before taxes necessary to cover the initial cost of R&D investment and to pay the corporate income tax so that it becomes profitable to perform research activities. Alternatively, the generosity of R&D tax incentives can be measured by annual R&D tax credits.

---

[25] The B-index is computed as the after-tax cost of a one Euro expenditure on R&D divided by one less the corporate income tax rate. The after-tax cost is the net cost of investing in R&D, taking account of all available tax incentives (corporate income tax rates, R&D tax credits and allowances, depreciation rates).

(e) R&D and innovation subsidies

Government-funded R&D performed by business firms primarily consists of contracts and non-repayable grants. Other forms of support are guarantees for bank loans, conditional loans and training grants. Government programs allocating direct subsidies are based on specific selection criteria. Firms applying for R&D projects must fulfil some predefined criteria in order to be funded. The indicators used in this study include government-funded BERD (Business Expenditure in R&D) as a percentage of total BERD and as a percentage of GDP and, alternatively, the level of R&D subsidies at the micro-level.

(B) Impact measures for public/government research and innovation intervention

(a) Private sector R&D expenditure

R&D expenditure is an indication of the level of R&D activity in an economy. It shows the amount of resources spent to increase the knowledge base. It is generally safe to assume that higher expenditure levels lead to higher gains in knowledge. R&D expenditure is widely used in empirical analyses to measure the magnitude of R&D activity on the company or the country level.

(b) Private sector innovation expenditure

Innovation expenditure is a broader concept than R&D expenditure. It recognises that successful product improvements require more activities than comprised under the heading of R&D expenditure. Innovation[26] expenditure also includes the purchase of patents and licenses, trial production and tooling-up, training of personnel, the acquisition of embodied technology, industrial design and market research.

(c) Patents

The number of **patent applications** is an indicator for the success of the innovative activities of a company, since patents relate directly to technological enhancements. As such, they are an indication of the increase in the knowledge stock of an economy. Additional knowledge is an important

contributor to economic growth. As governments are interested in bringing the generation of knowledge to a socially optimal level, patents are a useful indicator to judge the success of these endeavours. The short time-lag between R&D activity and patent application adds to its attractiveness as indicator for policy evaluations. National patent offices and the European patent office publish data on the number of patent applications that they receive. Because the data includes the name of the applicant, it is possible to relate the patent applications to specific companies for a deeper analysis. An important advantage for empirical research is the widespread availability of this indicator – patent office data is available for all developed countries. Furthermore, since this measure is a by-product of an administrative process, it is of high accuracy. Because of these advantages, 'raw patent counts are generally accepted as one of the most appropriate indicators that enable researchers to compare the inventive or innovative performance of companies' (Hagedoorn, Cloodt, 2003, p. 1368). A possible drawback of this indicator is that patents are also used for strategic purposes that go beyond mere protection against appropriability by others. Therefore, firm may patent useless inventions merely to signal their presence to competitors, to discourage new entrants, or to enter into cross-licensing agreements. Some firms prefer not to patent, keep their inventions secret and exploit the time lead on competitors to reap profits from their inventions.

(d) Products new to the firm

The Community Innovation Surveys (CIS) provide the share in total sales due to new or improved products as a measure of innovation output. The term 'new products' describes a product with new characteristics derived from the combination of existing technologies or from entirely new technologies. Cellular telephones with internet access are considered new products while cellular telephones that differ from old ones only by their shape or colour are not considered new. An improved product is a product with enhanced or upgraded performances, like ABS braking systems or cordless telephones. Most economists would agree that consumer utility increases as the number of products to choose from increases. Likewise, the productivity of firms is likely to increase with the range of intermediate inputs, as modelled in endogenous growth models. In the end, innovation outputs are a better innovation performance indicator than innovation inputs like R&D or innovation expenditures.

The share in sales due to new products can be considered as a sales weighted average of the

---

[26] The Oslo Manual (Eurostat/OECD, 1997) defines the term 'innovation' as follows: 'Technological product and process (TPP) innovations comprise implemented technologically new products and processes and significant technological improvements in products and processes. A TPP innovation has been implemented if it has been introduced on the market (product innovation) or used within a production process (process innovation). TPP innovations involve a series of scientific, technological, organisational, financial and commercial activities' (p. 47).

number of new products. New products are not collected on a systematic basis, whereas sales values on new products are easier to measure. Moreover, the simple count of new products does not account for differences in their value. In the share of innovative sales, a product innovation receives more weight if it is successful in the market, just like citation-based patents put more weight in the patents that receive more forward citations. However, the measurement of product innovation by the share of innovative sales has one major drawback: it may favour smaller firms, especially start-up firms, whose total sales is mainly composed of new products even though the absolute sales due to new products is much lower than for some larger firms producing predominantly unchanged products.[27]

(e) Products new to the market

The Community Innovation Surveys distinguish between products new to the firm and products new to the market. The former correspond to products that the firm introduces for the first time in the market, but that are not new to the market. The latter correspond to entirely new products that do not yet existed on the market. This distinction is important because it separates true innovation from imitation. The reasoning behind this distinction is that the impact on the economy is different depending on whether the first product of its kind is introduced (e.g. the mobile phone) or whether merely a different brand of an existing product is being produced. Products new to the market express radical innovations offering opportunities for further imitation. Products new to the firm, but not new to the market, instead signal diffusion of new products in the economy. While both notions are interesting to analyse, true innovations measure more fundamental innovation output with potentially more long-lasting effects.

(f) GDP per capita/labour productivity growth and other output measures of public sector research

At least some part of the increase in labour productivity or in GDP per capita can be assumed to reflect the impact of both public and private sector R&D. It is clear that government and university R&D have a direct effect on scientific and basic knowledge. However, modelling and measuring the productivity effects of public sector R&D is a difficult task. There are a number of reasons why it is difficult to measure rates of return on public sector R&D. It is

well known that public research takes a long time to affect production. Furthermore, public sector research may be undertaken for non-economic reasons and often produces public goods (Smith, 1991). In some cases the productivity effects of public research cannot be measured because the results are not accounted for in GDP (Guellec, van Pottelsberghe, 2003b). For example, health-related research improves the length and quality of life which is not taken into account in GDP measures. Overall, the expected effect of public sector R&D is positive, yet it remains unclear whether the impact is similar to private R&D. There are reasons to suppose that public R&D expenditures might be less productive at the margin if misdirected according to political, rent-seeking objectives. However, there are also reasons for a higher productivity of public R&D expenditures because the higher education sector concentrates more on basic research known to generate more externalities (Guellec, van Pottelsberghe, 2003b).

The principal output of university and government research is new knowledge - an output that is difficult to measure. The economically important outputs of university research include, among others, scientific and technological information, equipment and instrumentation, skills and human capital, networks of scientific and technological capabilities and prototypes for new products and processes (Sampat, 2003). Several useful indicators and proxies of the outputs of public research exist (see Box 2.1). One such indicator is publication counts. This indicator is frequently used to measure stocks and flows in the world knowledge base. Most

---

Box 2.1: Outputs of university research

The outputs of academic research can be classified into two major categories (National Science Foundation, 1998):

(i) Published outputs of academic research in referred journals

    (a) the output volume of research using article counts

    (b) patterns of research collaboration using multi-author articles

    (c) the use of research outputs in subsequent scientific research using citation counts

    (d) the potential practical utility of these research outputs using citation to these articles on patents;

(ii) Patents issued to universities and colleges, i.e. the number and types of patents and revenue generated by patents and licenses.

---

[27] For a discussion of various measures of product innovation, see Kleinknecht (1999).

publications result from research carried out by the academic sector. Besides the direct outcome of public sector research – publications and patents - the other outcomes occur through licensing and by creating spin-offs. However, it is important to keep in mind that patents are one of many channels through which university research contributes to innovation output. In a survey of R&D managers of firms in the U.S. manufacturing sector, Cohen, Nelson, and Walsh (2002) asked respondents to rank different channels through which they learn from university research. The authors found that in most industries, the channels reported to be most important were publications, conferences, and informal information exchange. Patents and licenses ranked near the bottom of the list.

In this chapter, scientific/research productivity is measured as outputs and outcomes related to inputs. The average number of papers produced by the researchers (or alternatively, number of papers in relation to public sector R&D as a percentage of GDP) is used as an indicator. The relevance and 'impact' of those publications can be measured by looking at the (relative) quantity of citations these publications receive from other, later, publications. Here we rely on citations relative to higher education sector expenditures on R&D and citations relative to the sum of HERD and government sector expenditures on R&D.

(g) Overview on further impact measures

Some other impact measures for public innovation intervention are available. First, innovation output can take the shape of new processes instead of new products. New processes allow existing products to be produced in a cheaper way, or more efficiently in terms of work safety or environmental protection. Second, the Community Innovation Surveys also contain information on ongoing innovation activities that have not yet lead to new products and processes, or that have failed to produce new products or processes. This is an indirect measure of innovation inputs. Third, CIS 3 asks firms explicitly about organisational innovations, i.e. changes in the way to do business. Fourth, another outcome of R&D activity is cost reduction. If cost reduction leads to lower prices, then the consumer surplus increases, whereas the producer surplus increases if prices are kept constant. This output of R&D is especially hard to measure because many additional factors influence cost reductions. Fifth, the count of patent applications gives equal weight to every innovation. By using patent counts that are weighted by the number of citations that the patent later received, it is possible to give more weight to

more significant innovations. Sixth, by econometric methods, one can estimate the capacity that a firm has to innovate and its intensity of innovation once it has reached the minimum capacity to innovate. It is then possible to construct from the estimates of both these two facets of innovation an expected innovation intensity for any firm given its characteristics (see Mohnen and Dagenais, 2002 and Mairesse and Mohnen, 2002).

2.2.3 Overview of the literature on the impact of public intervention

2.2.3.1 Impact of public sector research on industrial innovation, scientific output and overall productivity

The empirical literature on the effectiveness of public R&D spending investigates either its impact on output/productivity growth or its stimulative effect on business R&D. However, few studies investigate in detail the effects of research performed in the public sector. Bassanini and Scarpetta (2002) have reported cross-country regressions that suggest a negative return on public sector R&D. Subsequent research showed that the results of this study may be misleading because it fails to account for the time delay between public R&D and productivity outcomes. Guellec and van Pottelsberghe (2003a) explicitly examine the productivity effects of public sector R&D using panel data across 16 OECD countries. In particular, the authors analyse the relationship between national total factor productivity (TFP) levels and three distinct stocks of R&D capital based on (i) domestic business-performed R&D; ii) foreign business-performed R&D; and iii) public R&D performed in the higher education sector and in the government sector (public laboratories). They find evidence for lagged effects with a three-year time lag for the initial impact of public sector R&D capital. *The long-run elasticities of total factor productivity with respect to public sector R&D and business sector R&D capital are on average 0.17 and 0.13, respectively.* Thus, the long run impact of R&D seems to be higher when it is performed by the public sector than when it is performed by the private sector. Furthermore, the elasticity is higher for countries with a relatively large share of university-performed research compared to government laboratory research. The authors interpret this finding as evidence 'that much government performed R&D is aimed at public missions that do not impact directly on productivity (health, environment), whereas universities are providing the basic knowledge that is used in later stages by industry to perform technological innovation'. The elasticity of public research is also higher where the business R&D intensity is relatively high, indicating that the spillover benefits of public research are complementary with corporate research activities.

Another strand of the literature in this field investigates what proportion of firm's products could not have been developed without academic research. Mansfield (1991) illustrates the importance of academic research to the advance in industrial innovation using U.S firm data in seven manufacturing industries: information processing, electrical equipment, chemicals, instruments, drugs, metals, and oil. The author finds that about 11 % of the firms' new products and about 9 % of their new processes could not have been developed without substantial delay in the absence of recent academic research. Mansfield (1991) also identified inter-industry differences: the percentages of new products and processes steaming from recent academic research are highest in the drug industry. The average time lag between the conclusion of the relevant academic research and the first commercial introduction of the innovations based on this research was about 7 years. Finally, Mansfield (1991) estimated that the social rate of return from academic research in 1975–78 was 28 %. Using a large sample of German firms, Beise and Stahl (1999) find that about 5 % of new product sales could not have developed without academic research. Overall, one can conclude that academic research (e.g. scientific and engineering research) has a direct and significant impact on new products and processes and thus indirectly contributes to economic growth and productivity. Using time-series data for the US, Adams (1990) finds that there is a 20-year lag between the appearance of research in the academic community and its effect on productivity as measured by industry-absorbed knowledge.

Another strand of the literature addresses the spillover effect of academic research performed by universities and government research organisations (see Salter and Martin, 2001). The importance of universities in promoting technical change and innovation is widely recognized. Studies by Acz, Audretsch and Feldman (1992), Jaffe (1989) and Nelson (1986) have found a significant role for academic research in the innovation process. Jaffe (1989) has shown at a state level in the US that university research causes industry R&D and not vice versa. Another line of previous research of this type has utilised patent citations to identify positive knowledge spillovers. Studies, carried out in the US in particular, show that patents now rely more on academic scientific publications than they did in the past. Exploring the relationship among patent text

and the published research literature the authors find that only 27 % of the papers cited by US industry patents are authored by industrial scientists against 73 % written at institutions such as universities, government labs and other public agencies, both in the US and abroad (Narin et al., 1997). However, little work on this topic has been done for the EU.

The relationship between academic research and industrial innovation also depends on the structure of industry. A summary table developed by Marsili (1999) illustrates the patterns across industries. The author classified industries in terms of the contribution of academic research to innovation in each sector from very high to low (see Table 2.1). Not surprisingly, examples of industries that have been closely related to academic knowledge include computer hardware and software, biotechnology and pharmaceuticals.

2.2.3.2 Review of studies/reports on the impact of public/government innovation intervention on private R&D expenditures and innovation output

Macroeconomic studies

Macroeconomic studies typically exploit the time variation in the data. They use private R&D spending at the country or industry level and regress it on public R&D spending at the same level of aggregation. To avoid a spurious relationship between both variables, it is important to control for macroeconomic influences that can affect both private and public R&D (David et al., 2000).

The effect of public basic research on private basic research has been analysed for the US by Robson (1993) and Diamond (1998). Both authors find an effect of complementarity. There are also studies at country level for panels of OECD countries (Levy, 1990; von Tunzelmann and Martin, 1998) and at the industry level for Spanish data (Callejon and Garcia-Quevedo, 2003). For the majority of cases, complementary effects are found.

Guellec and van Pottelsberghe (2003b) examine the effect of government funding on business R&D across 17 OECD countries for the period 1981-1996. The authors report that government funding stimulates business R&D expenditure (BERD) if the government research is contracted to the business sector, but tends to partially crowd out BERD when performed in government laboratories. BERD is not affected by university research. They also find that tax incentives are effective in stimulating BERD.

Table 2.1: The role of academic research in different industries

Contribution of Academic Research	Development Activities Engineering Disciplines (mainly tacit)	Research-based Activities Basic and Applied Science
Very high	Computers	Pharmaceuticals
High	Aerospace Motor vehicles Telecommunications and electronics Electrical equipment	Petroleum Chemicals Food
Medium	Instruments Non electrical machinery	Basic metals Building materials
Low	Metal products Rubber and plastic products	Textiles Paper
Relevant scientific fields	Mathematics, Computer Science, Mechanical and Electrical Engineering	Biology, Chemistry, Chemical Engineering

Source: Adapted from Marisili (1999) cited in Salter and Martin (2001).

Guellec and van Pottelsberghe (2003b) quantify the average stimulatory effect of direct government funding of private R&D as a 0.70 marginal increase in business funded R&D for each dollar of direct non-defence government funding. This effect is found to be higher for those OECD countries with medium levels of subsidisation than for countries, such as Australia, with lower levels of public funding. Defence research carried out in the public sector does crowd out private R&D. They also report that the positive impact of government support on corporate research – through both direct funding and R&D tax incentives – is substantially enhanced when the levels of support are stable over time.

A related strand of literature investigates the impact of tax incentives for R&D on private expenditures. For instance, Bloom, Griffith and van Reenen (2002) examined the impact of taxes on R&D in eight countries over a 15 year period. They find that the considerable variation in the user cost of R&D within and across countries is induced by the very different tax systems. The econometric analysis suggest a quite substantial long-run elasticity of R&D with respect to user costs of about -1.0 after controlling for demand, country-specific fixed effects and world macroeconomic shocks. This suggests that a 1 % decrease in the user cost of R&D will lead to a 1 % increase in R&D expenditure. In a review of the literature, Hall and van Reenen (2000) conclude that the most plausible estimate of the long-run elasticity of R&D with respect to user costs of R&D is about -1.0.

Microeconomic studies

A crucial advantage of microeconomic studies is their ability to control for differences at the industry and company level. The industries can differ in the technological opportunities and in the appropriability of returns from innovation. Depending on the company size, one can expect important differences in innovative activities across companies. Studies in this area typically concentrate on one country and sometimes on a specific industry within a country.

Microeconomic studies using private R&D activity as an impact measure of public innovation intervention pose strong requirements on data availability. They require information on company characteristics *and* on public R&D subsidies. These studies have mostly been conducted for European countries and the US. The dependent variable of interest is usually the private R&D expenditure, and the question studied is whether public R&D subsidies succeed in raising private R&D expenditure. Some studies also use the R&D or innovation intensity as dependent variable.

Analyses of Spanish firms find a positive effect of subsidies on private R&D expenditures (Busom, 2000; González et al., 2004). These results are also confirmed by analyses of the German grant system (e.g. Licht and Stadler, 2003). The effect of R&D subsidies has also been tested for Israeli and French companies, again with a positive result. Toivanen and Niininen (2000) concentrate on the relationship between credit constraints and the effectiveness of R&D subsidies. Their empirical study of Finnish firms suggests that R&D subsidies are most effective when directed at firms affected by modest credit constraints. For the US, the Small Business Innovation Research Programme has been evaluated (Wallsten, 2000) and the author comes to the opposite conclusion: R&D grants are found to crowd out private R&D expenditure dollar for dollar.

Summing up, the majority of studies on the relationship between public and private funding of R&D finds that no complete crowding out takes place. Due to data restrictions, some analyses cannot differentiate between 'no complete crowding out' and 'complementarity'. But among the studies that are able to do so, many find indeed that public R&D and private R&D are in a complementary relationship. This is an important result in favour of government activities aiming to raise the economy-wide level of innovative activities.

2.3 The impact of public sector R&D and government support for R&D in the EU

2.3.1 General trends in public R&D

This section starts with a brief overview of the major trends in public sector R&D and publicly funded business enterprise sector R&D (for an extensive overview see European Commission, 2003b). Research and development activities in all EU countries are performed primarily by three sectors: business, institutions of higher education (primarily universities) and government institutions (see Box 2.2 for definitions of measures). While the EU-15 (1.30 %) lags significantly behind the US (1.86 %) and Japan (2.26 %) in terms of business sector R&D expenditure as a percentage of GDP, there is virtually no gap in public sector expenditures on R&D (including the government and higher education sector) which range between 0.68 % of GDP in the EU-15 and 0.65 % in the US in 2002 (see Table 2.2). However, both public sector and private sector expenditures on R&D are significantly lower in the new EU Member States than in the EU-15 at about 0.44 % and 0.39 % in 2000, respectively (see Table 2.2). In the new EU Member States the lower ratio of public sector R&D expenditures to GDP is mainly due to the low ratio of R&D performed by the higher education sector (HERD) to GDP. Furthermore, in the EU-15, HERD increased steadily relative to GDP over the 1980s and 1990s with a slowdown in the mid-1990s (see Graph 2.1). The ratio of

HERD to GDP reached 0.42 % in 2002 compared to 0.30 % in 1981. There seems to be a similar trend in the US, although the level is underestimated (see Box 2.2).

Box 2.2: Measuring public R&D expenditures

The public sector is a source of R&D funding and also a performer of R&D activity. When measuring public sector R&D by performing sector, it is useful to distinguish between the higher education sector and the government sector expenditures on R&D, HERD and GOVERD, respectively. It should be noted that values for the US and Sweden are seriously underestimated (OECD, 2003; European Commission, 2003b).

Data on GBAORD (government appropriations or outlay for R&D) concerns all appropriations by central government allocated to R&D in federal/central government budgets to be carried out in one of the four sector of performance – business enterprise, higher education, government and private non-profit sector. Data on government R&D appropriations therefore refers to budget provisions, not to actual expenditure, i.e. GBAORD measures government support for R&D using data collected from budgets. Data on GBAORD provides an indicator of the relative importance of various socio-economic objectives such as defence R&D, health R&D and environmental R&D in total public R&D spending (OECD, 2003; European Commission, 2003b).

Business expenditures on R&D (BERD) are the key component of all R&D activities. Funding for business R&D can come from any one of four sources: domestic business, government, other national institutions (for example charities funding medical research) and abroad; 'abroad' includes foreign businesses and foreign subsidiaries of domestic businesses.

In the EU-15, government sector expenditures on R&D as a percentage of GDP dropped from 0.32 % to 0.20 % during the same period, with the majority of this fall occurring during the 1990s - see Graph 2.1. The decline in funding for government labs in the EU-15 is largely due to drastic reductions in funding for government research organisations in countries such as France and the UK (OECD, 2002). It may also reflect restructuring of some government labs.

There is indication that the gap between the EU-15 and the US in terms of the ratio of BERD to GDP has increased significantly between 1995 and 2000 but decreased afterwards - see Graph 2.1. It should be noted that in EU countries the R&D expenditures of the higher education sector are primarily financed through public funding. However, the share of industry funding in the higher education sector

Table 2.2: R&D expenditures by performing sector (in percent of GDP)

	1998	1999	2000	2001	2002
EU-15					
Government sector	0.28	0.26	0.26	0.25	0.26
Higher education sector	0.39	0.39	0.40	0.41	0.42
Public sector	0.67	0.65	0.66	0.66	0.68
Business enterprise sector	1.20	1.25	1.27	1.30	1.30
New EU Member States					
Government sector	0.25	0.25	0.24		
Higher education sector	0.18	0.18	0.20		
Public sector	0.43	0.43	0.44		
Business enterprise sector	0.40	0.40	0.39		
US					
Government sector	0.20	0.20	0.19	0.21	0.23
Higher education sector	0.36	0.36	0.37	0.39	0.42
Public sector	0.56	0.56	0.56	0.60	0.65
Business enterprise sector	1.93	1.97	2.03	1.99	1.86
Japan					
Government sector	0.27	0.29	0.30	0.29	
Higher education sector	0.44	0.44	0.43	0.44	
Public sector	0.71	0.73	0.73	0.73	
Business enterprise sector	2.10	2.10	2.12	2.26	

Notes: The new EU Members States include CY, CZ, EE, HU, LV, LT, MT, PL, SK and SI.

Source: Eurostat, New Cronos and OECD, MSTI.

more than doubled between 1981 and 2001 (OECD, 2002). At the beginning of the 1990s, the EU-15 average for the share of HERD financed by the government was around 89 %. At the end of 1990s, the share of HERD financed by the government decreased slightly to 81 % (European Commission, 2003b). In the US, the share of HERD financed by the government decreased from 74 % to 71 % in the same period.

Measured as a percentage of GDP, public sector R&D spending (including the government and higher education sector) is highest in Finland, Sweden, France and the Netherlands. It is lowest in Portugal, Greece, Spain, Ireland, Luxembourg and in the new EU Member States - see Graph 2.2. Expenditures on

R&D in the higher education sector are highest in Sweden, Finland, Austria and the Netherlands with a share in GDP of 0.5 % and more. Public sector and private sector R&D expenditures are positively related across countries.[28] Countries with a higher ratio of expenditures on R&D in the higher education sector to GDP tend to have a higher ratio of business sector R&D expenditures to GDP but the correlation coefficient between the government expenditures on R&D and business sector R&D is not statistically significant at the 5 % level. Countries with a low initial level of public sector R&D (e.g. Portugal, Greece, Spain and Ireland) recorded the highest

[28] HERD and business R&D have a correlation coefficient of 0.72 and a p-value of 0.01 based on 25 EU countries, US and Japan.

Table 2.3: Trends in civilian and non-civilian GBAORD (in percent of GDP)

	total GBAORD, % GDP		Civil GBAORD, % GDP		non Civil GBAORD, % GDP	
	1995	2001	1995	2001	1995	2001
EU 15	0.83	0.75	0.69	0.63	0.11	0.13
EU 25	0.80	0.74				
United States	0.93	0.86	0.43	0.41	0.50	0.45
Japan	0.50	0.68	0.47	0.65	0.03	0.03

Source: Eurostat, New Cronos.

Graph 2.1: Evolution of R&D expenditure by performing sector

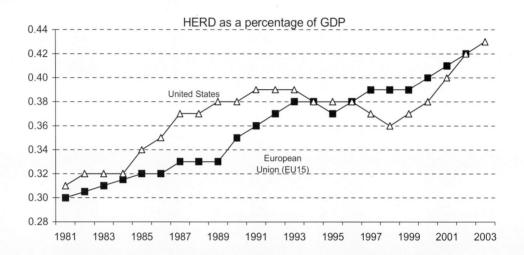

HERD as a percentage of GDP

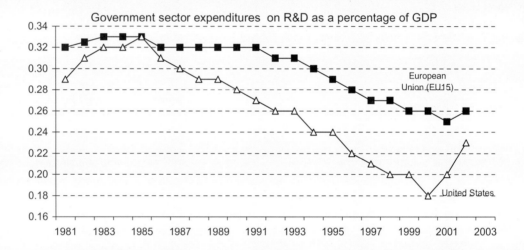

Government sector expenditures on R&D as a percentage of GDP

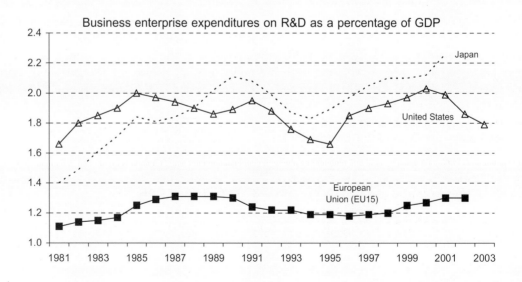

Business enterprise expenditures on R&D as a percentage of GDP

Source: Eurostat, New Cronos.

Graph 2.2: R&D by performing sector, 2001

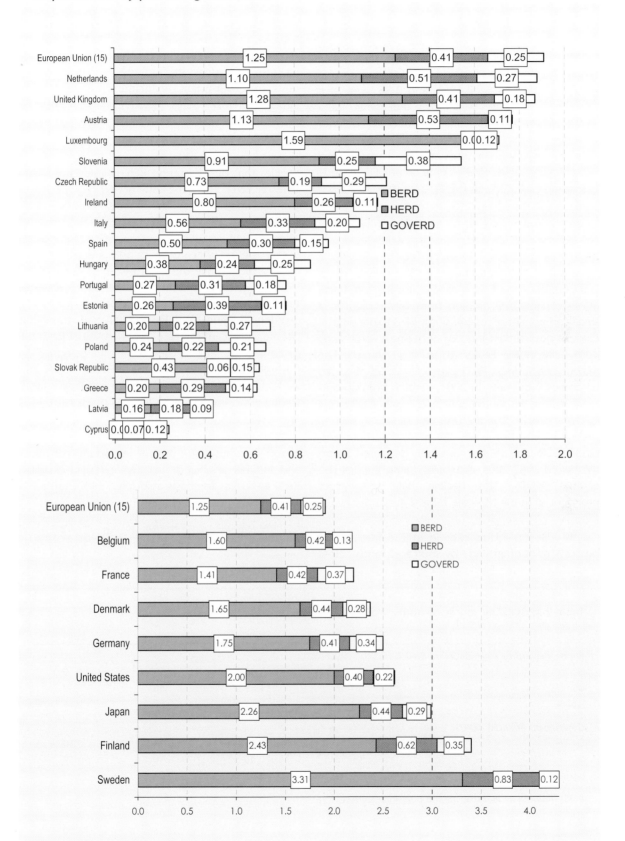

Source: Eurostat, New Cronos and OECD, MSTI. Data refers to 2001 or nearest available year.

Note: GOVERD stands for Government sector expenditures in R&D.

growth during the period 1995-2001. Some smaller EU countries (e.g. Finland and Denmark) also experienced an increase in public sector R&D (see European Commission, 2003b).

In 2001, the government budget appropriations or outlays for R&D (GBAORD) in EU-15, Japan and US amounted to 0.75 %, 0.68 % and 0.86 % of their GDP, respectively. It is well known that the EU has a smaller share of GBAORD devoted to defence compared to the US. In contrast, in the US, defence objective represents a substantial part of the total GBAORD and amounted to 0.45 % of GDP in 2001 compared to 0.13 % in the EU-15 - see Table 2.3

Given the significance of business R&D (BERD) as a component of all R&D activities, it is worth looking at the trends in government support for business R&D. Government support for business R&D includes direct R&D subsidies and fiscal incentives for R&D. In terms of direct subsidies, funding from government is a small component of total business R&D expenditures. Rates of government funding of business R&D range from 8 % in the EU-15 to 10 % in the US. The majority of business R&D expenditures are financed by domestic business. In 2001, funding from government sources accounted only for 0.1 % of GDP in the EU-15 and 0.19 % in the US – see Table 2.4. Both in the EU-15 and in the US, the ratio of government-funded BERD to GDP has constantly decreased during the period 1981-2001, especially during the first half of the 1990s. This decline has been more pronounced in the US – see Table 2.4.

Graph 2.3 shows the change in the intensity of business performed R&D by source of funds across

individual EU Member States. It is clear that the increases in the intensity of business sector R&D in some smaller Member States are largely driven by domestic industry funding, followed by foreign sources. The contribution of financing from government seems to be negligible. The US also saw large increases in business R&D, despite significant reductions in government financing. In several other large EU Member Sates, including Italy and the UK, both industry and government financed R&D declined as share of GDP.

Policies that directly target R&D include tax incentives for R&D. The generosity of R&D tax incentives can be measured by the B-index (Warda 1996, 2002, see also section 2.2.2). The relative generosity of R&D tax incentives differs significantly across the EU. According to this indicator, Spain and Portugal, have the most generous fiscal incentives for R&D - see Table 2.5. The least favourable tax environment can be found in Germany, Sweden, Belgium and Finland. Overall, there has been a significant increase in generosity of R&D tax incentives in the large company category in Portugal, Spain and the UK between 1995 and 2001. Furthermore, the UK, France and Japan significantly improved the attractiveness of their R&D tax systems in the period 2000-2004.[29]

Graph 2.4 shows the relative importance of direct and indirect financing (tax incentives) of business R&D as well as the costs associated with changes in

---

[29] France introduced the new Research Tax Credit 2004 (Crédit d'Impôt Recherche – CIR 2004). More information can be downloaded from the website of the Ministère délégué à la Recherche, http://www.recherche.gouv.fr/.

Table 2.4: BERD by source of funds, 1981-2001 (as percent of GDP)

	1981	1990	1995	2001
Business enterprise expenditure on R&D (BERD)				
EU-15	1.11	1.30	1.19	1.30
US	1.66	1.89	1.66	1.99
Japan	1.40	2.11	1.89	2.26
Government financed BERD				
EU-15	0.21	0.19	0.13	0.10
US	0.52	0.48	0.30	0.19
Japan	0.03	0.03	0.03	0.02
BERD financed by industry, abroad and other sources				
EU-15	0.90	1.11	1.06	1.20
US	1.14	1.41	1.36	1.80
Japan	1.37	2.08	1.86	2.24

Source: Eurostat, New Cronos and OECD, MSTI.

Graph 2.3: Change in BERD in % of GDP by source of funds, EU, US and Japan, 1990-2001

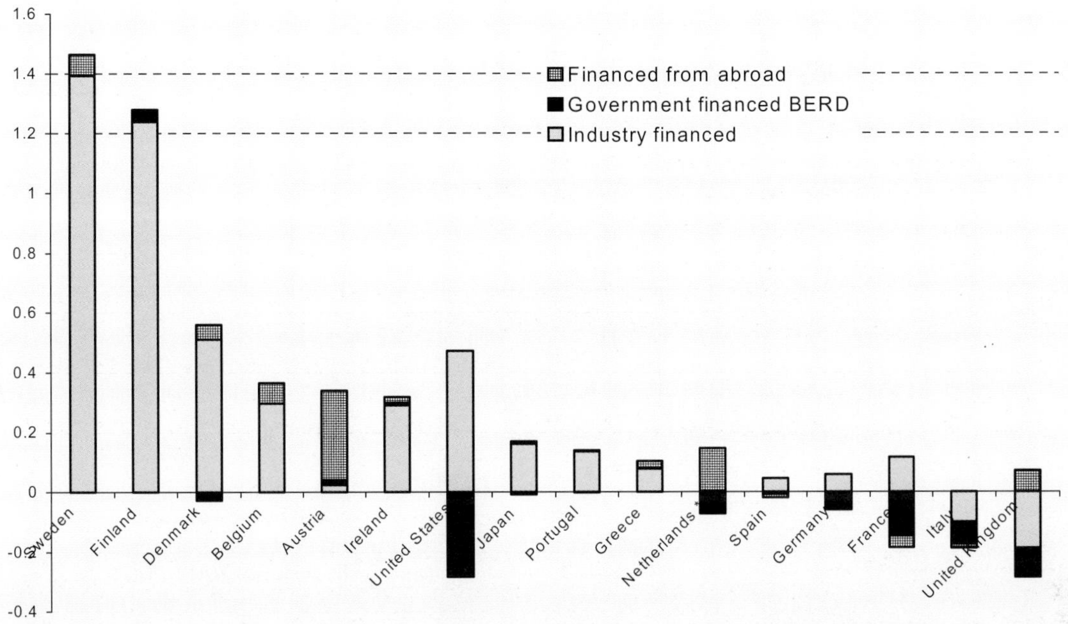

Legend:
- Financed from abroad
- Government financed BERD
- Industry financed

Source: OECD, MSTI. Data for 1990 (2001) or nearest available year.

Table 2.5: Rate of tax incentives for € 1 of R&D in 2001

	Large firms		SMEs
	2001	change between 1995-2001	2001
Belgium	-0.01	0.00	-0.01
Denmark	0.11	-0.02	0.11
Germany	-0.02	0.03	-0.02
Spain	0.44	0.16	0.44
Greece	-0.01		-0.01
France	0.06	-0.02	0.06
Ireland	0.00	0.00	0.00
Italy	-0.03	0.03	0.44
Netherlands	0.10	0.00	0.35
Austria	0.12	0.05	0.12
Portugal	0.34	0.36	0.34
Finland	-0.01	0.00	-0.01
Sweden	-0.01	0.00	-0.01
UK	0.10	0.10	0.11
EU (unweighted average)	0.08	0.05	0.14
US	0.07	0.09	0.07
Japan	0.01	0.02	0.12

Notes: Tax incentives are calculated as 1 minus the B-index. For example, in Spain, 1 unit of R&D expenditure by large firms results in 0.44 unit of tax relief.

Source: OECD, STI/EAS Division, May 2003.

Graph 2.4: Direct and indirect financing of business R&D and additional costs of changes in R&D tax credit regimes since 2002 (as percentage of business R&D)

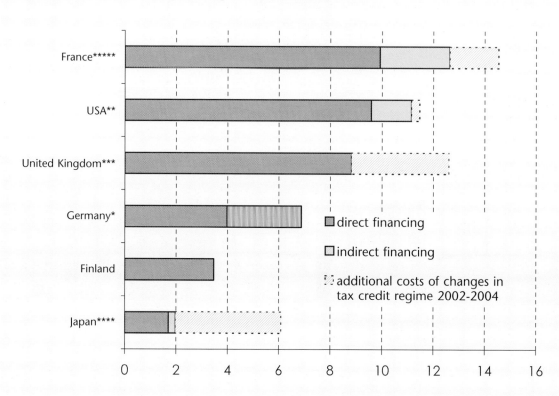

Notes: *Vertically striped: direct financing from regional funding agencies as a percentage of total business R&D spending. ** diagonally striped: estimated additional costs resulting from the introduction of the 'Alternative Incremental Credit' since the budget year 2002/03. *** diagonally striped: estimated additional costs resulting from the reform of the R&D tax system in 2000 (for SMEs) and 2002 (large firms). **** diagonally striped: estimated additional costs resulting from the by the change from the switch of incremental to a volume based R&D tax credit regime. ***** diagonally striped: estimated additional costs French NEW caused by the introduction of the new R&D Tax Credit regime (Crédit d'Impôt Recherche) in 2004.

Source: OECD, MSTI, Rammer et al. (2003).

R&D tax credit regimes since 2002 for a group of selected countries. Estimates indicate that in France the costs of R&D tax credits will increase from 2.7 to 4.7 % of total industry R&D expenditures due to the reform of the R&D tax system. In the UK the costs of the introduction of the new R&D tax credit regime in 2000 and 2002 were equivalent to 4 % of total industry R&D expenditures. In Japan a new volume-based R&D tax credit was introduced as an alternative to the existing incremental R&D tax credit starting from fiscal year 2003. This raises the costs to government of the R&D tax credit from 0.3 % to 4 % of total industry R&D expenditures. In the US, in contrast, R&D tax incentives represent 1.6 % of total industry spending. The costs will slightly increase from 1.6 % to 1.9 % as a result of the introduction of the alternative incremental credit regime.

In the new Member States tax incentives for R&D receive a low priority (European Commission, 2001). However, in those countries overall corpo-

rate tax ratios are already very low compared to the EU-15 countries.

The mix of direct financing and tax incentives for business R&D varies considerably across EU countries (see OECD, 2002; European Commission, 2003a). For example, with regard to large manufacturing firms, France and the UK have a relatively high share of R&D subsidies and offer a favourable tax treatment. Other countries, such as Finland, Italy and Sweden, focus more on direct subsidies. In contrast, Spain and Portugal have generous fiscal incentives combined with a relatively low subsidy rate. It is interesting to note that Sweden and Finland have neither substantial direct nor indirect funding although these countries have high levels of private business enterprise expenditures. In Finland, the substantial private R&D spending can be partly explained by an industrial structure focusing on ICT intensive, highly skilled, human-capital intensive production (Rouvinen and Ylä-Anttila, 2003). It is doubtful that tax incentives for

R&D can compensate for a lack of 'enabling conditions' in countries with low levels of R&D spending (OECD, 2002). Furthermore, tax incentives and direct subsidies may be either complements or substitutes. Data on R&D subsidy ratios and tax incentives for the 15 pre-accession Member States, the US and Japan for the period 1981-2002 indicate that countries with an increased level of tax concessions experienced a lower decrease in the R&D subsidy ratio. Also, econometric results suggest that both instruments are indeed complements.[30]

2.3.2 Empirical analysis of the impact of public support to R&D on business R&D

This section investigates the empirical relation between public support to R&D and business R&D by studying separately two channels through which public money spent on R&D can influence business R&D spending. The first concerns the relation between government-financed R&D expenditures (performed in the business sector) and business R&D spending; the second concerns the impact of public funding of R&D performed by universities and government institutions on business R&D.

Relationship between industry- and government-financed business R&D at the industry level

The aim here is to investigate whether government-financed R&D expenditures are complementary and thus 'additional' to private R&D spending, rather than substitutes for industry-financed R&D expenditures. The analysis, conducted for the business sector in the EU-15 at the industry level, extends previous work in two directions. First, the empirical analysis gives sector-specific estimates of the impact of government-funded R&D in the business sector; and, second, the use of industry-/country-level data allows the estimation of the R&D equation for each country separately.[31] The main hypothesis to be tested is whether R&D subsidies to a particular industry stimulate private R&D expenditures in that particular industry.[32] Complementarity between private and public BERD occurs when the estimated elasticity of government-funded BERD is significantly different from zero and positive. A negative estimated elasticity would indicate a substitution effect. A positive elasticity implies that the marginal

effect is also positive.[33] More specifically, the marginal effect measures the degree to which private R&D is stimulated by government-financed R&D.

The estimated elasticity of private business R&D with respect to publicly funded R&D ranges between 0.20 and 0.13 and is highly significant – see Table A.2.1 in Appendix 1. When controlling for output and R&D financed from abroad, in the EU, a marginal increase of € 1 in government-funded BERD leads to an increase in domestic business-funded R&D of € 0.93.[34] The funding effect on total R&D expenditures in the business sector is therefore € 1.93. The results are consistent with Guellec and van Pottelsberghe (2003b) who find a marginal effect of 0.70 in business-funded R&D for each dollar of direct non-defence government funding (total effect of 1.70). Moreover, the findings suggest a positive impact of R&D financed from abroad on domestic business R&D expenditures. A € 1 increase in BERD financed by abroad leads to an increase in domestic and privately funded R&D expenditures of about € 0.37.

For 17 out of 18 EU industries, the elasticity of industry-financed BERD with respect to R&D subsidies shows the expected positive sign.[35] Another result is that the elasticity estimates are generally higher in high-tech industries than in medium- and low-tech industries. The corresponding marginal effects of R&D subsidies show the opposite pattern as they depend on the R&D subsidy ratio.[36] In 10 out of 11 EU countries, private R&D is significantly positively associated with public R&D.[37]

The impact of government support and public sector R&D on business R&D

While most of the literature focuses on the impact of publicly funded R&D that is performed by private firms, few studies investigate the impact on private R&D of R&D performed by universities and government institutions. The aim in what follows is to analyse empirically the influence of both public sector R&D and government support for R&D on private R&D spending.

A large number of factors potentially have an impact on business sector R&D intensity. First and

---

[30] See 'European Productivity, Innovation and Public Sector R&D', background study prepared for the 2004 edition of the *European Competitiveness Report* for further details.

[31] The data used consists of an industry panel data set for 13 EU Member States in 25 industries for the period 1987-1999.

[32] In these regressions, possible (negative) spillover effects between industries are not addressed. It is well known that R&D subsidies may crowd out business R&D investments in other, closely related industries.

[33] The marginal effect is computed as the product of the estimated elasticity and the ratio of domestic industry-funded BERD to government-funded BERD evaluated at sample means.

[34] The elasticity estimates have been transformed into marginal effects based on sample means.

[35] For 15 industries, the elasticity is significantly positive at the 5 % level and for at least one more industry, it is significantly positive at the 10 % level.

[36] With a constant elasticity the marginal effect increases when the ratio of government financed R&D to industry financed R&D decreases.

[37] See 'European Productivity, Innovation and Public Sector R&D', background study prepared for the 2004 edition of the *European Competitiveness Report* for estimation results.

foremost, industry structure and the dynamics of output growth matter. If a country is specialised in industries typically characterised by a high degree of R&D intensity, then aggregate business R&D intensity will generally be high (European Commission 2003b, p. 59). Other factors affecting business R&D spending include competition and (de-)regulation policies as well as patent protection. In a narrower sense, the government provides for a research-prone, favourable business setting by funding universities as well as research in public laboratories: scientific knowledge from academic research generates positive knowledge spillovers thereby facilitating private business R&D and fostering productivity in the corporate world. As already discussed, apart from those indirect measures, the government can also stimulate business R&D with direct measures, either through fiscal incentives or by means of direct financial support.

The empirical literature evaluating the net effects of such intervention is concerned with basically three sources of negative (side-) effects. First, as discussed previously, the issue of 'input additionality' address the extent to which public R&D-assistance induces companies to spend more own *additional* resources on R&D than they would have spent without the public R&D assistance; second, and in the same vein as for direct support, indirect support through the promotion of R&D performed by universities and government research organisations may substitute for R&D projects which otherwise would have been undertaken by the corporate world. If private firms engage less in R&D because they cannot successfully compete against government-funded research, allocative distortions are said to prevail; finally, public sector R&D can act as a substitute to the private R&D sector, as it not only uses resources for R&D but also earns exclusive property rights to the research results. This potential source of crowding out arises if there is a shortage in the most decisive factor of the R&D process, that is, if high-skilled labour is scarce. Rising demand for high-skilled human resources by universities and government research organisations reduces the availability of the same for private sector usage. In this case, R&D subsidies could drive up the wages of scientists and engineers enough to prevent significant increases in real R&D (Goolsbee, 1998). For the US, Goolsbee (1998) finds that increases in funding for public R&D significantly raise the wages of scientists and engineers. Under these circumstances part of the gross R&D volume increase is eventually explained by an increase in its unit price (crowding out through prices).

Despite the potential negative effects of public R&D on private sector R&D discussed above, the public sector can also act as a complement to the private sector by lowering the cost of research for the industry. This can be achieved by conducting basic research and making its results publicly available. University research has historically been an important source of external knowledge, equipment and methodologies for industrial researchers in the development of new products and production processes. Graph 2.5 illustrates various types of public intervention and their potential impact on business R&D. Whether the positive stimulation and spillover effects dominate the negative effects discussed above is ultimately an empirical question and will be examined below.

The aim of this section is to estimate the impact of public sector intervention measures as outlined in Graph 2.5 on business expenditure on R&D. The econometric model used estimates the elasticities of BERD intensity (BERD/GDP) relative to the following variables:

-   Government-financed R&D expenditures in the business sector as a percentage of GDP which captures direct financial support in the form of grants, loans, etc.

-   B-index, measuring the generosity of the tax system[38], captures fiscal incentives. Decreases in the B-index mean that fiscal incentives for R&D have been increased, or, equivalently, that the cost of R&D-activities at the enterprise level has fallen. Accordingly, if fiscal incentives are effective in raising expenditures on R&D in the business sector, the estimated elasticity should be significantly negative.

-   R&D expenditures by the higher education sector (HERD) in percentage of GDP.

-   Government sector R&D expenditures (GOVERD) in percentage of GDP.

When estimating these elasticities, the level of development and the degree of specialisation in high-tech activities of the country are controlled for using the following explanatory variables in the regression:

-   GDP per capita in constant purchasing power parity.

---

[38]   For more details refer to Warda (1996) and OECD (2002).

Graph 2.5: Main policy tools towards business R&D and their potential impact

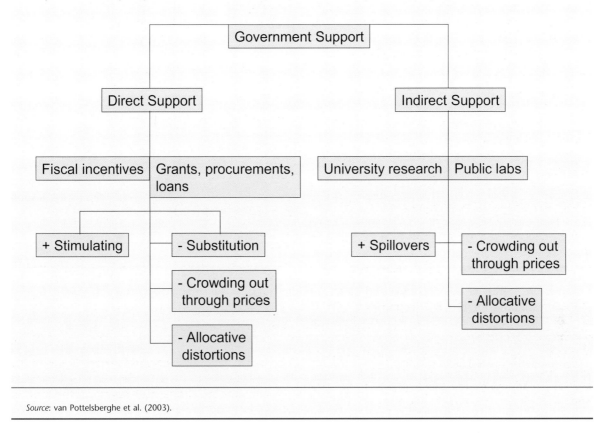

Source: van Pottelsberghe et al. (2003).

- Share of high-technology exports in total manufacturing exports. High-technology exports[39] are characterised by a high intensity of research and development and measure the technology-intensity of a country's exports. It could be argued that the share of high-technology exports is a measure of innovation output rather than a factor explaining innovation input. However, the share of high-technology exports also reflects the country's degree of specialisation in high-tech activities.[40]

The first question is whether **public sector R&D** is a complement or a substitute for private R&D, meaning whether it induces or crowds out private R&D. Overall, one can expect the positive spillover effects to dominate the potentially negative impacts discussed above so that the net effect of public sector R&D on business sector R&D is positive. Should, on the other hand, public sector R&D

generally crowd out private R&D, then the elasticities relative to higher education and government sector R&D would be negative.

A second aim of this section is to investigate the impact of **direct support measures** on business sector R&D: Is government-funded R&D performed by the business sector a substitute or a complement for private R&D? Do R&D tax credits foster business expenditure on R&D? The elasticities of business R&D relative to government-financed R&D expenditures in the business sector and relative to the B-index will provide an answer to these questions.

Table 2.6 presents estimation results for the elasticities of BERD with respect to R&D expenditures by the higher education sector (HERD) and the government sector (GOVERD), see Appendix 1 for complete estimation results. These estimates show that both government and university R&D are significantly positively related to R&D intensity in the business sector. As expected, HERD has a higher impact than government R&D. In terms of marginal impacts of public funding, a € 1 increase in R&D performed by universities leads to an additional € 1.3 in industry R&D while a € 1 increase in R&D performed by government institutions leads to €

---

[39] They include high-technology products such as aerospace, computers, pharmaceuticals, scientific instruments and electrical machinery (see OECD STI Scoreboard 2003).

[40] In the EU-15 countries, high-technology intensive exports account for 22 % of total manufacturing exports in 2001. Differences among EU countries are substantial: in 2001 the share of high-technology industries in total exports ranges from 54 % in Ireland to 9 % in Greece. Between 1991 and 2001, high technology exports as a proportion of total exports have grown rapidly in Finland, Ireland, the Netherlands and United Kingdom. During this period Finnish high technology exports as a percentage of total manufacturing exports grew faster than in any EU-15 country.

Table 2.6: Impact of public sector R&D on business expenditures for R&D (BERD): Panel estimates for 21 OECD countries

	(1) coeff.	(2) coeff.
log public sector R&D % GDP	0.95***	
log HERD % GDP		0.47**
log GOEVRD % GDP		0.24
log GDP per capita in constant PPP $	0.69*	0.56
period dummy 1990-1994	-0.07	-0.07
period dummy 1995-1999	-0.05	-0.03
period dummy 2000-2002	-0.03	0.00
constant	2.82**	2.74*

Notes: *, **, and *** denote significance at the 10 %, 5 %, and 1 % level respectively. Estimation period: 1986-2002 with data derived from three five-year intervals and one three-year interval. Excluding the non-EU countries has little effect on the regression results. Specification (1): HERD and GOVERD taken together as Public sector. Specification (2): separate impact-coefficients for HERD and intramural GOVERD.

Table 2.7: Impact of tax incentives and direct subsidies on business enterprise sector R&D (BERD): Panel estimates for 21 OECD countries

	including log HERD % GDP coeff
log government-funded BERD % GDP	0.15***
log B-index	-0.49*
log HERD % GDP	0.29***
log share of high-technology exports in total manufacturing exports	0.45***
log GDP per capita in constant PPP $	0.53**
period dummy 1985-1989	0.01
period dummy 1990-1994	-0.07
period dummy 1995-1999	-0.15
period dummy 2000-2002	-0.16
constant	3.67***
marginal effect of government-funded business R&D	1.4

Notes: *, **, and *** denote significance at the 10 %, 5 %, and 1 % level respectively. Estimation period: 1980-2002. Excluding the non-EU countries has little effect on the regression results. t-values are based on robust standard errors.

1.1 in industry R&D.[41] Finally, the coefficient of GDP per capita in constant PPP is positive and significant.

Table 2.7 shows inference on the R&D stimuli resulting from direct government intervention, i.e. from tax incentives and direct R&D subsidies. These results suggest that government-funded R&D in the business sector has a positive and significant impact on total business enterprise R&D. In order to test whether government-funded R&D in the business sector is a complement or a substitute to private R&D in the business sector,

the estimated elasticities are transformed into marginal effects. Note that the dependent variable is *total* R&D expenditures in the business sector, i.e. government-financed BERD is included. The results suggest that an increase of € 1 of R&D subsidies will generate an increase of total business sector R&D expenditures of € 1.4. Since this effect is higher than € 1, one can conclude that government-funded R&D is a complement for private R&D. The elasticity with respect to the share of high-technology exports in total manufacturing is positive and significant. This indicates that countries with a large share of exports in technology driven industries also have high business R&D intensity.

Changes in fiscal incentives for R&D as measured by the B-index significantly affect the R&D expenditure

[41] The marginal returns of HERD and GOVERD are calculated as the product of the respective elasticity estimates, 0.47 and 0.24, by the ratio of BERD to the variable. The ratios of BERD to HERD and of BERD to GOVERD are 2.85 and 4.68 respectively.

in the business sector. The elasticity of about -0.60 indicates that a 10 % reduction in the price of R&D (increase in generosity of tax incentives for R&D) leads to a 6 % increase in the amount of R&D.

Given these elasticity estimates, it is possible to calculate to what extent the observed change in the BERD intensity can be attributed to changes in tax incentives for BERD and direct R&D subsidies, initial BERD intensity, GDP per capita, industry structure and the spillover effects of higher education sector R&D, see Appendix 1 for further estimation results. Table 2.8 presents the results of the decomposition analysis for two periods. Generally, the predicted changes in BERD intensity are close to the observed ones. The average annual growth rate of BERD intensity over the period 1980-2002 is about 4.1 % which is close to the prediction of 3.7 %. The main cause of the increase in BERD intensity is the shift in industry structure towards high-technology industries which explains half of the change in BERD intensity. To the extent that reallocation of production factors towards high-technology industries is being hampered by lack of flexibility in factor markets, structural reforms aimed at rendering markets more flexible will play an important role in increasing the level of business R&D across the EU. Growth of GDP per capita is also an important factor explaining almost a third of the increased business R&D intensity. In contrast, the effects of direct subsidies and tax incentives for R&D are quite small. Finally, about 20 % of the increase in BERD intensity can be explained by the increase in HERD as a percentage of GDP, indicating substantial spillover effects from academic research.

In order to analyse whether the contribution of tax incentives has changed over time, the effects for the sub-period 1990-2002 are also estimated. Again, only 3 % of the increase in the ratio of BERD to GDP can be explained by the increase in fiscal incentives for R&D. In contrast, the decrease over time in government financed BERD as percentage of GDP has hampered the increase in R&D intensity in the business sector by 3 percentage points.

2.3.3 Impact of public sector R&D on economic growth and research output

Impact of public sector R&D on GDP per capita growth

University and government laboratory research has both direct and indirect impacts on the economy. Public sector research may directly lead to increases in productivity through increased knowledge and innovation. Examples include new information and

communication technologies and advances in the health sector through medical research. Indirect effects of public sector R&D can be caused by spillovers contributing to the productivity of private R&D. Examples include 'spin-off' projects from higher education or research institutes with R&D focus. In principle, total business expenditures on R&D could be split up into industry and government financed components. However, Griliches (1979) argue that there is no reason to separate private from government funds because a dollar is a dollar, whatever the source of funding. Guellec, van Pottelsberghe (2003b) argue that it is conceptually not feasible to distinguish spillovers from privately funded R&D from publicly funded R&D derived from a given R&D project. Therefore, the analysis here focuses on the effects of R&D performed by the public sector (understood as government sector and higher education institutions) and not on the effects of publicly funded business sector R&D.

An econometric model[42] is used to estimate the determinants of growth. The set of variables used to explain economic growth are: initial GDP per capita, the share of investment in GDP, population growth, human capital and the ratio of R&D expenditures to GDP by performing sector (i.e. higher education sector, government sector and business sector).[43] In the absence of spillovers, the effect of public sector R&D should be equal to its income share. The proxy measure for human capital used here is the average duration of education among the working age population (25 to 64 years of age).[44] The impact of average years of schooling is expected to be positive. The main data source is the OECD Economic Outlook database for the period 1960-2002.[45] In order to avoid the potential correlation between business cycles and the explanatory variables, the analysis uses data averaged over five-year periods rather than annual data.

Graph 2.6 displays the relationship between the change in public sector R&D as a percentage of GDP and GDP per capita growth. There is a positive correlation of 0.68 that is highly significant. This means that the change in R&D expenditures

---

[42] A dynamic panel data model is used. For more information see Appendix 2 or 'European Productivity, Innovation and Public Sector R&D', background study prepared for the 2004 edition of the *European Competitiveness Report*.

[43] Under the assumption of a steady-state long-run growth path for the period examined, growth rates can be expressed without reference to the stocks of physical or human capital.

[44] See de la Fuente, Domenech (2002). This indicator was also employed by Bassanini, Scarpetta (2002). It must be stressed that this variable is a weak indicator of human capital because it cannot account for differences in the quality of one additional year of education (see Wößmann, 2003).

[45] The group of countries include Australia, Austria, Belgium, Canada, Czech Republic, Denmark, Finland, France, Germany, Greece, Hungary, Iceland, Ireland, Italy, Japan, Netherlands, New Zealand, Norway, Poland, Portugal, Republic of Korea, Slovak Republic, Spain, Sweden, Switzerland, United Kingdom and the United States.

Table 2.8: Source of changes in BERD intensity (EU-15)

Observed percentage change in BERD % GDP	Predicted percentage change in BERD % GDP	Sources in percentage points (percent) of predicted change				
		Government-funded BERD % GDP	B-index	GDP per capita	High-tech export share	HERD % GDP
1980-2002						
4.1	3.7	-0.1	0.1	1.0	1.9	0.8
	(-2)	(3)	(28)	(51)	(20)	
1990-2002						
3.9	3.8	-0.3	0.1	1.2	2.5	0.5
	(100)	(-7)	(3)	(31)	(60)	(12)

Notes: For the period 1990-2002, UK and Italy are excluded because the growth of the business R&D intensity was negative. The contribution of the explanatory variables is calculated by multiplying the estimated coefficients from table 2.7 by the change in the observed explanatory variable.

performed by the public sector (measured as a percentage of GDP) is significantly higher in countries with a high GDP per capita growth. Since the causality is likely to work in both directions, one needs to be cautious in drawing conclusions.

Table 2.9 presents the results of the growth equation estimation with R&D expenditures disaggregated by performing sector. In specification 1, HERD as a percentage of GDP is included. Specification 2 is basically the same as specification 1 except that government sector expenditures on R&D as a percentage of GDP is also included. In specification 3, all three different categories of R&D expenditures are included. Given that the lagged endogenous variable is included, the coefficients are to be interpreted as short-run effects. Since the estimates of the adjustment coefficient are highly sensitive to the model specifications, the interpretation of results focuses on short-run elasticities.

The different R&D categories have the expected positive sign but government expenditures on R&D have a negative sign. The literature on the impact of both business-sector and public sector R&D capital on growth is quite thin. Using a panel of five-year averages for 17 OECD countries for the period 1980-1999, the German Council of Economic Advisors (Sachverständigenrat) (2002) investigates the relationship between R&D disaggregated by performing sector and GDP per capita and find a negative impact of government R&D as percentage of GDP on GDP per capita. Furthermore, HERD as percentage of GDP and BERD as percentage of GDP both have a significant and positive impact on GDP per capita. Guellec and Van Pottelsberghe (2004) examine the impact of domestic business-sector R&D, public sector and

foreign R&D capital stock on total factor productivity using panel data for 18 OECD countries covering the period 1980-1998. The authors find a positive and significant effect of total public sector R&D (measured as R&D capital stocks) on the level of total factor productivity. The results presented here differ from Guellec and Van Pottelsberghe (2004) in that an empirical growth equation is used to estimate the impact of private and public sector R&D. In particular, the R&D share of GDP by performing sector is used rather than the rate of growth of different types of R&D capital itself. In growth regressions this avoids the need to specify an initial R&D capital stock and assume a rate of its depreciation. However, R&D intensity can be a poor proxy for growth in R&D capital stocks.

Both HERD as percentage of GDP and BERD as percentage of GDP are significant at the 5 % level in the majority of cases, implying that increasing higher education sector expenditures on R&D and business enterprise R&D expenditures have a significantly positive impact on GDP per capita growth in the OECD area.

The short-run elasticity of GDP per capita with respect to HERD intensity is about 0.08 based on the third specification.[46] The effect of HERD is much higher than the income share of HERD of about 0.42 % in terms of GDP, indicating significant spillover effects. The short-run elasticity of BERD is about 0.05 and is

---

[46] Computed as 0.19*0.39, where 0.39 is the average HERD/GDP in percentage points The corresponding long-run elasticity of GDP per capita with respect to HERD is about 0.81 (=0.08/(1-0.91)). The large impact of HERD seems implausible. Closer inspection suggests that this implausible result may be due to the slow economic convergence in the 1980s and 1990s as indicated by the high impact of lagged GDP. The estimated values of the adjustment coefficients range between 0.16 (=1-0.84) and 0.09 (=1-0.91), implying that between 9 % and 16 % of the adjustment take place within five years.

Table 2.9: Impact of public sector R&D on GDP growth

	(1) coeff.	(2) coeff.	(3) coeff.
Δln GDP per capita (t-1)	0.84***	0.91***	0.91***
ΔInvestment, % GDP (t)	1.15***	1.17***	1.17***
ΔAverage years of schooling (t)	0.03	0.03	0.03
ΔHigher education sector expenditures R&D, % GDP (t)	0.18*	0.24**	0.19**
ΔGovernment expenditures on R&D, % GDP (t)		-0.29***	-0.36***
ΔBusiness enterprise sector expenditures on R&D, % GDP (t)			0.04**
Population 15-64, growth (t)	0.00	0.00	0.00
Year 1990-1994	-0.03**	-0.04**	-0.03*
Year 1995-1999	-0.01	-0.01	-0.01
Year 2000-2002	-0.03**	-0.04**	-0.04**
Constant	0.03*	0.02	0.01
Sargent test (p-value)	0.023	0.057	0.061
Number of observations (countries)	87 (27)	87 (27)	87 (27)
Short-run elasticities:			
Higher education sector R&D expenditures, % GDP (t)	0.07	0.09	0.08
Government expenditures on R&D, % GDP (t)		-0.08	-0.09
Business enterprise sector R&D expenditures, % GDP (t)			0.05
Long-run elasticities:			
Higher education sector R&D expenditures, % GDP (t)	0.44	1.01	0.81
Government expenditures on R&D, % GDP (t)	0.00	-0.82	-0.99
Business enterprise sector R&D expenditures, % GDP (t)			0.50

Notes: p-value in parentheses. Number of countries: 16 (US, Japan and 14 pre-accession EU countries). Public sector R&D is the sum of HERD and GOVERD. The relative citation index is a measure of relative prominence of scientific literature of a country. This index is the country's share of cited literature adjusted for its share of published literature. A value of 1 would indicate that the country's world share of cited literature is equal to the country's world share of scientific literature. A value greater (less) than 1 would indicate that the country is cited relatively more (less) often than indicated by the country's share of scientific literature.

Sources: OECD, MSTI and National Science Foundation.

Graph 2.6: Relationship between the GDP per capita growth and change in public sector R&D

Correlation=0.68; p-value: 0.006

y-axis: (average annual growth rate of GDP per capita in constant PPP $ between 1995-2002)

x-axis: (Absolute) change in public sector R&D expenditures in % GDP between 1995-2000.

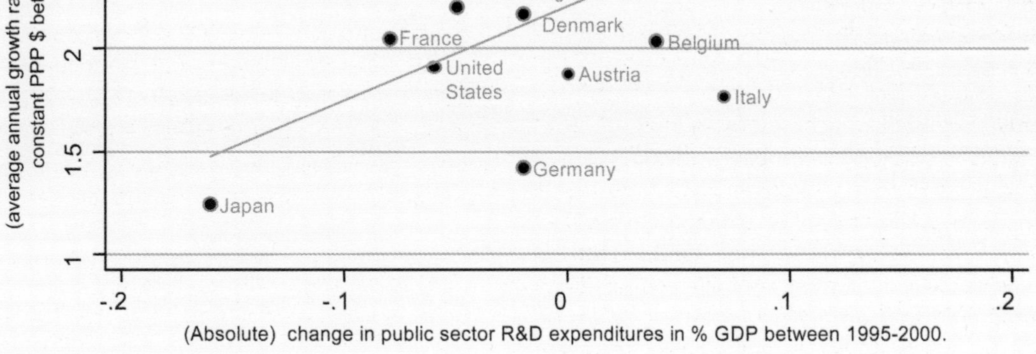

Notes: Ireland is excluded from the above analysis because of the extraordinary high growth rate during this period.

somewhat lower than the short-run elasticity of HERD. This is consistent with the hypothesis that the social rate of return of research in the higher education sector is higher than in the private R&D sector due to spillovers. It is interesting to note that the magnitude and statistical significance of HERD remains largely unchanged when business expenditures on R&D are included. This result concerning spillover effects from higher education research reinforces the need to integrate education policy reforms in the EU efforts to foster research and innovation throughout the economy. Unreported results show that there is a unidirectional causality from BERD in percentage of GDP and from HERD in percentage of GDP to growth in GDP per capita.[47] Furthermore, unreported results indicate that the impact of these R&D categories on growth is no different in EU countries than in the other countries in the sample.[48] Average years of schooling shows the correct sign, though not significant at the 5 % level. The poor performance of

average years of schooling as a measure of human capital could be largely due to the fact that the differences in educational quality between the countries are not captured.

The impact of public sector R&D on scientific output and patents

The number of scientific publications, the number of patents, the number of citations and the number of highly cited papers are basic indicators of the degree to which different R&D performers contribute to R&D knowledge.[49] This section looks at the evidence for relationships between public R&D and research output by means of a series of cross-plots of research output and various public R&D input indicators.

Table 2.10 shows the correlation coefficients between the average annual change in various

---

[47] Using panel Granger causality tests.
[48] Interaction effects between both HERD and BERD and a dummy variable for EU countries are not significantly different from zero.

[49] There are of course some new indicators measuring the scientific output such as the number of spin-offs generated by universities and government research centres. However, they are not available from internationally comparable sources (European Commission, 2003b).

Table 2.10: Correlation between the change in research output and public R&D

	Average annual growth rate of EPO patent applications per million population between 1990-1999	(Absolute) change in relative citation index between 1990-1999	Average annual growth rate of total scientific publications between 1990-1999
Average annual growth rate of public sector R&D in const. PPP US-$ (HERD + GOVERD) between 1990-2000	0.703 (0.002)	0.730 (0.001)	0.710 (0.002)
Absolute change in public sector R&D, % GDP between 1990-2000	0.645 (0.007)	0.579 (0.019)	0.556 (0.026)
Average annual growth rate of HERD in const. PPP US-$ between 1990-2000	0.541 (0.031)	0.753 (0.001)	0.609 (0.012)
Average annual growth rate of GBAORD in const. PPP US-$ between 1990-2000	0.574 (0.020)	0.572 (0.021)	0.712 (0.002)
Absolute change in government-funded R&D, % GDP between 1990-2000	0.293 (0.270)	0.604 (0.013)	0.029 (0.916)

Notes: p-value in parentheses. Number of countries: 16 (US, Japan and 14 pre-accession EU countries). Public sector R&D is the sum of HERD and GOVERD. The relative citation index is a measure of relative prominence of scientific literature of a country. This index is the country's share of cited literature adjusted for its share of published literature. A value of 1 would indicate that the country's world share of cited literature is equal to the country's world share of scientific literature. A value greater (less) than 1 would indicate that the country is cited relatively more (less) often than indicated by the country's share of scientific literature.

Sources: OECD, MSTI and National Science Foundation.

Graph 2.7: Correlation between the change in the relative citations index and change in public sector R&D (in percent)

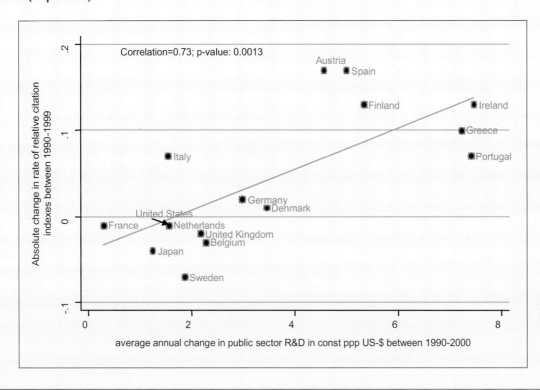

Source: OECD, MSTI.

measures of public sector R&D and changes in different types of research output based on data for the EU-15, Japan and the US. The correlation coefficient between the average annual growth rate of public sector R&D (measured in constant PPP) and the absolute change in the relative citation index is about 0.73 and highly significant - see Table 2.10, column 2.[50] This means that countries with a high growth rate of public sector expenditures on R&D experienced a rise in their relative citation index.

Graph 2.7 illustrates the fact that countries with the highest gains in the citation index such as Austria, Spain, Finland and Ireland have a higher-than-average growth of expenditures on R&D performed within the public sector. This indicates a higher marginal scientific productivity. In contrast, the opposite group of countries, showing a lower marginal scientific productivity are Japan, Sweden and Portugal.

The results are robust with respect to the measurement of public sector R&D expenditures (i.e. average annual growth rate of HERD in constant PPP, or alternatively the absolute change in public sector R&D expenditures as a percentage of GDP or the average annual growth rate of GBAORD in constant PPP). In all cases, the correlation coefficients are high and significant at the 1 % or 2 % level. Furthermore, the correlation between the absolute changes in government-funded R&D in percentage of GDP and the change in the relative citation index is high and significant.

Next the relationship between patents and public sector R&D is examined. In the US, universities have increased their patenting since the Bayh-Dole Act of 1980 which gave universities the right to patent and licence (National Science Foundation, 2002). The Bayh-Dole Act was introduced to encourage publicly funded research institutes and universities to file patents, exploit their research, and engage in collaborations with industry. In recent years, in Europe, several national legislations have converged to solutions of the Bayh-Dole Act type (European Commission, 2003c). Other Member States where provisions of this type have not yet been adopted are about to do

---

[50]   Note that citations are not a straightforward measure of quality for various reasons: self-citations by authors; authors citing colleagues, mentors, and friends; and a possible non-linear relationship of a country's number of publications and citations to that output (see National Science Foundation, 2002).

so. Column 1 in Table 2.10 shows the correlation coefficients between the average annual growth rates of EPO patent applications per million of population between 1990 and 1999 and the change in public expenditure on R&D (HERD and GOVERD) during the same period.

Again, there is a strong positive and significant relationship between the change in public sector expenditures on R&D and the change in EPO patent applications. The magnitude of the correlation coefficient is not very sensitive to the definition and measurement of public sector expenditures on R&D. Combining the change in the share of public sector R&D with the average annual growth rate of European patents per capita, it is clear that Portugal, Ireland and Finland have a higher-than-average marginal scientific productivity as the growth of EPO patents per capita is higher than the growth of public sector expenditures on R&D - see Graph 2.8.

Finally, the correlation coefficients between the growth of the number of total scientific publications between the period 1990-1999 and the growth of public R&D expenditures by performance/funds are presented in column 3 of Table 2.10. The results show that the correlation coefficients between the

growth rate of total scientific publications and different measures of public sector R&D are positive and significant at the 1 % level in all cases.

Some EU Member States have very low levels of patenting per capita at the beginning of the period but exhibit a strong upward growth trend. This also holds for the number of publications and the relative citation index. Therefore, the correlation coefficients, based on the levels for EU-25, Japan and the US, have also been computed and are presented in Table 2.11. However, it is well known that comparisons in the level of patents between the US and the EU may be biased due to the home advantage effect. This means that EU Member States will be dominant in EPO applications. Therefore, the correlation coefficients for the EU-15 countries are also presented in Table 2.11. For both sets of countries there is a large and significant correlation between EPO patents per capita (for the year 2000) and public sector R&D expenditures. Within the EU-15, countries with the highest level of patenting per labour force such as Sweden, Finland, Germany and the Netherlands spend a higher share of funds on the public R&D sector. Finally, the lowest level of both patenting and public sector R&D can be found in Cyprus, Slovak Republic and Latvia.

Graph 2.8: Correlation between the change in public sector R&D in percent and change in EPO patent applications in percent

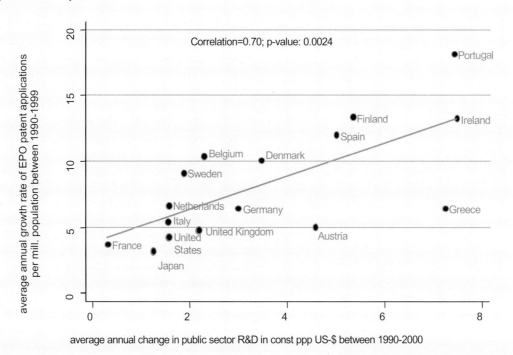

Source: OECD, MSTI.

Table 2.11: Correlation between research output and public

	Patents per LF 2000	RCI 1999	Articles per capita 2000
EU-25, USA and Japan			
GBAORD % GDP 2001	0.631	0.679	0.751
	(0.001)	(0.001)	(0.000)
Public sector R&D % GDP 2001	0.654	0.668	0.727
	(0.000)	(0.001)	(0.000)
Government-financed R&D, % GDP in 2001	0.705	0.745	0.723
	(0.000)	(0.000)	(0.000)
EU-15			
GBAORD % GDP 2001	0.539	0.700	0.666
	(0.038)	(0.005)	(0.007)
Public sector R&D % GDP 2001	0.627	0.825	0.745
	(0.012)	(0.000)	(0.001)
Government-financed R&D, % GDP in 2001	0.657	0.721	0.646
	(0.008)	(0.004)	(0.009)

Notes: p-value in parentheses. Relative prominence of scientific literature is measured on the basis of the relative citation index (RCI) of the country. This index is the country's share of cited literature adjusted for its share of published literature. An index of 1 indicates that the country's share of cited literature is equal to the country's world share of scientific literature. Values greater (less) than 1 indicate that the country is cited relatively more (less) than is indicated by the country's share of scientific literature (NSF 2002).

Source: National Science Foundation and Eurostat, New Cronos.

Again there is a high, positive and significant correlation between the relative citation index in 1999 and public sector R&D expenditures as a percentage of GDP in1998. This means that a country with higher public sector R&D expenditures as percentage of GDP has a larger number of frequently cited literature in relation to the country's share of world literature. Highly cited EU countries are the Nordic countries, Netherlands, Denmark, UK and Germany which also have a higher share of public sector R&D expenditures.

The next step in the analysis is to investigate the relationship between patent applications and public R&D when controlling for other factors such as business expenditures on R&D and country-fixed effects[51] as well as time effects. Again, a distinction is made between university and government laboratory expenditures on R&D.[52]

Table 2.12 presents the results for the relationship between public and private sector R&D and patent applications per capita. In specification (1), both private and public sector R&D are included while in specification (2) public sector R&D expenditures is disaggregated into higher education sector R&D

(HERD) expenditures and government sector expenditures on R&D, both measured as percentages of GDP. In addition, business enterprise sector R&D is split into publicly and privately financed R&D expenditures (specification 3) - see Appendix 2 for further details.

Table 2.12 shows that both the coefficients of private R&D (BERD) as a percentage of GDP and of public sector R&D (HERD and government expenditures combined) as a percentage of GDP are positive and significant, indicating a positive relationship between the R&D sectors and EPO patent applications per capita. This implies that countries with higher shares of R&D activities in the public sector have been able to achieve a higher level of patents per capita. This finding is consistent with the results of other empirical studies (see for instance Furman et al., 2002; Faber, Hesen, 2004). The elasticity of patents per capita with respect to public sector R&D is 0.64. This means that a ten percent increase in the ratio of public sector R&D to GDP (e.g. from 0.68 to 0.75) is associated with a 6.4 % increase in the number of patents per capita. Furthermore, the results indicate that the impact of public sector R&D is higher than that of business-funded R&D. The elasticity of patents per capita with respect to business enterprise sector R&D is 0.49. When breaking down public sector R&D into R&D conducted by the higher education sector and R&D done by the government sector, both R&D

---

[51] Country-specific effects control for factors such as the 'home advantage' bias.
[52] Furman et al. (2002) suggest that university research tends to be more accessible to industry researchers than government laboratory research.

Table 2.12: Relationship between public R&D and EPO patent applications: Panel estimates

Dependent variable: log EPO patent applications per capita

	(1) coefficient	(2) coefficient	(3) coefficient
log total BERD % GDP (t)	0.49***	0.47***	
log industry-financed BERD % GDP (t)			0.43***
log government-financed BERD % GDP (t)			0.10
log (HERD+GOVRD) R&D, % GDP (t)	0.64***		
log HERD % GDP (t)		0.36**	0.34**
log GOVRD, % GDP(t)		0.25*	0.23*
log years of schooling (t)	1.80*	1.68*	1.71*
Period dummy 1991-1994	0.03	0.04	0.04
Period dummy 1995-1999	0.32***	0.34***	0.34***
Constant	-0.30	0.39	0.59

Notes: *, **, and *** denote significance at the 10 %, 5 %, and 1 % level respectively. Estimation period: 1986-1999 with five-year interval data. Data for Germany refers to West Germany only until 1990; data for unified Germany during the period 1991-1995 is excluded. The group of countries includes Australia, Austria, Belgium, Canada, Denmark, Finland, France, Germany, Greece, Iceland, Ireland, Italy, Japan, Mexico, Netherlands, New Zealand, Norway, Poland, Portugal, Spain, Sweden, Switzerland, Turkey, UK and US; excluding the non-EU countries has little effect on the regression results.

sectors significantly contribute to the number of patents per capita. Furthermore, the ratio of government-funded BERD to GDP also has a small but positive effect on patents per capita.

A summing up

Using industry-level data for EU countries for the period 1987-1999, estimation results suggest that government-financed R&D expenditures complement domestic industry-financed expenditures on R&D. In terms of marginal impacts of public funding, € 1 increase in government financed R&D produces an additional € 0.93 in domestic industry R&D. Furthermore, using economy-wide data for a panel of OECD/EU countries for the period 1981-2002, the results suggest that both direct funding of business R&D and tax incentives for R&D have a significant and positive impact on business R&D spending in OECD and EU countries. These two policy instruments tend to complement each other. The empirical evidence suggests that R&D tax credits are an effective instrument.

The elasticity of tax incentives is about -0.5, indicating that a 10 % reduction in the price of R&D (i.e. an increase in the generosity of tax incentives for R&D) leads to a 5 % increase in the amount of R&D spending in the business sector in the long run. For the OECD/EU area during the period 1990-2002, the results suggest that the increase in fiscal incentives for R&D contributed 0.1 percentage points to the 3.9 increase in the ratio of business R&D to GDP. In contrast, the decrease in direct

R&D subsidies intensity has hampered increases in business R&D intensity by 0.3 percentage points. However, other factors such as the shift to R&D intensive industries seem to be more important than tax incentives or direct support for R&D in explaining the change in the R&D intensity in the business sector across EU countries. To the extent that reallocation of production factors towards high-technology industries is being hampered by lack of flexibility in factor markets, structural reforms aimed at rendering markets more flexible will play an important role in increasing the level of business R&D across the EU.

The results also support the importance of public sector R&D for productivity growth and for creating spillover effects to the private R&D sector. Expenditures on R&D performed by universities and public research organisations are significantly positively related to business enterprise sector expenditures on R&D, indicating that public sector R&D and private sector R&D are complements. For the period 1990-2002, a significant part of the increasing R&D intensity in the business sector can be explained by the increase in R&D expenditures performed by the higher education sector, indicating substantial spillover effects from academic research. When public sector R&D is disaggregated into its two main components, both government and university R&D spending are significantly positively related to the R&D intensity in the business sector, with the impact of higher education R&D larger than that of government R&D. In terms of marginal impacts of public funding, an additional €

1 spent in R&D performed by universities leads to an additional € 1.3 in industry R&D while € 1 increase in R&D performed by government institutions leads to an additional €1.1.

Estimation results of an economic growth equation for OECD/EU countries suggest that expenditures on R&D in the higher education sector significantly stimulate growth of GDP per capita. The effect of R&D performed by the higher education sector is higher than the income share of this sector, indicating substantial spillover effects. In addition, the impact of university research is somewhat higher than the impact of business R&D. This is consistent with the hypothesis that the social rate of return of research in the higher education sector is higher than in the private R&D sector due to spillover effects.

Finally, another important finding is that public sector R&D spending as a percentage of GDP has a positive and significant impact on EPO patent applications per capita, even after private R&D spending and country fixed effects have been controlled for. In particular, the impact of R&D performed by university and government research organisations is higher than the impact of business enterprise sector R&D. Also, correlation analyses of R&D expenditures performed by universities and public research organisations with indicators of research output suggest significant and positive associations with publication citations, number of patents per capita and number of publications. The role of higher education research in fostering R&D output and economic growth reinforces the need to integrate education policy reforms in the EU efforts to foster research and innovation throughout the economy.

2.4 Impact of public funding of business R&D on R&D/innovation and private patent outcome: country case studies

2.4.1 Public business R&D funding and private patent outcomes – Cross-country comparison and empirical analysis of Germany and Finland

2.4.1.1 Introduction

This section provides a comparison between Germany and Finland regarding public R&D funding and innovation support and their effects in innovation output as measured by patenting

performance. Despite the fact that these two countries have rather similar national innovation and R&D policies and very similar public funding systems and policy instruments, their innovation performance over the last years has been surprisingly different.

This section begins with an overview of general trends in innovation policy and of policy instruments fostering business R&D in Germany and Finland. It compares the most important innovation indicators and discusses the contribution of differences in innovation funding systems to the remarkable performance of Finland. In sub-section 2.4.1.2, input measures such as government budget appropriations and R&D personnel, and impact measures such as patent applications, are examined. The empirical analysis of the impact of public funding on patent outcome links innovative input and output and is presented in sub-section 2.4.1.3. A key question is whether public subsidies in co-operative R&D activities affect a company's probability to patent. A discussion on whether this particular policy tool is able to explain the remarkable differences in the innovation output (patents) between Finland and Germany closes the discussion.

2.4.1.2 General trends of innovation policy in Germany and Finland

Innovation is a priority of all Member States of the EU. Throughout Europe, a wide range of policy measures and support schemes aimed at fostering innovation have been implemented or are under preparation. The diversity of these measures and schemes reflects the diversity of the framework conditions, cultural preferences and political priorities in the Member States. As a distinctive feature, and in contrast to most European countries, Germany and Finland have (a) a comparable national innovation and R&D policy, (b) comparable policy instruments aimed to stimulate business R&D, and (c) a comparable public funding system.

(a) Innovation and R&D policies

In *Germany*, the main objective of innovation policy (in a broad sense) is to accelerate the diffusion of new technologies and to ensure that Germany is able to keep pace with international technological developments. In 2001, the Federal government's expenditure for R&D amounted to € 7 099 million, which represents a 2.8 % increase as compared to 2000 (OECD, 2003).

The contributions made by the Federal Ministry of Economics and Technology (BMWi), the Federal

Ministry of Defence (BMVg) and the Federal Ministry of Education and Research (BMBF) account for almost 90 % of total federal R&D funds. Nearly two-thirds of all federal R&D expenditure is financed by the BMBF's budget. In recent years, improvements have been achieved through three lines of promotion - innovation, cooperation, technological consulting. R&D expenditure growth for the BMBF has been stable and far higher than the average. An increase in 1999, when the BMBF's R&D expenditure was up 3.5 % from 1998 levels, was followed up in subsequent years - 2.9 % in 2000, 3.9 % in 2001 and 3.5 % in 2002 (cf. Fier, 2002; BMBF, 2000).

In recent years, *Finland's* technology policy has focused on the creation and application of new knowledge and skills, on the integration of sustainable development and the capacity for continuous renewal. Finland strives for the creation of an environment favourable to innovation and business activities. Finnish economic and societal development have been based on developing and diffusing high technology, both domestically and internationally, where the latter resulted in an increased effort to foster exports.[53] Eventually, the efforts resulted in a favourable international competitiveness of the Finnish economy. In various international comparisons, Finland ranks as one of the leading European countries for innovation measured in terms of growth, competitiveness, technological sophistication and infrastructure.

In Finland, the Science and Technology Policy Council, chaired by the Prime Minister, plays a key role in the coordination of innovation policy activities at the national level. The main tasks of the Council include directing science and technology policy, dealing with the overall development of scientific research and education, and issuing statements on the allocation of public science and technology funds to the various ministries and interested bodies.

Similar to the German structure of ministries, the two most important ministries in the Finnish national innovation system are the Ministry of Education and the Ministry of Trade and Industry. In 2003 the former administered 41.7 % and the latter 34.4 % of government outlays on R&D (Statistics Finland, 2004).

In general, Finland's performance has been determined by a fundamental structural shift from a resource-based economy to a knowledge-based economy. Clearly, R&D was a key factor in this development. R&D growth in Finland over the course of the 1990s outpaced that of all other OECD countries except Iceland, and by the end of the 1990s, Finland was by far the largest R&D spender (relative to GDP) of all OECD countries (cf. Werner, 2003). During this period, Germany has had to cope with the consequences of reunification. The transition to a market economy of the former DDR put strains on budgets and resources have been absorbed in the transformation process.

(b) Policy instruments fostering business R&D

Innovation policies rest on several pillars: Direct subsidies for research projects within thematic programmes, promotion of SMEs in three promotion lines (innovation, cooperation, technology consulting) and by four types of support (subsidies, loans, venture capital, and infrastructure supply) in the fields of information and consulting. In general, firms can compose an individual mix of public support out of the different pillars which best suits their specific challenges. In contrast to other Member States, Germany and Finland do not provide for special fiscal treatment of innovation - such as tax credits or tax subsidies.

Direct subsidies are the most important innovation policy tool in Finland and in Germany. Such subsidies belong to the group of policy instruments focussing on innovation financing, that is, the provision of finance for innovation activities, including measures designed to deliver or stimulate the delivery of financial support for innovation. Two important policy aspects must be stressed regarding direct subsidies for R&D and innovation: First, they are given as 'matching grants'[54] (cost sharing of total R&D project expenditures by the applicant and the government); second, they give preference to collaborative research projects (cooperative research of different firms and/or universities and/or research centres).

Matching grants for R&D projects are directed at thematic programmes, adoption of programme structures based on technology foresight, regular tenders and peer review-based selections, and special approaches (e.g. joint projects of industry and science or large firms and SMEs, regional networks, and start-ups). The administration of such

---

[53] High-tech products account for 20.6 % of exports.

[54] In Germany, direct project funding is carried out almost exclusively through grants, while the Finnish funding system also grants loans to the companies. As the loans amount to less than 20 % of the grants to firms and universities (Tekes, 2004b) no explicitly distinction between grants and loans is made here; furthermore, the source of the data used does not make possible this distinction.

business-related funding is delegated and carried out in Finland by Tekes (National Technology Agency) and in Germany by 'project leaders' (*Projektträger*).

Collaborative research for R&D projects is preferred because cooperation has advantages such as positive spillovers as well as cost and risk sharing (cf. Audretsch, 2003). In an empirical study, Cassiman, Veugelers (2002) and Dachs, Ebersberger, Pyka (2004) explore the effects of knowledge flows on R&D cooperation. Their results suggest that firms with higher incoming spillovers and higher appropriation ability have a higher probability of cooperating in R&D.

Networking and close cooperation between universities and industry are seen as a key strength in Finland as well as in Germany. About 50 % of the innovating companies in *Finland* have been involved in cooperative research and development. Judged by the frequency in 1998-2000, suppliers (41 %), customers and clients (38.1 %) as well as universities (29.1 %) are the most important partners for collaborative research (Statistics Finland, 2002). About one fifth of innovating firms collaborates with competitors and research labs, even though they are some of the least important collaboration partners. According to OECD data, Finland has the second largest share of firms with cooperation agreements with universities or government research institutes.[55] Finland is also engaged in international cooperation.

In *Germany,* during 1998-2000, 16.5 % of firms had cooperation agreements (corresponding to 15.1 % among SMEs and 46.4 % among firms with more than 500 employees). In total, 15.3 % of the German firms cooperate with partners in Germany and 6.7 % have foreign cooperation partners. Around 10 % of German firms cooperate with universities.[56] The share of firms with a cooperation partner has declined in 1998-2000 relative to 1994-1996. The only exception is the share of firms cooperating with commercial laboratories and R&D enterprises.[57]

The comparison between the German and the Finnish collaboration pattern reveals a strikingly higher propensity to collaborate in Finland (Foyn, 2000). Two reasons may explain this: First, the small size of the Finnish economy facilitates networking due to comparably low transaction costs in finding

the right collaboration partner. However, as rather large differences in the propensity to collaborate are found even in economies of comparable size such as Austria (cf. Dachs, Ebersberger, Pyka, 2004; Foyn, 2000), size cannot be the sole factor explaining the differences; secondly, strengthening of inter-firm networking and cooperation, as well as science-industry collaboration, has been a top priority of Finnish technology policy. One could argue that over the course of time, a collaboration culture has developed in Finland as the country experienced a longer history of collaboration-targeted public funding policy than most other European countries (Schienstock and Hämäläinen, 2001). Since the National Technology Agency (Tekes) started its first technology programme in the early 1980s, collaboration has been a part of the financing principles (see e.g. Lemola, 2002).[58]

(c) Public funding system

Within the administration of German and Finnish ministries, particular organisations (intermediaries) are responsible for the R&D and innovation funding process and have a central position in planning and financing. In Germany, the administration of public funds is mainly delegated to and carried out by 'project leaders' (*Projektträger*); in Finland this tasks belong to the National Technology Agency (Tekes).

The *German* 'project leaders', generally research centres and other organisations, are responsible for the technical and organisational realisation of ministerial projects. Through all stages of the project, qualified experts of different scientific and technical areas and competent contact persons perform several functions[59] and 'project leaders' are the key contact persons in the promotion of research. To cope with the responsibility of the funds entrusted to them[60], they must ensure that projects are realised at a high professional level and that the legal framework of the promotion of the project is considered.

In the *Finnish* innovation system, Tekes (National Technology Agency) is the counterpart to the German project leaders. It focuses on supporting firms as well as scientific institutes. It seeks to promote the competitiveness of the Finnish industry and service sector by promoting research and appli-

---

55   Sweden ranks first.
56   10.2 % (1998-2000) and 10.9 % (1994-1996).
57   Values based on CIS data.

58   Tekes' notion of collaboration includes different types of networks covering the wide spectrum of activities from basic R&D up to marketing.
59   In particular, the following functions: (i) Conceptual work at the preparation of new support programmes and emphases, (ii) project management (advisory service for applicants, professional and administrative phase-out of current projects, evaluation), (iii) supervision of EU support programmes, (iv) support in international research cooperations and (v) public relations.
60   'Project leaders' hold in trust subsidies amounting to up to € 500 million per year.

Graph 2.9: R&D funding systems in Finland and Germany

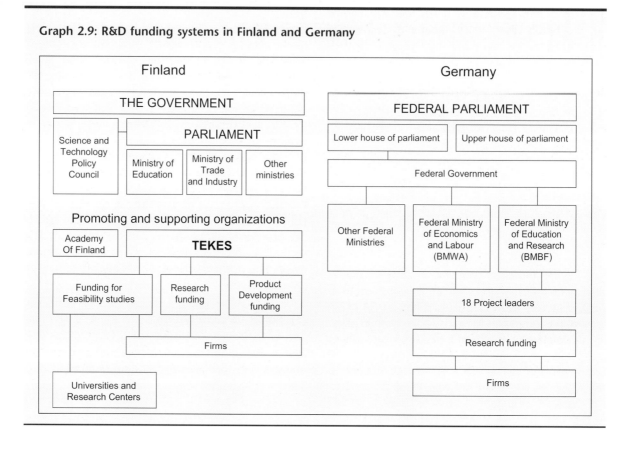

cations in the field of technological development. Tekes coordinates national technology programmes and provides funds for applied technical research. Being in the administrative domain of the Ministry of Trade and Industry, it also contributes to the preparation of national technology policy. With its share of 27.1 % of Government appropriations for R&D (€ 392 million in 2003), Tekes is the largest organisation in the field (Tekes, 2004a). In 2003, Tekes supported R&D efforts by means of industrial R&D grants (39.8 %), research funding to universities and research institutes (41.3 %), industrial R&D loans (10.2 %) and capital loans for R&D to companies (8.7 %). The type of funding for companies depends on the stage of innovation and the nature of the project.

In Germany and Finland, industrial R&D grants run from about 15 % to 50 %. Capital R&D loans run from 35 % to 60 % and industrial R&D loans from 45 % to 70 % of eligible costs (Finland). In both countries, funding is mainly restricted to domestically owned companies with domestic R&D activities. The funding share for research institutes and universities ranges from 50 % to 100 % of the eligible costs and is restricted to research work done at the institute or university. Those projects are usually cooperations with companies or other research facilities. Technology programmes are initi-

ated by Tekes or the German 'project leaders' and concentrate on specific technologies. The duration of the programmes is about three to five years. Both intermediators usually finance about half of the costs of the programmes. The remaining financing originates from the participating companies ('matched grant concept').

Input and output indicators on R&D and innovation

The Finnish government spent about € 1 400 million on R&D activities in 2002. Although this is less than one tenth of the German government support of about € 17 000 million, Finland spends 3.4 % of its GDP on R&D whereas Germany spends 2.5 % (2001). Moreover, the public R&D intensity in Finland at 0.96 % exceeds Germany's by 16 percentage points (OECD, 2003).

In the late 1990s, Finnish government outlays for R&D were markedly increased by a decision to allocate € 500 million to research and development over the years 1997 to 1999. This additional appropriation for R&D was financed by privatisation revenues. In 1999, an additional increment (€ 250 million) was introduced permanently. The objective of the additional appropriation was to foster the national system of innovation and to create a beneficial environment for business, employment and the economy. The final aim was to raise R&D to 2.9 % of GDP by 1999; this goal was already achieved in 1998.

Between 1995 and 2001 Finland's R&D expenditure increased by a higher rate (90 %) than the R&D expenditure in Germany (23 %). Aggregate R&D expenditure in Finland is shaped by the private ICT (Information and Communication Technology) sector (Nokia effect[61]). With increasing importance of the electronics industry its share of private R&D expenditure rose from about 25 % in 1990 to about 54 % in 1999 (Statistics Finland, 2001).

[61] The European Discussion on ICT up to the early 1990s was dominated by Finland and Nokia. (Finland as a typical large area country like Sweden has long years of experience in the sector of mobile communication. In contrast to other European countries, the infrastructural organisation is on behalf of the single communes and not centralised. The consequence is that regional traders have learned to provide common standards of technology.) Thus, Nokia became the 'third leg of Finland's economy' besides Wood and Paper, and Metal (see Mosaic Group, 1998). The 'Nokia Effect' described the ICT-led success of an economy. The term was established by the stock exchange speculators to describe decreases in the technology values of other countries' firm at the stock market caused by Nokia (cf. Ali-Yrkkö et al., 2000).

Concerning the outcome of funded R&D activities, Germany and Finland have different incentive structures. The German Federal Government stimulates the development of patent, licensing and exploitation expertise in their funding procedures. When an R&D recipient firm files an application it has also to submit a plan for the utilisation of the outcome – initially in form of an outline which subsequently will become more and more detailed. All publicly funded R&D recipients are expected and encouraged to assume responsibility for their exploitation management. Wherever possible, research findings have to be commercially utilised. In order to give an incentive to the grant recipients, the Federal Government allows them to keep all proceeds from the exploitation of patents for at least two years. If the recipient does not apply for a patent within two years, the R&D results become a public good (BMBF, 2000).In contrast to German practice, the funding scheme in Finland does not give the funded companies any additional incentive to patent the results of the funded research.Box 2.3 briefly presents the evolution of several R&D input and output indicators in Finland and Germany for the period since 1990.

Box 2.3

Gross Domestic Expenditure on R&D (GERD): Splitting GERD into its public and private shares shows that the ratio of public to private R&D in Germany is constant at about 1:2 in the period under consideration. In Finland, the relative importance of public R&D declined from 1990 to 2003: Public R&D expenditure could not keep pace with the fast increasing private R&D expenditure fuelled by the successful electronics industry.

Government Budget Appropriations or Outlays for R&D by socio-economic objectives (GBAORD): Although GBAORD is much lower in Finland than in Germany, it has grown at a higher rate in Finland. From 1990 to 2003 GBAORD rose by 113 % in Finland whereas in Germany 2002 it increased just by 50 % between 1990 and 2002. Relative to GDP, both GBAORD and GERD in Finland exceeded German figures by a small amount. Focussing on the composition of GBAORD in Germany during the period 1990-2003, the share of the defence budget declined continuously, whereas general university funding grew. In Finland, the most significant changes are a decline in space programme investments in favour of the share of non-oriented research programmes.

R&D Personnel (FTE): Whereas the absolute number of researchers is higher in Germany, the pattern of growth shows significant progress in Finland. In the period 1998-2000, the number of researcher grew by more than 30 % in Finland and by 17 % in Germany. It has been argued that the success of the Finnish innovation system can be attributed to the fact that, amongst other characteristics, it has been able to supply an ever-increasing number of science and engineering graduates (c.f. Georghiou et al, 2003).

Beside these R&D 'input' indicators, some innovation outcome indicators ('output') such as patents have displayed a remarkable catching-up in Finland in the 1990s. Patents play a key role in the innovation process, not only as an instrument to protect inventions, but also as a source of information for the planning of further R&D activities. The number of patents as an output variable is seen as an important indicator of a nation's technological competitiveness in the future.

Number of 'triadic' patent families[62]: The evolution in the number of triadic families in Germany is close to the evolution in the European Union with a small decrease in the 1991 and a growth of about 30 % since 1990. In contrast, Finland has experienced an increase of 170 % in this indicator, with a large increase in 1994 shortly before Finland became a member of the EU and of the EPC (European Patent Convention).

Number of patent applications to the European Patent Office (EPO): Germany shows a trend close to that of the European Union while in Finland this indicator had a much steeper growth. EPO applications in Finland show no significant increase in 1994: this suggests that the hump in the 1994 triadic patents is more a consequence of the developments in the electronics field than the result of Finland's EU or EPC membership.

Number of patents granted by the US Patent and Trademark Office (USPTO): Both Germany and Finland exceed the EU average growth in USPTO patent applications. In contrast to the EPO and triadic patents, German patent applications have grown much faster than Finnish applications at the USPTO. This suggests that German inventions, relative to Finnish ones, are more directed to the US markets.

[62] 'A patent is a member of the [triadic] patent families if it is filed at the European Patent Office (EPO), the Japanese Patent Office (JPO) and is granted by the US Patent and Trademark Office (USPTO)', (OECD, 2003).

2.4.1.3 Empirical analysis of public funding cooperation and patent outcome

Focus of the analysis

This section reviews how different firm characteristics affect the probability to patent. If significant spillovers are produced by collaborative research activities, firms participating in R&D networks will exhibit higher innovation productivity. Following the arguments by Hagedoorn, Cloodt (2003), the patenting behaviour of firms is used as a proxy for innovative performance. It is expected that R&D cooperations show a higher productivity in terms of patent applications due to positive spillover effects. However, it is unclear how publicly funded research networks differ from privately financed collaborations. On the one hand, it may be that public R&D networks are less productive. It could be the case that the focus on cooperative research of modern public technology policies forces firms to collaborate in order to receive public grants. If policy schemes had been different, those firms might have preferred to keep their knowledge secret and conduct only research projects on their own. In this case, the publicly funded R&D networks would not benefit from spillovers as firms pursue secrecy concerning their research when interacting with their research partners involved in the project. On the other hand, publicly funded networks and the partners involved may exhibit a 'higher quality' of research carried out as the research projects have passed the governmental quality control. Non-public R&D cooperations could have failed in such a process or only dealt with research less important for technological progress (cf. Czarnitzki, Fier, 2003).

The analysis focuses on the impact of public funding on innovative output. As public funding schemes both in Germany and in Finland focus on inducing companies to engage in collaborative research, both the effect of public funding and that of collaboration must be considered. The analysis addresses the following questions:

- Question 1: *Do funded companies have a higher innovation output than their output would have been, had they not received funding?*

- Question 2: *Do funded and collaborating companies exhibit a higher innovation output compared with the situation of neither collaboration nor funding?*

- Question 3: *Does collaboration increase innovation output, even if no funding is involved?*

- Question 4: *Does funding increase innovation output, even if no collaboration is involved?*

- Question 5: *Given that companies collaborate and receive funding, what would have happened if these firms had not received funding?*

- Question 6: *If a collaborating but non-funded company is funded, does this increase the innovative output?*

Neither the fact that companies receive public funding for their R&D nor the fact that companies collaborate for innovation can be reasonably interpreted as the result of a random process. Both receiving funding and collaboration are subject to a selection bias. Concerning funding, companies themselves choose to apply or not to apply for. Also, the funding agency selects from the pool of applications based on certain criteria. As collaboration for innovation is part of the companies' innovation strategy; it is the companies themselves that choose whether or not to collaborate. The selection bias results in the empirical fact that the group of funded companies is quite different from the group of non-funded ones, as well as the group of collaborating companies is quite different from the group of non-collaborating ones. The presence of this selection bias requires that an appropriate estimation procedure be used – see Appendix 3 for more information on data, methodology and estimation results.

Estimation results[63]

Variable description

The main question of this analysis is whether patent activities of firms are stimulated by public funding and/or cooperations. This patent activity is measured with a dummy variable (*PATENT*), indicating whether the particular firm has filed at least one patent application during the past three years. About 27 % of German and 16 % of Finnish firm in the sample have filed at least one application.[64]

Explanatory variables include two dummy variables: collaboration (*CO*), and subsidised arrangements

---

[63] Appendix 3 presents in more detail the data sources, methodology and econometric results. See also 'European Productivity, Innovation and Public Sector R&D', background study prepared for the 2004 edition of the *European Competitiveness Report*.

[64] The data used for the empirical analysis are from the Community Innovation Survey (CIS). In this analysis, the period used is 1994 to 2000 based on data from CIS II and CIS III. CIS data has been complemented by data taken from Statistics Finland's employment register as well as from patent statistics. With regard to the German database, West German companies instead of all German companies are used since West German firms are most similar to Finnish companies.

(FUNPUB).[65] The share of firms performing collaborative research is about 17 % (Germany) and 34 % (Finland). In the German (Finnish) sample, about 12 % (26 %) of all firms get an R&D subsidy. Other variables to control for firm heterogeneity are also used. Firm size is captured by number of employees, *EMPL*. The square of this variable, *EMPL²*, is also included to allow for non-monotonicity.[66] Export orientation, *EXQU*, is measures as exports divided by turnover. The patent stock, *PATSTOCK*, summarizes the historical technological experience and level of innovation activities. In addition to previous patenting activities, the current potential to patent clearly depends on the current R&D engagement of firms. This is measured by the number of R&D employees divided by number of employees (share of R&D employees, *RDEMP*) and its squared value is also included. Eight sector dummies capture different technological opportunities among business sectors. Finally, a time dummy reflects the changes in patenting activities over time.

Probability to patent

A first regression estimates the impact of the various explanatory variables on the probability to patent. Table 2.13 displays these results - the coefficients have no straightforward interpretation other than their sign and statistical significance.

A positive and significant coefficient for *FUNPUB* indicates that funded firms exhibit a significantly higher probability to file a patent than non-funded firms. This holds true for both Germany and

Finland. A positive impact of collaboration on the propensity to patent in both countries is also evident as is the impact of patenting history of the companies (captured by the variable patent stock). It is likely that this stems from experiences in the patent application procedure at the national or international patent offices.

Furthermore, larger firms are more likely to file a patent. The Finnish results suggest that beyond a size of approximately 1 700 employees, the propensity to patent declines with size, while the German sample suggests a turning point of 1250 employees[67]. Despite the statistical significance of the negative coefficient in the squared employment term, the employment values in the sample are mainly below the peak value in both countries[68] indicating a positive relationship between firm size measured by employment and propensity to patent. An inverted U-shaped influence can also be found for the R&D employment variable. In the Finnish case, the probability to patent increases up to a level of 18 % of highly educated employees and decreases beyond that value. The German estimates suggest a share of R&D employees of about 60 % to be the peak of influence of employment in R&D. The different results in magnitude of the peak values for Germany and Finland can be attributed to the different entities measured by the variable in both country samples (see Appendix 3). Again, the data show that in the region of declining influence of employment in R&D only few firms are present in both countries suggesting that in the relevant range the impact of R&D employment on the propensity to patent is positive. In general, these firms are small and operate in high-tech sectors. Here,

---

[65] Collaboration in this context means the active collaboration of all partners involved in the project; contracting-out of R&D is excluded.

[66] From a theoretical point of view, it would be desirable to include a variable indicating the age of the company. As the Finnish data does not contain reliable information on this an age variable is not included in either case.

[67] Employment is measured in thousands. The inverted U-shaped relation results from the negative sign of the coefficient of the squared size.

[68] Firms with size above the turning point are less than 0.5% in Finland and less than 4% in Germany.

Table 2.13: Estimation of patenting probability

	Germany	Finland
PATENT	Coefficient	Coefficient
EMPL	2.195***	1.241***
EMPL2	-0.878***	-0.370*
RDEMP	5.286***	4.433**
RDEMP2	-4.748***	-12.786*
PATSTOCK	0.871***	0.926***
EXQU	0.915***	0.526***
FUNPUB	0.375***	0.462***
CO	0.621***	0.688***
_CONS	-2.532***	-2.577***

Note: A Probit model was used in the estimation. *** (**, *) indicate a significance level of 1 % (5 %, 10 %); equations include eight industry dummies and one time dummy.

Table 2.14: Impact on probabilities of receiving funding and of cooperating

	Germany	Finland
FUNPUB	Coefficient	Coefficient
EMPL	1.181***	1.861***
EMPL2	-0.399**	-0.649***
RDEMP	6.252***	5.778***
RDEMP2	-5.110***	-13.607**
PATSTOCK	0.322***	0.555***
EXQU	0.213	0.833***
_CONS	-2.079***	-1.588***
CO	Coefficient	Coefficient
EMPL	1.374***	3.165***
EMPL2	-0.442***	-1.470***
RDEMP	5.831***	2.555**
RDEMP2	-4.809***	-4.190
PATSTOCK	0.289***	0.496***
EXQU	0.533***	0.742**
_CONS	-1.917***	-1.100
RHO	0.459***	0.737***

Note: Bivariate probit estimation on *FUNPUB* and *CO*. *** (**, *) indicate a significance level of 1 % (5 %, 10 %). All estimations include eight industry dummies and one time dummy.

secrecy instead of patenting may be preferred because with the patent disclosure, knowledge assets become at least partly public.[69]

Table 2.14 presents the impact of the different explanatory variables on the probability of being funded (upper panel) and on the probability of collaborating (bottom panel).

Probabilities of collaborating and of being funded

Fundamentally, the data support the hypothesized selection bias as the group of funded (collaborating) companies is significantly different from the group of non-funded (non-collaborating) companies. The regressions yield comparable results for both countries. One of the differences relates to the significant influence of the squared R&D intensity in the estimation of the German sample. For companies with more than 60 % R&D employees, the regressions reveal a decreasing likelihood to collaborate on innovation. As mentioned previously, these companies are generally small and operate in high-tech sectors, where innovation competition can be regarded as exceptionally fierce. The reluctance to collaborate may be caused by the companies' fear of losing marketable knowledge. This effect is not present in the Finnish data.[70]

The second difference is the influence of the export orientation on the companies' propensity to receive funding. In the Finnish sample, there is a highly significant positive influence. In the German sample, the influence is not significant at the 10 % level. As the National Technology Agency (Tekes), which distributes the largest fraction of project-related funding in Finland, puts strong focus on the economic viability of the results of the funded project, special effort is put on the companies' competitiveness and the competitive advantage of the technology involved in the project (cf. Tekes, 2004a). In a small open economy, the companies' competitiveness leads to an emphasis on export-oriented companies.

Finally, on the basis of an econometric technique that addresses the selection bias problem, the main conclusions concerning each of the six questions dealing with the influence of R&D collaboration and public funding on patenting activity are summarised below.[71]

Question 1: *Do funded companies have a higher innovation output than their output would have been, had they not received funding?*

---

[69] Note that patents are published in Europe 18 months after the (first) application, even though the patent may not have been granted yet (see e.g. OECD, 1994, p. 27).

[70] The coefficient of the squared R&D employment is not statistically significant for Finland, therefore the higher the share of R&D employees the higher propensity to collaborate.

[71] These results are based on a matching estimator using the propensity scores on the collaboration and funding variables derived from the regression presented in Table 2.14. More details on this estimator and on the econometric results can be found in Appendix 3 or in 'European Productivity, Innovation and Public Sector R&D', background study prepared for the 2004 edition of the *European Competitiveness Report*.

This question concerns the differences between companies that receive funding and those that do not. In both countries, the average company not receiving funds is smaller, less R&D-intensive, has a lower level of past technological experience and a lower export orientation. Also, the average funded company reveals a significantly higher propensity to patent than the average non-funded company. The differences in the propensity to patent in the German and the Finnish sample are most likely caused by the different composition of the samples.

Funded companies in Finland are smaller but considerably more export-oriented than the German companies. About 63 % of the funded German companies, but only 37 % of the Finnish companies, have patented before. After controlling for other characteristics that differentiate these two groups, differences in the average funded and the average non-funded company vanish: on average, both groups have an equal probability of receiving funding and of collaborating. Yet, a significant difference in the propensity to patent remains. Funded companies have a higher likelihood to patent than non-funded companies. Funding increases the probability to patent by 75 % in Germany. In Finland, however, funding causes the patenting probability to double. This means that both in Germany and in Finland public funding exerts a positive influence on the funded companies' propensity to patent. Regardless of their collaboration behaviour, public funding exhibits a positive impact on the funded companies innovative output.

Question 2: *Do funded and collaborating companies exhibit a higher innovation output compared with the situation of neither collaboration nor funding?*

After controlling for firms' characteristics, on average, the initial dissimilarity between the two groups (firms which collaborate and are funded vs. those which do neither) vanishes. In both groups, Germany shows a relatively higher propensity to patent (70.8 % in the collaborating/funded group and 47.1 % in the other group after controlling for characteristics) than Finland (46 % and 12.8 %, respectively). Yet, the impact of simultaneous collaboration and public funding is larger in Finland (33.2 %) than in Germany (23.7 %). Both effects are significant. The impact of public funding is even more pronounced if public funding induces companies to collaborate.

Question 3: *Does collaboration increase innovation output, even if no funding is involved?*

This question focuses on the impact of collaboration in the absence of public funding. There is a significantly positive impact of collaboration, even in the

situation where no public funding is granted. The magnitude of the impact, however, differs between German and Finnish firms. In the absence of public funding, collaboration increases the propensity to patent by 22.4 percentage points in the German sample, whereas the increase in the Finnish sample only amounts to 14.4 percentage points. Thus, even without public funding, increased collaboration has a positive impact on companies that collaborate, compared with their situation had they not collaborated.

Question 4: *Does funding increase innovation output, even if no collaboration is involved?*

This case investigates whether funding increases innovative output even if companies do not collaborate. The results reveal a significantly positive impact of public funding, even if companies do not change their collaboration behaviour. For the sample of non-collaborating firms, public funding has a positive impact on the innovative output of funded companies.

Question 5: *Given that companies collaborate and receive funding, what would have happened if these firms had not received funding?*

This case investigates whether funded and collaborating companies would have achieved equal innovative output had they not been funded. The results for the German sample suggest that, once companies collaborate, funding does not increase the innovative output. Having concluded that funding together with collaboration (Question 2) has an impact on the innovative output and collaboration without funding also yields positive effects (Question 3), it can be said that in Germany, funding does not significantly increase innovative output once companies collaborate. The result on Question 4 for the German sample indicates that among the companies that do not collaborate, public funding does cause an increase in innovative output. The result here suggests that the impact of public funding varies according to the collaboration decision of the firms. In the Finnish sample, however, even if companies decide to collaborate, funding has a positive impact. In contrast to the results for Germany, funding exerts a positive impact regardless of the collaboration decision in the case of Finland.

Question 6: *If a collaborating but non-funded company is funded, does this increase the innovative output?*

This question investigates whether removing funding has a negative impact on the innovative output.

Consistent with the findings for Question 5, there is no impact in the German sample but in the Finnish data the impact is significant. Even more so, it is of the same magnitude (but the opposite sign, of course) as the impact in the context of Question 4.

A Summing up

The evidence reviewed here concerns the significance of innovation policies and R&D collaboration in Germany and Finland as representative of the set of such policies used in the Member States. Although both countries have very similar innovation policies, they have very different records of success. In Germany, as in other large EU Member States, there has been a moderate increase of R&D investments whereas Finland is representative of the success smaller Member States have seen in recent years.

Particular attention was paid to the significance of collaborative research. The effects on the innovative output of companies, measured by their patenting activity, of both public funding and R&D collaboration were analyzed. The main conclusion from this case study is that public funding and collaboration have a positive impact on innovative output for firms in Finland. In Germany, however, only collaboration and the combination of subsidies with collaboration show significant effects. Through this crucial mechanism policy makers can improve Europe's innovative performance by means of the 'Action Plan 2010' - incentives for R&D collaboration seem a particularly promising recipe. The relevance of collaboration in fostering innovative performance identified in this analysis reflects the importance of the interconnections between public and private agents in driving innovation. It is precisely in this area that the EU tends to score low relative to the US where public and higher education research institutions have developed a far more effective system of linkages with the world of innovation.

In Germany there appears to be a large innovation potential in the group of firms that receive R&D subsidies but do not engage in collaboration. This potential could be exploited by having recourse to R&D collaborations. In Finland this effect is substantially smaller, possibly due to the high share of firms already engaged in collaboration.

2.4.2 Impact of government funding on R&D and innovation: the case of Austria

2.4.2.1 Introduction

This second country case study is devoted to Austria, another typical medium-size country. Con-

trary to the case study of Germany and Finland, which focused on the propensity to patent, the present one measures the outcome of public support for innovation in terms of innovation inputs and outputs. The input side of innovation is measured by the intensity of R&D expenditures.[72] The output of innovation is measured by the share of total sales due to innovative products, i.e. new or substantially modified products. Moreover, the share in sales of new products can relate to products new to the firm or new to the market. The former includes true innovation and imitation, the latter only true innovations. Both dimensions of novelty will be examined.

The objective is to evaluate whether firms that receive government support are performing better than those that do not receive funding for innovation. Public support can relate to R&D expenditures but also to other innovation activities like promoting new products and providing informational support for the introduction of new products. The relative effectiveness of national versus EU-originating public support is also considered here.

As before, the analysis uses micro data from the latest Community Innovation Survey, CIS 3, covering the years 1998-2000. The data make it possible to examine the effect of government support both on the propensity to be innovative and on the amount of innovation.

2.4.2.2 Data

The analysis is based on the CIS 3 microdata for Austria covering the period 1998-2000.

Respondents were asked the following questions:

- During the period 1998-2000, has your enterprise introduced into the market any new or substantially improved products?

- During the period 1998-2000, has your enterprise introduced any new or substantially improved production process?

- By the end of 2000, did your enterprise have any ongoing innovation activities?

---

[72] The Community Innovation Surveys contain information on another (broader) definition of innovation inputs, the expenditures on innovation, comprising intramural and extramural R&D, acquisition of machinery and equipment for the production of new goods, the costs of acquisition of patents, licenses, know-how, training for innovation, design, and market introduction of new products. Statisticians do not consider these responses very reliable and report many non-responses on this question. It was therefore decided to consider only R&D expenditures as a measure of innovation inputs.

Table 2.15: Distribution of innovator types in Austria, 1998-2000

	Number of observations	Percentage all firms	Percentages with respect to innovating firms
Total	1287	100 %	
Innovators	546	42 %	100 %
New to firm product innovators	418	32 %	77 %
New to market product innovators	190	15 %	35 %
Process innovators	346	27 %	63 %
Ongoing innovation activities	409	32 %	75 %
Abandoned innovation activities	63	5 %	12 %

• During the period 1998-2000, did your enterprise have any innovation activities that were abandoned?

A first way to characterize innovators is to consider as innovators those that have responded 'yes' to any of those four questions. It is also possible to consider different types of innovators - product innovators are those who have responded affirmatively to the first question, process innovators those who responded affirmatively to the second question and potential innovators those who had either ongoing but incomplete innovation activities or those who were not successful in their innovation activities in the three year time-span. Among product innovators, it is possible to identify innovators with products new to the firm but not to the market, those who are imitators, and those with products new to the market who can be regarded as true innovators.

The final data set[73] consists of 1287 observations. Of those, 42 % declare themselves as innovators. Among those, 77 % are product innovators offering products new to the firm and a lower fraction, 35 %, have come up with products new to the market, 63 % innovate in processes, 75 % are unsuccessful or not yet successful innovators, and 12 % have had to abandon some innovation projects - see Table 2.15. Clearly, a firm may belong to various groups of innovators. Almost half of the Austrian innovators are both product and process innovators, and many successful innovators during the period 1998-2000 have ongoing innovation activities which might produce new processes or new products in the future. The remainder of the analysis focuses on product innovators because only for these does the CIS 3 dataset contains data on innovation.

Distribution of various types of government support

In the CIS 3 dataset, firms are asked about four sources of public support for innovation: local and regional government, central government, the EU and, in particular, the EU 4th and 5th Framework Programmes for RTD. The central government, including agencies working for the central government, is the most often cited source of public support for innovation, followed by the local government, the EU and the Framework Programmes for RTD, be it for innovators, R&D performers, new to firm or new to market product innovators. Again a firm may receive various kinds of public support.

Table 2.16 indicates that R&D performers are more likely to obtain support for innovation than the innovators. Support for innovation is thus more concentrated on the input side than on the output side of innovation. It is also noticeable that new to market product innovators are more likely to receive public support of some kind than new to firm product innovators.

2.4.2.3 Methodology

Are firms that receive government support more innovative than those that receive no governmental support? Two sides of the innovation process can be examined: on the input side, R&D expenditures, and on the output side, the share of innovative sales. Graph 2.10 illustrates the relation between government intervention and innovation activities. R&D feeds into the innovation process, which yields new products while government intervention can affect the input and/or the output side of innovation.

Econometric model

Since the CIS 3 questionnaire asks only innovators about sources of government funding, it is not

---

[73] For details on how the final dataset was constructed from the original dataset see 'European Productivity, Innovation and Public Sector R&D', background study prepared for the 2004 edition of the *European Competitiveness Report*.

Table 2.16: Distribution of government support among innovators, Austria, 1998-2000

	All Innovators		R&D performers		New to Firm Product innovation		New to Market Product innovation	
	Nb	Perc.	Nb	Perc.	Nb	Perc.	Nb	Perc.
Local Government funding	113	(20.7 %)	78	(25.8 %)	89	(21.3 %)	56	(29.5 %)
Central Government funding	172	(31.5 %)	150	(49.7 %)	145	(34.7 %)	91	(47.9 %)
EU funding	64	(11.7 %)	51	(16.9 %)	51	(12.2 %)	32	(16.8 %)
4th or 5th RTD Framework	46	(8.4 %)	40	(13.2 %)	39	(9.3 %)	22	(11.6 %)

possible, as in the cross-country comparison between Germany and Finland, to compare the means of innovation output between supported and non-supported firms but only the means among innovators of different types. This leaves too few observations to use a matching estimator where each firm receiving support is matched to a similar firm receiving no support, thereby controlling for other determinants like size, network or industry affiliation. The alternative is then to model the endogeneity of innovation and of public support.

The model treats government support, R&D and innovative sales as endogenous. Box 2.4 describes the model in a formal way and specifies the distribution assumptions about the error term.[74]

- The first two equations deal with the determinants of government support for innovation. Two sources of support are considered: those emanating from the central government and

those emanating from the EU.[75] As modelled in González, Jaumandreu, Pazó (2004), firms form expectations about government funding for innovation from domestic and EU sources. These expectations then enter the R&D and innovation output equations.

- The third equation concerns the determinants of (intramural and extramural) R&D. Since not all firms are R&D performers, there might be a selection bias if only firms that perform R&D are considered. To correct for selectivity, a Tobit model, which posits a latent variable that explains simultaneously the R&D intensity equation and the observed non-R&D performing enterprises for which the latent variable falls below a critical threshold, is used.

- The fourth equation concerns innovation output. The focus is on product innovations for which the dataset provides both qualitative and quantitative information. Since there are

[74] For a presentation of the asymptotic least squares estimation procedure that is used to estimate this model see 'European Productivity, Innovation and Public Sector R&D', background study prepared for the 2004 edition of the *European Competitiveness Report*.

[75] The CIS 3 dataset for Austria is too small to analyse separately the four sources of government support contained in the questionnaire.

Graph 2.10: Government funding and innovation activity

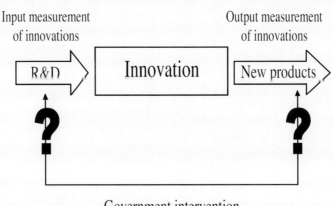

Box 2.4: Model equations

$$g_{dom} = 1 \text{ if} \qquad g_{dom}^* = \alpha_1 z_1 + \varepsilon_1 > 0; \ = 0 \text{ otherwise}$$

$$g_{EU} = 1 \text{ if} \qquad g_{EU}^* = \alpha_2 z_2 + \varepsilon_2 > 0; \ = 0 \text{ otherwise}$$

$$R\&D = 0 \text{ if} \quad R^* = \beta_{r1} z_3 + \beta_{r2} g_{dom}^* + \beta_{r3} g_{EU}^* + \varepsilon_r \leq 0;$$

$$= R^* \text{ if } R^* > 0$$

$$inno = 0 \qquad \text{if } inno^* = \beta_{i1} z_4 + \beta_{i2} g_{dom}^* + \beta_{i3} g_{EU}^* + \beta_{i4} R^* + \varepsilon_i \leq 0;$$

$$= inno^* \text{ if } inno^* > 0$$

where

ε_1, ε_2, ε_r, ε_i are normally distributed error terms with zero means and, respectively, 1, 1, σ_r and σ_i standard deviations;

z_1, z_2, z_3, and z_4 are control variables;

g_{dom} (domestic government support), g_{EU} (EU government support), R&D (R&D/sales), and $inno$ (share of innovative sales) are the endogenous variables.

---

both innovators and non-innovators, it is necessary to use again a Tobit model with a latent variable that is equal to the observed intensity of innovation for innovators and which falls below the innovation threshold for non-innovators. Two variants of this model are used, in one the innovation output is composed of products new to the firm (corresponding to imitators and true innovators) and in the other it consists of products new to the market (characterizing true innovators). The latent variable for R&D enters the latent variable for innovation. The more R&D firms do, the higher the chance they come up with a new product. Government support for innovation can thus affect innovation output directly or indirectly by stimulating R&D.

This model allows to analyse which type of government support has a significant effect on innovation, and whether is affects innovative sales directly or via R&D. Endogeneity and selectivity are explicitly taken into account in the estimation of the model.

Information necessary to estimate this model is only available for the 42 % of firms in the sample that are innovative in some way. The analysis is done only for this sub-sample of innovating firms.

Control variables

In each equation, there are controls variables for determinants other than the policy and innovation variables. The main control variables used are:[76]

Industry Dummies

Dummy variables account for industry specific effects in each equation. The government might be more willing to foster certain industries, like biotechnology, because it is promising to invest in new technologies. Due to data restrictions, industries are classified in three clusters: the high-tech cluster (vehicles, chemicals, machinery, electrical products, plastics, telecommunication, computer services, engineering services, support auxiliary transport activities, and not elsewhere classified industries), the low-tech cluster (food, textiles, wood, non-metallic mineral products, basic metals, supplies, finance and transportation), and wholesale industry, which is strongly represented in the sample;

---

[76] The choice of the control variables in the model is not a trivial one. To identify the parameters of the model it is necessary to impose exclusion restrictions, i.e. exclude some explanatory variables in some of the equations in order to identify the other ones. The choice of exclusion restrictions is partly done on theoretical grounds (sources of information are more likely to determine innovation directly than through government support), and partly based on the significance of estimated coefficients. Non-significant coefficients might be bad instruments to identify other key parameters of the model.

Domestic Group

Governments might be less willing to intervene if firms belong to a group because it is expected that these firms benefit from group support;

Foreign Group

Government might be even less willing to finance projects of subsidiaries of foreign companies using taxpayers' money but to favour domestic firms. The group variables are dichotomous appearing only as determinants of financial support;

Size

Large firms might innovate more and do more R&D. Government support may be targeted more towards SMEs but it might also be concentrated in large firms if government is too risk averse to finance R&D in small firms. Size is measured by the logarithm of the number of employees and enters as an explanatory variable in each equation;

Competition

The more competition a firm faces, the more assistance might be considered to be a good policy. Competition is measured by whether or not the international market is the perceived predominant market;

Cooperation

When financing research or innovation, the government normally supports the collaboration of firms at the research stage, especially with universities and research institutes. Cooperation is a dichotomous variable directly constructed from CIS 3. Competition and cooperation affect R&D and innovation only through government support.

Human Capital

The higher the qualification of workers, the higher the capacity of the firm to succeed in the innovation process. Human capital is constructed as the number of workers with higher education divided by the total number of workers in the firm. It enters as a determinant of R&D intensity.

Appropriability problems

The capacity to appropriate the output of research, be it by patenting, by secrecy or other means, is regarded as a significant determinant of R&D (see Cohen, Levin, 1989). Appropriability problems are proxied by the perceived importance of economic risk as an obstacle to innovation.

Financial difficulties

Because the market failures in information goods, innovators might find it difficult to obtain appropriate financing for their innovation. Financial difficulties are measured by the perceived difficulty in access to finance.

Externalities form science

The other possible important source of information necessary to control for are externalities deriving from basic research at universities and public research institutions. Appropriability, access to finance and externalities are binary variables. Human capital, appropriability problems, financial difficulties and externalities from science enter as determinants in the R&D intensity equation.

Externalities form clients

Clients are often recognized as an important source of information concerning the needs in the market (see von Hippel, 1988). In the case of product innovations, it seems reasonable to expect information from clients to have an influence.

2.4.2.4 Results

Table 2.17 presents the magnitude and the direction of the marginal effects of the various explanatory variables on the probability of receiving government support for innovation. When a firm shifts from a low-tech industry to a high-tech industry it increases its probability of obtaining government support. For example, support from the central government increases in that case by 11.1 percentage points, EU support by only 3 percentage points. In Austria, the wholesale trade sector is more likely to get support from the national government or the EU than the low-tech sectors. Firms that belong to a group are less likely to get innovation support, probably because they are supposed to have access to resources emanating from the group. Government is even less likely to finance firms belonging to foreign groups, probably because taxpayers' money is supposed to help domestic firms. The national government prefers funding firms that are independent, that have a certain size, that operate mostly in foreign markets, that cooperate in innovation activities and that

Table 2.17: Marginal effects of determinants of various sources of innovation support, Austria, 1998-2000, CIS 3, probit estimation

Explanatory variables	Support from central Government	Support from the European Union	Support from national sources (local or central Government)	Support from European Union and 4th or 5th RTD Framework Programmes
High-tech sectors	-0.513***	-0.389***	-0.470***	-0.408***
Low-tech sectors	-0.624***	-0.419***	-0.586***	-0.435***
Wholesale trade	-0.598***	-0.363***	-0.530***	-0.379***
Austrian group	-0.141***	-0.084***	-0.197***	-0.085***
Foreign group	-0.126***	-0.121***	-0.216***	-0.122***
Size	0.077***	0.046***	0.083***	0.048***
Competition	0.152***	- 0.180***	-	-
Cooperation	0.129***	0.113***	0.121***	0.111***
Financial difficulties	0.105***	- 0.117***	-	-

*Significant at 10 %, **significant at 5 %, ***significant at 1 %

experience difficulties in financing their innovation. Firms that face international competition have a 15 percentage points higher probability to be funded by the central government. Enterprises which cooperate in innovation are more likely to get help from both national and EU sources. Doubling size increases by 7.7 percentage points the probability of receiving support from the central government and by 4.6 percentage points from the EU. Support from national sources is more responsive than from EU sources. There is not a substantial difference in the factors determining local and central government support or EU and RTD support for innovation, but there is some difference between national and EU support in general.

Table 2.18 reports the estimation results obtained with the broad measure of innovation: products new to the firm, i.e true product innovators together with imitators. Table 2.19 reports the results for the narrower measure of innovation: products new to the market, corresponding to true product innovators. As expected, the major difference between the two variants of the model is in the innovation equation. Since the variant with true innovators selects a more homogeneous set of firms, the estimates of variant 2 are slightly more precise.[77]

As the comparison of columns 1 and 3 of Table 2.18 reveals, when government support is treated as endogenous, as it should be, the effect on R&D intensity of some of the exogenous variables (central government support, human capital and science externalities) doubles. Central government support appears to be one of the most important determinants of R&D. Receiving central government support increases by 2.3 percentage points the intensity of R&D, which is a high value given that the mean R&D intensity is 2.8 %. Doubling the number of employees decreases R&D intensity by half a percentage point. One percentage point increase in human capital, which is large given the mean value of human capital of 5.2 percentage points, is connected to only one tenth of a percentage point increase in R&D intensity. The only other significant effect comes from the science push: ceteris paribus, firms that benefit from information emanating from universities or government labs have an R&D intensity 1.1 percentage point higher.

Unlike for R&D intensity, treating government support measures as endogenous or exogenous makes hardly any difference on the estimates of the innovation equation (compare columns 2 and 4 in Table 2.18). R&D has a significant effect on innovation. The rate of return of R&D in terms of innovative sales is of the order of 10 %. The externalities due to clients increase the innovation intensity by half a percentage point. The higher intensity of innovation in high-tech than low-tech and in low-tech compared to wholesale trade reflects and confirms the ad-hoc classification used here.

Columns 5 and 6 report the marginal effects when central and local government support are merged (under the title 'national government support') and EU support is merged with RTD support from the

[77] In both cases, the Sargan test of overidentifying restrictions does not reject the null hypothesis that the overidentifying restrictions hold, even with a 10 % margin of error, when government support is explained by the model. In this sense the data do not reject the model specification. When government support is treated as exogenous, however, the Sargan test rejects the model specification at the 5 % level.

Table 2.18: Marginal effects of determinants of new to firm product innovations, Austria, 1998-2000, CIS 3, ALS estimation

	Exogenous support		Endogenous support					
	R&D	Innovative sales	R&D	Innovative sales	R&D	Innovative sales	R&D	Innovative sales
Central government support	0.010***		0.023***				0.023***	-0.004
EU support	0.004		0.000				-0.001	0.016
National government support					0.017***			
All EU support					0.000			
R&D		1.106***		1.097***		1.070***		1.087**
High-tech industries	-0.008**	0.143***	0.022	0.150***	0.009	0.150***	0.021*	0.187**
Low-tech industries	-0.017***	0.115***	0.015	0.123***	0.001	0.122***	0.013	0.156**
Wholesale trade	-0.018***	0.080***	0.010	0.085***	-0.003	0.084**	0.009	0.113
Size	-0.000	-0.010	-0.005***	-0.010	-0.003**	-0.010	-0.005***	-0.013
Human capital	0.064***		0.130***		0.113***		0.128***	
Appropriability	0.001		0.005		0.003		0.005	
Financial difficulties	0.003		-0.004		-0.002		-0.004	
Externalities from science	0.005***		0.011***		0.010***		0.011***	
Externalities from clients		0.052***		0.050**		0.051**		0.053**

* Significant at 10 %, **significant at 5 %, ***significant at 1 %.

Notes: Columns 1 and two report the results of the estimation treating innovation support as exogenous; the remaining columns treat support as endogenous. Columns 5 and 6 presents results using 'national government support' by merging central and local government support, and 'all EU support' by merging EU support with RTD support from the 4th and 5th Framework Programmes. Estimation results presented in columns 7 and 8 allow for a direct effect of support measures on innovation.

4th and 5th Framework Programmes (under the title 'all EU support').[78] The effects are of similar magnitude as when only two of the four measures are singled out (previous columns).

The last two columns of Table 2.18 report the results of the experiment when government support measures are allowed to affect innovation directly in addition to their indirect effect through R&D. The results suggest that direct effects are not significant.

It is noticeable that EU support always turns out to be non-significant. Since a large fraction of firms that receive central government support also get EU support it is likely that the effects of the latter are confounded with those of the former. It may also be the case that some EU money is handed out by national agencies and is perceived by firms as being nationally funded. Financial difficulties and appropriability problems play no significant role on R&D, nor does size on innovation.

Table 2.19 reports the marginal effects of the explanatory variables for the *new-to-market product innovations*. An increase in the marginal effects when the public support measures are treated as endogenous is again apparent, also in the effect of R&D on innovative sales. The robustness of the results to the use of two specific versus two merged government

[78] Collinearity would not allow the estimation of the separate effects of all four sources of innovation support.

support measures is also confirmed. The marginal effects of the explanatory variables on new to market product innovations are similar to those on new-to-firm product innovations, except for the rate of return on R&D: where € 1 of R&D generates € 0.53 of sales of products new to the market against € 1.1 of sales of products new to the firm. Therefore, the rate of return on R&D is only half as high in generating sales of products new to the market as in generating sales of products new to the firm only.[79] The major difference between true innovators and the group true innovators together with imitators is in the specification presented in the last two columns of Tables 2.19 and 2.18 which allows for direct effects of government support on innovation. Central government support leads to an increase of 2.7 percentage points in innovative sales (for an average of 2.8 percent) in addition to the 0.7 (0.023*0.303) percentage points due to the indirect effect through R&D. The total effect of central government support measures amounts to 3.3 percentage points.

2.5 Conclusions

The aim of this chapter was to analyse empirically the influence of public sector R&D on output and industrial innovations in the European Union. Since the gap in public research spending (measured as higher education and government sector R&D) between the European Union and the United States is quite small, government policies should be directed at stimulating business R&D spending. The two main policy tools are to provide favourable tax treatment for firms who undertake R&D or to directly subsidise private R&D projects.

Using industry-level data for EU countries for the period 1987-1999, the results suggest that government-financed R&D expenditures complement domestic industry-financed expenditures on R&D. In terms of marginal impacts of public funding, an increase of € 1 on government financed R&D produces an additional € 0.93 in domestic industry R&D. Furthermore, using economy-wide data for a panel of OECD/EU countries for the period 1981-2002, the results suggest that both direct funding of business R&D and tax incentives for R&D have a significant and positive impact on business R&D spending in OECD and EU countries. These two policy instruments tend to complement each other. The empirical evidence suggests that R&D tax credits are an effective instrument. A 10 % reduction in the price of R&D (i.e. an increase in the generosity of tax

incentives for R&D) leads to an 8.1 % increase in the amount of R&D spending in the business sector in the long run. For the OECD/EU area during the period 1990-2002, the results suggest that 0.01 percentage points of the increase in the ratio of business R&D to GDP can be explained by the increase in fiscal incentives for R&D (representing 3 % of total increase). In contrast, the decrease over time in government financed BERD as percentage of GDP has hampered the increase in R&D intensity in the business sector by 3 percentage points. However, the majority of the increase in the average R&D intensity cannot be explained neither by the tax credits nor by direct funding. Thus, other factors such as the shift to R&D intensive industries seem to be more important than direct support for R&D in explaining the change in the R&D intensity in the business sector across EU countries. To the extent that reallocation of production factors towards high-technology industries is being hampered by lack of flexibility in factor markets, structural reforms aimed at rendering markets more flexible will play an important role in increasing the level of business R&D across the EU.

Another conclusion from this chapter is the importance of the public R&D sector for productivity gains and spillover effects to the private R&D sector. Expenditures on R&D performed by universities and public research organisations are significantly positively related to business enterprise sector expenditures on R&D, indicating that public sector R&D and private sector R&D are complements. For the period 1990-2002, a significant part of the increasing R&D intensity in the business sector can be explained by the increase in R&D expenditures performed by the higher education sector, indicating substantial spillover effects from academic research. When public sector R&D is split up into the two main parts, both government and university R&D spending are significantly positively related to the R&D intensity in the business sector, with the impact of higher education R&D being larger than that of government R&D spending. In terms of marginal impacts of public funding, an additional euro in R&D performed by universities leads to an additional 1.3 euro in industry R&D while a an euro increase in R&D performed by government institutions leads to 1.1 euro in industry R&D.

Results for OECD/EU countries suggest that expenditures on R&D in the higher education sector significantly stimulate growth of GDP per capita. The effect of R&D performed by the higher education sector is higher than the income share of this sector, indicating substantial spillover effects. In addition, the impact of university research is somewhat higher than the impact of business R&D. This

---

[79] Part of the difference may be due to the fact that these results do not account for distributed lags or mark-ups which could differ between products new to the market and products new to the firm only.

is consistent with the hypothesis that the social rate of return of research in the higher education sector is higher than in the private R&D sector due to spillover effects.

Another important finding is that public sector R&D spending as a percentage of GDP has a positive and significant impact on EPO patent applications per capita, even after private R&D spending and country fixed effects have been controlled for. In particular, the impact of R&D performed by university and government research organisations is higher than the impact of business enterprise sector R&D. Also, correlation analyses of R&D expenditures performed by universities and public research organisations with indicators of research output suggest significant and positive associations with the citations of publications, number of patents per capita and the number of publications.

The analysis of the effectiveness of public support to R&D and innovation using microdata for three member countries (Germany, Finland and Austria) suggested that the public sector has an important role to play in innovation by giving financial support and/or stimulating cooperation. The largest impact is achieved when collaboration and public funding are conducted simultaneously. In Germany, public funding has no additional impact once firms cooperate already, but it does have an impact in Finland. In Austria, central government support increases the companies' share of products new to the firm in total sales by 2.5 percentage points (for an average of 19.8 percent) and the companies' share of products new to the market in total sales by 3.3 percentage points (for an average of 5.8 percent). The relevance of collaboration in fostering innovative performance identified in this analysis reflects the importance of the interconnections

Table 2.19: Marginal effects of determinants of new to market product innovations, Austria, 1998-2000, CIS 3, ALS estimation

	Exogenous support		Endogenous support					
	R&D	Innovative sales	R&D	Innovative sales	R&D	Innovative sales	R&D	Innovative sales
Central government support	0.010***		0.026***				0.023***	0.027**
EU support	0.003		-0.004				-0.001	-0.016
National government support					0.018***			
All EU support					-0.003			
R&D		0.376***		0.530***		0.506***		0.303*
High-tech industries	-0.008**	-0.080***	0.021*	-0.085***	0.007	-0.084***	0.021*	-0.076**
Low-tech industries	-0.017***	-0.091***	0.015	-0.090***	0.000	-0.090***	0.014	-0.075**
Wholesale trade	-0.018***	-0.093***	0.011	-0.093***	-0.004	-0.093***	0.009	-0.078***
Size	-0.000	0.008***	-0.005***	0.008**	-0.003**	0.008**	-0.005***	0.004
Human capital	0.059***		0.115***		0.097***		0.123***	
Appropriability	0.002		0.005		0.004		0.006	
Financial difficulties	0.003		-0.005		-0.003		-0.005	
Externalities from science	0.005***		0.012***		0.010***		0.012***	
Externalities from clients		0.028**		0.027**		0.027**		0.025**

* Significant at 10 %, **significant at 5 %, ***significant a 1 %

Notes: Columns 1 and two report the results of the estimation treating innovation support as exogenous; the remaining columns treat support as endogenous. Columns 5 and 6 presents results using 'national government support' by merging central and local government support, and 'all EU support' by merging EU support with RTD support from the 4th and 5th Framework Programmes. Estimation results presented in columns 7 and 8 allow for a direct effect of support measures on innovation.

between public and private agents in driving innovation. It is precisely in this area that the EU tends to score low relative to the US where public and higher education research institutions have developed a far more effective system of linkages with the world of innovation.

These results have some implications for public policy. Given the significant and positive impact of tax incentives on R&D spending, increasing the generosity of R&D subsidies may become instrumental in increasing business R&D to levels closer to those of other main world players. This is likely to be particularly true for countries with little or no tax incentives (e.g. the new EU member countries and some large EU countries, notably Germany and Italy for large firms). Firm level results suggest that university-industry partnerships appear to accelerate technological diffusion via patents. Policies should improve the collaboration of public research organisations with firms and foster technology transfer through funding and specific programs. There is also a need to improve the infrastructure for commercialisation of research findings such as technology transfer offices and providers of risk capital.

Furthermore, one can conclude that governments should provide appropriate funding of R&D conducted by public institutions, in particular research and development in the higher education sector. The role of higher education research in fostering R&D output and economic growth reinforces the need to integrate education policy reforms in the EU efforts to foster research and innovation throughout the economy. Government research institutions are asked to contribute more directly to social economic welfare by demonstrating the relevance of their research. However, the decline in funding for government research organisations in the EU implies that restructuring will be accomplished through the reallocation of existing resources. There is also an increasing pressure on public sector organisations to engage in the systematic evaluation of their programs. The evaluation should include researchers and programmes as well as institutions.

The Royal Netherlands Academy of Arts and Sciences proposed a list of indicators that might be used to evaluate the social benefits of public research. These indicators include a number of aspects such as scientific excellence (measured by the number of publications and citations analysis), products (e.g. healthcare technologies and services, instruments, programmes), and presentations for a non-scientific audience.

As the analysis above implies, the public sector appears to play an important role in stimulating the basic scientific and technical knowledge that firms then incorporate into patents and hopefully into licences, new products, processes or services. Yet, even though these results support innovation policy interventions such as matched grants and the stimulation of cooperations, several important questions, such as the optimal mix of different innovation instruments, remain. If European Member States target to become the most competitive federation by 2010, they still have to exchange their experiences on the impact of R&D policies and evaluations to learn from each other.

References

Acs, Z.J., Audretsch, D.B. and Feldman, M.P. (1992): 'The Real Effects of Academic Research: A Comment', American Economic Review, 82, pp. 67-76.

Adams, J.D. (1990): 'Fundamental Stocks of Knowledge and Productivity Growth', Journal of Political Economy, 98(4), pp. 673-703.

Adams, J.D. (2004): 'US Defence R&D Spending: An Analysis of the Impacts', Rapporteur's Report for the EURAB Working Group ERA Scope and Vision.

Ali-Yrkkö, J., Paija, L., Reilly, C. and Ylä-Anttila, P. (2000): Nokia—A Big Company in a Small Country, ETLA, Helsinki.

Anderson, T. and Hsiao C. (1982): 'Formulation and Estimation of Dynamic Models using Panel Data', Journal of Econometrics, 18, pp. 47-82.

Arellano, M. and Bond, S. (1991): 'Some Tests of Specification for Panel Data: Monte Carlo Evidence and an Application to Employment Equations', Review of Economic Studies, 58, pp. 29-51.

Arrow, K. (1962): 'Economic Welfare and the Allocation of Resources for Inventions', in: Nelson, R. (ed.), The Rate and Direction of Inventive Activity, pp. 609-625, Princeton University Press, Princeton.

Audretsch, D.B. (2003): 'Standing on the Shoulders of Midgets: The U.S. Small Business Innovation Research Program (SBIR)', Small Business Economics, 20, pp. 129-135.

Bassanini, A. and Scarpetta, S. (2002): 'The Driving Forces of Economic Growth: Panel Data Evidence for the OECD Countries', in: *OECD Economic Studies*, 2, pp. 9-56, OECD, Paris.

Beise, M. and Stahl, H. (1999): 'Public Research and Industrial Innovations in Germany', Research Policy, 28, pp. 397-422.

Bloom, N., Griffith, R. and Van Reenen, J. (2002): 'Do R&D tax credits work?: Evidence from a Panel of Countries 1979–1997', Journal of Public Economics, 85, pp. 1-31.

BMBF (2000): *Bundesbericht Forschung*, Bonn.

Boden, R., Cox, D., Georghiou, L. and Barker, K. (2001): 'Administrative Reform of United Kingdom Government Research Establishments: Case Studies of New Organisational Forms', in: Cox, D., Gummett, P. and Barker K. (eds.), *Government Laboratories. Transition and Transformation*, pp. 77-96, IOS Press, Amsterdam.

Bönte, W. (2003): 'Does federally financed business R&D matter for US productivity growth?', Applied Economics, 35, No. 15, pp. 1619-1625(7).

Bozeman, B. (1994): 'The Cooperative Technology Paradigm: An Evaluation of U.S. Government Laboratories' Technology Transfer Activities', Policy Studies Journal, 22, pp. 322-327.

Busom, I. (2000): 'An Empirical Evaluation of the Effects of R&D Subsidies', Economics of Innovation and New Technologies, 9, pp. 111-148.

Callejon, M. and Garcia-Quevedo, J. (2003): 'Public Subsidies to Business R&D. An Industry-Level Analysis', mimeo.

Cassiman, B. and Veugelers, R. (2002): 'R&D Co-operation and Spillovers: Some Empirical Evidence from Belgium', American Economic Review, 92, pp. 1169-1184.

Cohen, W.M. and Levin, R.C. (1989): 'Empirical studies of innovation and market structure', in: Schmalensee, R. and Willig, R.D. (eds.), *Handbook of Industrial Organization*, vol. II, chapter 18, pp. 1060-1107, Elsevier Science Publishers.

Cohen, W., Nelson, R. and Walsh, J. (2002): 'Links and impacts: The influence of public research on industrial R&D', Management Science, 48(1), pp. 1-23.

Czarnitzki, D. and Fier, A. (2003): 'Publicly Funded R&D Collaborations and Patent Outcome in Germany', ZEW Discussion Paper No. 03-24.

Dachs, B., Ebersberger, B. and Pyka, A. (2004): 'Why do Firms Co-operate for Innovation? - A Comparison of Austrian and Finnish CIS 3 Results', Working Paper 255, Department of Economics, University of Augsburg.

David, P.A., Hall, B.H. and Toole, A.A. (2000): 'Is Public R&D a Complement or Substitute for Private R&D? A Review of the Econometric Evidence', Research Policy, 29, pp. 497-529.

De la Fuente, A. and Doménech, R. (2002): 'Educational Attainment in the OECD, 1960-1995', CEPR DP 3416, OECD, Paris.

Diamond, A.M. (1998): 'Does Federal Funding Crowd Out Private Funding of Science?', presentation at the American Economics Association meetings, January, Chicago.

European Commission (2001): 'Innovation policy issues in six candidate countries: the challenges', Office for Official Publications of the European Communities, Luxembourg.

European Commission (2003a): Raising EU R&D Intensity - Improving the effectiveness of public support mechanisms for private sector research and development: (i) Direct measures and (ii) Fiscal measures, ISBN 92 894 5578 0/5575 6/5574 8, Luxembourg.
http://europa.eu.int/comm/research/era/3pct

European Commission (2003b): 'Third European Report on Science & Technology Indicators, Towards a Knowledge-based Economy', Brussels.

European Commission (2003c): Communication from the Commission, 'The role of the Universities in the Europe of Knowledge', COM(2003)58 final.

European Commission (2003d): 'Investing in research: an action plan for Europe 2003', SEC(2003)489.

Eurostat and OECD (1997), 'Proposed Guidelines for Collecting and Interpreting Technological Innovation Data', Paris.

Faber, J. and Hesen, A.B. (2004): 'Innovation capabilities of European Nations: cross-national analyses of patents and sales of product innovations', Research Policy, 33, pp. 193-207.

Fier, A. (2002): 'Staatliche Förderung industrieller Forschung in Deutschland. Eine empirische

Wirkungsanalyse der direkten Projektförderung des Bundes', ZEW Wirtschaftsanalaysen, Band 62, Baden-Baden.

Foyn, F. (2000): 'Community innovation survey 1997/98— final results', Statistics in focus, Research and Development, Theme 9—2/2000 Eurostat.

Furman, J.L., Porter, M.E. and Stern, S. (2002): 'The determinants of national innovative capacity', Research Policy, 31(6), pp. 899-933.

Georghiou, L., Smith, K., Toivanen, O. and Ylä-Anttila, P. (2003): Evaluation of the Finnish Innovation Support System, Ministry of Trade and Industry, Finland, Helsinki.

German Council of Economic Advisors (Sachverständigenrat), Gutachten (2002/03): 'Determinants of Economic Growth in Industrialised Countries: A panel data analysis' (Einflussfaktoren des wirtschaftlichen Wachstums in Industrieländern: Eine Analyse mit Paneldaten).

Goolsbee, A. (1998): 'Does Government R&D Policy Mainly Benefit Scientists and Engineers?', NBER Working Papers 6532, National Bureau of Economic Research.

González, X., Jaumandreu, J. and Pazó, C. (2004): 'Barriers to innovation and subsidy effectiveness', mimeo.

Greene, W.H. (2002): Econometric Analysis, 4th ed., Upper Saddle River, Prentice-Hall.

Griffith, R. (2000): 'How important is business R&D for economic growth and should the government subsidise it?', Institute of Fiscal Studies briefing notes (published online at: www.ifs.org.uk).

Griliches, Z. (1979): 'Issues in Assessing the Contribution of Research and Development to Productivity Growth', Bell Journal of Economics, 10, pp. 92-116.

Guellec, D. and Van Pottelsberghe, B. (2001): 'R&D and Productivity Growth: Panel Data Analysis of 16 OECD Countries', OECD Economic Studies, 2, pp. 103-126, OECD, Paris.

Guellec, D. and Van Pottelsberghe, B. (2003a): 'From R&D to Productivity Growth: Do The Institutional Setting and The Source of Funds of R&D Matter?', IIR Working Paper 03-26, Hitotsubashi University IIR.

Guellec, D. and Van Pottelsberghe B. (2003b): 'The impact of public R&D expenditure on business R&D', Economics of Innovation and New Technologies, 12(3), pp. 225-244.

Guellec, D. and Van Pottelsberghe B. (2004), 'From R&D to productivity growth: do the institutional settings and the source of funds of R&D matter?', Oxford Bulletin of Economics and Statistics, 66(3), pp. 353-378.

Hagedoorn, J. and Cloodt, M. (2003): 'Measuring Innovative Performance: Is There an Advantage in Using Multiple Indicators?', Research Policy, 32, pp. 1365-1379.

Hall, B.H. and Van Reenen, J. (2000): 'How effective are fiscal incentives for R&D? A review of the evidence', Research Policy, 29, pp. 449-469.

Heckman, J.J., Ichimura, H. and Todd, P. (1997): 'Matching as an Econometric Evaluation Estimator: Evidence from Evaluating a Job Training Program', Review of Economic Studies, 46, pp. 605-654.

Heckman, J.J., Lalonde, R.J. and Smith, J.A. (1999): The Economics and Econometrics of Active Labour Market Programs, in: Aschenfelter, A. and Card, D., Handbook of Labour Economics, 3, pp. 1866-2097, Amsterdam.

Islam, N. (1995): 'Growth Empirics: A Panel Data Approach', Quarterly Journal of Economics, 110, pp. 1127-1170.

Jaffe, A.B. (1989): 'Real effects of Academic Research', The American Economic Review, 79, pp. 957-970.

Kleinknecht, A. (1999), 'Indicators of Manufacturing and Service Innovation: Their Strengths and Weaknesses', in: Metcalfe, J.S. and Miles, I. (eds.), Innovation Systems in the Service Economy: Measurement and Case Study Analysis, pp. 169-186, Kluwer Academic Publishers, London.

Kutinlahti, P. and Oksanen, J. (2003): Trend Chart Country Report Finland, Covering Period: September 2002 to August 2003.
(http://www.vtt.fi/ttr/pdf2003/trend03.pdf)

Lemola, T. (2002): 'Convergence of National Science and Technology Policies: the Case of Finland', Research Policy, 31, pp. 481-1490.

Levy, D.M. (1990): 'Estimating the Impact of Government R&D', Economic Letters, 2, pp. 69-173.

Licht, G. and Stadler, M. (2003): 'Auswirkungen öffentlicher Forschungsförderung auf die private F&E-Tätigkeit: Eine mikroökonometrische Evaluation', University of Tübingen, Discussion Paper No. 56.

Mairesse, J. and Mohnen, P. (2002): 'Accounting for Innovation and Measuring Innovativeness: An Illustrative Framework and an Application', American Economic Review, Papers and Proceedings, 2(2), pp. 26-230.

Mansfield, E. (1991): 'Academic Research and Industrial Innovation', Research Policy, 20(1), pp. 1-12.

Marsili, O. (1999): 'The anatomy and evolution of industries, technical change and industrial dynamics', Doctoral thesis, SPRU, University of Sussex, Brighton.

Mohnen, P. and Dagenais, M. (2002): 'Towards an Innovation Intensity Index. The Case of CIS-I in Denmark and Ireland', in: Kleinknecht, A. and Mohnen, P. (eds.), Innovation and Firm Performance. Econometric Explorations of Survey Data, Palgrave, Hampshire and New York.

Mowery, D. and Sampat, B. (2002): Universities and Innovation, in: Fagerberg J., Mowery D. and Nelson R. (eds.), The Handbook of Innovation, forthcoming.

Mosaic Group (1998): The Global Diffusion of the Internet, March, http://mosaic. unomaha.edu/GDI1998/5FINLAND.PDF.

Narin, F., Kimberley, S., Hamilton, S. and Olivastro, D. (1997): 'The Increasing Linkage between U.S. Technology and Public Science', Research Policy, 26(3), pp. 17-330.

National Academy of Engineering (2003): Impact of Academic Research on Industrial Performance, National Academies Press, Washington DC.

National Science Foundation, (1998): 'Science and Engineering Indicators - 1998', Division of Science Resources Statistics, Arlington.

National Science Foundation (2002): 'Statistics, Science and Engineering Indicators–2002', Arlington, VA (NSB 02-01).

Nelson, R. (1959): 'The simple Economics of Basic Scientific Research', Journal of Political Economy, 67, pp. 97-306.

Nelson, R. (1986): 'Institutions supporting technical advance in industry', The American Economic Review, 76(2), pp. 186-189.

OECD (1998): 'University Research in Transition', OECD, Paris.

OECD (2001): 'The New Economy: Beyond the Hype', Final report on the OECD growth project for the meeting of the Council at Ministerial level, OECD, Paris.

OECD (2002): 'Science, Technology and Industry Outlook', OECD, Paris.

OECD (2003): 'Main Science and Technology Indicators', OECD, Paris.

OTA (1986): 'Research Funding as an Investment: Can We Measure the Returns?-A Technical Memorandum', Washington DC: US Congress, Office of Technology Assessment.

Rammer, C. (2003): European Trend Chart on Innovation, Country Report Germany 2003, Covering period: October 2002-September 2003, EU, DG Enterprise, Mannheim.

Rammer, C., Polt, W., Egeln, J., Schibany, A., Fier, A. and Licht, G. (2003): 'Internationaler Vergleich der Forschungs- und Innovationspolitik', unpublished report sponsored by the German Ministry of Education and Research.

Robson, M. (1993): 'Federal Funding and the Level of Private Expenditure on Basic Research', Southern Economic Journal, 60, pp. 63-71.

Rosenbaum, P.R. and Rubin, D.B. (1983): 'The Central Role of the Propensity Score in Observational Studies for Causal Effects', Biometrika, 70, pp. 41-55.

Rouvinen, P. and Ylä-Anttila, P. (2003): 'Case Study: Little Finlands's Transfor-mation to a Wireless Giant', in: Dutta S., Lanvin, B. and Paua, F. (eds.), The Global Information Technology Report 2003-2004, New York, Oxford University Press (for the World Economic Forum).

Royal Netherlands Academy of Arts and Sciences (2001): 'The societal impact of applied health research: towards a quality assessment system', Health Sciences Subcommittee of the Medical Committee of Royal Netherlands Academy of Arts and Sciences, Amsterdam, KNAW, www.knaw.nl/cg.

Salter, A.J. and Martin, B.R (2001): 'The economic benefits of publicly funded basic research', Research Policy, 30, pp. 509-532.

Sampat, B.N. (2003): 'The Effects of Bayh-Dole on Technology Transfer and the Academic Enterprise: A Survey of the Empirical Literature', Georgia Institute of Technology, mimeo.

Schienstock, G. and Hämäläinen, T. (2001): *Transformation of the Finnish Innovation System: A Network Approach*, Sitra Reports Series 7, Sitra, Helsinki.

Smith, K. (1991): 'Economic Returns to R&D: Method, Results, and Challenges', Science Policy Support Group Review Paper No. 3, London.

Statistics Finland (2001): *Science and Technology in Finland 2000*, Helsinki, Statistics Finland.

Statistics Finland (2002): *EU Innovation Survey 2000*. http://www.stat.fi/tk/yr/ttinno00_en.html

Statistics Finland (2004): *Tutkimus- ja kehittämisrahoitus valtion talousarviossa*, Helsinki, Statistics Finland.

Tekes (2004a): *Tekes in a nutshell*, www.tekes.fi/eng/ (as of March 4 2004).

Toivanen, O. and Niininen, P. (2000): 'Investment, R&D, Subsidies and Credit Constraints', Helsinki.

Von Tunzelmann, N. and Martin, B. (1998): 'Public vs. Private Funding of R&D and Rates of Growth: 1963-1995', Working Paper, Science Policy Research Unit, University of Sussex.

Wallsten, S.J. (2000): 'The Effects of Government-Industry R&D Programs on private R&D: The Case of the Small Business Research Program', RAND Journal of Economics, 31(1), pp. 82-100.

Warda, J. (1996): 'Measuring the Value of R&D Tax Provisions', in: OECD, *Fiscal Measures to Promote R&D and Innovation*, pp. 9-22, OECD, Paris.

Warda, J. (2002): 'Measuring the Value of R&D Tax Treatment in OECD Countries', STI Review, 27, pp. 185-211.

Werner, R. (2003): 'Finland: A European Model of Successful Innovation', Chazen Web Journal of International Business Fall 2003, http://www. gsb. columbia.edu/chazenjournal.

Wößmann, L. (2003), 'Specifying Human Capital', Journal of Economic Surveys, 17(3), pp. 239-270.

Impact of public sector R&D and government support on business R&D

Relationship between industry- and government-financed business R&D at the industry level

Table A.2.1 presents the results for the impact of publicly funded business R&D on business R&D using industry data for 13 EU countries under three specifications.

Impact of government support and public sector R&D on business R&D

Table A.2.2 presents estimation results under two specifications of the model and two estimation approaches (fixed effects model and a dynamic panel data model). The first specification deals with the more indirect channels of public R&D assistance (HERD and GOVERD). In a second specification, separate impact-coefficients for HERD and intramural GOVERD are also reported.[80] Since the lagged

dependent variable is not significant, the discussion of the results should focus on the fixed effects model.

Table A.2.3 shows inference on the R&D stimuli resulting from direct government intervention, i.e. from tax incentives and direct R&D subsidies. Note that the lagged dependent variable is not significantly different from zero and hence the discussion of the results should rely on static fixed effects model. However, in order to compare the results with previous studies using a dynamic model, the dynamic panel data models are presented as well. This also indicates that there is hardly any catch-up observable in private R&D levels across OECD/EU countries. The dynamic specification finds a long-run elasticity of -1.05. This finding is consistent with former evidence on the triggering effect of tax incentives. Bloom et al. (2002), for instance, find a long-run price elasticity of industry-financed and industry–performed R&D with respect to the price of R&D of about -1.0. Their estimates are based on data for eight OECD countries for the period 1979-1997. European Commission (2003a) suggests a median price elasticity of -0.81. Guellec and van Pottelsberghe (2003b), however, find the long-run elasticity of the B-index to be somewhat lower; using OECD data for 17 countries, they obtain a coefficient of about -0.31.

---

[80] Contrary to Guellec and van Pottelsberghe, annual data are not employed. Instead, averages derived from five-year periods and one three-year period (2000-2002) are used. First and foremost, the rationale for doing so lies in the limited availability of relevant data for many countries. Also, it can be argued that the B-index displays little annual variation and that only a longer period interval is suitable to capture the effects of changes in the fiscal system. This approach using averages leaves only five data points for each country.

Table A.2.1: Relationship between industry- and government-financed BERD (pooled over EU industries and countries)

	ln government-financed BERD, constant prices	ln BERD financed from abroad, constant prices	ln real value added	Constant	Number of observations	Number of groups	R^2 (within)	marginal effect Government funded BERD	marginal effect Financed from abroad
(1)	0.21***			3.85***	1319	255	0.22	1.69	
(2)	0.19***	0.03**		3.77***	1035	226	0.25	1.14	0.26
(3)	0.13***	0.04***	0.37***	2.50***	687	156	0.28	0.93	0.37

Notes: *, **, and *** denote significance at the 10 %, 5 %, and 1 % level respectively. Dependent variable: log domestic industry-financed BERD measured in constant $ 1995 prices and PPPs. Unbalanced industry panel over the period 1987-1999. Fixed effects estimates, time effects are included, but not reported. The sample includes data for Austria, Belgium, Denmark, Finland, France, Germany, Greece, Ireland, Italy, Portugal, Spain, Sweden and United Kingdom. The marginal effect is calculated as the product of the estimated elasticity and the ratio of industry-funded BERD to government-funded BERD. Specification (2) controls for BERD financed from abroad and specification (3) controls for both BERD from abroad and for real value added.

Table A.2.2: Impact of public sector R&D on business expenditures for R&D (BERD): Panel estimates for 21 OECD countries

	fixed effects model				dynamic panel data model			
	(1)		(2)		(1)		(2)	
	coeff.	t-value	coeff.	t-value	coeff.	t-value	coeff.	t-value
log BERD % GDP (t-1)					0.14	1.10	0.15	1.22
log public sector R&D % GDP (t)	0.95	3.95			0.65	3.64		
log HERD % GDP (t)			0.47	2.61			0.47	4.52
log GOEVRD % GDP (t)			0.24	1.65			0.12	1.41
log GDP per capita (t)c	0.69	1.93	0.56	1.47	0.89	3.13	0.70	2.62
period dummy 1990-1994	-0.07	-1.13	-0.07	-0.97	-0.22	-3.43	-0.25	-3.83
period dummy 1995-1999	-0.05	-0.53	-0.03	-0.33	-0.14	-2.67	-0.15	-2.84
period dummy 2000-2002	-0.03	-0.22	0.00	0.03	-0.13	-2.30	-0.12	-2.17
constant	2.82	2.15	2.74	1.93	0.12	2.67	0.14	2.96
number of observations	72		72		72		72	
R² (within)	0.48		0.43					

Notes: The dynamic panel data model is estimated using the one-step GMM estimator in first differences. Dependent Variable is log total BERD % GDP (within-transformed or in first differences). The long-run elasticity of BERD % GDP with respect to public sector R&D % GDP is 0.76 (=0.65/(1-0.14)). Estimation period: 1986-2002 with data derived from three five-year intervals and one three-year interval. Excluding the non-EU countries has little effect on the regression results.

Table A.2.3: Impact of tax incentives and direct subsidies on business enterprise sector R&D (BERD): Panel estimates for 21 OECD countries

	fixed effects model				dynamic panel data model			
	excluding log HERD % GDP		including log HERD % GDP		excluding log HERD % GDP		including log HERD % GDP	
	(1)		(2)		(3)		(4)	
	coeff	t-value	coeff	t-value	coeff	t-value	coeff	t-value
log BERD % GDP (t-1)					0.16	0.82	0.07	0.41
log government-funded BERD % GDP (t)	0.23	5.70	0.15	3.10	0.15	4.13	0.11	2.94
log B-index	-0.60	-2.26	-0.49	-1.90	-0.88	-3.76	-0.75	-3.46
log HERD % GDP (t)			0.29	2.98			0.28	2.17
log share of high-technology exports in total manufacturing exports	0.46	5.49	0.45	5.71	0.37	3.74	0.35	3.29
log GDP per capita in constant PPP $	0.58	2.17	0.53	2.06	0.69	2.36	0.65	2.51
period dummy 1985-1989	0.03	0.54	0.01	0.23				
period dummy 1990-1994	0.01	0.15	-0.07	-0.97	-0.06	-1.27	-0.11	-2.86
period dummy 1995-1999	-0.04	-0.39	-0.15	-1.44	-0.08	-2.71	-0.10	-3.74
period dummy 2000-2002	-0.05	-0.39	-0.16	-1.26	-0.04	-0.97	-0.04	-1.42
constant	3.67	2.04	3.67	2.04	0.09	1.82	0.10	2.01
number of observations	99		99		73		73	
R² within	0.78		0.81					
marginal effects of government-funded business R&D								
short run					1.5		1.0	
long run	2.2		1.4		1.7		1.1	
long run elasticity of the B-index					-1.05		-0.81	

Notes: The dynamic panel data model is estimated using the one-step GMM estimator in first differences. Dependent variable is log BERD % GDP (within-transformed or in first differences). The long-run elasticity of BERD % GDP with respect to the B-index is public sector R&D % GDP is -0.81 (=-0.75/(1-0.07)). Estimation period for the dynamic model: 1985-2002 with data derived from three five-year intervals and one three-year interval. Estimation period for the static model: 1980-2002. Excluding the non-EU countries has little effect on the regression results. t-values are based on robust standard errors. Long-run elasticities are calculated as the ratio between short-run elasticities (i.e. estimated beta-coefficients) and the partial adjustment coefficient. The partial adjustment coefficient is defined as (1 – coefficient on the lagged endogenous variable).

**Decomposition of changes in BERD intensity
as presented in Table 2.8
(sub-section 2.3.2)**

Taking the total differential for the estimated R&D equation and rewriting in terms of growth rates, the percentage change in BERD intensity can be written as:

$$\frac{\Delta x_{nt}}{x_{nt}} \approx \sum_{j=1,2,3,4} \varepsilon_x z_j \frac{\Delta z_{jnt}}{z_{jnt}},$$

Where $\Delta \chi_{nt}/\chi_{nt}$ and $\Delta z_{nt}/z_{nt}$ denote the actual growth rate of the BERD intensity and the explanatory variables respectively and $\varepsilon_\chi z_j$ denotes the elasticity of BERD intensity with respect to variable z_j. The actual growth rate should be close to the predicted one.

Impact of public sector R&D on economic growth and research output

Impact of public sector R&D on GDP per capita growth

Using panel data, the steady-state GDP per capita equation can be written as:

$$\ln(y_{i,t}) = \beta \ln(y_{i,t-r}) + (x_{i,t-r})\delta + \eta_i + \lambda_t + \varepsilon_{t,t} \quad (3)$$

where $y_{i,t}$ is per capita GDP (expressed in 1995 purchasing power parities) in country i in period t, $x_{i,t-r}$ is a row vector of determinants of economic growth, η_i is a country-specific effect, y_t is a period-specific effect and $\varepsilon_{t,t}$ is an error term. The choice of the variables $x_{i,t-r}$ depends on the particular variant of the neoclassical growth model one wishes to examine. The country-specific effect captures the existence of time-invariant determinants of a country's steady state that are not already controlled for by $x_{i,t-r}$. The obvious candidates for these determinants are differences in the technology level (Islam, 1995). The equation in first differences can be written as:[81]

$$\ln(y_{i,t}) - \ln(y_{i,t-r}) = \beta(\ln(y_{i,t-r}) - \ln(y_{i,t-r-1})) +$$

$$+ ((x_{i,t-r}) - (x_{i,t-r-1}))\delta + \lambda_t + (\varepsilon_{t,t} - \varepsilon_{t,t-r}) \quad (4)$$

Impact of public sector R&D on scientific output and patents

The following equation describes the relationship estimated in Table A.2.4.

$$\ln\left(\frac{PAT_{it}}{L_{it}}\right) = \beta_i + \beta_1 \ln\left(\frac{PAT_{it-1}}{L_{it-1}}\right) + \beta_2 \ln\left(\frac{SUB_{it}}{GDP_{it}}\right) + \beta_3 \ln\left(\frac{INDBERD_{it}}{GDP_{it}}\right)$$

$$+ \beta_4 \ln\left(\frac{HERD_{it}}{GDP_{it}}\right) + \beta_5 \ln\left(\frac{GOVRD_{it}}{GDP_{it}}\right) + \beta_6 \ln(schooling) + \lambda_t + u_{it} \quad (5)$$

where PAT_{it}/L_{it} denotes EPO patent applications per capita. SUB_{it}/GDP_{it}, $INDBERD_{it}/GDP_{it}$ denote government- and industry-funded BERD expenditures as a percentage of GDP, $HERD_{it}/GDP_{it}$ denotes the ratio of higher education section R&D expenditures to GDP and $GOVERD_{it}/GDP_{it}$ denotes the ratio of government sector R&D expenditures to GDP; schooling denotes the average years of education among the working age population; λ_t is a period-specific effect and u_{it} is an error term. Country dummies are included to control for omitted country-specific fixed factors such as the 'home advantage' bias. The 'home advantage bias' means that a country generally takes more patents in its domestic market than in other regions.[82]

The upper panel shows the results for the dynamic panel model using GMM first-differences, while the lower panel shows the results using the fixed-effects estimator. Since the coefficient on the lagged dependent variable is not significantly different from zero, it appears that very little or no 'catch-up' in patents per capita among the OECD countries took place between 1986 and 1999.

Note that when interpreting the coefficients on government-funded BERD as a percentage of GDP, one has to take into account the high collinearity between government-funded and industry-funded BERD with a correlation of 0.71. An F-test for the joint significance of industry- and government-funded R&D reveals that both variables are significant at the one percent level.

---

81 This introduces a moving-average with unit root in the disturbance. Instrumental variables methods applied to first differences can be employed (see Anderson and Hsiao, 1982; Arellano and Bond, 1991). In this case, lagged values (using lags t minus 2 or earlier) can be used as valid instruments for the lagged change in per capita GDP. For the other explanatory variables, all (or selected) past values are used as instruments in the regression.

82 One method which has been proposed for eliminating the 'home advantage' bias is the usage of triad patents (i.e. those patents that are applied for at all three patent systems (EPO, USPTO and JPO).

Table A.2.4: Relationship between public R&D and EPO patent applications: Panel estimates

Dynamic panel data estimates using GMM first differences
(Change in dependent variable: Δlog EPO patent applications per capita)

	(1)		(2)		(3)	
	coefficient	t-value	coefficient	t-value	coefficient	t-value
Δ log EPO patent applications per capita (t-1)	0.10	0.59	0.05	0.32	0.08	0.52
Δ log total BERD % GDP (t)	0.33	3.03	0.26	2.34		
Δ log industry financed BERD % GDP (t)					0.22	2.20
Δ log government financed BERD % GDP (t)					0.07	1.58
Δ log (HERD+GOVRD) R&D, % GDP (t)	0.44	1.92				
Δ log HERD % GDP (t)			0.23	1.84	0.21	1.63
Δ log GOVRD, % GDP(t)			0.35	2.51	0.30	2.07
Δ log years of schooling (t)	4.10	3.97	4.15	4.03	3.65	3.37
Period dummy 1991-1994	-0.15	-1.22	-0.18	-1.45	-0.14	-1.15
Period dummy 1995-1999	0.15	1.01	0.13	0.86	0.16	1.06
Constant	0.08	0.55	0.14	0.95	0.12	0.82
Number of observations (countries)	68 (25)	68 (25)	68 (25)			

Fixed effects estimates (Dependent variable: log EPO patent applications per capita)

	(1)		(2)		(3)	
	coefficient	t-value	coefficient	t-value	coefficient	t-value
log total BERD % GDP (t)	0.49	4.93	0.47	4.75		
log industry-financed BERD % GDP (t)					0.43	4.66
log government-financed BERD % GDP (t)					0.10	1.58
log (HERD+GOVRD) R&D, % GDP (t)	0.64	2.93				
log HERD % GDP (t)			0.36	2.58	0.34	2.37
log GOVRD, % GDP(t)			0.25	1.89	0.23	1.76
log years of schooling (t)	1.80	1.96	1.68	1.75	1.71	1.80
Period dummy 1991-1994	0.03	0.68	0.04	0.77	0.04	0.82
Period dummy 1995-1999	0.32	4.26	0.34	4.34	0.34	4.34
Constant	-0.30	-0.14	0.39	0.17	0.59	0.26
Number of observations (countries)	68 (25)		68 (25)		68 (25)	
R^2 (within)	0.93		0.93		0.93	

Notes: Upper panel: One-step GMM estimates (in first-differences); the long-run elasticity of EPO patents per million of population with respect to public sector R&D is 0.44; estimation period: 1986-1999 with five-year interval data; it should also be noted that data for Germany refers to West Germany only until 1990; data for unified Germany during the period 1991-1995 is excluded; the group of countries includes Australia, Austria, Belgium, Canada, Denmark, Finland, France, Germany, Greece, Iceland, Ireland, Italy, Japan, Mexico, Netherlands, New Zealand, Norway, Poland, Portugal, Spain, Sweden, Switzerland, Turkey, UK and US; excluding the non-EU countries has little effect on the regression results.

Public funding of business R&D and private patent outcomes: empirical analysis of Germany and Finland – Econometric results

This analysis concerns the impact of public funding on innovative output. Since public funding schemes both in Germany and in Finland focus on inducing companies to engage in collaborative research, both the effect of public funding and that of collaboration must be considered. The analysis encompasses several questions that are analysed structurally in the same way: A (sub)sample of companies will be described by one (or more) properties. Companies within this (sub)sample will be characterised by an additional property. Companies with this property are the **treated** companies, whereas companies without this additional property are the **control** group. The basic question is: 'What would have been the innovative output of treated companies if they had not been treated'. Table A.2.5 summarises the research questions. For both groups of companies the characteristics of the treated and the control group are given in terms of public funding and collaboration.

Data and methodology

Data sources

The data used for the empirical analysis are from the Community Innovation Survey (CIS).[83] The CIS surveys collect firm-level data on inputs and outputs of the innovation process across a wide range of industries and across Member States and regions. These data are collected at enterprise level and comparable at the European scale. Data collection is done at regular intervals, now for the third time. This continuity in CIS provides a major source of information on innovation at the enterprise level for firms in the EU Member States. In this analysis, the period used is 1994 to 2000 based on data from

CIS II and CIS III. CIS data has been complemented by data taken from Statistics Finland's employment register as well as from patent statistics. With regard to the German database, West German companies instead of all German companies are used since West German firms are most similar to Finnish companies.

Methodology

Evaluation problem and selection bias

Each research question addresses a counterfactual situation[84] 'What would a treated firm with given characteristics have done if it had not been treated?' This is central to assessing the impact of treatment (funding or collaboration) as the impact is the difference between the output of the firm under treatment and the output of the firm had it not been treated.[85] As the counterfactual situation cannot be observed, it has to be estimated.

Neither the fact that companies receive public funding for their R&D nor the fact that companies collaborate for innovation can be reasonably interpreted as the result of a random process. Both receiving funding and collaboration are subject to a selection bias. Concerning funding, companies themselves choose to apply or not to apply. Also, the funding agency selects from the pool of applications based on certain criteria. As collaboration for innovation is part of the companies' innovation strategy; it is the companies themselves that choose whether or not to collaborate. The selection bias results in the empirical fact that the group of funded companies is quite different from the group

---

[83] The CIS, launched in 1991 jointly by Eurostat and the Innovation and SME Programme, aims at improving the empirical basis of innovation theory and policy at the European level through surveys of innovation activities at the enterprise level in the Member States.

[84] For the treated companies, only their output under treatment can be observed but not their output if they had not been treated. The latter situation is called counterfactual as it cannot be observed.

[85] A more technical exposition of the evaluation problem can be found in 'European Productivity, Innovation and Public Sector R&D', background study prepared for the 2004 edition of the *European Competitiveness Report*.

Table A.2.5: Research questions

	Treated		Control		Research question
Case	Fund.	Coll.	Fund.	Coll.	
1	yes	–	no	–	Do funded companies have a higher innovation output compared with the case if these companies had not received funding?
2	yes	yes	no	no	Do funded and collaborating companies exhibit a higher innovation output compared with the situation of neither collaboration nor funding?
3	no	yes	no	no	Does collaboration increase innovation output, even if no funding is involved?
4	yes	no	no	no	Does funding increase innovation output, even if no collaboration is involved?
5	yes	yes	no	yes	Given companies collaborate and receive funding, what would have happened had these firms not received funding?
6	no	yes	yes	yes	If a collaborating but non-funded company is funded, does this increase the innovative output?

of non-funded ones, as well as the group of collaborating companies is quite different from the group of non-collaborating ones. Assessing the impact of the treatment based on a comparison of the treated group (funded and/or collaborating) and the group of non-treated companies may generate dubious results as the groups are not comparable due to the selection bias.

Matching

The matching approach has been developed to identify treatment effects when the available observations on individuals or firms are subject to a selection bias (see Heckman et al., 1999, Heckman et al., 1997 for surveys). Hence, the matching estimator generates the counterfactual situation and controls for the selection bias simultaneously. The matching is based on the insight that the counterfactual situation for the treated companies can be estimated from the sample of non-treated observations. The matching estimator amounts to creating (i.e. estimating) from the control group a sample of non-treated observations which is comparable to the sample of treated observations, whereas comparability relates to a set of a priori defined characteristics (x). In the empirical application below, the estimated sample of non-treated observations is denoted *matched controls*.

As the matching procedure requires the definition of the characteristics x, dimensionality problems might occur. If the number of matching criteria is large, it will hardly be possible to find any control observation. Therefore, the propensity score matching will be used (see Rosenbaum and Rubin,

1983). The idea is to estimate the propensity score of participation for the whole sample and find pairs of participants and non-participants that have the same probability value of participation.[86]

Estimation results

Variable description

The main question of this analysis is whether patent activities of firms are stimulated by public funding and/or cooperations. This patent activity is measured with a dummy variable (*PATENT*), indicating whether the particular firm has filed at least one patent application during the past three years. Exogenous variables are basically two dummy variables: collaboration (*CO*), and subsidised arrangements (*FUNPUB*).[87] Other variables to control for firm heterogeneity are also used. Firm size is captured by number of employees, *EMPL*. The square of this variable, $EMPL^2$, is also included to allow for non-monotonicity.[88] Export orientation, *EXQU*, is measures as exports divided by turnover. The patent stock, *PATSTOCK* (), summarizes the historical technological experience and level of

---

[86] In this analysis, a 'kernel-based matching' is used that estimates the counterfactual on the basis of all non-treated companies in the sample. As matching criteria, both the propensity score for the subsidy dummy (*funpub*) and also the propensity score obtained by regressing the innovative activities dummy (*innov*) on the exogenous variables are used. This selection of matching criteria ensures the similarity of the treated and the non-treated companies both in terms of funding probability and in terms of the likelihood of carrying out innovative activities. For more details on this methodology see 'European Productivity, Innovation and Public Sector R&D', background study prepared for the 2004 edition of the *European Competitiveness Report*.

[87] Collaboration in this context means the active collaboration of all partners involved in the project; contracting-out of R&D is excluded.

[88] From a theoretical point of view, a variable indicating the age of the company would be desirable to include. As the Finnish data does not contain reliable information on this an age variable is not included in either case.

Table A.2.6: Bivariate probit estimation on the funding (FUNPUB) and the cooperation (CO)

	Germany		Finland	
FUNPUB	Coefficient	Standard error	Coefficient	Standard error
EMPL	1.181***	0.237	1.861***	0.267
EMPL2	-0.399**	0.128	-0.649***	0.193
RDEMP	6.252***	0.621	5.778***	1.592
RDEMP2	-5.110***	0.648	-13.607**	5.280
PATSTOCK	0.322***	0.842	0.555***	0.071
EXQU	0.213	0.163	0.833***	0.974
_CONS	-2.079***	0.141	-1.588***	0.096
CO	Coefficient	Standard error	Coefficient	Standard error
EMPL	1.374***	0.223	3.165***	0.269
EMPL2	-0.442***	0.122	-1.470***	0.190
RDEMP	5.831***	0.578	2.555**	1.097
RDEMP2	-4.809***	0.612	-4.190	2.634
PATSTOCK	0.289***	0.077	0.496***	0.071
EXQU	0.533***	0.151	0.742**	0.095
_CONS	-1.917***	0.130	-1.100	0.087
RHO	0.459***	0.041	0.737***	0.021

Note: *** (**, *) indicate a significance level of 1 % (5 %, 10 %). All estimations include eight industry dummies and one time dummy.

innovation activities and is computed by the perpetual inventory method.[89] In addition to previous patenting activities, the current potential to patent clearly depends on the current R&D engagement of firms. This is measured by the number of R&D employees divided by number of employees (share of R&D employees, *RDEMP)* and its squared value is also included.[90] Eight sector dummies based on the NACE classification capture different technological opportunities among business sectors. In principle, these dummies are created according to the NACE two-digit sectoral classification. However, some sectors are merged due to a low number of observations. Finally, a time dummy reflects the changes in patenting activities over time.

Matching estimations

As it is inappropriate to assume that the errors of the estimation of *CO* and *FUNPUB* to be independent, a bivariate probit model to regress the collaboration dummy and the public funding dummy on the exogenous variables is used (Greene, 2002, Ch. 19.6). Results are presented in Table A.2.6.

Fundamentally, the data support the hypothesized selection bias as the group of funded (collaborating) companies is significantly different from the group of non-funded (non-collaborating) companies.

The matching estimator is computed using the propensity scores (*XBCO* and *XBFUNPUB*) derived from the regression above. The correlation coefficient (*RHO*) is significant because collaboration and funding are linked to each other, ex post supporting the hypothesis leading to the application of the bivariate probit estimation. Tables A.2.7 to A.2.12 report the results. They illustrate that the selection bias is removed by the matching procedure: If the mean of the treated group and the control group was significantly different before the matching, this significance vanishes after the matching. The main conclusions concerning each of the six questions dealing with the influence of R&D collaboration and public funding on patenting activity are summarised below.

---

[89] The patent stock *PATSTOCK* ($\prod$) is computed by the perpetual inventory method: $\prod_{i,t} = (1-\delta) \prod_{i,t-1} + \pi_{i,t}$, where $\pi_{i,t}$ denotes the number of patent applications and δ represents the depreciation rate of knowledge assets and is set to $\delta = 0.15$ (see e.g. Hall, 1990). The initial value of the variable, in 1980, is set to zero. The bias arising from this assumption should be negligible because the patent data are available since 1980, but the period under review in the regressions starts in 1994.

[90] In the Finnish data set, the share of highly educated employees with a technical education as proxy for the R&D employees is used. The data is from Statistics Finland's employment register and merged with the CIS data. As the share of highly educated technical employees is available for the whole population of firms, using this variable eliminates the effect that only innovators answered the R&D input question in the innovation survey.

Case 1: Do funded companies have a higher innovation output compared to the case if these companies had not received funding?

Table A.2.7

	Germany			Finland		
	Treated Mean *Std,err*	Control	Matched control	Treated Mean *Std,err*	Control	Matched control
EMPL	0.415	0.204***	0.410	0.221	0.090***	0.234
	0.028	0.007	0.010	0.012	0.004	0.009
EMPL2	0.419	0.152***	0.399	0.153	0.035***	0.197*
	0.054	*0.011*	*0.014*	0.016	*0.010*	*0.015*
RDEMP	0.152	0.046***	0.148	0.018	0.001***	0.017
	0.014	*0.003*	*0.007*	0.002	*0.004*	*0.000*
RDEMP2	0.087	0.023***	0.082	0.003	0.002***	0.003
	0.014	*0.003*	*0.004*	0.001	*0.000*	*0.000*
PATSTOCK	0.632	0.318***	0.614	0.374	0.113***	0.366
	0.027	*0.010*	*0.013*	0.018	*0.007*	*0.012*
EXQU	0.291	0.180***	0.288	0.415	0.226***	0.410
	0.014	*0.005*	*0.005*	0.012	*0.006*	*0.007*
XBFUNPUB	-0.788	-1444.107***	-0.797	-0.275	-0.936***	-0.287
	0.033	*0.011*	*0.032*	0.025	*0.012*	*0.025*
XBCO	-0.563	-122.464***	-0.568	0.002	-0.595***	0.001
	0.036	*0.013*	*0.034*	0.026	*0.011*	*0.023*
PATENT	0.635	0.220***	0.476***	0.408	0.075***	0.205***
	0.027	*0.009*	*0.012*	0.018	0.006	*0.007*
# obs	310	2,232	310	713	2,082	713

Note: *** (**,*) indicate the significance level of 1 % (5 %, 10 %) in a two-tailed t-test on equal means of the corresponding group and the treated firms. Here the treated group consists of the funded companies and the control group contains all not funded firms, The column 'matched control' displays the control group after the matching. Mean differences of sectors are not presented. However, the distribution over industries differs before matching and vanishes after the estimation of the control group.

Both in Germany and in Finland public funding exerts a positive influence on the funded companies' propensity to patent. Regardless of their collaboration behaviour, public funding exhibits a positive impact on the funded companies innovative output.

Case 2: Do funded and collaborating companies exhibit a higher innovation output compared to the situation of neither collaboration nor funding?

Table A.2.8

	Germany			Finland		
	Treated Mean Std,err	Control	Matched control	Treated Mean Std,err	Control	Matched control
EMPL	0.494	0.182***	0.439	0.257	0.076***	0.241
	0.045	0.007	0.017	0.015	0.004	0.012
EMPL2	0.569	0.128***	0.449	0.186	0.030***	0.176
	0.092	0.011	0.027	0.020	0.005	0.018
RDEMP	0.172	0.037***	0.173	0.020	0.009***	0.022
	0.021	0.003	0.010	0.002	0.001	0.001
RDEMP2	0.099	0.018***	0.096	0.003	0.002	0.004
	0.021	0.003	0.008	0.001	0.000	0.000
PATSTOCK	0.689	0.284***	0.635	0.408	0.093***	0.380
	0.037	0.010	0.016	0.021	0.007	0.014
EXQU	0.318	0.166***	0.316	0.430	0.212***	0.412
	0.020	0.005	0.009	0.014	0.007	0.009
XBFUNPUB	-0.675	-1.507***	-0.694	-0.207	-0.994***	-0.239
	0.042	0.011	0.028	0.041	0.013	0.028
XBCO	-0.400	-1.303***	-0.421	0.105	-0.666***	0.076
	0.043	0.013	0.042	0.030	0.011	0.029
PATENT	0.708	0.168***	0.471***	0.460	0.041***	0.128***
	0.036	0.008	0.017	0.021	0.005	0.011
# obs	161	1,963	161	553	1,690	553

Note: *** (**,*) indicate the significance level of 1 % (5 %, 10 %) in a two-tailed t-test on equal means of the corresponding group and the treated firms. Here the treated group consists of the funded and collaborating companies and the control group contains the not funded and not collaborating firms. The column 'matched control' displays the control group after the matching. Mean differences of sectors are not presented. However, the distribution over industries differs before matching and vanishes after the estimation of the control group.

The impact of public funding is even more pronounced if public funding induces companies to collaborate.

Case 3: Does collaboration increase innovation output, even if no funding is involved?

Table A.2.9

	Germany			Finland		
	Treated Mean Std,err	Control	Matched control	Treated Mean Std,err	Control	Matched control
EMPL	0.360	0.182***	0.379	0.148	0.076***	0.148
	0.026	0.007	0.014	0.010	0.004	0.010
EMPL2	0.315	0.128***	0.353	0.061	0.030***	0.074
	0.046	0.011	0.020	0.009	0.005	0.008
RDEMP	0.107	0.037***	0.106	0.015	0.009**	0.014
	0.012	0.003	0.008	0.002	0.001	0.001
RDEMP2	0.052	0.018***	0.056	0.003	0.002	0.003
	0.012	0.003	0.006	0.000	0.000	0.001
PATSTOCK	0.564	0.284***	0.562	0.204	0.093**	0.195
	0.030	0.010	0.016	0.020	0.007	0.013
EXQU	0.283	0.166***	0.268	0.290	0.212***	0.283
	0.015	0.005	0.007	0.016	0.015	0.010
XBFUNPUB	-1.002	-1.507***	-1.022	-0.679	-0.994***	-0.707
	0.036	0.011	0.035	0.030	0.013	0.029
XBCO	-0.673	-1.303***	-0.695	-0.283	0.667***	-0.315
	0.036	0.013	0.035	0.031	0.011	0.030
PATENT	0.598	0.168***	0.374***	0.220	0.041***	0.076***
	0.030	0.008	0.015	0.021	0.005	0.005
# obs	266	1,963	266	387	1,690	387

Note: *** (**,*) indicate the significance level of 1 % (5 %, 10 %) in a two-tailed t-test on equal means of the corresponding group and the treated firms. Here the treated group consists of the not funded but collaborating companies and the control group contains the neither funded nor collaborating firms. The column 'matched control' displays the control group after the matching. Mean differences of sectors are not presented. However, the distribution over industries differs before matching and vanishes after the estimation of the control group.

Even without public funding, increased collaboration has a positive impact on companies that collaborate, compared with their situation had they not collaborated.

Case 4: Does funding increase innovation output, even if no collaboration is involved?

Table A.2.10	Germany			Finland		
	Treated Mean Std,err	Control	Matched control	Treated Mean Std,err	Control	Matched control
EMPL	0.306	0.182***	0.347	0.081	0.076	0.072
	0.029	0.007	0.017	0.012	0.004	0.008
EMPL2	0.219	0.128*	0.316*	0.027	0.030	0.021
	0.046	0.011	0.027	0.014	0.005	0.007
RDEMP	0.115	0.037***	0.117	0.012	0.009	0.012
	0.018	0.003	0.010	0.003	0.001	0.002
RDEMP2	0.060	0.018**	0.064	0.002	0.002	0.002
	0.018	0.003	0.006	0.001	0.000	0.000
PATSTOCK	0.559	0.284***	0.554	0.243	0.092***	0.231
	0.041	0.010	0.022	0.035	0.007	0.024
EXQU	0.261	0.166***	0.251	0.358	0.211***	0.372
	0.021	0.005	0.010	0.023	0.006	0.018
XBFUNPUB	-0.954	-1.507***	-0.968	-0.532	-0.994***	-0.550
	0.046	0.011	0.045	0.047	0.013	0.046
XBCO	-0.776	-1.303***	-0.789	-0.396	0.667***	-0.413
	0.054	0.013	0.053	0.043	0.011	0.041
PATENT	0.545	0.168***	0.372***	0.209	0.041***	0.072***
	0.041	0.008	0.019	0.034	0.005	0.011
# obs	145	1,963	145	148	1,690	148

Note: *** (**,*) indicate the significance level of 1 % (5 %, 10 %) in a two-tailed t-test on equal means of the corresponding group and the treated firms. Here the treated group consists of the funded but not collaborating companies and the control group contains the neither collaborating nor funded firms. The column 'matched control' displays the control group after the matching. Mean differences of sectors are not presented. However, the distribution over industries differs before matching and vanishes after the estimation of the control group.

Public funding has a significantly positive impact, even if companies do not change their collaboration behaviour. For the sample of non-collaborating firms, public funding has a positive impact on the innovative output of funded companies.

Case 5: Given companies collaborate, and receive funding, what would have happened, if these firms had not received funding?

Table A.2.11

	Germany			Finland		
	Treated Mean Std,err	Control	Matched control	Treated Mean Std,err	Control	Matched control
EMPL	0.500	0.370**	0.434	0.221	0.148***	0.186**
	0.045	0.027	0.022	0.013	0.010	0.009
EMPL2	0.579	0.330**	0.419	0.141	0.061***	0.081***
	0.092	0.047	0.037	0.018	0.009	0.008
RDEMP	0.179	0.109***	0.166	0.018	0.017	0.021
	0.021	0.012	0.013	0.002	0.003	0.001
RDEMP2	0.106	0.053**	0.096	0.003	0.004	0.004
	0.021	0.012	0.013	0.001	0.002	0.000
PATSTOCK	0.693	0.565***	0.730	0.371	0.204***	0.373
	0.036	0.030	0.021	0.021	0.020	0.015
EXQU	0.318	0.286	0.345	0.410	0.289***	0.402
	0.020	0.015	0.011	0.014	0.016	0.010
XBFUNPUB	-0.658	-0.986***	-0.670	-0.301	-0.690***	-0.317
	0.043	0.036	0.041	0.027	0.032	0.026
XBCO	-0.385	-0.654***	-0.394	0.016	-0.285***	0.005
	0.044	0.037	0.043	0.028	0.026	0.027
PATENT	0.712	0.602**	0.712	0.430	0.219***	0.352***
	0.036	0.030	0.019	0.021	0.021	0.012
# obs	163	269	163	530	392	530

Note: *** (**,*) indicate the significance level of 1 % (5 %, 10 %) in a two-tailed t-test on equal means of the corresponding group and the treated firms. Here the treated group consists of the both funded and collaborating companies and the control group contains the collaborating but not funded firms. The column 'matched control' displays the control group after the matching, Mean differences of sectors are not presented. However, the distribution over industries differs before matching and vanishes after the estimation of the control group.

In Germany: once companies collaborate, funding does not increase the innovative output. Given that funding together with collaboration (Case 2) has an impact on the innovative output and collaboration without funding also yields positive effects (Case 3), funding does not significantly increase innovative output once companies collaborate. Among the companies that do not collaborate, public funding does cause an increase in innovative output (Case 4). The result here suggests that the impact of public funding varies according to the collaboration decision of the firms.

In Finland: Even if companies decide to collaborate, funding has a positive impact. In contrast to the results for Germany, funding exerts a positive impact regardless of the collaboration decision.

Case 6: If a collaborating but not funded company is funded, does this increase the innovative output?

Table A.2.12

	Germany			Finland		
	Treated Mean *Std,err*	Control	Matched control	Treated Mean *Std,err*	Control	Matched control
EMPL	0.375	0.516***	0.398	0.149	0.281***	0.164
	0.027	0.046	0.018	0.010	0.016	0.010
EMPL2	0.335	0.607***	0.407	0.062	0.220***	0.087
	0.047	0.093	0.036	0.009	0.023	0.010
RDEMP	0.111	0.186***	0.114	0.015	0.020	0.011
	0.013	0.021	0.007	0.002	0.002	0.001
RDEMP2	0.054	0.110**	0.058	0.003	0.003	0.002
	0.012	0.021	0.006	0.001	0.001	0.000
PATSTOCK	0.574	0.699***	0.571	0.205	0.419***	0.202
	0.030	0.036	0.023	0.020	0.020	0.012
EXQU	0.290	0.324	0.283	0.290	0.439***	0.305
	0.015	0.020	0.011	0.016	0.014	0.010
XBFUNPUB	-0.941	-0.633***	-0.933	-0.673	0.163***	-0.664
	0.034	0.044	0.033	0.030	0.030	0.029
XBCO	-0.647	-0.357***	-0.644	-0.278	0.148***	-0.272
	0.037	0.047	0.035	0.031	0.031	0.025
PATENT	0.611	0.717**	0.572	0.220	0.475***	0.292**
	0.030	0.035	0.021	0.021	0.021	0.012
# obs	265	166	265	389	586	389

Note: *** (**,*) indicate the significance level of 1 % (5 %, 10 %) in a two-tailed t-test on equal means of the corresponding group and the treated firms. Here the treated group consists of the not funded but collaborating companies and the control group contains the both funded and collaborating firms. The column 'matched control' displays the control group after the matching. Mean differences of sectors are not presented. However, the distribution over industries differs before matching and vanishes after the estimation of the control group.

Consistent with the findings in Case 5, removing funding has no impact in the German sample but in the Finnish data the impact is significant. Even more so, it is of the same magnitude (but the opposite sign, of course) as the impact in Case 4.

## Chapter 3:

Performance in the EU Health Sector

3.1 Introduction

The health care sector is one of the most important sectors in any economy, representing one of the largest service industries in developed countries. Currently its output accounts for about 7 % of GDP in the EU-15, larger than the roughly 5 % accounted for by the financial services sector or retail trade sector (O'Mahony and van Ark, 2003). Therefore trends in productivity and efficiency in this sector will have a large impact on these performance measures in economies as a whole. Moreover, the performance of the health sector will affect the competitiveness of the overall economy via its effect on labour costs, labour market flexibility and the allocation of resources at the macroeconomic level. The final output of this sector – ensuring a healthy population – will have an impact on the productive capacity of the workforce in general and so have consequences across all sectors of the economy. Hence the functioning of the health sector will have an important impact upon the standards of living of Europe's citizens. However, evaluating performance in services, and the public sector in particular, is fraught with difficulties (O'Mahony and Stevens, 2002). Doing so for the health sector is more difficult than in other service sectors since both the system of provision and the nature of the production process have a number of unique features.

This chapter examines the economic, organisational and innovation characteristics of the health sector and reviews some evidence on performance. To place current trends in context, section 3.2 begins with an account of how health care systems have developed over time, before outlining the nature of the production process in health, with particular emphasis on why the health sector differs from other service sectors. Developments in the health sector have significant consequences for the overall economy, hence a discussion of this critical relationship follows.

Given the significant nature of this link, the importance of evaluating health sector performance is clear.

The structure of the health care system is an important factor for consideration in the assessment of performance. Differences across countries in preferences between equity and efficiency considerations mean that health care systems have developed in different ways; section 3.3 presents an overview of current systems of provision in the Member States. Section 3.4 then discusses the theoretical framework underlying attempts to understand developments in health care performance, concentrating on efficiency arguments but also considering the impacts on equity. The influence of technology on performance is also explored. Available evidence on performance of the EU health care sector is then reviewed in section 3.5. The health sector possesses several distinctive features that complicate the measurement of performance. Therefore, performance is evaluated through more than one approach. Section 3.5 begins by considering evidence regarding health outcomes and expenditures, taken from both macroeconomic studies covering the entire sector or large sub-sectors and microeconomic studies focusing on specific diseases. A discussion of the use of capital, labour and pharmaceuticals follows, as the utilisation of inputs also plays a significant role in determining performance. Finally, this section considers recent attempts to improve efficiency through reform in the context of organisational changes. Section 3.6 concludes by drawing some conclusions for policy.

3.2 The characteristics of the health sector

3.2.1 The system of health provision

The health care sector is subject to a high degree of government intervention. Governments intervene both directly, through provision and funding, but also indirectly, through regulation. Governments have to balance the often conflicting goals of equity and efficiency of health provision. The potential conflict between these goals is fundamental to understanding both the development of systems of provision and attempts to reform these systems. Hence it is important to place the development of the health care system in historical context. In a recent overview of international trends in health care performance, Cutler (2002) divides the development of the sector into a number of stages. He suggests that the origins of medical care systems in most countries were fundamentally driven by equity considerations, with little concern about efficiency. Guarantees of equal access to medical care for all citizens led to the development of universal insurance coverage. Initially governments could ignore efficiency considerations since medical care could do little for sick people. However, beginning with the development of antibiotics, the post-war period has been one of rapid change in our understanding of the causes of illness and technological change in treating illness. This in turn gave rise both to rising costs associated with new treatments and increasing demand as citizens became more aware of the benefits of medical interventions. These increases in costs and demand led to an increasing conflict between the two goals of equity and efficiency. Cutler (2002) suggests that since the 1960s the rapid increase in medical care expenditure led to governments facing severe financial constraints and so commitments to complete equality became unaffordable. The initial response of many countries was first to place regulatory limits on costs, reducing provider fees and rationing access in the 1970s and 1980s. While these policies had some success in cost containment, the controls led to increased waiting times and greater access restrictions with resulting dissatisfaction on the part of consumers. The result was a greater emphasis on ensuring efficiency with many countries moving away from regulation towards more market-oriented solutions in the 1990s. A consequence is that systems have become less equitable – the poor do not have the same access to health care as the rich in price-rationed systems. Hence the equity/efficiency trade-off has become more apparent, with differences across countries in the preferences of policy makers with regard to these two goals leading to differences in the extent to which market-based reforms have been implemented.

3.2.2 The nature of the production process

In some ways, the health sector is just like any other service sector. Inputs such as capital, labour, and materials are employed to produce health care outputs. However there are reasons why standard assumptions employed to measure productivity in private market services do not translate easily to measuring performance in the health sector. In many countries, public provision means that market prices for outputs are not readily available. An alternative might be to use quantity indices, but the nature of the output is such that it is difficult to define what precisely is being produced. Health care is a sector where information asymmetries abound, since service provision through public funding or insurance schemes creates a wedge between the final consumers and service providers. It is relatively easy to measures the activities of the sector, e.g. number of medical treatments, but the extent to which alternative treatments lead to improvements in the health of the consumer is difficult to gauge.

Another impediment to an analysis of the performance of the health sector is the fact that the output of medical care treatments is difficult to disentangle from other influences on health, such as lifestyle and diet. In the health care sector extraneous influences tend to be very large and often dominate changes in medical care provision. For example Tunstall-Pedoe et al. (1999) emphasise the importance of declining incidence of heart disease episodes in explaining the reduction in mortality rates from heart disease over a ten year period. In turn, this declining incidence is likely to be most influenced by lifestyles and changes in risk factors such as smoking.

On the input side developments in technology have an important influence on all three main categories, labour, capital and materials. The health care sector is regarded as being highly skill-intensive and there are likely to be complementarities between the use of high technology equipment – e.g. CT scanners – and skilled labour. Drug use is an important intermediate input and so rapid technological change in the pharmaceuticals sector will be an important contributory factor to performance. Also, the use of new treatments is frequently embodied in capital equipment. Hence, it is important to take account of both the quality of inputs used as well as their quantities in evaluating productivity performance across countries.

A further potential difference between health care and private service provision is the possibility of diminishing returns. Baily and Garber (1997) suggest diminishing returns are fundamental to the sector. They suggest that many conditions will respond to additional units of treatment or resources devoted to diagnostic and other management with successively smaller units of health output. In addition, if patients who derive the greatest benefit from care are the first to receive it, diminishing returns are also likely to characterise the expansion in the number of patients treated. Against this, Berndt (1997) argues that physicians may in fact treat patients on a first come, first served basis and that it is not clear that the most cost effective treatments are undertaken first. The possible existence of diminishing returns has the implication that a country that devotes more resources to a disease will have lower average productivity than other countries.

Finally the nature of technological change also has features that distinguish the health care sector from other services. Changes in medical technology are generally considered to add to, rather than replace, old methods. It is a sector where advances in knowledge have increased the capabilities of medical interventions, and so have led both to rapidly rising costs and increased demand. The Technological Change in Health Care (TECH) Global Research Network (2001) suggests that technological change is responsible for much of the increased expenditure on health care world-wide, arguing that other factors that contribute to expenditure growth appear to only explain a small fraction.

3.2.3 The effects of the health sector on competitiveness

Developments in the health sector have significant consequences for the competitiveness of the economy. On the one hand the health sector is very different from other sectors; there is very little international trade in health services and so EU health providers face little competition. This lack of international competition may lead to inefficiencies which have a knock-on effect on the rest of the economy, leading to the potential for misallocation of resources. In addition the output of the sector, ensuring a healthy population, may affect productivity and competitiveness in the economy in general.

Poor relative performance in the healthcare sector may affect competitiveness through the misallocation of resources at the macroeconomic level. Excessive expenditure in the healthcare sector will shift resources away from other, potentially more productive, sectors of the economy. In addition, there are two main channels whereby the health sector will affect the competitiveness of the overall economy. The first is the effect that the system has on labour costs, and hence international competitiveness. The second is the effects the system will have on job mobility and hence labour market flexibility. If the health sector is allowed to expand without control, this will affect labour costs via tax rates and insurance contributions. Labour costs are an important determinant of international competitiveness and increased taxation or insurance contributions will affect it negatively, unless the increased health spending brings with it a parallel increase in productivity, such as reductions in the numbers of days lost through ill-health. If there is over-consumption of healthcare services – due to problems of supplier induced demand for example – the increase in costs is unlikely to result in such an increase in productivity.

The method of healthcare funding will have implications for job mobility and thus labour market flexibility. Unlike general taxation or national insurance schemes, occupational insurance schemes (whether social or private) will increase the costs of moving job. Research in the US suggests that many workers are reluctant to move jobs because of the fear of losing insurance coverage (General Accounting Office, 1995; Gruber, 1998). However, research on Germany, where the price (although not the benefits) of insurance may change after a job move, has found little evidence for this theory (Holtz-Eakin, 1994).

The output of the health sector is the increase in the health of the population. A healthier economy is in general a wealthier one. Health has been shown to play a significant role in determining economic growth (Bloom, Canning and Jamison, 2004). For example, improved health has been identified as one of the key factors behind the East Asian growth 'miracle' (Bloom, Canning and Malaney, 2000). Jamison, Lau and Wang (2004), using data on 53 countries, found that over the period 1965-1990, approximately 11 % of growth could be attributed to improvements in health, as proxied by the survival rate of males aged between 15 and 60 years old. However, this effect was strongest in those countries that initially had lower levels of health. Their analysis suggests that health impacts on growth through its direct effect on output levels rather than by changing the rate of technological advancement. Nevertheless, there are considerable difficulties in measuring the precise relationship between health and economic performance because the causality may work in both directions and dynamic influences may come into play.

Graph 3.1 illustrates how a country's economic growth is affected by the health of its population, drawing on work by Bloom, Canning and Jamison (2004). Bloom et al. (2004) suggest two channels through which health affects GDP.

Graph 3.1: The relationship between health and GDP

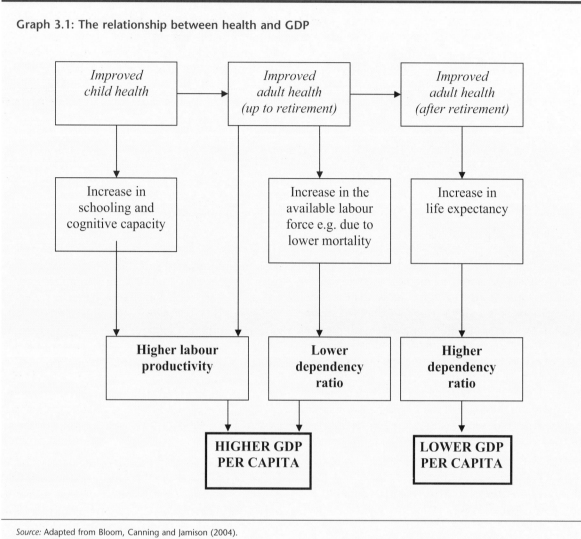

Source: Adapted from Bloom, Canning and Jamison (2004).

First, health affects GDP via its impact on labour productivity. An individual in good health is, *ceteris paribus*, more productive than an individual in poor health. However it is not only adult health that plays a role here. Child health is also important as this influences adult health. It is also of considerable significance with regard to future labour productivity. A healthier child is likely to gain more from their education and their cognitive ability is enhanced. This provides the grounding for a well-skilled labour force in the future, boosting labour productivity and therefore GDP.

Second, Bloom *et al.* (2004) note that a healthier adult population increases the size of the available labour force. A larger labour force results in a lower dependency ratio, which in turn boosts GDP per capita. Although this is true for countries with a very low life expectancy, it is likely to be of less relevance when considering the EU and other developed countries. While better health among adults of working age serves to reduce the depend-

ency ratio, this may not be the case if improvements in health are mainly experienced by those adults past retirement age. If such improvements in health lead to an increase in life expectancy, this may actually cause the dependency ratio to rise, having a negative impact on GDP. This is particularly relevant in current worries about aging populations in many developed countries. The increase in the numbers of retired people will create an increasing burden similar to that being placed on countries' pension systems, where fewer workers are contributing per retirees claiming. A relatively stable or even declining workforce in most EU states has to finance the healthcare for increasing numbers of elderly citizens.

Graph 3.1 depicts the channels through which increased health may affect GDP but the causality could run both ways. In countries with low levels of health, economic growth provides the resources to be able to provide a better health system, but this becomes increasingly difficult (Clarke and Islam,

2003). However, economic growth may also have a negative effect on health, for example due to increased pollution or facilitating lifestyle changes, such as over-consumption of fatty foods, both of which can be damaging to health. Finally the chart depicts a static situation but there may well be dynamic impacts that are difficult to gauge. For example one solution to the ageing population problem is to extend the age of retirement. Better provision of medical care may facilitate this since increased health makes it more likely that people are able and willing to work for a greater number of years.

3.3 Overview of EU Health Systems

The structure of the health care system is a key factor for its efficiency. Across the EU, and indeed internationally, a number of different approaches to providing health care are apparent. An overview of the EU and US systems, including the ways in which health care is both financed and delivered, is provided in Box 3.1.[91]

Ensuring that all residents have access to health services is an important goal in all EU countries, and as such all have universal or almost universal coverage. Even in the Netherlands, where only 65 % of the population are covered by a compulsory scheme, with voluntary private insurance available to the remainder, only 1.6 % of the population are without health insurance. This is in stark contrast to the US, where 16 % of the population aged under 65 are uninsured.

Most health care in the EU is publicly financed. Taxation or social insurance schemes provide the main sources of funding. Taxation may be collected at either the national or local level, or both. Social insurance contributions are generally made by both employee and employer. Some countries have a small number of health insurance or sickness funds, such as France, while some have many, such as Germany. Individuals may have free choice of insurance fund, or membership may be determined by occupation. Although one system will generally predominate, most countries use a combination of insurance and taxation to finance health care.

The role of private insurance varies between countries. In most EU countries, there is the option to take out voluntary health insurance; this is insurance that an individual may choose to purchase, either directly or through an employer scheme. However, this is generally a supplement to, rather than a substitute for, the main health care system. The exceptions are Germany and the Netherlands, where some of the population are covered by substitutive private insurance. In the US, most health care is funded by private insurance, although the public sector still provides a significant amount of health care funding.

Individuals are increasingly required to pay part of the cost of medical care received. This cost-sharing may, for example, comprise co-payments (the payment of a fixed amount for a service) or co-insurance (where the individual pays a proportion of the cost of care). Their use varies among countries, with countries such as the UK restricting these to services such as pharmaceuticals, dental and optical care, while countries such as Finland also use cost-sharing for ambulatory and inpatient care. Cost-sharing can help to reduce unnecessary demand for services by making consumers bear some of the expense of treatment, and may therefore help to improve efficiency. However, it also has negative implications for equity in situations where individuals do not receive the treatment they require because they cannot afford the cost. To combat this, exemptions and limits are in place in all the countries reviewed here to ensure that the poorer and more vulnerable groups of society are not adversely affected by these measures.

The payment system used for physicians is also an important factor as this can affect expenditure and impact on incentives. For example, some doctors receive salaries, some are paid on a fee-for-service basis, and some are paid on a capitation basis. Fee-for-service means that a payment is made for each service provided, while capitation systems involve the payment of a fixed amount for each patient enrolled per time period. Fee-for-service systems tend to be more expensive as they can lead to over-supply of services. Salaries tend to be better at containing costs but may provide little incentive to increase output. In response to these problems, some countries have introduced payment systems that combine two or more of these methods.

Delivery of health care can be provided by either the public or private sector, and is most commonly provided by a combination of both. Increasingly, contracts are used whereby purchasers contract with either public or private providers to deliver

---

[91] This lists the main features of the systems of health care provision, under the broad headings of finance, delivery and other important attributes. Typologies of health care systems, focusing on the extent of public/private financing and service provision, are common in the literature (see e.g. OECD, 1994). These, however, become less useful when dealing with a large number of countries. In particular it is difficult to classify the health care systems in the new member states to these typologies.

services. Alternatively, care may be provided directly, through an integrated model. Choice of provider varies between countries. Some allow free choice of both doctor and hospital, which may serve to increase competition and is also partly aimed at increasing patient choice and satisfaction. Some countries allow direct access to all levels of health care, while others employ a gatekeeping system where a referral is necessary to obtain hospital and sometimes specialist care. Gatekeeping can help to improve the continuity of health care services that a patient receives.

The EU enlargement has introduced even greater diversity into the range of health care systems in the EU. The consequences of enlargement and the challenges that lie ahead not only for the new Member States but also the impact on the existing members are the subject of much current discussion; see for example, MacLehose and McKee (2002) and Busse (2002). A brief description of current health systems amongst the new Member States is presented in the second half of Box 3.1.

The new Member States have seen dramatic change in their health systems in recent years. They have moved from highly centralised, planned systems to a much more decentralised approach. Reforms are ongoing, and in particular these countries have continued to undergo change in order to comply with the conditions necessary for EU accession. Although some provide universal coverage, others are yet to achieve this completely.

These countries now all have a health system based to varying degrees on a compulsory social insurance system. The most notable exception to this is Latvia, where most health care is financed through taxation, and although there is a so-called 'health insurance system', in reality the main role of the sickness funds is administration of the health care budget.

Voluntary health insurance (VHI) generally plays a small role, if any. Cost-sharing has been established in all systems, for example with the introduction of co-payments. An important additional feature of health systems is informal payments, which are an area for concern. Murthy and Mossialos (2003) discuss a number of reasons why such payments take place, including poorly paid health care professionals, limited private provision, and a lack of both transparency and funding in the health system, as well as cultural factors. They also propose that this is one possible reason why the market for VHI is often small in such cases, as individuals would rather make direct payments to the doctor than make contributions to a private insurance company.

Two new Member States, Cyprus and Malta, have very different historical backgrounds to the central and eastern European countries. However, their health systems are also undergoing significant change, with both countries currently in the process of introducing social insurance systems.

Box 3.1: Overview of Health Systems in the EU and US[92]

Belgium

Finance: Mandatory health insurance system, 65 % funded by social insurance contributions, 35 % by federal government subsidies. Co-payments apply for several services, including in ambulatory and inpatient care. Most doctors are paid on a fee-for-service (FFS) basis. Increase in popularity of supplementary voluntary health insurance (VHI), provided by both mutualities and private insurers.

Delivery: Health care is mostly privately provided. Primary care is mostly provided by independent doctors. Approximately 60 % of hospitals are private, non-profit making organisations, remainder are publicly owned. Free choice of provider and hospital. No formal gatekeeping system, although a patient would generally be referred to a hospital by a general practitioner (GP) or specialist.

Other: Almost universal coverage. 88 % are covered by the main insurance scheme for both major and minor risks, while the self-employed are only covered for minor risks.

---

[92] The descriptions below draw heavily on information from the European Observatory on Health Care Systems, in particular the 'Health Care Systems in Transition' publications (see references). Information was also obtained for the fifteen existing EU member states from Jakubowski and Busse (1998), and for the new EU member states from the World Health Organisation (2000, 2001) 'Highlights on health' publications and the Gesellschaft für Versicherungswissenschaft und -gestaltung e.V. (2003). In addition, the following country-specific sources were used: Riesberg and Busse, 2003 (Germany); Hellenic Republic, Ministry of Health and Welfare (Greece); Imai, Jacobzone and Lenain, 2000 (France); Department of Health and Children, 2001, 2004 (Ireland); Schaapman, 2003 (Netherlands); Department of Health, 2004a (UK); Royal College of General Practitioners, 2002 (UK); Republic of Cyprus, 2003 (Cyprus); Palu and Kadakmaa, 2001 (Estonia); Ministry of Health, 2004 (Malta); Jasiutowicz, 2000 (Poland); Girouard and Imai, 2000 (Poland); Docteur, Suppanz and Woo, 2003 (US) and National Center for Health Statistics, 2003 (US). Helpful advice on updating these descriptions was received from the following individuals: Klara Frecerova, Director of Department of Foreign Relations, Ministry of Health; Dr. Svatopluk Hlavacka, Director of Health Care Department, Ministry of Health, Slovak Republic; Jarno Habicht, WHO Representative for Estonia; Catharina Hjortsberg, The Swedish Institute for Health Economics (IHE); Maria Hofmarcher, Institute for Advanced Studies, Austria; Jutta Järvelin, Centre for Health Economics at Stakes (CHESS), Finland; Jautrite Karaskevica, Health Statistics and Medical Technology Agency, Latvia; Liuba Murauskiene, Director, Health Economics Center, Lithuania; Frances O'Brien, Department of Health and Children, Ireland and Sarah Thomson, London School of Economics. While we have endeavoured to ensure that each country profile is as up-to-date as possible to the best of our knowledge, the constantly evolving nature of health care systems means that it is possible that changes have occurred to the descriptions reported here.

Denmark

Finance: National health service (NHS), financed mainly through state, county and municipal taxation. Co-payments apply for some pharmaceuticals, dental care, physiotherapy and spectacles, also for group 2 GP option (see below). GPs are mainly paid by a combination of capitation and fee-for-service payments. Approximately 28 % of the population have some form of additional VHI, often in order to obtain cover for co-payments.

Delivery: State-controlled but highly decentralised. Most primary care is provided by self-employed GPs. Most hospitals are publicly owned and managed at the county level, private sector accounts for less than 1 % of hospital beds. Free choice of hospital offered since 1993, but not widely used.

Other: Universal coverage. There are two options for GP care; in group 1, restricted choice of GP and free access to secondary care requires referral, while group 2 allows for free choice of GP or specialist but the patient must pay extra for this privilege (1.7 % of population).

Germany

Finance: Compulsory social insurance scheme, financed mainly by insurance contributions. Above a certain income level, it is possible to opt out of the statutory system and purchase private insurance – applies to about 9 % of the population (including some employees covered by employers). Use of co-payments has recently increased, including for ambulatory and inpatient care, following implementation of the Statutory Health Insurance Modernization (SHIM) Act. Doctors working in ambulatory care are paid FFS. Largest VHI market in Europe, all are entitled to purchase supplementary private insurance.

Delivery: Strict separation between primary and hospital care. Most primary care is provided by private doctors – free choice of GP, direct access to specialists. Hospital care is provided by both public and private providers – very few are for-profit. A referral is generally required for access to hospital care. Free choice of hospital in theory, but in practice this is not always possible.

Other: Almost universal coverage, less than 0.2 % are uninsured.

Greece

Finance: Mix of NHS and social insurance system, funded 46 % by social insurance contributions, 12 % from taxation (in 2000). 42 % of health care expenditure financed privately, mainly direct payments to private providers, but also some co-payments. Mix of physician payment systems, including FFS in private sector and for those on contract to insurance funds, while those employed by health centres are generally salaried.

Delivery: Mix of public and private providers, health care is delivered through health care units belonging to the NHS, the insurance funds and the private sector. 25 % of hospital beds are provided by the private sector. Individuals can choose any public or private hospital that is contracted by their fund, but must pay if they choose a non-contract private hospital.

Other: Almost universal coverage. Those who are not insured have free access to public hospitals and health centres. They can also pay directly for private treatment if they wish.

Spain

Finance: National health service, mainly financed through general taxation. Co-payments of 40 % for prescription phar-maceuticals, but not for public primary, outpatient or inpatient care. Hospital doctors are paid by salary, as are most primary care doctors (with some capitation). Some supplementary voluntary private insurance.

Delivery: Most health care provided publicly. Primary care is publicly managed and delivered. Patients have the right to choose a GP but unlikely to consult a GP outside of their health area. Most hospitals are publicly owned. 'Three-stage' gatekeeping system in operation – to access hospital care, required to first see a GP then an ambulatory specialist.

Other: Almost universal coverage - 99.8 % in 2000.

France

Finance: Compulsory health insurance system, mainly funded by insurance contributions - most of the employee's component replaced by the 'general social contribution' tax since 1998. Co-payments apply for a wide range of services. Over 90 % of the population now have some form of supplementary VHI, since free VHI cover was made available to those on low incomes in 2000. GPs and specialists in ambulatory care are generally paid by FFS, while hospital staff are normally salaried.

Delivery: Free choice of provider (doctor and hospital). Most ambulatory care is provided privately. No referral system, an attempt to encourage this has not been widely taken up. About 2/3 of hospital care is provided by the public sector.

Other: Universal coverage attained following introduction of Universal Health Coverage Act (CMU) in 2000.

Ireland

Finance: National health service system, mainly financed through general taxation. Some voluntary private insurance, accounting for roughly 6.8 % of total health spending in 2001. Co-payments apply, additional charges for non-medical cardholders for certain services, including GP visits. GPs are paid by capitation for patients who are medical cardholders, but FFS for non-medical cardholders (no set charges).

Delivery: Mix of public and private provision. Most hospitals are publicly owned. Some purely private hospitals, but often possible to receive private care in a public hospital. GPs are independent, those belonging to the General Medical Services (GMS) scheme can provide services to medical cardholders through contracts with the health boards. Some choice of GP. A referral from a GP is normally required in order to access hospital care.

Other: All residents are entitled to health care, but while approximately 30 % are medical cardholders (those aged over 70 years old as well as those on low incomes) and entitled to mainly free services, the remainder are subject to charges for some services.

Italy

Finance: National health service, mainly financed by taxation. A regional tax on productive activities replaced social insurance contributions in 1997. Use of co-payments, including for diagnostic services, pharmaceuticals and specialist visits. Some supplementary private insurance. GPs are paid on a capitation basis, hospital doctors are salaried.

Delivery: Most health care is publicly managed. The majority of hospitals are publicly owned. Gatekeeping system – a visit to a specialist must be authorised by a GP, but the patient has free choice of any NHS accredited specialist.

Other: Universal coverage.

Luxembourg

Finance: Compulsory health insurance. State contributes a maximum of 40 % to the health insurance system, the remainder is funded through insurance contributions. Co-payments apply for various health services. 75 % of the working age population have voluntary complementary private health insurance. GPs are paid by FFS.

Delivery: Primary health care is provided mainly by independent GPs. Patients have free choice of GP or specialist, with direct access. No gatekeeping system. One private for-profit hospital, remainder are divided between non-profit organisations and those run by local authorities.

Other: Almost universal coverage.

Netherlands

Finance: Mixed insurance system. All residents are covered for long term and high cost care under the Exceptional Medical Services Act (AWBZ). General health care provided through compulsory membership under the Sickness Funds Act (ZFW) for individuals below a certain income level (65 % of population). AWBZ and ZFW are mainly funded by insurance contributions, also receive state subsidies. Those not covered by ZFW can purchase voluntary private insurance instead. Supplementary private insurance is available to all from both the sickness funds and private insurers. GPs are paid by capitation for those patients insured under ZFW, but FFS for those with private insurance. Co-payments apply for various health services, under all three insurance components.

Delivery: Ambulatory care mainly provided by private GPs. Over 90 % of hospitals are private non-profit institutions. Free choice of GP. Gatekeeping system – a referral is needed from a GP in order to access specialist care, but there is free choice of specialist.

Other: 1.6 % of population are uninsured. New insurance system proposed from 2006.

Austria

Finance: Compulsory social insurance. Social insurance contributions fund just over half of health care expenditure. Increasingly, a greater proportion of health care is financed through private expenditure. Approximately 1/3 of the population have supplementary private insurance. Several co-payments apply, in both primary and hospital care. GPs are mainly paid FFS - with higher fees charged by 'non-contract' doctors.

Delivery: Most primary care is provided by private self-employed doctors, although increase in outpatient care in hospitals is resulting in a mix of public and private provision in ambulatory care. Most hospital care is provided publicly. Some use of gatekeeping. A patient is free to choose any doctor contracted by their fund – can also choose to see a 'non-contract' doctor but rate of reimbursement is lower.

Other: Universal coverage, not possible to opt out of the insurance system.

Portugal

Finance: National health service, mainly funded by general taxation. In addition, 'health sub-systems' provide health care for particular professions (about 25 % of population), funded by employer and employee contributions. Co-payments for pharmaceuticals, as well as for other services including consultations, emergency and home visits. About 10 % of the population have supplementary voluntary health insurance. NHS doctors are salaried, private doctors are paid FFS. Many doctors combine NHS work with private practice.

Delivery: Primary care is publicly and privately provided. Free choice of GP. Under the NHS, GPs act as gatekeepers for secondary care, but members of health subsystems can directly access any specialist or hospital allowed by their scheme. Most hospital care is provided directly by the NHS.

Other: Universal coverage.

Finland

Finance: National health service, most health care funded through taxation, with shift in financing from the state to the municipalities in recent years. In 2000, 18 % of total health expenditure was paid by the state, 42 % by the municipalities and 15 % by the National Health Insurance (NHI). Patients pay directly for private care and generally can reclaim one-third of the cost through NHI. Co-payments apply for various services, including in ambulatory and hospital care. Very small voluntary insurance sector. Private doctors are paid FFS. Hospital doctors receive salaries. So are most health centre doctors, although some receive a combination of salary, capitation and FFS.

Delivery: Primary care generally provided through publicly owned health centres. Hospitals are mostly publicly owned. Little choice of GP – some choice within health centre. Patients need a referral to access specialist care at hospitals. Direct access to specialists in the private sector, who can also refer to public hospitals. No real choice of hospital.

Other: Universal coverage.

Sweden

Finance: National health service, mainly funded through local taxation, with some subsidies from national government. In 1999, social insurance contributions funded 21-25 % of health spending. Co-payments include flat-rate fees for many health services, set by county councils. Very small market for supplementary VHI. Public doctors in ambulatory care are salaried.

Delivery: Ambulatory care is provided by public and private doctors, and hospital outpatient departments. Free choice of first-contact provider. Hospitals are publicly owned, very few private hospitals. It is possible to access secondary care directly through a hospital outpatient department. Some choice of hospital, a referral is not always necessary.

Other: Universal coverage.

UK

Finance: National health service, mainly funded through general taxation. Almost 10 % of total health care expenditure financed through national insurance contributions. Co-payments apply for some services, including for pharmaceuticals, dental and optical care. Some supplementary private VHI. GPs are paid by a combination of capitation, allowances and fees for particular services. Hospital staff are salaried. Private doctors are usually paid by FFS.

Delivery: Primary care is provided mainly by GPs, together with other health care professionals, through primary care trusts (PCTs). PCTs play an increasingly important role in the health system. Some choice of GP, but must live within designated area. Very small number of private sector GPs. GPs act as gatekeepers to secondary care. Most hospitals are publicly owned, less than 5 % of hospital beds are in the private sector.

Other: Universal coverage.

Cyprus

Finance: The public health sector, accounting for less than 40 % of total health care spending, is financed through general taxation. This provides free or reduced rate health care to those who are eligible – approximately 55 % of the population. Emergency services are available to the entire population at no charge. The private sector plays a significant role, this is mostly financed by direct payments; the private insurance market is fairly small. In addition, there are schemes that cover certain sections of the population, these are generally organised and funded by employers.

Delivery: Mix of public and private provision. Health services are provided publicly under the government health system. The 'special schemes' may sometimes use both the public and private sectors to deliver health care.

Other: A National Health Insurance System (NHIS) is to be implemented by 2006. This should lead to universal coverage. The Health Insurance Organisation will contract both public and private providers to deliver health care services. All individuals will be able to choose a GP to register with; some choice of specialist and hospital will also be possible.

Czech Republic

Finance: Compulsory health insurance system, financed by contributions from individuals, employers and the state. Health insurance finances more than 80 % of health care expenditure. Some use of cost-sharing, mainly for certain pharmaceuticals, dental care and medical aids. Very small market for supplementary voluntary insurance. Doctors in public hospitals are salaried, while, since 1997, GPs are paid mostly by capitation with some FFS.

Delivery: Mix of public and private providers, who enter into contracts with the insurance funds to provide care, regardless of ownership. Most ambulatory care is privately delivered. Patients have free choice of doctor. No gatekeeping system as yet. Most hospitals are publicly owned – only roughly 10 % of total beds are in private hospitals.

Other: Universal coverage, not possible to opt out of insurance system.

Estonia

Finance: Social health insurance system, accounts for approximately 65 % of total health care expenditure. General taxation accounts for approximately a further 10 %. Use of cost-sharing, including co-payments for pharmaceuticals, most dental care, visit fees for outpatient care and bed-day fees for inpatient care. Private VHI plays a very small role, accounting for 1 % of total health care spending. Primary care doctors are independent, entering into contracts with the insurance fund to provide services, and physician payment methods vary. Hospital doctors are paid mainly by salary, but hospitals may also choose to include a performance related component.

Delivery: Reforms to primary care introduced in the 1990s were largely implemented by 2003. GPs are now independent contractors. All Estonian citizens have enrolled with a GP, patients have free choice of any GP or specialist that is contracted by their insurance fund. GPs have some gatekeeping role, but patients can still access certain outpatient specialists directly. Outpatient care providers and hospitals are also contracted by the Estonian Health Insurance Fund. At present, most hospitals are publicly owned, but this is an area currently undergoing reform.

Other: In 2001, estimates suggest that 93.5 % of the population were covered by health insurance. Emergency medical care is available to those who are not insured.

Hungary

Finance: Compulsory National Health Insurance Fund, accounts for the majority of health care expenditure. In addition to insurance contributions, a health care tax, payable since 1997, is another important source of funding for the insurance system. Co-payments apply for some services. Very small VHI sector. Most doctors are public employees and receive a salary. However, the majority of GPs are now paid mainly on a capitation basis.

Delivery: Public sector is dominant in the provision of health care, the private sector plays only a small role. Free choice of GP. Most GPs now operate under a contract system, but some are employed directly by local government. Some use of gatekeeping, but not particularly strict, still possible to access some specialists directly. Delivery of health care is still largely hospital-centred. Only a small percentage of hospital beds are under private ownership.

Other: Almost universal coverage, roughly 1 % are not insured.

Lithuania

Finance: Compulsory health insurance system introduced in 1997. Health expenditure is financed by a combination of insurance contributions and taxation. Small VHI market. Some co-payments apply, mainly for pharmaceuticals and medical aids. Doctors in public hospitals and clinics are paid mainly by salary. Health care providers contracted by the Health Insurance Fund are permitted to charge for some services, in line with legal regulations. Primary care is now remunerated on a capitation basis.

Delivery: Most health care is publicly provided. Some private sector involvement, mostly in the provision of outpatient care. Growing private provision of primary care. Choice of primary care facility and of GP within this. A referral is required to access specialist care. Without a referral, the patient must pay, except in an emergency case. Hospitals are publicly owned.

Other: All residents should be covered by the health insurance system, but if no contributions are paid a patient receives care at no cost only in an emergency.

Latvia

Finance: Most health care expenditure is financed by taxation collected at the central level. A 'health insurance system' is in place, but the main purpose of the sickness funds is actually to administer the health care budget. Resources are allocated to the sickness funds, who contract with providers to deliver health care. Cost-sharing applies to many health care services. The market for voluntary private health insurance is small but increasing. Variety of physician payment systems.

Delivery: On-going reforms to primary care. Free choice of GP, although in practice this may not be possible in more rural regions. Primary health care doctors may be directly employed or work on a contract basis. A referral is necessary to access most specialists and secondary care. Hospital care is mostly provided by the public sector, small number of private hospitals. Patients have free choice of hospital among those that are contracted by their sickness fund.

Other: Universal coverage in theory, in practice some individuals experience difficulty in accessing care due to not being able to afford treatment and because of distance from health care facilities.

Malta

Finance: National health service, funded from general taxation. Cost-sharing applies for pharmaceuticals, some dental and optical care. Significant private sector - increasing role of voluntary private insurance, but many also pay directly to see private GPs and specialists. Doctors in the public sector are salaried, those in the private sector are paid FFS. Most doctors working in the public sector also provide health care privately.

Delivery: Most health care is hospital-based. Hospital care is available from public hospitals under the NHS. A few private hospitals also exist. Under the state system, primary care is provided mainly in public health centres. Patients are not registered with their own GP, seen by duty doctor. Although a gatekeeping system is in operation, not always effective. Possible to indicate a preference for a certain specialist. Many choose to pay for private primary care – estimates suggest that 2/3 of primary care is provided privately. Private specialists can be accessed directly.

Other: Universal coverage. Malta is currently reforming its health system, funding will in future come from the National Insurance Fund rather than general taxation, and the current integrated model will be replaced by a contract system.

Poland

Finance: Compulsory national health insurance system, introduced in 1999, financed mainly by insurance contributions. Some co-payments, mainly for pharmaceuticals, dental care and medical aids. Small role for private health insurance. Remuneration in primary care is mainly by capitation. Hospital physicians working in the public sector are mostly paid by salary with some additional payments, for example, for providing specific services. FFS is the usual method of payment for private care.

Delivery: Health care is provided by both the public and private sectors. The sickness funds contract with providers from both sectors to deliver services. Some use of gatekeeping, a referral is generally needed to access secondary care, although some specialists are directly accessible. Free choice of any provider that is contracted by the sickness fund. It is also possible to receive care from a private provider not contracted by the fund but in this case the individual must bear the cost. Most hospitals are publicly owned.

Other: Almost universal coverage.

Slovenia

Finance: Health insurance system, statutory insurance contributions fund the majority of health care spending. Co-payments apply for various services. Supplementary VHI is available in order to cover cost of co-payments and some extra services. Doctors employed in the public sector are paid mainly by salary with some incentive payments. Private sector doctors working on a contract basis are paid according to the terms of the contract, those without contracts are paid FFS.

Delivery: Primary care is provided by both the public and private sectors. Patients can choose a primary care doctor in a public health centre or a private doctor that is contracted by the insurance fund. Use of gatekeeping – a referral is required to access secondary care but patient has choice of provider. Most hospitals are publicly owned.

Other: Almost universal coverage, not possible to opt out of the mandatory insurance system.

Slovak Republic

Finance: Compulsory health insurance system, mainly funded by insurance contributions. Some use of cost-sharing, including for certain pharmaceuticals and medical aids. Public sector doctors are salaried. Independent GPs (98 %) are paid by capitation, private specialists (75 %) are paid on a FFS basis.

Delivery: Primary care doctors are independent and have contractual agreements with the health insurance funds to provide care. Individuals have choice of GP although in certain areas this may be limited. Gatekeeping system, although some specialists can be accessed without a referral. Private specialists, working on a contract basis, operate alongside public sector specialists. Most hospitals are publicly owned.

Other: Universal coverage.

United States

Finance: Mostly private insurance, with the majority of the working-age population covered by employer insurance schemes. Public sector involvement still significant, particularly, for example, with the Medicare and Medicaid programmes. Co-payments apply. Variety of payment systems for doctors, including FFS and capitation.

Delivery: Mostly privately managed and delivered. Most hospitals are community hospitals, of which 2/3 are private, not-for-profit organisations. A few are operated by federal government. Significant increase in 'managed care' during 1990s, these plans sometimes involve use of gatekeeping. However, the restrictions on freedom of both consumers and physicians led to considerable dissatisfaction, and there has been a shift away from very tight management in recent years.

Other: Approximately 16 % of the population under 65 years of age were uninsured in 2001.

3.4 The determinants of health sector performance

This section considers factors affecting the performance of the health sector, how EU governments have responded and the effectiveness of these policies. It is important to note that the health sector is the subject of considerable governmental intervention across the world, even in the US. In order to understand the performance of the sector, it is important therefore to understand why this is so. Essentially, the health sector is subject to a number of market imperfections that are likely to increase the consumption and supply of and hence expenditure on healthcare.

3.4.1 Reasons for government intervention

There are two main sets of justifications for government intervention in the health sector: equity considerations and reasons of economic efficiency. The health sector is subject to a number of – often interrelated – market imperfections and information asymmetries. These problems impinge upon the efficiency of the sector as they affect incentive structures, resource allocation and the development and dissemination of technological advances. Perverse incentives may be created, encouraging over-consumption/provision of health services.[93]

3.4.2 The efficiency of the health sector

Economic efficiency is made up of two components: technical and allocative efficiency. Technical efficiency refers to the ability to obtain maximal output from its inputs. Allocative efficiency refers to whether the outputs and inputs are used in the correct proportions, given their prices. Efficiency problems can often create or exacerbate inequality in the availability of healthcare, as in the case of risk selection. However, often the cures for inefficiency have a negative impact on the equitable distribution of healthcare. One example of this is the use of cost-sharing to overcome the moral hazard created by the availability of care at zero marginal cost. The majority of the discussion of this chapter involves technical efficiency, but allocative efficiency will also impact upon the competitiveness of EU economies.

The funding system for healthcare can affect allocative efficiency at three levels (Mossialos and Dixon, 2002): allocation of resources between healthcare and the rest of the economy; how they are allocated to areas within the healthcare system; and within areas. Clearly, over-consumption or over-supply in the healthcare sector may shift resources away from other, potentially more productive, sectors of the economy, either through increased insurance premiums and taxation or through the reduction of government spending from potentially more productive areas. Other problems of allocative inefficiency include the relative demand for different factors of production, such as capital versus labour, or different types of labour.

3.4.3 The influence of market structure on performance

Healthcare is essentially provided by insurance, either private or social insurance or through taxation. This enables the risk surrounding the demand for healthcare to be pooled. In common with other insurance markets, the health sector is liable to a number of imperfections. In addition, the market for health care may be such that it produces an unsatisfactory or inappropriate outcome, from the point of view of society as a whole. Some aspects of healthcare – for example infectious diseases – have the features of a public good, in particular the presence of positive externalities, i.e. external benefits to other members of society from the provision of a health service. If individuals, their insurance funds, or the government pays the marginal private benefit of a medical intervention for its provision, society as a whole will under-consume healthcare.[94] In addition to the issue of externalities, there are three main mechanisms whereby the structure of the market will impact on equity and efficiency in the health sector resulting from imperfect information: moral hazard, adverse selection and risk selection. Their effects will generally be to increase consumption and expenditure.

3.4.3.1 Moral Hazard

A healthcare system based on insurance or taxation will suffer from problems of moral hazard because the very act of being insured creates incentives for individuals to change their behaviour in two important ways. First, they may seek less diligently to prevent illness, knowing that their insurance will cover the monetary costs arising. Second, in the light of any health problem, they are likely to over-consume healthcare because of its low cost

---

[93] It is possible that they will also lead to under-consumption in certain sectors of the economy, because of risk-selection and wealth effects, which will lead to an inequitable health outcome.

[94] Unless there is only one insurer, in which case the externality is internalised because the additional costs will be borne by the insurer.

compared to the situation where they pay the full cost of their actions. This is exacerbated by supplier-induced demand whereby health providers understand many aspects of a patient's medical state more than they themselves or their insurers do and they also are more aware of the potential medical interventions. The possession of this knowledge can be exploited to the provider's gain by manipulating the quantity, quality and price of healthcare services in ways not readily apparent to the patient. Another aspect of this is the incentive to demand new – and possibly more expensive – medical technology over old (Zweifel and Manning, 2000; Weisbrod, 1991).

A number of policies have been implemented to overcome the problem of moral hazard, primarily with the intention to mitigate its effects on expenditure. Many countries have implemented budget caps in an attempt to contain spending, with varying degrees of success. Experience suggests that such measures are most effective in health systems where financing and delivery of health care are or have been integrated, for example in Denmark and the UK. However, this is not always the case, as other countries with integrated health systems, including Greece, Italy, Portugal and Spain have not enjoyed similar success (Docteur and Oxley, 2003). Budgetary measures have generally not been particularly successful in health systems financed by social insurance, such as France. Alternatively, some more indirect measures to contain expenditure have been applied; for example, during the mid-1990s, Germany restricted spending to the rise in revenue from insurance contributions, which were set at fixed rates (Docteur and Oxley, 2003).

Most EU countries have increased their use of cost-sharing for pharmaceuticals, dental and ophthalmic treatments, especially during the 1990s. The effect of this is to reduce expenditure by directly shifting expenditure from the government or insurer to the individual. By shifting part of the cost to the consumer, such policies can also reduce over-consumption. However, research by Siu et al. (1986) suggests that it is not the case that co-payments reduce 'unnecessary' treatment by any more than 'necessary' treatment – both types of care appear to be affected to the same extent. Cost-sharing may even lead to a decline in efficiency if it results simply in a shift in the place where individuals seek treatment – from general practitioners to hospitals, for example (Docteur and Oxley, 2003).

One way to overcome the problem of supplier induced demand via the incentive structure is

through capitation.[95] Capitation attempts to predict the demand for healthcare by the population and pay healthcare providers the expected costs. This can be done simply at an aggregate level, or it may depend on personal characteristics, such as age, morbidity and social circumstances. Capitation can be done simply by assigning an equal amount of funding to every citizen, regardless of their characteristics or circumstances, as it is in Spain. Alternatively it can depend on personal characteristics, such as age (as in France), or a progressively more sophisticated set of demographic, morbidity and social circumstances from gender (as in Germany) through to marital status, housing tenure and employment status (as in Stockholm County).

3.4.3.2 Adverse selection

Asymmetric information between population and insurer in voluntary insurance schemes can result in *adverse selection* as insurers cannot calculate an actuarial premium for each individual and so charges an average premium. This will create the incentive for above average risk individuals to purchase insurance but those with below average risk to forego it, causing overall risk, and hence premiums, to increase. Governments attempt to overcome this problem by financing the system through taxation or by legislating to make contributions to insurance compulsory.

3.4.3.3 Risk selection

The converse of adverse selection is *risk-selection*, where insurers will refuse insurance to individuals with above-average risk. High risk individuals will not reap the benefits of risk pooling and therefore may not be able to afford insurance. As with adverse selection, governments attempt to overcome this problem by financing the system through taxation or by legislating to make access to insurance, and hence health services, open to all.

3.4.3.4 Lack of competitive forces

It has long been known that a major potential problem with public sector service provision is the lack of a price mechanism to allocate resources. Public sector intervention, therefore, is likely to eliminate or at least reduce the financial incentives

---

[95] A market solution to over-consumption, over-supply or over-pricing is managed care, whereby an agent (typically the insurer) attempts to control costs by directly managing the relationship between provider and insured individual. This can include many situations from the restriction of the set of providers to fully integrated systems of insurance and service providers (Glied, 2000). However, the evidence on managed care is mixed. Whilst there may have been an initial effect on total expenditure, these were short lived (Maynard and Bloor, 1998; Maynard and Dixon, 2002).

increasing productivity or promoting technological advances. The effects of this may be felt throughout the sector. For example, if individuals do not have any choice with regard to their service provider, the latter have little incentive to maintain 'competitive' prices. Governments have attempted to overcome the lack of a functioning market by introducing wage or price controls or by creating some form of pseudo markets.

Wage controls have been most commonly used in those countries with integrated health care systems. This has been applied to both the hospital sector, as in Denmark, Ireland and the UK, and also in ambulatory care where staff are salaried, for example, in Finland, Spain and Sweden (Docteur and Oxley, 2003). Price controls have also been widely applied. A variety of approaches have been taken to controlling prices, including the direct setting of prices by government. With the exception of Germany, all other EU countries have some form of price controls for pharmaceuticals (Docteur and Oxley, 2003). Another approach to controlling prices has been used both in Germany, in its ambulatory sector, and Austria, in its hospital sector. These countries have introduced systems which exert control over prices by adjusting these according to the quantity of services provided, in order to remain within a set budget.

In systems where a purchaser/provider distinction is in place, price negotiations may take place between the two parties, introducing potentially competition between providers. The UK is one example but competition, notably at the level of hospitals, can also be found in Denmark, Finland and some Swedish counties. Docteur and Oxley (2003) note that sometimes such negotiations have collapsed, for example, as has previously occurred in Belgium, France and Luxembourg, and prices have had to be set directly as a result.

Systems based on salaries provide little incentive to increase output; hence the introduction of fee-for-service contracts in some countries (e.g. Belgium, Denmark, Greece, France, Luxembourg, the Netherlands, Austria, and Finland), usually in the private sector. Fee-for-service systems tend to be more expensive and can lead to over-supply of services, as opposed to salaries, which tend to be better at containing costs. This has led to some countries introducing combined payment systems.

Box 3.2: The influence of market structure on performance

Moral Hazard

Problem: low or zero marginal cost of service

Effects: increase in demand for services by individuals and supplier induced demand leading to increased overall costs

Policies: cost-sharing, capitation, managed care

Adverse selection

Problem: asymmetric information between population and insurer/funding body

Effects: the use of average risk premiums leads to high risk individuals taking up insurance and low risk ones foregoing it.

Policies: compulsory contributions, taxation

Risk selection

Problem: asymmetric information between population and insurer

Effects: private firms tend to 'cherry-pick' insurees, no insurance for high risk people

Policies: compulsory contributions, taxation

Lack of competitive forces

Problem: public sector intervention reduces or eliminates financial incentives increasing productivity or promoting technological advances.

Effects: high prices of services, equipment and pharmaceuticals as well as high wages.

Policies: purchaser-provider split, price and wage controls, fee-for-service, contracting-out

3.4.4 Technology and innovation in the healthcare sector

Technology is an important determinant of the performance in the health sector where technology is changing rapidly. Sixty years ago, the healthcare system involved mainly diagnosis, prediction of the likely outcome and guidance while illness took its own course; nowadays there are a wide variety of possible interventions (Weisbrod, 1991). Technology is generally accepted as the main explanatory factor behind increasing health expenditure (e.g. Newhouse, 1992, Moise, 2003a). Gelijins and Rosenberg (1994) identify three ways in which health expenditure is influenced by technological developments. First, expenditure may increase when a new technology is introduced. Second, expenditure will be affected by the intensity with which existing technology is applied. Finally, expenditure will also be affected by the rate and extent of expansion of use of new technology. However, recent research (Cutler and McClellan (2001) suggests that while new technology generally increases expenditure, the benefits of improved technology may outweigh the extra costs. New developments can be cost-enhancing by increasing the quality of treatments or cost-reducing by increasing the efficiency with which a given problem is treated. Although the latter will increase the productivity of the sector, the effect of the former is ambiguous and its evaluation requires difficult measurement of quality change.

Basic research in health care is global, with advances in knowledge publicly available in medical journals or disseminated at conferences. Also knowledge about new health care products is widely disseminated as drugs and other medical devices are often sold on world markets. However, while new technologies are used in all countries quickly after they are available, the extent of use varies enormously. According to McClellan and Kessler (2003, p. 4): 'although technological change in health care may be driven ultimately by discovery and invention of new techniques and devices, cross national studies of the cause and consequences of technological change focus on differences in rates of actual use of technologies.' Thus, when considering the impact of technology on productivity the primary interest is in diffusion.

The organisation of the health sector will have an important influence on the development, dissemination and implementation of new technology. The funding mechanism will have an important influence on the type of research that is undertaken via the incentives it provides to practitioners and researchers (Weisbrod, 1991). The structures of health care systems also have consequences for the diffusion of technology, especially supply-side factors such as physician and hospital payment mechanisms, as well as the regulation of technology (Moise, 2003a).

Any health system that does not create an incentive for agents to consider the costs of treatment (i.e. moral hazard) is likely to promote cost-raising R&D. As with any investment, if there is no return to cost-reducing R&D, there is no incentive to undertake it. It has been argued that the greater emphasis on cost control in the predominantly state-controlled (whether by taxation or social insurance) EU health sector has led to a slower implementation of cost-enhancing technology (Weisbrod, 1991; Cutler, 2002). The EU health sector has, therefore, been able to take advantage of the development of new technologies elsewhere as it has been able to introduce them slowly, after the expensive early stages of implementation. Whilst there is little evidence on the overall impact on productivity in the EU, the result is likely to be lower average costs at the expense of a delay in implementation.

3.5 The performance of the EU health sector

Given the share of the health sector in national income, measurig its performance is extremely important. Unfortunately, as with many public services, the measures employed for private services do not easily translate to deriving internationally comparable measures in the health sector. National accounts sources, which often form the bedrock of estimates for private services, cannot be used in this sector given the past propensity to measure outputs by inputs. While EU countries are embarking on employing quantity indicators to measure real output changes in the national accounts, this process is still at the experimental stage. In addition, national accounts statisticians are concerned with measuring quality change, an important consideration in the health care sector given the rapid progress of knowledge and technology, but agreed methods to adjust for quality have not yet emerged.

Considering sources other than national accounts, international comparisons of health sectors are fraught with problems. Whilst measures of aggregate expenditure are readily available (see below), comparisons of aggregate health expenditure have been hampered by the lack of theoretical basis for the determinants of health expenditure (Gerdtham and Jönsson, 2000).

This section first considers aggregate performance indicators, examining the cost of providing health care and whether variations in costs are related to outcomes; next it examines why expenditures vary across countries and whether EU countries have been successful in containing costs; and, finally, it looks at the relationship between expenditures and economic growth. In addition, selected studies at the microeconomic, disease-based, level are reviewed; these, are increasingly seen as an important method to fill the gaps in aggregate indicators. Input use and organisational change are also discussed separately.

3.5.1 Macro indicators

3.5.1.1 How much does health care cost?

Graph 3.2 shows total health spending as a proportion of GDP in the EU and the US in 2000. It is clear that despite the variation in expenditure within the EU, all EU countries spend substantially less on health care as a percentage of GDP than does the

US. In 2000, the highest spender in the EU was Germany, at 10.6 % of GDP compared to 13.1 % in the US. In the future, expenditure in the EU and US must consider the implications of the expansion of Medicaid in the US to cover the 16 % of the US population currently without health insurance of any kind. Given the fact that coverage is almost universal across Europe, this is likely to increase the gap in spending between the US and the EU Member States.

Graph 3.3 shows the total amount of spending on health care *per capita*, broken down into public and private sectors. The picture of overall expenditure is similar to that in Graph 3.2 but there are changes in the ordering within the EU. Luxembourg has a slightly higher per capita spending on healthcare than Germany. The most notable difference between Graph 3.2 and Graph 3.3 is the relative size of the health sectors in EU-15 and in the new Member States measured as a percentage of GDP and in absolute $PPP terms. One implication of this is that differences in *per capita* spending between the EU-15 and new Member States are largely due

Graph 3.2: Total Health Expenditure in the EU and US, 2000 (percent of GDP)

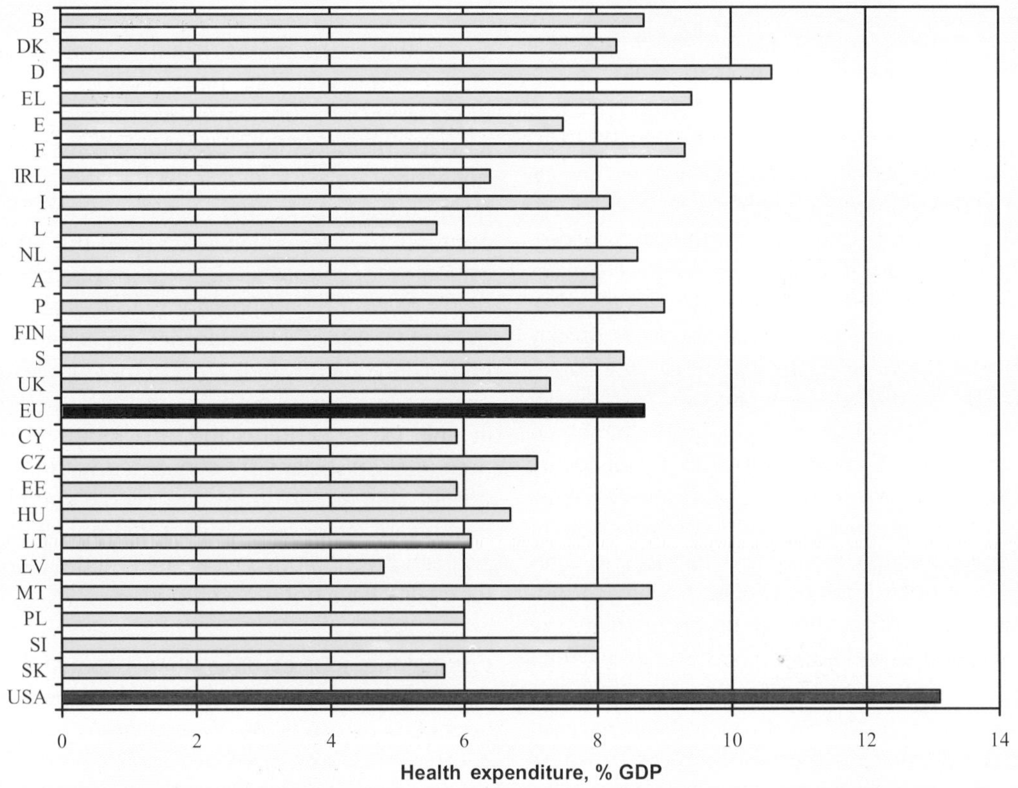

Health expenditure, % GDP

Notes: EU refers to the EU-15.

Source: WHO European Health for All Database, 2004 and OECD Health Data 2003, 2nd edition.

Graph 3.3: Public and Private Per-Capita Health Expenditure in the EU and US, 2000 (USD in PPP)

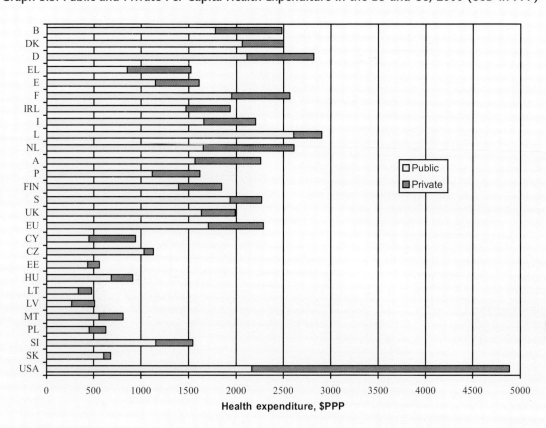

Notes: EU refers to EU-15.

Source: WHO European Health for All Database, 2004 and OECD Health Data 2003, 2nd edition.

to differences in GDP. Graph 3.3 also shows that although public expenditure in the US accounts for a considerably smaller proportion of total health expenditure than the EU, *per capita* public health expenditure in the US is still higher than all EU countries but Luxembourg.

The reasons for the variations in health expenditure are unclear. Expenditure may be greater because the output of its health sector is higher, but also because it does not operate efficiently or its population are generally more prone to illness. Both output and efficiency may be a function of the type of system in place. The overall income of the nation also affects the overall expenditure on healthcare.

3.5.1.2 Is expenditure related to outcomes?[96]

The health of a country's population is both an input to and output of the health sector. This is because the health status of a population reflects

not only the quality of health care in the country, but also its dietary and other socio-economic factors. Countries with higher consumption of alcohol and tobacco, for example, are likely to place a heavier burden on their health sectors than others. Some have argued that differences in health are due almost entirely to differences in socio-economic and demographic factors. It is argued that the amount that can be attributed to the health sector is minimal (Wilkinson, 1996; Navarro, 2000). Clearly, variables such as wealth, health expenditure and technology are highly collinear.

Life expectancy, which has been rising over time, is a commonly used measure of the health status of a population. There is little variation in this indicator across the Member States as shown in Table 3.1 but the US is at the bottom end of the country distribution, in stark contrast to its position in terms expenditure per capita, even if on the basis of life expectancy at age 65 it fares more favourably. Also, the US has considerably higher neonatal mortality rates than the EU (Baily and Garber, 1997) which is likely related to the lack of universal insurance

---

[96] There are a large number of output/outcome indicators provided by the World Health Organisation (WHO).

129

Table 3.1: Life expectancy in the EU and US

	Male life expectancy at birth, years		Female life expectancy at birth, years		Life expectancy at 65 years, male and female	
	1990	2000	1990	2000	1990	2000
Belgium	72.8	74.2‡	79.6	80.8‡	16.9	17.6‡
Denmark	72.3	74.1*	78.0	78.9*	16.2	16.8*
Germany	72.1	75.2	78.6	81.3	16.4	18.1
Greece	74.8	75.8*	79.6	81.0*	17.1	18.0*
Spain	73.4	76.0	80.6	83.0	17.5	19.0
France	73.4	75.2*	81.8	82.8*	18.7	19.2*
Ireland	72.1	74.0	77.7	79.3	15.2	16.5
Italy	73.8	76.8	80.5	83.0	17.3	19.0
Luxembourg	72.2	75.0	78.7	81.9	16.5	18.5
Netherlands	73.9	75.7	80.4	80.8	17.1	17.6
Austria	72.5	75.6	79.1	81.5	16.8	18.4
Portugal	70.5	72.6	77.5	79.7	15.7	16.7
Finland	71.0	74.3	79.1	81.3	16.2	17.9
Sweden	74.9	77.5	80.7	82.3	17.5	18.7
United Kingdom	73.1	75.7	78.7	80.5	16.4	17.7
EU-15	73.1	75.6	79.8	81.7	17.1	18.4
USA	71.8	74.1	78.8	79.5	17.2	18.0
Cyprus	na	75.6	na	80.2	na	17.3
Czech Republic	67.6	71.8	75.5	78.6	13.8	15.8
Estonia	64.7	65.4	75.0	76.3	14.5	15.3
Hungary	65.2	67.6	73.9	76.3	14.0	15.2
Lithuania	66.5	66.8	76.4	77.6	15.7	16.3
Latvia	64.2	64.9	74.6	76.1	14.5	15.3
Malta	73.8	76.0	78.4	80.3	15.7	17.0
Poland	66.6	69.8	75.6	78.1	14.6	15.9
Slovenia	70.0	72.3	78.0	80.1	15.8	17.0
Slovak Republic	66.8	69.3	75.8	77.6	14.4	15.2

Notes: * indicates 1999 data, ‡ indicates 1997 data.

Source: OECD Health Data 2003; WHO European Health for All Database 2004; Health, United States, 2003, National Center for Health Statistics.

coverage amongst the poorer sections of the population and immigrants. Clearly, if the sole interest were in the performance of the providers of health care then the US position is not too bad. But if equity considerations are also given a weight in performance measures then the relevant outcome (life expectancy) show the US in a very poor relative position.

Graph 3.4 plots the relationship between expenditure and life expectancy at age 65. The data suggest that countries that spend more on health per capita record higher life expectancy. However, it is clear that there are two distinct groups, the EU-15 and the new Member States. For EU-25, the correlation coefficient between life expectancy and expenditure is 0.75 and is significant at the 5 % level (although not at the 1 % level) but for EU-15 alone there is no evidence of such relationship.[97] One reason for this is likely the general impact of income on life expectancy. As there may be a positive relationship between GDP and life expectancy, using expenditure as a percentage of GDP, rather than per capita spending, may weaken the relationship between expenditure and life expectancy at 65. For example, Luxembourg and the Slovak Republic both spend a smaller proportion of GDP on health than all other EU countries (except Latvia), but have much different life expectancies – Slovakia one of the lowest and Luxembourg one of the highest. The first panel of the graph shows that this may in part be because the two countries spend much different amounts per capita on healthcare, with the relatively wealthy Luxem-

---

[97] This is also true if health expenditure as percent of GDP is used although the overall relationship is weaker.

bourg spending over three times as much. Clearly, many other factors contribute to life expectancy beyond the health care system (such as wealth, diet and lifestyle) and it is difficult to determine whether there is a significant relationship.

Life expectancy is just one outcome which the health sector seeks to influence. The evidence on the relationship between overall spending and age-standardised death rates (SDR) for ischaemic heart disease, cerebrovascular disease and malignant neoplasms are shown in Graph 3.5.

Unlike life-expectancy at 65, there does appear to be a relationship between overall health expenditure and the SDR for ischaemic heart disease in the

new Member States but not for the EU-15. Within the former, countries with higher health expenditure per capita and GDP tend to have lower SDRs for ischaemic heart disease. Also new Member States with higher health expenditure per capita also tend to have lower SDRs for cerebrovascular disease. There is no evidence of a relationship between expenditure and the SDRs from malignant neoplasms at any level. However in the latter case expenditure on health care is frequently palliative, relieving symptoms, rather than life enhancing so that outcomes should also take account of quality of life.

It is important to note that these indicators relate only to a small subsection of the health sectors' services. One attempt to obtain an overall perform-

Graph 3.4: Life expectancy at 65 years and expenditure on health, in $PPP per capita and as a percentage of GDP

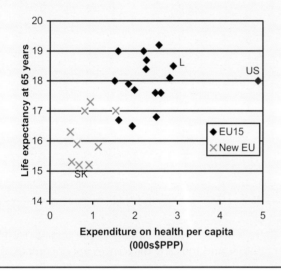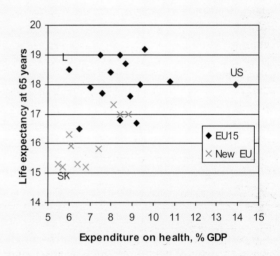

Graph 3.5: Age-standardised death rates (SDR) for major illnesses and expenditure on health

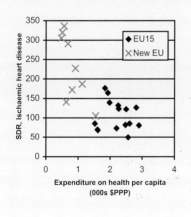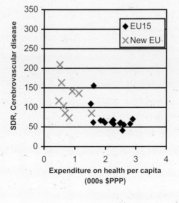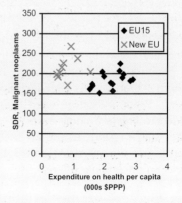

Table 3.4: WHO overall attainment indicators and rankings

	Index	Uncertainty interval	Rank*	Uncertainty interval
Belgium	91.29	90.21 - 92.31	13	7 - 18
Denmark	90.86	89.98 - 91.83	20	13 - 24
Germany	91.28	90.36 - 92.23	14	8 - 20
Greece	90.52	89.70 - 91.32	23	17 - 25
Spain	90.96	90.10 - 91.81	19	12 - 23
France	91.93	91.01 - 92.91	6	3 - 11
Ireland	90.23	89.33 - 91.11	25	20 - 26
Italy	91.35	90.47 - 92.24	11	7 - 21
Luxembourg	92.00	90.97 - 93.00	5	2 - 11
Netherlands	91.62	90.70 - 92.55	8	4 - 15
Austria	91.47	90.52 - 92.44	10	6 - 18
Portugal	87.64	86.31 - 88.86	32	29 - 32
Finland	90.78	89.82 - 91.72	22	13 - 25
Sweden	92.01	91.08 - 92.97	4	2 - 11
UK	91.61	90.87 - 92.34	9	6 - 13
Cyprus	88.58	87.42 - 89.61	28	27 - 31
Czech Republic	87.77	86.90 - 88.68	30	28 - 33
Estonia	81.75	80.18 - 83.14	48	44 - 55
Hungary	83.35	82.19 - 84.39	43	39 - 47
Lithuania	81.04	79.53 - 82.46	52	48 - 59
Latvia	77.96	76.23 - 79.86	67	63 - 88
Malta	87.72	86.89 - 88.54	31	29 - 32
Poland	85.77	85.00 - 86.61	34	33 - 37
Slovenia	87.92	86.49 - 89.20	29	27 - 32
Slovakia	84.68	83.01 - 86.02	39	35 - 43
USA	91.07	89.86 - 92.28	15	7 - 24

* Rankings are relative to all 191 WHO states included

Source: WHO World Health Report 2000

ance measure that accounted for the many – often conflicting – goals of health systems was attempted by the World Health Organisation (WHO). The *World Health Report 2000* (WHR) was a comprehensive and controversial attempt to create a measure of the overall attainment and performance of the health sector. Overall attainment was considered in terms of three goals – not only better health, but also the fairness of financial contribution and the responsiveness of the health system in terms of respecting individual's dignity, autonomy and confidentiality. Given the WHO's belief in the importance of equity issues, distribution of both health and system responsiveness were included as well as their levels. These indicators were then weighted and added to create a single index of 'attainment'. The index and rankings of the EU Member States and the US are presented in Table 3.4, along with the reported uncertainty interval.

The data suggest that, as with the individual outcome indicators, the main difference is between the EU-15 and new Member States. In particular,

there is little to separate many of the original EU-15 countries and that any differences are encompassed by the uncertainty intervals surrounding the data. Therefore, despite the variation in health systems and overall expenditure, there is little evidence that these are reflected even in this broad measure of outcomes. By comparison, the attainment of the US health system is around the middle of the EU-15 countries, but higher than all of the new Member Sates.

The *World Health Report 2000* also considered the efficiency of health provision.[98] While the overall attainment index shown in Table 3.4 provides an absolute measure of achievement, the performance indices, shown in Table 3.5, provide an indication of a country's performance in relation to its expenditure. Performance is considered both in terms of overall health system attainment and level of health. The first panel is based on overall attainment from Table 3.4 relative to expenditure. In the second

[98] Although puzzlingly the WHO called it 'performance' – it has since changed this confusing nomenclature.

Table 3.5: WHO overall performance indices and rankings

	Performance				Health Level (DALE)			
	Index	Uncertainty interval	Rank*	Uncertainty interval	Index	Uncertainty interval	Rank*	Uncertainty interval
Belgium	0.915	0.903 - 0.926	21	18 - 24	0.878	0.860 - 0.894	28	23 - 30
Denmark	0.862	0.848 - 0.874	34	32 - 36	0.785	0.769 - 0.801	65	61 - 72
Germany	0.902	0.890 - 0.914	25	22 - 27	0.836	0.819 - 0.852	41	39 - 47
Greece	0.933	0.921 - 0.945	14	13 - 19	0.936	0.920 - 0.951	11	9 - 13
Spain	0.972	0.959 - 0.985	7	4 - 8	0.968	0.948 - 0.989	6	3 - 8
France	0.994	0.982 - 1.000	1	1 - 5	0.974	0.953 - 0.994	4	2 - 7
Ireland	0.924	0.909 - 0.939	19	14 - 22	0.859	0.840 - 0.870	32	29 - 38
Italy	0.991	0.978 - 1.000	2	1 - 5	0.976	0.957 - 0.994	3	2 - 7
Luxembourg	0.928	0.914 - 0.942	16	13.5 - 21	0.864	0.847 - 0.881	31	27.5 - 35
Netherlands	0.928	0.914 - 0.942	17	14 - 21	0.893	0.875 - 0.911	19	17 - 24
Austria	0.959	0.946 - 0.972	9	7 - 12	0.914	0.896 - 0.931	15	13 - 17
Portugal	0.945	0.931 - 0.958	12	10 - 15	0.929	0.911 - 0.945	13	10 - 14.5
Finland	0.881	0.866 - 0.895	31	27 - 33	0.829	0.812 - 0.844	44	41 - 50
Sweden	0.908	0.893 - 0.921	23	20 - 26	0.890	0.870 - 0.907	21	18 - 26
UK	0.925	0.913 - 0.937	18	16 - 21	0.883	0.866 - 0.900	24	21 - 28
Cyprus	0.906	0.879 - 0.932	24	16 - 30	0.885	0.865 - 0.898	22	19 - 28
Czech Republic	0.805	0.781 - 0.825	48	43 - 54	0.765	0.749 - 0.779	81	73 - 83
Estonia	0.714	0.684 - 0.741	77	68 - 85	0.677	0.657 - 0.694	115	107 - 118.5
Hungary	0.743	0.713 - 0.768	66	59 - 74	0.698	0.682 - 0.714	105	101 - 111
Lithuania	0.722	0.690 - 0.750	73	65 - 82	0.724	0.705 - 0.742	93	89 - 103
Latvia	0.630	0.589 - 0.665	105	94 - 118	0.655	0.631 - 0.677	121	115 - 125
Malta	0.978	0.965 - 0.993	5	3 - 7	0.989	0.968 - 1.000	2	1 - 4
Poland	0.793	0.762 - 0.819	50	45 - 59	0.742	0.723 - 0.758	89	84 - 94
Slovenia	0.838	0.813 - 0.859	38	34 - 46	0.797	0.781 - 0.813	62	55 - 66
Slovakia	0.754	0.721 - 0.781	62	54 - 73	0.742	0.729 - 0.757	88	85 - 92
USA	0.838	0.817 - 0.859	37	35 - 44	0.774	0.758 - 0.789	72	67 - 78

Source: WHO World Health Report 2000

* Rankings are relative to all 191 WHO states included

panel, the level of health is measured by disability-adjusted life expectancy (DALE), defined as 'expectation of life lived in equivalent full health' (WHO World Health Report, 2000). For each country, the performance index for the level of health is calculated as the difference between the observed DALE in that country and that which would exist in the absence of modern health system, divided by the difference between the maximum DALE achievable given health expenditure per capita and the DALE in the absence of a modern health system.[99]

There is greater variation in these indices and rankings and, by implication, differences in EU countries are largely due to inefficiency (although it cannot

---

[99] The *World Health Report 2000* was the first concerted attempt to provide a comprehensive comparative analysis of health systems. However, it has been criticised at many levels in many respects (e.g. Almeida *et al*, 2000; Mulligan, Appleby and Harrison, 2000; Navarro, 2000; Williams, 2000; McKee, 2001; Asada and Hedemann, 2002). Nevertheless, the important issue here is the difficulty in distinguishing the health sectors within the original EU-15 and within the new Member States. Just like the single dimensions of heath we discussed earlier, it is impossible to come to any conclusions about the influence of health systems on performance within the EU beyond the fact that performance appears to be higher in the EU-15 countries than the new Member States.

be ruled out that the DALE calculations are influenced by unmeasurable exogenous influences). On both measures some of the Member States show better than average performance (France, Italy) and others score significantly below average (Denmark, Finland). Nevertheless, as with the overall WHO attainment index, the main difference is between the EU-15 and the new Member States.

3.5.1.3 Why then does expenditure vary?

If differences in expenditure do not lead to differences in health outcomes, how can we explain the substantial differences in health expenditure across countries, and in particular between the EU and the US? One possibility is that this may be due to the different structure of health systems. For instance, the main source of funding could be related to the level of expenditure.

The public sector has a larger role in the health sector in general in EU economies than in the US (Table 3.6). Again there is fairly wide variation within EU

Table 3.6: Public health expenditure as a percentage of total health expenditure

| | Public expenditure as % of total health expenditure | | |
	1980	1990	2001
Belgium	na	na	71.1
Denmark	87.8	82.7	82.4
Germany	78.7	76.2	74.9
Greece	55.6	53.7	56.0
Spain	79.9	78.7	71.4
France	na	76.6	76.0
Ireland	81.6	71.9	76.0
Italy	na	79.3	75.3
Luxembourg	92.8	93.1	87.8
Netherlands	69.4	67.1	63.3
Austria	68.8	73.5	67.9
Portugal	64.3	65.5	69.0
Finland	79.0	80.9	75.6
Sweden	92.5	89.9	85.2
United Kingdom	89.4	83.6	82.2
EU-15	*na*	*77.3*	*75.0*
USA	*41.5*	*39.6*	*44.4*
Cyprus	52.4	40.0	33.4
Czech Republic	96.8	97.4	91.4
Estonia	na	na	77.8
Hungary	na	na	75.1
Lithuania	na	90.0	71.6
Latvia	na	100.0	68.3
Malta	na	na	65.7
Poland	na	91.7	71.1
Slovenia	100.0	100.0	86.7
Slovak Republic	na	na	89.3

Note: 2001 data is not available for Luxembourg, graphs shown here are for 2000; most recent data for Poland is for 1999.

Source: WHO European Health for All Database, 2004 and OECD Health Data 2003, 2nd edition.

economies, with the public sector accounting for over 80 % of total health expenditure in Denmark, Luxembourg, Sweden and the UK in 2001, against less 60 % in Greece. The US stands out as having a far lower public input. Nevertheless, the general trend in EU economies has been to reduce the proportion of total health expenditure accounted for by the state. It is only in Greece and Portugal that the proportion of public health expenditure has increased over the past twenty years, although it has increased in Ireland during the 1990s after falling previously.

As noted previously, a free market in health care may result in over-consumption. This possibility is consistent with the data of Graph 3.6. The Graph suggests a weak relationship between total expenditure on health care and the proportion of this expenditure made by the public sector. The highly market-orientated US health sector is very different with its low levels of state intervention and high total expenditure compared to the EU countries. However, within the EU, this relationship is weaker with the economies with the highest and lowest expenditure on health care (Germany and Latvia, respectively) having similar levels of public involvement in terms of expenditure.

3.5.1.4 Have EU countries been successful in containing costs?

It was noted earlier that rising expenditure on health care is an important concern in all EU countries. Table 3.7 shows the growth in total health expenditure as a percentage of GDP. For the period 1990-2000, this increased by 1.2 percentage points in the US, compared to 1.0 percentage points in the EU-15. In the 1980s, however, growth in the US was much higher than all EU countries for which data were available.[100] The US did not impose limitations on costs to the same extent as other countries did (Cutler, 2002). In contrast in some Member States growth was negative for that time period. Finally, the 1970s was a period where healthcare expenditures grew as a percent of GDP in most countries, with EU growth generally higher than in the US.

---

[100] One exception to this is Ireland, which saw a large fall in spending during the 1980s, but this was after a decade of falling spending.

Graph 3.6: The relationship between public and total health expenditure in 2000

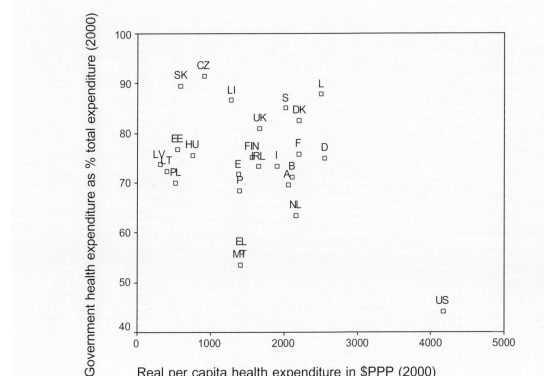

Source: OECD Health Data 2003, 2nd edition.

3.5.2 Microeconomic studies of performance

The difficulties in tying macroeconomic indicators to resource use and a desire to understand the process of technology diffusion and links with supply side constraints has in recent years led to a focus on disease specific microeconomic studies. These studies concentrate on persons diagnosed with specific diseases, and frequently also particular population cohorts thus controlling to some extent for extraneous influences. The analysis is generally based on micro data from administrative records, individual data and surveys. Many studies were multi-disciplinary involving, among others, medical researchers and health economists. This section outlines briefly some main findings from these studies, especially those that include some international comparisons.

The McKinsey Global Institute published one of the first international comparative studies in 1996 (McKinsey, 1996, summarised in Baily and Garber, 1997). This study had two main objectives. The first

was to assess differences in relative productivity at the disease level comparing the US, the UK and Germany. Productivity is defined as the physical inputs used to achieve a given level of health outcomes. The second was to examine the causes of observed differences in terms of variations in diagnostic and treatment approaches and to relate these to each country's system of provision, concentrating on provider incentives and supply constraints.

The project focused on four specific common diseases - diabetes, gallstones, breast cancer and lung cancer - with data from the late 1980s. Inputs were measured as labour (physicians, nurses, technicians and others), supplies (drugs, surgical instruments etc.) and capital, with the weighted sum of inputs used to measure aggregate physical inputs for each disease treatment process in each country. Outcome measures were derived by comparing the expected health outcomes with treatment in each country to the outcomes without treatment.

- The diabetes study was carried out only for the UK and the US. Inputs were measured by

Table 3.7: Growth in total health expenditure as a percentage of GDP

	Growth in total health expenditure as a % of GDP			
	1960-70	1970-80	1980-90	1990-2000
Belgium	na	2.4	1.0	1.3
Denmark	na	na	-0.6	-0.2
Germany	na	2.5	-0.2	2.1
Greece	na	0.5	0.8	2.0
Spain	na	1.8	1.3	0.8
France	na	na	na	0.7
Ireland	1.4	3.3	-2.3	0.3
Italy	na	na	na	0.2
Luxembourg	na	2.3	0.2	-0.5
Netherlands	na	na	0.5	0.6
Austria	1.0	2.3	-0.5	0.9
Portugal	na	3.0	0.6	2.8
Finland	1.8	0.8	1.4	-1.1
Sweden	na	2.1	-0.6	0.2
United Kingdom	0.6	1.1	0.4	1.3
EU-15	na	na	na	1.0
USA	1.9	1.8	3.2	1.2
Cyprus	na	na	1.7	1.4
Czech Republic	na	na	na	2.1
Estonia	na	na	na	na
Hungary	na	na	na	na
Lithuania	na	na	na	2.8
Latvia	na	na	0.4	2.3
Malta	na	na	na	na
Poland	na	na	na	0.7
Slovenia	na	na	1.2	2.4
Slovak Republic	na	na	na	na

Source: WHO European Health for All Database, 2004 and OECD Health Data 2003, 2nd Edition.

labour since this is by far the most important for this disease and outcomes focused on the relative rates of developing selected complications. Baily and Garber showed that diabetics in the UK were less likely to develop complications than those in the US, resulting in superior outcomes in the UK. Since the UK also used some 34 % fewer inputs, productivity was found to be significantly higher in the UK.

- In the case of gallstones, treatment is costly and invariably involves surgery. Here, the UK - US comparisons showed that on a per operation basis the US and the UK had similar outcomes but the US used 71 % fewer inputs leading the authors to conclude that the US had higher average productivity. The authors also conclude that the US was also more productive than Germany.

- In the case of breast cancer, inputs included all labour, supplies and capital employed in the four phases of treatment (screening, assessment, therapeutic and follow-up) and outcomes were five year age-adjusted survival rates following diagnosis. The results show the US and the UK with much greater productivity than Germany but it was not possible to distinguish between the UK and US. Screening had a significant effect on differences in overall input consumption and productive efficiency, with the greater screening in the US coming at a relatively high cost. The main reason behind the poor relative German performance was the much longer length of hospital stays. Finally in the case of lung cancer, the US was found to have higher average productivity followed by Germany with the UK very far behind. The US had shorter hospital stays and greater use of outpatient chemotherapy and better targeting of those most likely to benefit from treatments (using CT scans), with again some small offset from higher staffing levels in the US. Surgical frequency was highest in Germany.

In explaining the differences across countries, the McKinsey report emphasises differences in regulation and competition. They suggest that the per-diem payment system in Germany gave greater incentives to extend hospital stays than the generally fee-for-service payment system in the US although this effect may be overstated. In addition, McKinsey point to the separate control and regulation of primary and hospital care in Germany which hampers substitution of outpatient for inpatient treatments. They also emphasise the lower diffusion of technological changes in Britain and link this again to provider payment systems and lack of competition.

The McKinsey report suggests higher productivity in the US relative to other countries in contrast to many of the findings using macroeconomic indicators. In terms of reconciling these differences McKinsey point to higher incidence of disease in the US, greater US administrative costs, higher neonatal mortality in the US and higher costs of inputs, in particular payments to physicians and drugs. Of these, higher payments to physicians were found to be by far the most important explanation.

Grieve *et al.* (2001) found, on the basis of detailed patient data from European hospitals, a very wide variation in costs and outcomes and in the amount of staff time allocated and the type of staff used across 13 centres covering ten European countries. The evidence suggests some positive relationship between resource use and outcomes. The authors conclude that the way resources are organised, in addition to the level of resources used, may be important in explaining variations in outcomes.

Perhaps one of the most systematic and detailed international comparative study of the performance of health sectors was the OECD age related disease (ARD) project. This focused on a particular age cohort, the elderly, with, to date, results available for three diseases, ischaemic heart disease, breast cancer and stroke; results are summarised in OECD (2003).

Ischaemic Heart Disease (IHD) is the world's leading cause of death and accounts for about 10 % of total expenditures on health. The ARD project (summarised in Moise, 2003b) showed that, while there was little cross-country correlation between intensity of use and outcomes, the US did show lower fatality rates than other countries. The author concludes that the results show some support that supply side constraints have an impact on intensity of treatment and the diffusion of technology. Results for stroke (Moon, 2003) did show a relationship between the use of resources and health outcomes with the important exception of the UK where high fatality rates went hand in hand with high resource use. Confirming the findings of Grieve *et al.* (2001) the ARD project suggests that it is not just how much money is spent but how it is spent that is important. In the case of breast cancer the results suggest that there is no clear association between technological inputs and survival rates, except in the UK where much lower availability of machines was associated with very poor outcomes. Also, state-of-the-art machinery alone is not sufficient to achieve high performance rates; better performance arises from well organised screening programs and following the latest clinical guidelines.

The TECH Global Research Network 2003 study (McClellan and Kessler, 2003) links differences across countries to economic and regulatory incentives. They find that financial and regulatory incentives for technological change differ enormously across countries, providing a potentially useful foundation for careful cross-country comparisons of the diffusion of technology and its consequences. The results suggest that supply side incentives appear to be important determinants of trends in high-tech treatments but are less so for low-tech treatments. Utilisation is likely to be higher in fee-for-service systems than in those where physicians are paid salaries. Macro technology regulation was also found to be a key determinant of technological change.

In summary, the microeconomic studies highlight the difficulties in matching resource use and technological diffusion to outcomes in order to explain why little hard evidence can be gleaned using macroeconomic indicators. In particular these studies suggest much of the observed improvement in health outcomes are likely to fall outside the health care system and that diminishing returns are an important issue in evaluating relative performance. Nevertheless the studies suggest that variations in supply-side incentive systems do have an impact on utilising cost-effective treatments and technology diffusion. Hence, even if it is not possible to precisely quantify performance, changes to the systems of provision are likely to impact on productivity.

3.5.3 Use of inputs

3.5.3.1 Labour input

The labour force is probably the most important resource in any health care system, and its utilisa-tion is certainly a significant determinant of the performance of the health sector. Expenditure on the labour force accounts for the greatest proportion of current spending – estimates suggest that in many countries this is between 60 and 80 % (Buchan, 2000). This section first considers employment trends using national accounts sources and then discusses issues relating to the deployment of labour input in the health care sector.

Trends in employment and total hours worked can be obtained on a reasonably consistent basis from national accounts sources for the combined health and social services sector. Table 3.8, using data in O'Mahony and van Ark (2003), shows labour input, either measured by numbers employed or total hours worked, growing faster in the US than in the EU-15, with the percentage point differences more pronounced in the 1980s than in the decade since 1990. For both the US and the EU-15, growth in hours worked has been higher in the health sector than in the total economy (O'Mahony and van Ark, 2003). Data for selected Member States highlight variation across countries. Thus, both Germany and the Netherlands show considerably larger increases in labour input than do France or the UK.

Trends in aggregate labour input conceal considerably diversity by type of labour employed. Many countries are currently facing a shortage of health professionals, and without an adequate number of staff a country's ability to improve its performance will be impaired. Equally important is that the labour force possesses the necessary skills, particularly in the face of continuing advances in technology and knowledge. It is also crucial to find a suitable balance between different types of workers. Consideration should be given to the roles of health care professionals, as in certain circumstances it may enhance efficiency if use of overqualified and

Table 3.8: Growth in number employed and hours worked in the health and social work sector

	US	EU-15	France	Germany	Netherlands	UK
Growth in total number employed, average % per annum						
1979-1990	3.9	2.7	2.3	3.6	2.8	2.8
1990-1995	3.1	1.7	1.4	3.8	2.4	1.5
1995-2001	1.9	1.7	1.0	2.8	3.2	0.5
Growth in total hours worked, average % per annum						
1979-1990	4.1	2.0	0.6	2.9	1.0	2.4
1990-1995	3.0	1.4	1.3	2.8	1.6	1.8
1995-2001	2.3	1.4	0.3	2.3	2.7	-0.2

Source: O'Mahony and van Ark (2003).

expensive staff is avoided where it is possible for the same tasks to be carried out perfectly adequately by others. While medical professionals are the first group that spring to mind when we think of the health sector workforce, the role of managerial and administrative staff should not be forgotten. Training of non-medical staff is therefore also crucial if the performance of the health system is to be maximised.

Considerable variation exists between countries in terms of the number of health care professionals. Table 3.9 shows the number of physicians per 100,000 population in 1980, 1990 and 2000. The ratio of physicians to the population in those countries with the highest number of doctors is more than double that of the ratio observed in the countries with the fewest. Thus in 2000, the greatest number of physicians per 100,000 population were in Italy (599) and Greece (444) with both Belgium and Lithuania, also having ratios of more than 400 physicians for every 100,000 of the population. This

compares with 223 physicians in Ireland, 218 in Slovenia and 220 in Poland. Recent data on a comparable basis are not available for the UK, but OECD suggest a graph of about 200, placing it among those countries with the fewest physicians (OECD Health Data, 2003). Similarly OECD data for the US puts the number of practising physicians in the middle to low range. The number of physicians has been increasing over time in all EU countries, with the exception of Estonia and Latvia, which have seen some decline between 1990 and 2000, and Lithuania, which has experienced a very slight fall.

A shortage of health care professionals is an issue of concern in many countries. Even in countries where there is no overall shortage of workers, it may be the case that certain rural areas are not well served (Docteur and Oxley, 2003). In other countries there is an oversupply of physicians, generally in the Southern European countries - for example in Spain where oversupply has led to unemployment among this group. While a country may not have an overall

Table 3.9: Physicians per 100,000

	Physicians per 100,000		
	1980	1990	2000
Belgium	249	344	414
Denmark	218	311	345
Germany	n.a.	300	326
Greece	243	338	444
Spain	n.a.	226	324
France	201	305	328
Ireland	131	156	223
Italy	312	462	599
Luxembourg	148	201	249
Netherlands	191	251	319
Austria	165	222	312
Portugal	196	283	318
Finland	174	242	307
Sweden	220	259	304
United Kingdom	140	160	200**
EU-15	216	299	349
USA	n.a.	240**	270**
Cyprus	110	207	259
Czech Republic	226	271	337
Estonia	294	350	322
Hungary	250	280	310*
Lithuania	340	403	401
Latvia	362	412	320
Malta	n.a.	201	265
Poland	n.a.	214	220
Slovenia	177	199	218
Slovak Republic	255	294	323

Source: WHO European Health for All Database.

Notes: * indicates 1999 data, ** OECD estimates.

shortage of physicians, in some countries there is a tendency to have an oversupply of certain specialists while at the same time experiencing a shortage of generalists (Saltman and Figueras, 1997).[101]

The WHO data suggest even greater variation in the number of nurses per capita. Nurses account for a very significant part of the health care labour force. While some countries suffer from a shortage of doctors and others have an oversupply, the lack of nurses is a concern in many countries. Fawcett-Henesy (2000) notes that a shortage of nurses and midwives is a problem for almost all of Western Europe. Nursing is currently underdeveloped in many Central and Eastern European (CEE) countries, and is an issue that needs to be addressed.

In some countries, the increasing emphasis on primary care and the contemporaneous restructuring of the health system has led to an oversupply of specialists with a shortage of general practice physicians. This has been a particular problem for Central and Eastern European countries and needs to be resolved if primary care reforms are to be successful. Changes to training are required to rectify this imbalance, both in the short-term to provide specialists with the necessary skills to work in general practice, but also over the longer term, requiring changes to the teaching curricula of medical schools. Estonia, for example, has introduced a specialist training programme for GPs (Saltman and Figueras, 1997).

As labour accounts for such a large proportion of recurrent expenditure, some countries have attempted to reduce spending on staff in efforts to contain total health expenditure. Indeed, the variation in the number of health care professionals across countries may indicate that there are gains to be made by reducing the number of staff in some countries (Docteur and Oxley, 2003). However, while this may have helped to control spending in the short run, in the longer term difficulties may arise. Firstly, if the number of professionals is reduced, this is likely to increase the workload of those remaining and can have damaging effects on morale and can affect the ability to recruit staff in the future. In both the UK and Denmark, earlier reforms to control spending have meant that the health systems are now currently struggling to meet demand even as financial resources have been increased. Such shortages also give medical profes-

sionals greater bargaining power to increase their wages as strikes in France and Finland have demonstrated.

To boost supply of professionals in the UK in recent years there has been a 60 % increase in the number of medical school places since 1997 (Department of Health, 2004b). A measure to restrain the rising number of professionals has been to restrict the number of doctors allowed to bill public insurers, as in Denmark and the Netherlands, and in Austria professional associations restrict the number of ambulatory care physicians (Docteur and Oxley, 2003). However, some countries have struggled to contain growth in the number of professionals despite such constraints. As noted previously, it is not only the physical number of health care professionals that matters but also that they are appropriately skilled. Implementation of health care reform depends on the availability of appropriately skilled labour and with continuing advances in technology and knowledge, it is increasingly difficult to remain up-to-date and requires that training continues to adapt to changing circumstances. There is also increased emphasis on the development of new skills in the face of changing working environment, such as teamwork and communication skills.

The escalating shortage of nurses has created much concern, and appears to be a global phenomenon. Irwin (2001) reports that the International Council of Nurses (ICN) found nursing shortages across much of Europe. For example, in 2001, the Netherlands had a shortage of 7000 nurses, and the UK a shortage of 22000. Fewer individuals are training to become nurses, and experienced nurses are leaving their profession. Irwin notes that both demand and supply factors have contributed to the nursing shortage. Demand has increased as a result of a greater emphasis on primary care, technological change and an ageing population. Supply has fallen as nursing has decreased in popularity as an occupation. Women, who were traditionally the main recruits, now have a greater variety of career opportunities. There has also been much interest in how nurses, and the appropriate use of their skills, may enhance the cost-effective use of resources. Increasing the autonomy of nurses is part of a wider move concerned with redefining the roles of health professionals. Fawcett-Henesy (2000) notes that nurses are now carrying out some of the duties that would previously have been the responsibility of doctors, while similarly, health care assistants and other professionals are adopting some of the work previously performed by nurses. This trend has been particularly apparent in primary care. Some countries, including the Netherlands, UK and the Scandi-

---

[101] Saltman and Figueras (1997) discuss some of the factors that have resulted in an oversupply of physicians in certain areas of Europe, which include historical and cultural factors and a tendency to substitute labour for capital. They report that medical unemployment has not lessened this problem and suggest that entry to (especially private) medical schools should be monitored.

navian countries have improved opportunities for nursing education and training an measures have been adopted to retain nurses in the profession.

The mobility of nurses has already been the subject of considerable debate. The nursing shortage in the UK led to considerable recruitment from abroad, including Australia, South Africa, the Philippines and Nigeria in addition to recruits from EU countries (Irwin, 2001). Tjadens (2002) reports that, while other European countries have also recruited from abroad, this has generally not been so extensive. There are some concerns regarding recruitment and training costs and subsequent retention rates (Irwin, 2001), as well as ethical questions relating to recruiting nurses from countries that may themselves face shortages.

There are concerns over whether the new Member States can retain sufficient health care professionals to provide the services required in their own country, when it may be unable to compete with other countries in terms of pay and standards of living. Dubois, Nolte and McKee (2004) cite the example of Poland, which has invested heavily in changes to the training of health professionals, particularly nurses, and may now lose these skilled workers to other countries. However, enlargement is unlikely to result in a dramatic surge in general labour migration (European Commission, 2001) and, besides, increased labour mobility will create a need to harmonise training across countries to ensure comparable levels of quality and skills.

A factor that will soon have greater effect on health care professionals is the EU working time directive. Pickersgill (2001) points out that many European health systems will be affected by changes in August 2004, when junior doctors will be restricted to working 58 hours per week, decreasing to 48 hours by 2009. There is also concern that many European countries will be confronted with a loss of a considerable number of professionals as the baby-boom generation retires while the population will be ageing and demand will be increasing as supply falls.

3.5.3.2 Capital input

For selected countries data are available from national accounts, on investment in the health sector (including social services). From these data capital stocks were estimated assuming geometric decay. Buildings represent a significant component of investment in the health sector, equal to about 70 % of total investment in the European countries and about 40 % in the US since 1979. Given the

fact that much of new technology is embodied in equipment investment, capital stocks were estimated separately for structures and equipment.[102]

Table 3.10 presents growth rates of capital stock for selected time periods for the US and four EU Member States. There is large variation across the countries considered but, in general, growth rates in equipment tend to be larger than structures. The US shows high growth rates in equipment capital throughout and higher than in the EU countries other than France before 1995. From the latter date there was a pronounced acceleration of growth of equipment capital in the US not matched in the EU countries. For the total economy since 1979, annual average growth rates of US structures and equipment investment were about 1.8 % and 3.3 %, respectively; in the UK investment was about 2.5 % for both assets and in France 1 % and 4 % for structures and equipment, respectively. Thus it appears that capital growth in the health sector has been rising faster than in the economy as a whole.

Much of the greater US investment is in information and communications technology (ICT). The European countries have also increased their shares of ICT but at lower rates than in the US, mirroring total economy trends presented in O'Mahony and van Ark (2003). O'Mahony and van Ark classify health and social work as a non-ICT intensive service sector, with average ICT use lower than in private (for example, financial and business) services. In terms of high technology capital, increased investment in advanced medical equipment and instruments is likely to be more important in driving equipment investment rates. Unfortunately the national accounts data do not contain sufficiently disaggregated data by asset type to allow examination of trends in medical equipment.

Anell and Barnum (1998) find that differences in the accumulation of capital have occurred for a variety of reasons, including institutional arrangements and geographical factors. Hospitals comprise the greatest part of the health system capital stock. This is partly a result of past investment patterns, but also because the nature of hospital care is more capital intensive compared to other areas such as primary care (Anell and Barnum, 1998). Recent years have seen a reduction in the number of hospital beds per capita across Europe, in Western Europe from the 1980s and in Central and Eastern Europe since the 1990s.

---

[102] Depreciation rates were set at 0.021 for structures and 0.167 for equipment, based on investment by asset type and depreciation rates employed in the US; see Inklaar et al. (2003) for further details on methods to estimate capital stocks and data sources.

Table 3.10: Growth rates of capital stock in the health sector

	US	France	Germany	Netherlands	UK
Growth in real capital stock, % per annum					
Structures					
1979-1990	6.90	1.23	1.58	4.33	4.10
1990-1995	3.34	1.53	3.21	3.64	4.61
1995-2001	4.37	0.64	2.40	2.99	3.34
Equipment					
1979-1990	5.69	8.92	3.29	3.48	5.60
1990-1995	6.67	7.56	6.02	1.15	5.94
1995-2001	9.29	6.33	5.65	3.51	3.29
Real Investment shares, annual average					
Structures (1979-2001)					
	0.39	0.46	0.53	0.71	0.69
Share ICT investment in equipment					
1979-1989	0.116	0.073	na	0.104	0.122
1990-1995	0.198	0.091	na	0.171	0.061
1996-2001	0.337	0.197	na	0.326	0.269

Sources for investment data: US, Bureau of Economic Analysis; France, INSEE; Germany, Statistisches Bundesamt; Netherlands, Statistics Netherlands; UK, Office for National Statistics – see Inklaar et al. (2003) for details.

Note: ICT assets comprise, computing equipment, software and communications. The UK investment statistics do not show computers and communications equipment separately from other tangible equipment so were estimated using data from Input output and supply use tables.

This has partly been the result of reforms to contain costs but advances in technology have also reduced the need for some forms of hospital care. How to account for variations in quality and technology use is, of course, an issue. Technology has reduced the length of stay required for many illnesses and it thus affects the desirable allocation of capital. Anell and Barnum (1998) note that a conflict arises here as changes to the capital stock occur gradually, while advances in technology and knowledge are rapid. This creates difficulties in planning capital investment and in achieving efficient use of resources. In general then, there is little systematic evidence across countries on the utilisation of capital inputs in the health sector.

3.5.3.3 Intermediate input: Pharmaceuticals

Pharmaceuticals are crucial to the performance of the health sector since they influence health outcomes. At the same time, expenditure on pharmaceuticals has been increasing, contributing to the general rise in health spending.

Expenditure on pharmaceuticals has been increasing as a proportion of GDP over the last three decades and accounts for an average of approximately 15 % of total health expenditure in OECD countries (Jacobzone, 2000). Pharmaceutical expenditure generally accounts for a higher proportion of GDP in poorer countries (*ibid*). In 2000, the proportion of total health spending accounted for

by pharmaceuticals and other medical non-durables varied among countries, from 8.7 % in Denmark to 34 % in the Slovak Republic (OECD Health Data, 2003). This compares with a share of 11.9 % in the US. Differences in expenditure may also reflect different patterns of usage. The use of pharmaceuticals differs greatly across Europe. This is particularly true when we consider certain drugs – the consumption of antibiotics in France, for example, is four times higher than in the Netherlands (Maynard, 2003).

Why has expenditure on pharmaceuticals risen? There are many reasons, including the development of expensive new drugs and an ageing population increasing demand for pharmaceuticals (Mossialos, 1998). The higher growth in pharmaceutical spending relative to GDP may also be a consequence of the stronger growth of the pharmaceutical sector compared to the overall economy (Jacobzone, 2000). Another explanation is that countries spending a higher proportion of GDP on health tend to have higher usage of new pharmaceuticals than others.

In the face of pressure to contain health care costs generally, countries have attempted to restrain the increase in pharmaceutical expenditure in order to contain total health spending. Actions have been taken to influence both the demand for and supply of pharmaceuticals. Cost-sharing, which has been widely used, may take various forms including flat-rate payments per prescription, co-payments of a fixed percentage of the cost or a requirement to pay the difference if the patient opts to use a branded drug rather than a cheaper generic alternative. By transferring some of the cost of the medicine to the consumer, this should help to reduce any unnecessary consumption; there is some evidence that co-payments reduce consumption.[103] Reference price systems, where the consumer pays the difference if they request a branded drug when a cheaper generic alternative is available, can also help to reduce expenditure on pharmaceuticals. These have gained in popularity in recent years and the use of generics appears to have increased as a result (Jacobzone, 2000).

Several countries have also introduced prescribing guidelines to encourage the appropriate use of pharmaceuticals. Doctors' prescribing patterns are influenced by the incentives implicit in their reimbursement system. Doctors working in the tax-financed national health systems in Northern Europe tend to be less likely to over-prescribe, for example (Jacobzone, 2000). Prescribing patterns may also be influenced by the pharmaceutical industry itself, which invests heavily in marketing its new products to physicians (Maynard, 2003). On the supply-side, most countries control pharmaceutical prices to some extent. Some countries, such as Italy and the Netherlands have set pharmaceutical prices with reference to prices in other countries (Docteur and Oxley, 2003). It may be the case that such price controls have led to partial convergence of pharmaceutical prices across Europe (Ljungkvist *et al*, 1997; Jacobzone, 2000). Clearly, developing new pharmaceuticals is a lengthy and expensive process and prices must be set so as to reward innovation but also to avoid possible abuse of monopoly power while the drug is under patent. Finally, because consumers will not generally possess the knowledge to assess the safety, quality and effectiveness of medicines and intervention, rectifying this information asymmetry has led to all countries to develop strict pre-marketing rules and the establishment of the European Medicinal Products Evaluation Agency in 1995 (Docteur and Oxley, 2003).[104] Maynard (2003) points out that the aim of this is to promote the efficient allocation of resources, not to reduce overall expenditure. In health systems with strict price controls, industry has tended to concentrate on developing products

where the innovation element is relatively small (Jacobzone, 2000). In this way, the industry may be avoiding strict price regulation, but not contributing greatly to improving treatment.

The pharmaceutical market is different to other parts of health care systems, partly because of its international nature. There is some evidence to suggest that the European pharmaceutical sector has become less competitive in comparison to the US (Gambardella, Orsenigo and Pammolli, 2000). However, there are considerable differences across countries, with the deteriorating competitive position largely the consequence of the performance of the industry in Germany and Italy. In contrast, the pharmaceutical sectors in the UK, Denmark, Sweden and Ireland have performed rather well. Several reasons are responsible for this loss of competitiveness, including that growth in both capital and R&D seems to result in less growth in pharmaceutical sales than in the US; others include the stricter requirements for the testing of pharmaceuticals and the effect of policies to contain health spending. However, others have suggested (GAO, 1994) that reforms to contain costs in some countries do not necessarily lead to a reduction in global R&D, as firms still have the opportunity to earn profits in the international market.

3.5.4 Organisational change

Organisational changes are increasingly being recognised as an important channel through which productivity can be improved and have recently become the focus of considerable research in market sectors (e.g. Bresnahan, Brynjolfsson and Hitt, 2002). The drive to improve efficiency in the health care sector in many EU countries in the 1990s led to a number of organisational changes. This section describes two such sets of changes that have had particular impact in the health sector, decentralisation and increasing patient choice.

Devolution and decentralisation in the health sector

Decentralisation has been a common theme in health care reform across the EU although no Member State has an either completely decentralised or completely centralised system. Decentralisation is a broad concept permitting to classify various reforms under this heading. The European Observatory on Health Care Systems (2000) defines decentralization as '(c)hanging relations within and between a variety of organizational structures/bodies, resulting in the transfer of the authority to plan, make decisions or manage public functions

---

[103] For example, the Rand Health Insurance Experiment (Newhouse, 1993) found that co-payments of 25 % decreased demand by around one quarter.

[104] There is also increasing interest in evaluating the cost-effectiveness of pharmaceuticals, with several countries having introduced new authorities for this purpose, such as the National Institute for Clinical Excellence (NICE) in England and Wales and the Agence nationale pour le développement de l'évaluation médicale (ANDEM) in France. The increasing use of such 'pharmacoeconomic assessment', has been found to be useful for determining the value-for-money of new pharmaceuticals, as well as for aiding reimbursement and pricing decisions (Dickson, Hurst and Jacobzone, 2003).

from the national level to any organization or agency at the sub-national level'.[105]

Various factors have led countries to pursue decentralisation. One is dissatisfaction with centralised systems whose disadvantages include an overly bureaucratic nature and inefficiency, slow reactions to changing needs and circumstances, and few incentives for innovation. Decentralisation in health care is not an isolated issue – it is often part of a much wider political change, as in the new Member States where there has been a move towards much more decentralised systems since the breakdown of the previous regimes.[106]

Intuition suggests that by decentralising decision-making to a lower level, health care should become more responsive to the needs of the actual population.[107] If resources are allocated more appropriately to reflect local circumstances, this may be beneficial for both efficiency and equity.[108] While in theory decentralisation should allow greater responsiveness to the local population, in reality they may not possess this freedom. Wilkin *et al.* (2001) report that, in the UK, primary care groups have been subject to numerous performance targets and directives, leading to tensions between the different levels of management. Decentralisation may also speed up responsiveness to changing circumstances, particularly if communication improves as a result.[109]

The effect of decentralisation on equity is unclear. Decentralisation has the potential to reduce inequity, for example, if it leads to a better geographical distribution of resources. However, if it reduces uniformity in decision making across regions, it may increase inequality. So far, research has not shown any direct relationship between decentralisation and reduction in equity, as there are many other contributory factors.[110] Finally, significant disadvantages of decentralisation are the possibility of fragmentation and duplication of services.

Privatisation has raised particular concerns with regard to equity. Privatisation of financing is much more likely to affect equity than privatisation of service provision, but there is still some dispute.[111] It is possible that privatisation of services increases consumer choice, but equity may be adversely affected, if choice is increased for the wealthy but not for the poor. Privatisation in some countries has also led to problems with cost containment. When delivery is privatised, but funding is provided by the public sector, this can lead to considerable increase in expenditure with greater difficulty in containing costs, as the experience of some county councils in Sweden, where they have chosen to increase private sector involvement in provision (Diderischen, 1999), has shown.

While decentralisation has been a popular component of health care reform, there are considerable differences between countries in their approach reflecting political and social factors that exert considerable influence. Broadly speaking, those countries with NHS style health systems have tended to be more centralised while those with social insurance models have been more decentralised (Hunter *et al.*, 1998). Leys (1999) suggests that differences in culture and particularly expectations will play an important role. He cites Spain and the UK, arguing that the Spanish, who have historically been much more accustomed to variations in health care across regions, will have different expectations with regard to equity than those in the UK where the national health service, with equity as a fundamental principle, has been in place for a longer period of time. Therefore any inequalities arising as a result of decentralising reforms are more likely to be tolerated in Spain.

Despite the potential advantages of decentralisation, evidence has shown that there are particular

---

[105] Decentralisation is commonly classified into four types; de-concentration, devolution, delegation and privatisation (e.g. Hunter *et al.*, 1998; Cheema and Rondinelli, 1983). De-concentration or 'administrative decentralisation' refers to the passing of administrative responsibility to a lower level. Devolution, or 'political decentralisation, involves the transfer of responsibility to a lower political level. Delegation occurs where responsibility for certain tasks are transferred to a lower organisational level (Hunter *et al.*, 1998). The fourth type of decentralisation, privatisation, refers to the shift of public sector functions to the private sector, although commentators acknowledge that this last channel is somewhat different from the previous three. The potential advantages of decentralisation have been widely documented. Indeed, Hunter *et al.* (1998) note that all too often policymakers have been quick to acknowledge the advantages without paying full attention to the associated disadvantages.

[106] Although in some cases the disadvantages have led some countries to reverse direction; for example, in Hungary, the former 19 regional health insurance funds were brought together into one national fund (Mossialos *et al.*, 2002).

[107] This was one of the main factors behind Sweden's decision to devolve responsibility for health care to county councils in 1982 (Diderischen, 1999).

[108] The importance of this is noted by Reverte-Cejudo and Sánchez-Bayle (1999) in a discussion of decentralisation in the Spanish health care system. Spain established a National Health Service system in 1986 with 17 autonomous health services, but currently only seven of the Autonomous Communities have considerable responsibility for health care. There are a number of areas where the system could still be improved, for example there is inequity both within and between regions, excessive regional bureaucracy, and also some duplication.

[109] Enthoven (2000), in an article discussing modernisation of the NHS in the UK, argues that decentralisation allows important local information to be taken account of, that may not be available to central authorities, especially if there are weak information systems.

[110] For example in the highly decentralised health care system in Finland, when costs had to be contained during the economic crisis in the 1990s, certain groups, including alcoholic and psychiatric patients, were more likely to have access to care reduced and expenditure on services contained (Koivusalo, 1999). Similarly in Sweden, Diderischen (1999) argues that while in theory the decentralised system has allowed greater responsiveness to the local population, with adjustments in funding across counties to take account of differences in income and health, recent pressure to contain costs has reduced access to care.

[111] Sweden, for example, has recently banned any further privatisation of hospitals largely as a result of concerns about equity (Burgermeister, 2004). Private companies will no longer be allowed to run hospitals that treat both state insured and privately insured patients, although they will be allowed to treat just privately insured patients.

activities of the health care sector that should not be subject to decentralisation (Hunter *et al.*, 1998). Firstly, general health policy decisions should not be decentralised. Secondly, decisions regarding the future of health sector resources, such as the number of health care professionals to be trained, are probably best made at the national level. Some regulation is also required at a centralised level, although it is crucial to find the appropriate level of effective regulation. Finally, monitoring of population health and of health care services should be carried out centrally.

Improving choice

The UK was the first EU member to launch competition in the public health market, via provider competition, in the 1980s (Le Grand, Mays and Mulligan, 1998). In the early 1990s, Nordic countries, like Sweden, also adopted some aspects of provider competition (Saltman *et al.* 1997 and 1998). In tax-financed countries like the UK and the Nordic countries, the main element of health sector reform was to introduce purchaser-provider splits. In social health insurance countries like Germany and the Netherlands, the focus was on introducing competition on the demand side in the mid 1990s.

The extent of patient choice of health care provider varies considerably among EU countries (see section 3.3). However, most countries have tried to increase consumer choice in recent years, particularly in primary, but also in secondary, care. Reforms have attempted to improve patient choice in order to increase quality and accountability of services, improve patient satisfaction and ultimately raise health outcomes. There is evidence to suggest that improvements in health outcomes have been achieved by patients becoming increasingly involved in managing their own health (Wold-Olsen, 2003). But greater consumer choice and involvement in health care depends on an ability to make choices and as well as on whether consumers wish to actually choose (Rijckmans *et al*, 2002). There is evidence from some Member States that resource allocation and patient satisfaction can be improved through greater consumer choice.[112]

3.6 Conclusions

Given its significant share of aggregate economic activity, and its consequences for the competitiveness and functioning of the overall economy, it is clear that measuring the performance of the health sector is important. While the health economics literature generally emphasises the unique nature of this sector, it is necessary to analyse its performance in a wider framework than is usual for service industries. Its unique features range from its historical development, with its original concentration on equity rather than efficiency goals, to the high degree of government intervention and regulation and to the importance of technological change in understanding both expenditure increases and input use. In addition information asymmetries make it difficult to distinguish between activities and outputs, whereas final outcomes are highly influenced by extraneous influences such as lifestyle changes. Thus performance is difficult to measure as is drawing conclusions on the relative efficiency of systems of provision.[113]

The health sector is characterized by a number of market imperfections, including moral hazard, adverse selection and the presence of externalities. Recently many EU Member States have embarked on reforms in order to promote efficiency and productivity growth. The relationship between technology and performance is critical. While rapid advances in technology are responsible for much of the increase in health expenditure, this must be weighed against the considerable benefits that they produce in terms of improvements in health outcomes.

Both the macro aggregate indicators and micro studies show some weak evidence that increased expenditure on health care leads to better outcomes, with the evidence somewhat stronger in the case of microeconomic disease based studies. Attempts to ascertain the presence of a relationship between health expenditure and outcomes based on macro indicators produced mixed results. The findings of micro studies suggest that health sector productivity may well be affected by changes to the system of health care provision, with supply-side incentives influencing the use of treatments and technology diffusion. However, a significant point to note is that much of the observed improvements in health outcomes appear not to be a result of the health care system itself but to depend on other outside factors which exert a much greater influence. The evidence

---

[112] In Denmark, for example, individuals can choose from two possibilities for primary care and it appears that the' system is performing well (Vallgårda *et al*, 2002). Vallgårda *et al.* (2002) also note that reforms introduced in 1993 that gave patients free choice of hospital have had a relatively small effect, although there is evidence to suggest that this may now be rising. In the UK, patient choice of provider is more limited than in some other European countries. Reforms thought have been introduced to increase responsiveness to patients needs and further reforms are underway to increase patient choice; by December 2005, all patients will be offered a choice of 4-5 different providers when referred to secondary care (Hutton and Enqvist, 2003). Sweden's 1999 reforms increased patient rights, including choice of primary care doctor, provision of more information, choice of treatment where possible and the option to obtain a second opinion. In 2003, the county councils extended choice to other health care providers, accompanied by the introduction of a database which allows patients to view waiting times across hospitals (Hutton and Enqvist, 2003).

[113] A step towards developing a more comprehensive and comparable empirical basis for the analysis of the health sector is the work on the System of Health Accounts undertaken by Eurostat and the Member States.

to date, even from the microeconomic studies, highlights the diversity across countries in outcomes, resource use and adoption of technological changes and hence renders it difficult to draw concrete conclusions. Demand-side incentives, such as cost-sharing, may also influence health system efficiency, although there is little by way of concrete evidence on the impact of such policies.

Currently, many EU countries are engaged in a process of reform with greater emphasis on efficiency targets. Despite the paucity of evidence at the country level, there is general agreement that the rise in expenditures in health care provision world-wide requires more consideration of efficiency than has hitherto been the case. But the pace of reform will be determined by the historical evolution of systems of provision and preferences regarding equity. It is unlikely that there are easy solutions to these issues. In private market services, for example, a common argument is that less competition and excess regulation in the EU may hinder productivity growth (see the review in Mason et al., 2003). To date there is little hard evidence to support this thesis but proponents at least can point to considerably higher productivity in the past decade in the US, probably the most competitive and least regulated industrial economy. In the health care sector, in contrast, the US experience is not consistent with a preference for unfettered competition and deregulation. Although there is a general recognition that providing greater incentives may enhance efficiency, equity considerations reveal the weaknesses in the US health care sector.

On the input side, there appears to be some scope for better use of resources, in particular labour. Thus oversupply of physicians in some EU countries coincide with shortages in others and in many there is also scope to improve the mix between general and specialist physicians and nurses. Better and more co-ordinated training programs may be a policy change that is worth exploring. Expenditure on pharmaceuticals has been rising and therefore subject to numerous cost containment reforms. At the same time, pharmaceuticals contribute enormously to improvements in health outcomes. A balance therefore must be achieved between cost containment and ensuring sufficient incentives for continued innovation. Far less systematic evidence is available to compare the role of capital across countries, in both quantity and quality terms.

Finally, organisational change may play an important role in performance. Reforms under way suggest that each country needs to find the appropriate mix of both decentralisation and centralisation for its individual circumstances. The extent of patient choice varies among EU countries. Many have chosen to increase choice in order to improve health outcomes, as well as the quality of care and patient satisfaction. However, the literature suggests that the success of such reforms is dependent on the information available to individuals. Improving the efficiency of the heath sector, securing benefits from advanced technology at reasonable cost, and ensuring equity and quality of services and products are major challenges facing the EU.

References

Anell, A. and Barnum, H. (1998): 'The allocation of capital and health sector reform', in: Saltman, R.B., Figueras, J. and Sakellarides, C. (eds.), *Critical Challenges for Health Care Reform in Europe*, Buckingham, Open University Press.

Almeida, C., Braveman, P., Gold, M.R., Szwarcwald, C.L., Ribeiro, J.M., Miglionico, A., Millar, J.S., Porto, S., Costa, N.R., Rubio, V.O., Segall, M., Starfield, B., Travessos, C., Uga, A., Valente, J. and Viacava, F. (2000): 'Methodological concerns and recommendations on policy consequences of the World Health Report 2000', The Lancet, 357, pp. 1692-7.

Asada, Y. and Hedemann, T. (2002): 'A problem with the individual approach in the WHO health inequality measurement', International Journal for Equity in Health, 1, pp. 2-6.

Baily, M. and Garber, A. (1997): 'Health care productivity', Brookings Papers on Economic Activity: Microeconomics, pp. 143-202.

Berndt, E. (1997): 'Comment on Health care productivity', Brookings Papers on Economic Activity: Microeconomics, pp. 203-209.

Bloom, D., Canning, D. and Jamison, D. (2004): 'Health, wealth and welfare', Finance and Development, pp. 10-15, March.

Bloom, D., Canning, D. and Malaney, P. (2000): 'Demographic change and economic growth in Asia', Supplement to Population and Development Review, 26, pp. 257-90.

Bresnahan, T., Brynjolfsson, E. and Hitt, L. (2002): 'Information technology, workplace organisation and the demand for skilled labour: firm-level evidence', Quarterly Journal of Economics, 117(1), pp. 339-376.

Buchan, J. (2000): 'Health sector reform and human resources: lessons from the United Kingdom', Health Policy and Planning, 15(3), pp. 319-325.

Buchan, J. (2002): 'Global nursing shortages', British Medical Journal, 324, pp. 751-752.

Burgermeister, J. (2004): 'Sweden bans privatisation of hospitals', British Medical Journal, 328, p. 484.

Busse, R. (2002): 'Health Care Systems in EU Pre-Accession Countries and European Integration', Arbeit und Sozialpolitik.

Cheema, G. and Rondinelli, D. (1983): Decentralisation and Development, Newbury Park, Sage.

Clarke, M. and Islam, S.M.N. (2003): 'Health adjusted GDP (HAGDP) measures of the relationship between economic growth, health outcomes and social welfare', CESIFO Working Paper No. 1002.

Culyer, A. and Simpson, H. (1980): 'Externality models and health: a Rückblick over the last twenty years', Economic Record, 56, pp. 222-230.

Cutler, D. (1997): 'Comment on Health care productivity', Brookings Papers on Economic Activity: Microeconomics, pp. 209-215.

Cutler, D. (2002): 'Equality, efficiency and market fundamentals: the dynamics of international medical care reform', Journal of Economic Literature, pp. 881-906, September.

Cutler, D. and McClellan, M. (2001): 'Is Technological Change in Medicine worth it?', Health Affairs, 20(5), pp. 11-29, September/October.

Department of Health (2004a): 'The NHS explained', (http://www.nhs.uk/thenhsexplained/default.asp).

Department of Health (2004b): 'More doctors in training than ever before', Press release, 8 March 2004.

Department of Health and Children (2001): 'Health Strategy 2001', Department of Health and Children, Ireland, (http://www.doh.ie/hstrat/index.html).

Department of Health and Children (2004): Health Information page, (http://www.doh.ie/ hinfo /index.html).

Dickson, M. and Jacobzone, S. (2003): 'Pharmaceutical Use and Expenditure for Cardiovascular Disease and Stroke: A Study of 12 OECD Countries', OECD Health Working Papers, No. 1.

Dickson, M., Hurst, J. and Jacobzone, S. (2003): 'Survey of Pharmacoeconomic Assessment Activity in Eleven Countries', OECD Health Working Papers, No. 4.

Diderischen, F. (1999): 'Devolution in Swedish health care', British Medical Journal, 318, pp. 1156-1157.

Docteur, E. and Oxley, H. (2003): 'Health-care systems: lessons from the reform experience', OECD Economics Department Working Papers, No. 374, December, OECD, Paris, (http://www.olis.oecd.org/olis/2003doc.nsf/linkto/e co-wkp(2003)28).

Docteur, E., Suppanz, H. and Woo, J. (2003): 'The US Health System: An Assessment and Prospective Directions for Reform', OECD Economics Department Working Papers, No. 350, OECD, Paris.

Dubois, C., Nolte, E. and McKee, M. (2004): 'Human resources for health in Europe', A proposal for a study by the European Observatory on Health Care Systems, (http://www.who.dk/ observatory/ Studies/20031111_1).

Enthoven, A.C. (2000): 'Modernising the NHS: A promising start, but fundamental reform is needed', British Medical Journal, 320, pp. 1329-1331.

European Commission (2001): Information Note: 'The free movement of workers in the context of enlargement', Brussels, European Commission, 6 March.

European Observatory on Health Care Systems (1996): 'Health Care Systems in Transition: Greece'.

European Observatory on Health Care Systems (1999): 'Health Care Systems in Transition: Luxembourg'.

European Observatory on Health Care Systems (1999): 'Health Care Systems in Transition: Portugal'.

European Observatory on Health Care Systems (1999): 'Health Care Systems in Transition: United Kingdom of Great Britain and Northern Ireland'.

European Observatory on Health Care Systems (1999): 'Health Care Systems in Transition: Hungary'.

European Observatory on Health Care Systems (1999): 'Health Care Systems in Transition: Poland'.

European Observatory on Health Care Systems (2000): Care Systems in Transition (HiT)-template, Copenhagen, WHO Regional Office for Europe, cited in European Observatory on Health Care Systems Glossary (see above).

European Observatory on Health Care Systems (2000): 'Health Care Systems in Transition: Belgium'.

European Observatory on Health Care Systems (2000): 'Health Care Systems in Transition: Germany'.

European Observatory on Health Care Systems (2000): 'Health Care Systems in Transition: Spain'.

European Observatory on Health Care Systems (2000): 'Health Care Systems in Transition: Czech Republic'.

European Observatory on Health Care Systems (2000): 'Health Care Systems in Transition: Estonia'.

European Observatory on Health Care Systems (2000): 'Health Care Systems in Transition: Lithuania'.

European Observatory on Health Care Systems (2000): 'Health Care Systems in Transition: Slovak Republic'.

European Observatory on Health Care Systems (2001): 'Health Care Systems in Transition: Austria'.

European Observatory on Health Care Systems (2001): 'Health Care Systems in Transition: Denmark'.

European Observatory on Health Care Systems (2001): 'Health Care Systems in Transition: Finland'.

European Observatory on Health Care Systems (2001): 'Health Care Systems in Transition: Italy'.

European Observatory on Health Care Systems (2001): 'Health Care Systems in Transition: Sweden'.

European Observatory on Health Care Systems (2001): 'Health Care Systems in Transition: Latvia'.

European Observatory on Health Care Systems (2002): 'Health Care Systems in Transition: Slovenia'.

European Observatory on Health Care Systems (2002): 'Health care systems in eight countries: trends and challenges', Dixon, A. and Mossialos, E (eds.).

European Observatory on Health Care Systems (2004): The Observatory's Health Systems Glossary, (http://www.who.dk/observatory/Glossary/Toppage).

Fawcett-Henesy, A. (2000): 'Nursing in the WHO European Region in the 21st Century', Eurohealth, 6(5), pp. 29-31, Winter 2000/2001.

Gambardella, A., Orsenigo, L. and Pammolli, F. (2000): 'Global competitiveness in pharmaceuticals. A European Perspective', report prepared for the Directorate General Enterprise of the European Commission.

Gelijins, A. and Rosenberg, N. (1994): 'The dynamics of technological change in medicine', Health Affairs, 13, pp. 28-46, Summer.

General Accounting Office (1994): *Companies typically charge more in the United States than in the United Kingdom*, GAO/HEHS 94-29.

General Accounting Office (1995): *Health insurance portability: reform could ensure continued coverage for up to 25 million Americans*, Washington, GAO.

Gerdtham, U.-G. and Jönsson, B., (2000): 'International Comparisons of Health Expenditure', in: Culyer, A.J. and Newhouse, J.P. (eds.), *Handbook of Health Economics*, 1a, chapter 1, pp. 11-53, Amsterdam, North Holland.

Gesellschaft für Versicherungswissenschaft und -gestaltung e.V. (GVG) (2003): 'Study on the Social Protection Systems in the 13 Applicant Countries: Cyprus', Country Study, prepared for the European Commission, (http://europa.eu.int/comm/employ-ment_social/soc-prot/social/cyprus_final.pdf).

Gesellschaft für Versicherungswissenschaft und -gestaltung e.V. (GVG) (2003): 'Study on the Social Protection Systems in the 13 Applicant Countries: Czech Republic', Country Study, prepared for the European Commission, (http://europa.eu.int/ comm/employ-ment_social/soc-prot/social /czech_ republic _final.pdf).

Gesellschaft für Versicherungswissenschaft und -gestaltung e.V. (GVG) (2003): 'Study on the Social Protection Systems in the 13 Applicant Countries: Estonia', Country Study, prepared for the European Commission, (http://europa.eu.int/comm/employ-ment_social/soc-prot/social/estonia_final.pdf).

Gesellschaft für Versicherungswissenschaft und -gestaltung e.V. (GVG) (2003): 'Study on the Social Protection Systems in the 13 Applicant Countries: Hungary', Country Study, prepared for the European Commission, (http://europa.eu.int/comm/employment_social/soc-prot/social/hungary_final.pdf).

Gesellschaft für Versicherungswissenschaft und -gestaltung e.V. (GVG) (2003): 'Study on the Social Protection Systems in the 13 Applicant Countries: Latvia', Country Study, prepared for the European Commission, (http://europa.eu.int/comm/employment_social/soc-prot/social/latvia_final.pdf).

Gesellschaft für Versicherungswissenschaft und -gestaltung e.V. (GVG) (2003): 'Study on the Social Protection Systems in the 13 Applicant Countries: Lithuania', Country Study, prepared for the European Commission, (http://europa.eu.int/ comm/ employment_social/soc-prot/social/lithuania_final.pdf).

Gesellschaft für Versicherungswissenschaft und -gestaltung e.V. (GVG) (2003): 'Study on the Social Protection Systems in the 13 Applicant Countries: Malta', Country Study, prepared for the European Commission, (http://europa.eu.int/comm/employment_social/soc-prot/social/malta_final.pdf).

Gesellschaft für Versicherungswissenschaft und -gestaltung e.V. (GVG) (2003): 'Study on the Social Protection Systems in the 13 Applicant Countries: Poland', Country Study, prepared for the European Commission, (http://europa.eu.int/comm/employment_social/soc-prot/social/poland_final.pdf).

Gesellschaft für Versicherungswissenschaft und -gestaltung e.V. (GVG) (2003): 'Study on the Social Protection Systems in the 13 Applicant Countries: Slovak Republic', Country Study, prepared for the European Commission, (http://europa. eu.int/ comm/employment_social/soc-prot/social/slovak_republic_final.pdf).

Gesellschaft für Versicherungswissenschaft und -gestaltung e.V. (GVG) (2003): 'Study on the Social Protection Systems in the 13 Applicant Countries: Slovenia', Country Study, prepared for the European Commission, (http://europa.eu.int/comm/employment_social/soc-prot/social/slovenia_final.pdf).

Girouard, N. and Imai, Y. (2000): 'The health care system in Poland', OECD Economics Department Working Papers, No. 257.

Glied, S. (2000): 'Managed Care', in: Culyer, A.J. and Newhouse, J.P. (eds.), Handbook of Health Economics, pp. 707-53, Amsterdam, North Holland.

Grieve, R., Hutton, J., Bhalla, A., Rastenytë, D., Ryglewicz, D., Sarti, C., Lamassa, M., Giroud, M., Dundas, R. and Wolfe, C.D.A., on behalf of the Biomed II European Study of Stroke Care (2001): 'A Comparison of the Costs and Survival of Hospital-Admitted Stroke Patients Across Europe', Stroke, 32, pp. 1684-1691.

Grossman, M. (1972a): 'On the concept of health capital and the demand for health', Journal of Political Economy, 80, pp. 223-55.

Grossman, M. (1972b): The Demand for Health: A Theoretical and Empirical Investigation, Columbia University Press, New York.

Grossman, M. (2000): 'The Human Capital Model', in: Culyer, A.J. and Newhouse, J.P. (eds.), Handbook of Health Economics, 1b, chapter 34, pp. 347-408, Amsterdam, North Holland.

Gruber, J. (1998): 'Health Insurance and the Labor Market,' NBER Working Paper No. 6762, October.

Hellenic Republic, Ministry of Health and Welfare, 'Health, health care and welfare in Greece', edited by Sissouras, A. and Souliotis, K. (http:// www. ypyp.gr/EN/health/HEALTH.pdf).

Holtz-Eakin, D. (1994): 'Health Insurance Provision and Labor Market Efficiency in the United States and Germany', in: Blank, R. and Freeman, R. (eds.), Social Protection Versus Economic Flexibility: Is There a Tradeoff?, Chicago, University of Chicago Press.

Hunter, D.J., Vienonen, M. and Wlodarczyk, W.C. (1998): 'Optimal balance of centralized and decentralized management', in: Saltman, R.B., Figueras, J. and Sakellarides, C. (eds.), Critical Challenges for Health Care Reform in Europe, Buckingham, Open University Press.

Hutton, J. and Engqvist, L. (2003): 'Making publicly funded health services more responsive', Eurohealth, 9(3), Autumn.

Imai, Y., Jacobzone, S. and Lenain, P. (2000): 'The changing health system in France', OECD Economics Department Working Paper, No. 269.

Inklaar, R., Stokes, L., Stuivenwold, E., Timmer, M. and Ypma, G. (2003): 'Data Sources and Methodology', in: O'Mahony, M. and van Ark, B. (eds.), EU *productivity and competitiveness: a sectoral perspective. Can Europe resume the catching-up process?*, European Commission, Brussels.

Irwin, J. (2001): 'Migration patterns of nurses in the EU', Eurohealth, 7(4), pp. 13-15, Autumn.

Jacobzone, S. (2000): 'Pharmaceutical policies in OECD countries: reconciling social and industrial goals', OECD, Labour Market and Social Policy - Occasional Papers, No. 40.

Jakubowski, E. and Busse, R. (1998): 'Health care systems in the EU. A comparative study', Chambers, G.R. (ed.), Public Health and Consumer Protection Series SACO 101, European Parliament, Luxembourg.

Jamison, D., Lau, L. and Wang, J. (2004): 'Health's contribution to economic growth in an environment of partially endogenous technical progress', Working Paper No. 10, Disease Control Priorities Project, Bethesda, Maryland: Fogarty International Center, National Institutes of Health. Forthcoming in: Lopez-Casasnovas, G., Rivera, B. and Currais, L. (eds.), *Health and Economic Growth: Findings and Policy Implications*, Cambridge, MA, MIT Press.

Jasiutowicz, K.P. (2000): 'Health Care Reform in Poland 1999', (http://republika. pl/kpjas/en /basics.html).

Jones, C. (2002): 'Why have health expenditures as a share of GDP risen so much?', National Bureau of Economic Research Working Papers, No. 9325.

Koivusalo, M. (1999): 'Decentralisation and equity of healthcare provision in Finland', British Medical Journal, 318, pp. 1198-1200.

Le Grand, J., Mays, N. and Mulligan, J. (eds.) (1998): *Learning from the internal market: a review of the evidence*, London, Kings Fund.

Leys, C. (1999): 'The NHS after devolution', British Medical Journal, 318, pp. 1155-1156.

Ljungkvist, M.O., Andersson, D. and Gunnarson, B. (1997): 'Cost and utilisation of Pharmaceuticals in Sweden', Health Policy, 41, S55-S69.

MacLehose, L. and McKee, M. (2002): 'Gateway to the European Union: Health and EU enlargement', Eurohealth, 8(4), Special Issue, Autumn.

Marshall, M.N., Shekelle, P.G., Leatherman S. and Brook R.H.(2000): 'The public release of perform-ance data: what do we expect to gain? A review of the evidence', Journal of the American Medical Association, 283(14), pp. 1866-1874, April 12.

Mason, G., O'Mahony, M. and van Ark, B. (2003): 'The Policy Framework: Does the EU need a Productivity Agenda', in: O'Mahony, M. and van Ark, B. (eds.), *EU productivity and competitiveness: a sectoral perspective. Can Europe resume the catching-up process?*, European Commission.

Maynard, A. (2003): 'Drug dealing and drug dependency', Eurohealth, 8(5), pp. 8-10, Winter 2002/2003.

Maynard, A. and Bloor, K. (1998): 'Managed care: palliative or panacea', Occasional Papers in Health Economics, No. 8, London, Nuffield Trust.

Maynard, A. and Dixon, A. (2002): 'Private health insurance and medical savings accounts: theory and experience', in: Mossialos, E., Dixon, A., Figueras, J. and Kutzin, J., *Funding health care: options for Europe*, European Observatory on Health Care Systems Series, Buckingham, Open University Press.

McClellan, M.B. and Kessler, D.P. (2003): 'Introduction: a global analysis of technological change in health care, with a focus on heart attacks', in: McClellan, M.B. and Kessler, D.P. (eds.), *Technological change in health care. A global analysis of heart attack*, chapter 1, University of Michigan Press.

McClellan, M.B. and Kessler, D.P. (eds.) (2003): *Technological change in health care. A global analysis of heart attack*, University of Michigan Press.

McKee, M. (2001): 'Measuring the efficiency of health systems', British Medical Journal, 323, pp. 295-296.

McKinsey Global Institute and the McKinsey Health Care Practice (1996): 'Health Care Productivity', Los Angeles, McKinsey and Co. Inc. summarised in: Baily, M. and Garber, A. (1997), Health care productivity, Brookings Papers on Economic Activity: Microeconomics, pp. 143-202.

Ministry of Health (2004): 'The health care system in Malta', last edited 21 January 2004, (http://www.gov.mt/frame.asp?l=2&url=http://www.health.gov.mt).

Moise, P. (2003a): 'The technology-health expenditure link. A perspective from the Ageing-Related

Diseases Study', in: *A Disease-based comparison of health systems. What is best and at what cost?*, chapter 12, OECD, Paris.

Moise, P. (2003b): 'The heart of the health care system: summary of the ischaemic heart disease part of the OECD Ageing-related Diseases study', in: *A Disease-based comparison of health systems. What is best and at what cost?*, chapter 2, OECD, Paris.

Moon, L. (2003): 'Stroke Treatment and Care: A Comparison of Approaches in OECD Countries', in: *A Disease-based comparison of health systems. What is best and at what cost?*, chapter 3, OECD, Paris.

Mossialos, E. (1998): 'Regulating Expenditure on Medicines in European Union Countries', in: Saltman, R.B., Figueras, J. and Sakellarides, C. (eds.), *Critical Challenges for Health Care Reform in Europe*, Buckingham, Open University Press.

Mossialos, E. and Dixon, A. (2002): 'Funding health care: an introduction', in: Mossialos, E., Dixon, A., Figueras, J. and Kutzin, J. (2002), *Funding health care: options for Europe*, European Observatory on Health Care Systems Series, Buckingham, Open University Press.

Mossialos, E., Dixon, A., Figueras, J. and Kutzin, J. (eds) (2002): *Funding health care: options for Europe*, European Observatory on Health Care Systems Series, Buckingham, Open University Press.

Mossialos, E. and Le Grand, J. (1999): *Health Care and Cost Containment in the European Union*, Aldershot, Aldgate, 1999.

Mulligan, J., Appleby, J. and Harrison, A., (2000): 'Measuring the performance of health systems', British Medical Journal, 321, pp. 191-192.

Murthy, A. and Mossialos, E. (2003): 'Informal payments in EU Accession Countries', Euro Observer, 5(2), European Observatory on Health Care Systems.

National Center for Health Statistics (2003): *Health, United States, 2003*, Department of Health and Human Services, Center for Disease Control and Prevention, Hyattsville, Maryland.

Navarro, V. (2000): 'Assessment of the World Health Report 2000', The Lancet, 356, pp. 1598-1601.

Newhouse, J.P. (1992): 'Medical care costs: how much welfare loss?', Journal of Economic Perspectives, 6, pp. 3-21.

Newhouse, J. (1993): 'Free for All? Lessons from the RAND Health Insurance Experiment', The Insurance Experiment Group Coauthors, Harvard University Press.

OECD (1992): 'The Reform of Health Care Systems: A Review of Seven OECD countries', OECD, Paris.

OECD (1994): 'The Reform of Health Care Systems: A Review of Seventeen OECD countries', OECD, Paris.

OECD (1995b): 'New directions in health policy', Health Policy Studies, No. 7, OECD, Paris.

OECD (2003): *OECD Health Data 2003*, OECD, Paris.

OECD (2003): *A Disease-based comparison of health systems. What is best and at what cost?*, OECD, Paris.

O'Mahony, M. and Van Ark, B. (2003): *EU Productivity and Competitiveness: An Industry Perspective. Can Europe Resume the Catching-up Process?*, European Commission.

O'Mahony, M. and Stevens, P. (2002): 'Measuring performance in the provision of public services: A review', mimeo, National Institute of Economic and Social Research, London.

Palu, T. and Kadakmaa, R. (2001): 'Estonian hospital sector in transition', Eurohealth, 7(3), pp. 61-64.

Pickersgill, T. (2001): 'The European working time directive for doctors in training', British Medical Journal, 323, p. 1266.

Pritchard, C. (2002): 'The social and economic impact of emerging health technologies: mechanisms for diffusion/uptake of technology and evidence-based planning', DSTI(2002)1/ANN1.

Republic of Cyprus (2003), 'About Cyprus', (http://www.cyprus.gov.cy/cyphome/govhome.nsf/0/36037CA698754C7AC2256B8300340FD0?OpenDocument&languageNo=1)

Reverte-Cejudo, D. and Sánchez-Bayle, M. (1999): 'Devolving health services to Spain's autonomous regions', British Medical Journal, 318, pp. 1204-1205.

Riesberg, A. and Busse, R. (2003): 'Cost-shifting (and modernisation) in German health care', Euro Observer, 5(4), European Observatory on Health Care Systems.

Rijckmans, M., Garretsen, H., van de Goor, I. and Bongers, I. (2002): 'Demand-orientation and demand-driven care: conceptual confusion in health care', Eurohealth, 8(5), pp. 33-35, Winter 2002/2003.

Royal College of General Practitioners (2002): 'General Practice in the UK', RCGP Information Sheet, No. 4, June.

Saltman, R.B. and Figueras, J. (1997): European health care reforms: analysis of current strategies, WHO Regional Publications, European Series No. 72, Copenhagen: WHO Regional Office for Europe.

Saltman, R.B., Figueras, J. and Sakellarides, C. (eds.) (1998): Critical Challenges for Health Care Reform in Europe, Buckingham, Open University Press.

Schaapman, M. (2003): 'Debate over healthcare system reform', Hugo Sinzheimer Institute, Faculty of Law, University of Amsterdam, April. (http://www.eiro.eurofound.eu.int/2003/03/feature/nl0303103f.html).

Siu, A.L., Sonnenberg, F., Manning, W.A., Goldberg, G.A., Bloomfield, E.S., Newhouse, J.P. and Brook, R.H. (1986): 'Inappropriate use of hospitals in a randomized trial of health insurance plans', New England Journal of Medicine, 334(10), pp. 635-641.

Technological Change in Health Care (TECH) Research network (2001): 'Technological Change Around the World: Evidence from Heart Attack Care', Health Affairs, 20(3), May/June.

Tjadens, F. (2002): 'Health care shortages: where globalisation, nurses and migration meet', Eurohealth, 8(3), pp. 33-35, Summer.

Tunstall-Pedoe, H., Vanuzzo, D., Hobbs, M., Mähönen, M., Cepaitis, Z., Kuulasmaa, K. and Keil, U. (2000): 'Estimation of contribution of changes in coronary care to improving survival, event rates, and coronary heart disease mortality across the WHO MONICA Project populations', The Lancet, 355, iss. 9205, pp. 688-700.

Tunstall-Pedoe, H., Kuulasmaa, K., Mähönen, M., Tolonen, H., Ruokokoski, E. and Amouyel, P. (1999): 'Contribution of trends in survival and coronary-event rates to changes in coronary heart disease mortality: 10-year results from 37 WHO MONICA Project populations', The Lancet, 353, iss. 9164, pp. 1547-57.

Vallgårda, S., Thomson, S., Krasnik, A. and Vraengbaek, K. (2002): 'Denmark', in: Dixon, A. and Mossialos, E. (eds.), Health care systems in eight countries: trends and challenges, European Observatory on Health Care Systems.

Weisbrod, B.A. (1991): 'The health care quadrilemma. An essay on technological change, insurance, quality of care, and cost containment', Journal of Economic Perspectives, 29, pp. 523-52.

Wilkin, D., Gillam, S. and Smith, K. (2001): 'Primary care groups: Tackling organisational change in the new NHS', British Medical Journal, 322, pp. 1464-1467.

Wilkinson, R. (1996): Unhealthy societies, London: Routledge.

Williams, A. (2000): 'Science or Marketing at WHO? A Commentary on 'World Health 2000', Health Economics, 10(2), pp. 93-100.

Wold-Olsen, P. (2003): 'The customer revolution: the pharmaceutical industry and direct communication to patients and the public', Eurohealth, 8(5), pp. 11-13.

World Health Organisation (2000): 'The World Health Report 2000. Health Systems: Improving Performance'.

World Health Organization (2000): 'Highlights on health in Hungary', WHO Regional Office for Europe, prepared for European Commission. (http://europa.eu.int/comm/health/ph_projects/1999/monitoring/hungary_en.pdf).

World Health Organization (2001): 'Highlights on health in Czech Republic', WHO Regional Office for Europe, prepared for European Commission. (http://europa.eu.int/comm/health/ph_projects/1999/monitoring/czech_republic_en.pdf).

World Health Organization (2001): 'Highlights on health in Estonia', WHO Regional Office for Europe, prepared for European Commission. (http://europa.eu.int/comm/health/ph_projects/1999/monitoring/estonia_en.pdf).

World Health Organization (2001): 'Highlights on health in Latvia', WHO Regional Office for Europe, prepared for European Commission. (http://europa.eu.int/comm/health/ph_projects/1999/monitoring/latvia_en.pdf).

World Health Organization (2001): 'Highlights on health in Lithuania', WHO Regional Office for Europe, prepared for European Commission. (http://europa.eu.int/comm/health/ph_projects/1999/monitoring/lithuania_en.pdf).

World Health Organization (2001): 'Highlights on health in Poland', WHO Regional Office for Europe, prepared for European Commission. (http://europa.eu.int/comm/health/ph_projects/1999/monitoring/poland_en.pdf).

World Health Organization (2001): 'Highlights on health in Slovakia', WHO Regional Office for Europe, prepared for European Commission. (http://europa.eu.int/comm/health/ph_projects/1999/monitoring/slovakia_en.pdf).

World Health Organization (2001): 'Highlights on health in Slovenia', WHO Regional Office for Europe, prepared for European Commission. (http:// europa.eu.int/comm/health/ph_projects/1999/monitoring/slovenia_en.pdf).

World Health Organisation (2003): WHO Mortality Database.

World Health Organisation (2004): European Health for All Database, WHO Regional Office for Europe.

Zweifel, P. and Manning, W.G. (2000): 'Moral Hazard and Consumer Incentives in Health Care', in Culyer, A.J. and Newhouse, J.P (eds.), *Handbook of Health Economics*, vol. 1b, chapter 8, pp. 409-60, Amsterdam, North Holland.

Chapter 4:
The European Automotive Industry: Competitiveness, Challenges, and Future Strategies

4.1 Introduction

The purpose of this Chapter is to present an overview of the European automotive industry and the sources of its competitiveness. The analysis of competitiveness in this Chapter focuses on the ability to defend and/or to gain market shares in open, international markets by relying on price and/or the quality of goods. This ability is affected by a wide range of factors and conditions ranging from production costs to technological and organisational innovation, from the regulatory framework to macroeconomic developments. In view of this, the Chapter compares a wide set of indicators internationally and assesses their development over time.

The Chapter is organized as follows: the industry's economic importance, structure and major economic actors are discussed in Section 2. Section 3 focuses on market performance. The international markets are explored by looking at the terms of trade and foreign direct investment. Moreover, a more detailed review of the developments in China and in the Russian Federation is provided. Section 3 examines the characteristics of the European home market as well as the consequences of enlargement. Section 4 discusses labour costs and productivity, R&D and innovation patterns and trends. Section 5 focuses on regulatory issues. In Section 6, an analysis of strengths, weaknesses, opportunities and threats (SWOT) draws together the possible implications of the various elements identified in the previous sections. Section 7 concludes.

4.2 The European automotive industry in a global context

This Section describes the European automotive industry by reviewing industry specific indicators such as value added and employment as well as capital stock, investment and R&D. The importance of the industry is illustrated by looking at its share in total manufacturing, as well as by comparisons across different economic regions and over time. The industry is divided into car, truck and bus segments. The key indicator is output measured in terms of production units. The section also includes a description of the supplier industry and its role for manufacturers. The discussion singles out the restructuring and consolidation process among manufacturers and suppliers and, in particular, how technology shapes the value chain. Finally, capacity utilisation issues are discussed in some detail.

4.2.1 Economic importance

The automotive industry is one of Europe's major industries. It contributes about 6 % to total European manufacturing employment and 7 % to total manufacturing output. In the EU-15, US and Japan, the automotive industry accounts for less than two percent of GDP and provides less than 1.5 percent of total employment. The importance of the automotive industry derives, to a large extent, from its linkages within the domestic and international economy. There is evidence that domestic upstream inputs into the production of the automotive industry amount to up to two times the volume of value added in the automotive industry itself.

The automotive industry in the EU-15 is highly concentrated, with Germany alone accounting for close to half of total value added. In addition to Germany, also Sweden, Germany and France, as well as the Czech Republic, Slovakia and Hungary show a specialisation in auto manufacturing.

While the automotive industry is not a high-tech industry, it is a major driver of new technologies and the diffusion of innovations throughout the economy. Almost 20 % of all R&D in manufacturing is undertaken by car manufacturers. Its close links with many other manufacturing sectors (such as chemicals, plastics, electrical and electronic parts, etc.) contribute to the rapid diffusion of new technologies. Moreover, the industry is an important demand source for innovations from other industries, including high-tech sectors such as ICT.

Finally, motor vehicles are one of the most important consumer goods in terms of total household expenditures. As the largest durable consumer good in terms of expenses (next to housing), demand for motor vehicles is highly correlated with the general business cycle.

4.2.1.1 Value added

The automotive industry contributes about 7 % to total manufacturing output in Europe. Total value added produced in the motor vehicles industry in the EU-15 in 2002 was roughly the same as in the US, some € 114 billion. The value added in the production of motor vehicles in Japan was some 35 % lower, € 74 billion – see Table 4.1.

Within the EU, the production of motor vehicles is rather concentrated in a few countries. The largest producers are Germany (which accounts for 45 % of total EU-15 value added in motor vehicles production), France (17 %), the United Kingdom (11 %), Italy (7 %), Spain (7 %) and Sweden (6 %). Together, these six countries account for about 93 % of motor vehicle production within the EU-15.

The share of motor vehicles in total manufacturing value added has been stable since 1991 in Japan and the EU-15, but has increased significantly in the US.[114] In 1991, the share was about 8 % in Japan (9 % in 2000), 4 % in the US (8 % in 2000), and 6 % in the EU-15 (7 %). Within the EU, motor vehicles production is most prominent in terms of its

---

[114] Source: OECD/STAN data.

share in total manufacturing in Sweden (15 % of total manufacturing value added in 2002), Germany (13 %), France (10 %), Spain (7 %), Belgium (7 %), Austria (6 %), UK (5 %) and Italy (4 %).

In the new Member States, the size of the automotive industry in the Czech Republic, Hungary and Poland, and possibly Slovakia, is similar to that of Austria and the Netherlands, and they rank in the lower middle field of European automobile producers. The other new Member States belong to the group of minor producers of parts, as do Denmark, Finland, Greece and Ireland.

Although the automotive production of the new Member States occupies rather small a share in the overall European production, at national level this industry is a major driver of the economy in those new Member States that are specialised in it. In 2001, the share of the automotive industry in total manufacturing value added reached 10.9 % in the Czech Republic, 10.1 % in Hungary, 8.2 % in Slovakia and 4.5 % in Poland. Due to the many assembly plants, the value added shares of the automotive industry in the new Member States are typically lower than their production shares.

4.2.1.2 Employment

In 2002, the motor vehicle industry employed 1.91 million workers in the EU-15, 1.15 million in the US, and 0.65 million in Japan (Table 4.2). The past years have been difficult for the industry, where employment declined by about 12 % in the US, 2 % in EU-15 and 5 % in Japan between 2000 and 2002.

Data on value added and employment suggest much higher labour productivity levels in the Japan and the US than in the EU. Recent trends indicate a further widening of EU's productivity gap in the auto industries since the turn of the millennium.

Table 4.1: Value added in the production of motor vehicles in EU, US and Japan (current exchange rates)

		2000	2001	2002
EU-15	€ million	117,154	118,156	114,170
US	USD million	120,400	109,334	120,800
	€/USD	1.086	1.118	1.062
	€ million	110,866	97,794	113,748
Japan	Yen billion	8,129	8,753	9,254
	1000JPY/€	0.1078	0.1215	0.1253
	€ million	75,408	72,041	73,855

Source: The German Association of the Automotive Industry (VDA), International Auto Statistics 2003. OECD/STAN and ZEW calculations.

Table 4.2: Employment in the production of motor vehicles in EU-15, US and Japan (thousands)

	1999	2000	2001	2002
EU-15	1,901	1,944	1,933	1,907
US	1,312	1,313	1,212	1,151
Japan	705	683	664	646

Source: The German Association of the Automotive Industry (VDA), International Auto Statistics 2003. OECD/STAN and own calculations.

Between 1991 and 2000, the share of the motor vehicles industry in total manufacturing employment increased in Japan, the US and the EU-15. In Japan, the share of motor vehicles rose from about 6.5 % of all manufacturing jobs in 1991 to 7.5 % in 2000, in the EU, from 5.5 % to 6.5 % and in the US from 4.5 % to 5.5 %.[115] Between 1995 and 2000, the share of motor vehicles production in total employment in the economy remained close to 1.4 % in Japan, 0.7 % in the USA, and 1.1 % in the EU-15.

At the EU-25 level, total employment in the auto industry in 2002 amounted to 2.13 million. Percentages of manufacturing employment in the motor vehicle industry were largest in Germany (11 %), Sweden (10 %), the Czech Republic (8 %), Belgium (8 %), Spain (7 %) and France (7 %). These shares have increased since 1991 by about half to one percentage point in all these countries with the exception of France, where the share remained stable.

4.2.1.3 Capital stock and investment

Motor vehicle manufacturing is an investment-intensive industry. This is borne out by consistently high levels of investment in fixed capital, plant and equipment. In comparison to other manufacturing sectors, its capital intensity (investment per person employed) is inferior only to Mining, Oil Refining, Chemicals, Paper and Basic metals.[116]

Trends in investment activity[117] in the motor vehicle industry are similar to those in total manufacturing. Investment levels as percent of value-added and production tend to remain stable.

4.2.1.4 Production, backward and forward linkages

Beyond its own production, the automotive industry generates economic activity through back-ward and forward linkages. A first indicator of the backward linkages is the ratio of value added in an industry to its total production (the difference between production and value added represents the inputs). Between 1991 and 2000, this ratio varied between 20 % and 30 % in car manufacturing in the EU, US and Japan.[118] Over the period, the ratio increased in Japan (from 25 % to 27 %) and the US (from 22 % to 30 %), but fell in the EU-15 (30 % to 22 %).[119]

The above figures illustrate the large importance of inputs from other sectors in the production of motor vehicles. Since a part of the inputs are foreign imports, they must be subtracted to obtain the domestic backward linkage effect. As imports account on average for approximately 25 % of total production, the backward linkage is of a magnitude of 2 – each euro of value added in motor vehicles demands approximately two euros of domestic inputs. A similar effect would be expected for employment relationships.

A more precise way of quantifying the magnitude of backward linkages is through input-output tables. The analysis is restricted to the latest available Input-Output (I-O) tables for Germany (published by the Statistical Office in December 2003) since EU-wide I-O tables are not available. Graph 4.1 shows the impact of a € 1 increase in final demand for cars on production values and imports (in €) of goods produced by the automotive sector itself and other sectors.[120] The main impact of an increase in final demand for cars is visible in the automotive sector where the production of automotive products (including parts) increases by € 1.4. Not surprisingly, an increase in the demand for cars has a large impact on steel production, the metal working industry, high-tech manufacturing (i.e. mechanical and electrical engineering, measurement and control, electronics, etc.), chemical prod-

---

[115] Source: OECD/STAN data.
[116] Source: European Commission, *Pocketbook of EU Sectoral Indicators*, forthcoming.
[117] Source: OECD/STAN data.

[118] Source: OECD/STAN and own calculations.
[119] In Europe, the value of automobile production increased faster than the value added of the sector while in the US, the reverse happened. A possible explanation for the diverging movements in value added relative to production might be that outsourcing developed to a higher degree in the EU than in the US.
[120] These estimates also account for secondary effects i.e. the additional demand for cars resulting from the increase in the induced output of other sectors.

Graph 4.1: Backward Linkages of Final Demand for Automotive Products in Germany, 2000

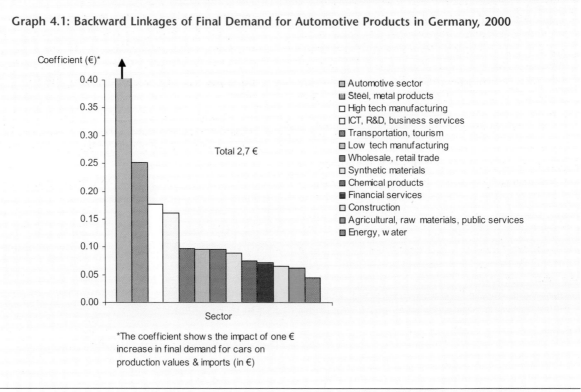

Total 2,7 €

- Automotive sector
- Steel, metal products
- High tech manufacturing
- ICT, R&D, business services
- Transportation, tourism
- Low tech manufacturing
- Wholesale, retail trade
- Synthetic materials
- Chemical products
- Financial services
- Construction
- Agricultural, raw materials, public services
- Energy, water

*The coefficient shows the impact of one €
increase in final demand for cars on
production values & imports (in €)

Source: ZEW calculations using data from the Federal Statistical Office Germany.

ucts and rubber. There are strong links between car production and several service sectors, namely business services (including R&D and IT services), financial services, transport and trade, and service sector output is raised by nearly half a euro. These links through the value chain demonstrate the importance of the automotive sector as an engine for growth and employment.

The structure of the I-O tables masks major downstream effects for the automotive repair and maintenance services industries, since these services are contracted through final users of vehicles. Domestic demand for these services originates from, and is proportional to, the total stock of new and used vehicles owned by domestic firms and consumers.

4.2.1.5 Expenditure on R&D

The increasing importance attached to R&D by European car manufactures is shown by the rising share of the motor industry in R&D expenditures of total manufacturing. Between 1995 and 2000 this share increased by 20 % to reach around 19 % of the total manufacturing R&D-see Graph 4.2. This level exceeded comparable figures of the US (~15 %) and Japan (~13 %).

At country level, R&D expenditures by German car manufactures account for more than 30 % of total manufacturing R&D expenditures in Germany. In Sweden the share is 18 %, in France and in Italy 16 %. In these countries, R&D activities undertaken by manufactures of cars and other transport equipment have a significant impact on the national R&D investments. It is the spectacular increase of the R&D intensity of the German car industry that accounts for the expansion of the EU's worldwide share in automotive R&D.

4.2.2 Industry profile: main actors

The automotive industry is characterised by large internationally owned manufacturers and suppliers as well as a number of small and medium sized companies which meet the criteria of component suppliers.

The definition of the European Automotive Industry used in this report comprises the production of light vehicles, heavy-duty vehicles i.e. trucks and buses, as well as the manufacture of parts, systems and technical units (in statistical terms, comprising NACE 34) taking place within the EU-15, and as far as possible in the EU-25. The car, truck and bus sectors will be discussed individually.

The following definitions[121] are used throughout the report.

---

[121] See Plunkett´s Industry Almanac.

- An *Original Equipment Manufacturer* (OEM) is a company that manufactures and/or assembles the final product. In other words, while a car made under a brand name by a given company may contain various components, such as tires, brakes or entertainment features which are manufactured by different suppliers, the firm responsible for the final assembly/manufacturing is the OEM;

- *Tier 1 supplier*: A component manufacturer delivering directly to final vehicle assemblers.

Tier 1 suppliers work hand-in-hand with automobile manufacturers to design, manufacture and deliver complex automobile systems and modules, such as significant interior, exterior or drive train units. Tier 1 suppliers in turn purchase from tier 2 and tier 3 suppliers;

- *Tier 2 supplier*: These companies produce value-adding parts in the minor sub-assembly phase. Tier 2 suppliers buy from tier 3 and deliver to tier 1;

- *Tier 3 supplier*: A supplier of engineered mate-

Graph 4.2: Share of R&D expenditures in the motor industry 1995 and 2000 (in % of total manufacturing)

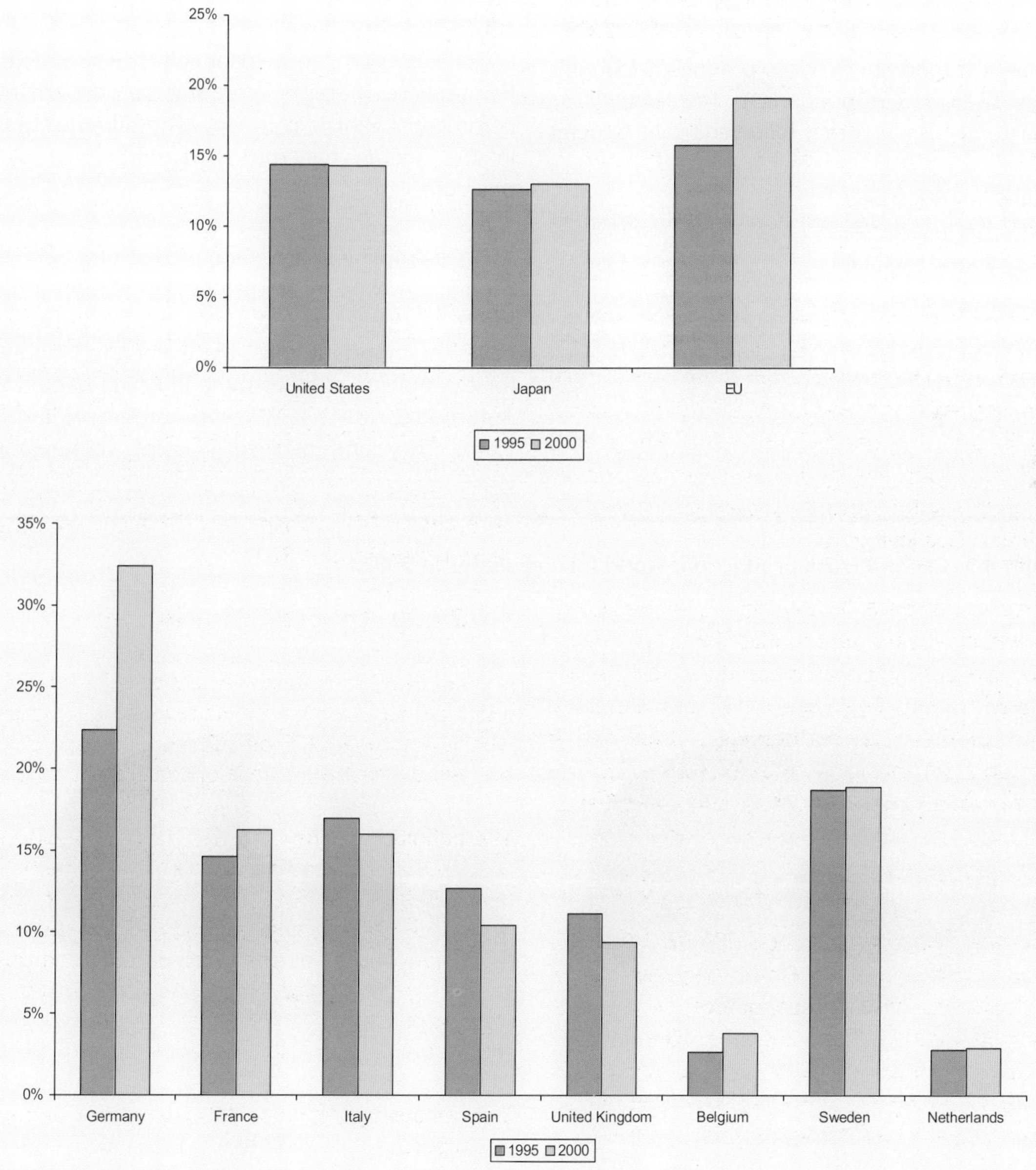

Source: OECD Research and Development Expenditure in Industry database, 1987-2001.

rials and special services, such as rolls of sheet steel, bars and heat and surface treatments. Tier 3 suppliers rank below tier 2 and tier 1 suppliers in terms of the complexity of the products that they provide.[122]

4.2.2.1 Manufacturers

Global vehicle production consists of passenger cars, commercial vehicles and buses.[123] In the following, each of these will be discussed in turn.

4.2.2.1.1 Passenger cars

In the production of passenger cars for the world market, Europe leads with a share of 42 % of world production, followed by Asia-Oceania with 35 % and America with 21 % (Graph 4.3).

In terms of the number of cars produced, Europe's share is 37 % (15 million units). The leading car manufacturer is Toyota, followed by General

Motors, Volkswagen, Ford, Honda and PSA (Graph 4.4). Within Europe, Germany has the highest production share (29 %), followed by France (18 %), Spain (13 %) and the UK (9 %).

4.2.2.1.2 Trucks

Also the commercial vehicles sector is dominated by the big three: America, Europe and Asia-Oceania – see Graph 4.3. In contrast to the car sector, America takes the biggest share of the market with 56 % of total production volume, followed by Asia-Oceania with 30 %. Europe is number three with just 14 %. One reason for the strong positions of America and Asia are the long distances in countries such as the USA, Brazil, China or India. DaimlerChrysler – which has a number of different assembly plants in North and South America – covers Asia with an investment in FUSO, an Asian commercial vehicle manufacturer. Its purchase of Freightliner, originally an American commercial vehicle company with different brands in this sector, has further reinforced its global position.

Asian companies are more important in truck production than in car production (Graph 4.5). In the truck market, also some Chinese manufacturers have an important role. The company Dongfeng, for example, is number three in China behind First Automotive Works (FAW) and Automotive Industry Corp. They are involved in joint ventures with

---

[122] See Plunkett´s Industry Almanac.

[123] Passenger cars are motor vehicles with at least four wheels, designed and constructed for the transport of passengers, and comprising no more than eight seats in addition to the driver's seat. Light commercial vehicles are motor vehicles with at least four wheels, designed and constructed for the carriage of goods. Mass given in tons (metric tons), is used as a limit between light commercial vehicles and trucks. Minibuses, derived from light commercial vehicles, are designed and constructed for the carriage of passengers, comprising more than eight seats in addition to the driver's seat and having a maximum mass not exceeding 5 tons. Trucks are vehicles designed and constructed for the carriage of goods. Maximum authorised mass is above 3.5 tons. They include tractors designed for towing semi-trailers. Buses and coaches are designed and constructed for the carriage of passengers, comprising more than eight seats in addition to the driver's seat, and having a maximum mass exceeding 5 tons.

Graph 4.3: Car and truck production: world market shares in 2002

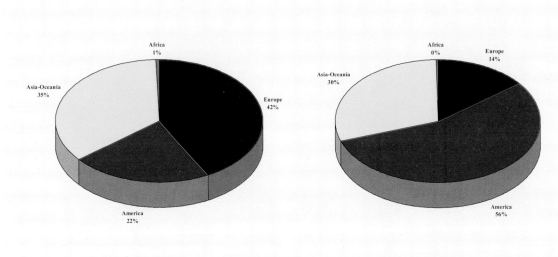

Cars　　　　　　　**Trucks**

Source: International Association of Motor Vehicle Manufacturers (OICA).

Graph 4.4: Ranking of car manufacturers 2002 – Output in units

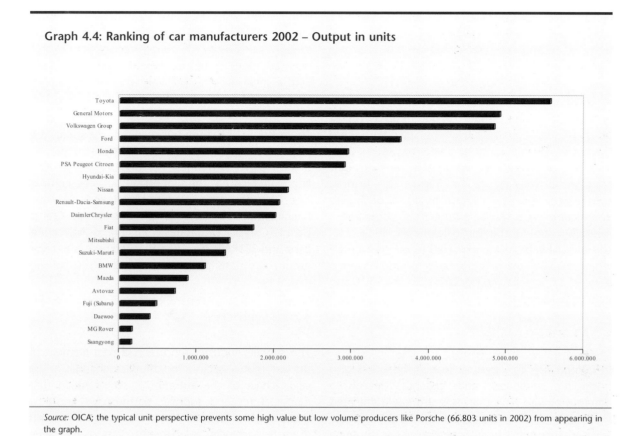

Source: OICA; the typical unit perspective prevents some high value but low volume producers like Porsche (66.803 units in 2002) from appearing in the graph.

Graph 4.5: Ranking of truck manufacturers – Output in units 2002

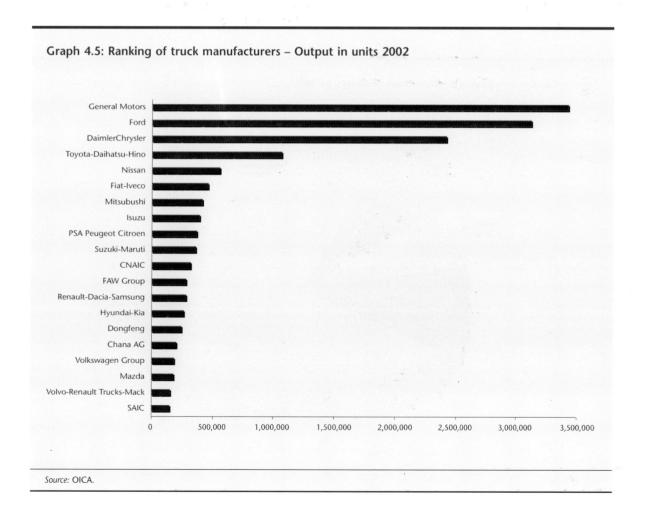

Source: OICA.

Nissan, Peugeot and Kia which enable them to supply over 240,000 commercial vehicles, more than the output of Volkswagen or Volvo in this segment.

In Europe, Spain, France, Germany and Italy produce the largest share of output in terms of units. The first position is taken by Spain with more than 580,000 units, or a share of 24 %. The majority of output is accounted for by light commercial vehicles up to 3.5 t. The leading company is PSA which produces 40 % of Spain's entire commercial vehicle output. This production is not designated for the domestic market; 85 % of all commercial vehicles are exported to the 'rest of the world'. France takes the second position with a share of 17 %, followed by Germany with 14 % and Italy with 12 %.

4.2.2.1.3 Buses

In comparison to cars and trucks, the bus sector (including minibuses and coaches) reveals a different picture. This market is strongly dominated by Asian manufacturers (Graph 4.6). The region of Asia-Oceania and China in particular constitutes a huge market for buses. China has a share of 70 % of output i.e. a production volume of more than

one million units in 2002. Number two in this market is South Korea with a share of 14 %. Interestingly, the Russian Federation steps ahead of European countries to be number three in this market with a share of 4 %. The Western European countries, headed by Sweden, trail behind.

The majority of the big bus manufacturers originate in Asia and primarily supply this region only. The biggest player is Hyundai (Graph 4.7) and its affiliate Kia which has the highest output. The companies Changan Auto, Harbin Harfei and Changhe Aircraft Industry dominate production in China. DaimlerChrysler Omnibus with its brands Mercedes-Benz and SETRA is strong in Europe and has a major production basis for chassis in Brazil, supplying global markets.

4.2.2.2 Suppliers

The supplier industry represents a vital element of the automotive sector. The dramatic changes in the value chain of the automotive sector mean that manufacturer and supplier partnerships are now indispensable. Suppliers are assuming more and more responsibility for different parts of the value chain, even the lion's share in some cases. This trend is expected to continue. According to a study

Graph 4.6: Bus production: world market shares in 2002

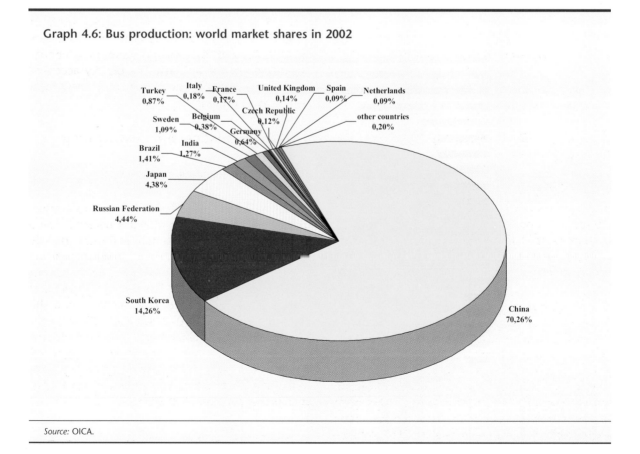

Source: OICA.

Graph 4.7: Ranking of bus manufacturers – Output in units, 2002

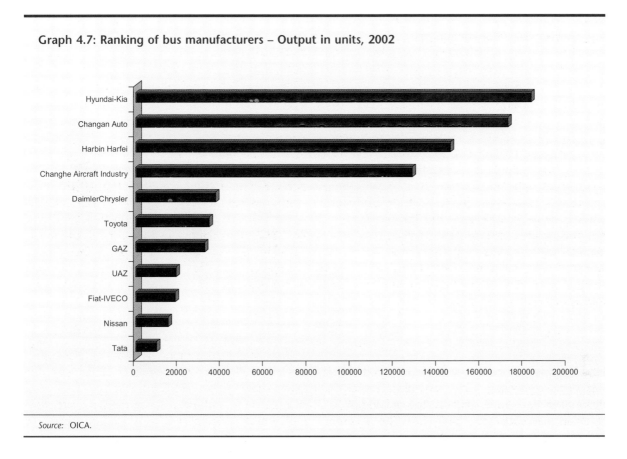

Source: OICA.

by the German Association of the Automotive Industry (VDA)/CAR there will be at least three sources of opportunities for future growth in the supplier industry:

- access to new markets,

- increased vehicle value, e.g. through innovations in electronics,

- benefits from manufacturers' outsourcing strategies.

These developments will necessitate major inputs in terms of manpower, R&D expertise and financial resources, if suppliers want to be able to accompany manufacturers at their assembly plants all over the world. All of the top 100 suppliers are internationally operating firms with a turnover of at least € 940 million.

The largest twenty supplier companies (see Annex Table A4.1) fall into three geographical groups dominated by the US, Germany, France and Japan. There are traditional links between US OEM and US first tier suppliers, French OEMs and French first tier suppliers, and between German OEMs and German first tier suppliers. As a rule, Japanese OEMs prefer to use suppliers from their own conglomerates. These traditional links are in decline. OEM globalisa-

tion tends to favour larger suppliers, resulting in increasing M&A activity in this sector.

Graph 4.8 presents the new business locations selected by German suppliers in the last five years (1997-2002) and illustrates the increasing internationalisation of the industry. The priority accorded to Eastern Europe,[124] with 26 % of all new locations, is worth noting.

4.2.3 Consolidation and restructuring

4.2.3.1 The consolidation process

Consolidation and restructuring have radically transformed the industry during the last decades. These developments have accelerated in the last decade with the opening to international competition of new and increasingly important markets such as Eastern Europe, China and Russia. The search for scale and scope economies by large manufacturers and the difficulty for smaller ones to sustain the investment race have led to an ever decreasing number of independent manufacturers in the market. Graph 4.9 illustrates this trend which resulted in the reduction of the number of independent manufacturers from 36 in the seventies to 14 in 2003.

---

[124] Poland, Czech Republic, Slovakia, Hungary.

163

Graph 4.8: New business locations chosen by German automotive industry suppliers in 1997-2002

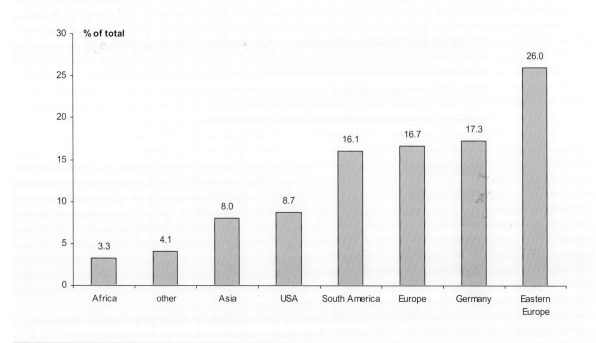

Source: The German Association of the Automotive Industry (VDA).

Graph 4.9: Restructuring in the European, U.S. and Japanese car industry[125]

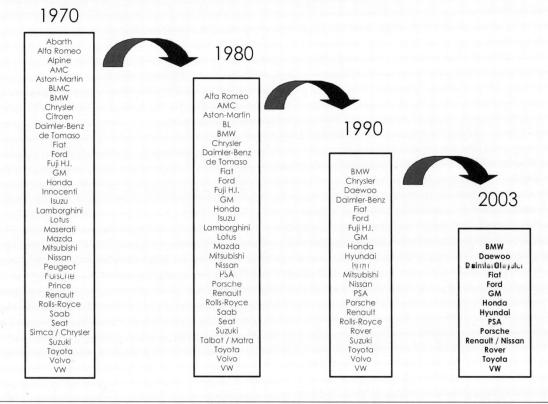

Source: Associated Press (AP).

---

[125] A truly global perspective should certainly include producers from China, India and Russia. Given the focus of this study and the lacking availability of comparable historical information, narrowing the scope to the major producing areas Europe, Japan and the USA should provide useful insights nevertheless.

Despite the decline in the number of car manufacturers, competition in the regional, local and niche markets has increased as larger companies are now present in all of them. Mergers and acquisitions (M&A) have played an important role in the process by giving instant access to particular regions and niche markets and continue to do so. As a result, manufacturers have transformed themselves from automobile companies to automobile groups.

A parallel adjustment is taking place also within the supplier industry, in its search for more product responsibility, larger innovation capabilities and global presence[126] (see Annex Tables A4.2 and A.4.3 for recent M&A transactions concerning, respectively, the manufacturers and the supply industry).

Links within the automobile industry go far beyond equity deals; each of the following types of linkage is quite common:

- Joint venture;

- Interchange or buy-off of products;

- Marketing or distribution agreement;

- Technology or R&D agreement; and

- Assembly agreement.

Manufacturers maintain a complex web of several such relationships, both among themselves and with tier 1 suppliers, by which they manage the organisation and strategic control of the whole value chain. This is of paramount importance, especially in mature markets such as Western Europe where customers expect additional enhancements from vehicle manufacturers, but are not willing to pay higher prices. Therefore, product innovations have to be financed with an increased efficiency along the value chain which includes component suppliers as well after-sales-services.

4.2.3.2 Restructuring of the value chain: the role of technology

Future innovations in vehicle manufacturing will be closely intertwined with electronics and software control systems. These innovations have to be linked with the traditional mechanical automobile components. The traditional component supplier or new entrants in the sector will take over these new value-added activities. The result will be that more R&D will shift to them. The vehicle manufacturer will try to ensure his added value share with cost pressure on the component supplier and cost optimisation on the side of their retail business. The changes in organisation and market strategies which will arise from technological innovations are described below.

In the 1980s, the modern passenger car consisted of up to 10,000 different parts. The special knowledge of vehicle manufacturers concerned the management of the complexity of the production process, which required co-ordinating up to 2,500 suppliers (Womack and Jones, 1991). In general, contract periods for standard products were short and suppliers were regarded as commodity suppliers rather than strategic partners in innovation.[127] For manufacturers, a very high integration of the production was an advantage in competition. Above all, American manufacturers like General Motors purchased 70 percent of their parts from own production which required considerable innovation capabilities and capital lockup (Terporten, 1999).

At the beginning of the nineties, the pressure to innovate and to cut costs led to a reduction of manufacturing tasks to the 'core' (Terporten, 1999). In Germany, the share of the vehicle manufacturer in total automotive value added declined from 18 % in 1995 to 12.8 % in 2001 (Graph 4.10). Similar declines were registered for the UK (about –5.9 percentage points), Italy (about –5.3 percentage points), Spain (-3.8 percentage points) and France (-2.1 percentage points). Only in Sweden did the vehicle manufacturers' share in the total value added of the automobile industry increase. Simultaneously, the number of employees declined in the automotive industry as a whole, whereas within the supplier industry (NACE 34.3) employment and gross value added increased.

The changes have not reduced the complexity of the process of vehicle manufacturing, but rather have relocated the tasks along the value chain. Some suppliers are taking the responsibility for larger systems (components/modules), for example the petrol injection. The responsibilities of first tier suppliers not only include the construction of systems, the just-in-time delivery to vehicle manufacturers and the co-ordination of second and third tier suppliers, but also the corresponding R&D. In the last years, half of the total R&D activity of the automobile industry has been carried out by the

---

[126] A small number of transactions though seem to follow a financial investment logic.

[127] See Fieten (1995).

Graph 4.10: Share of 'Manufacture and assembly of motor vehicles and engines' (NACE 34.1) in gross value added of the automotive industry (NACE 34.1-34.3)

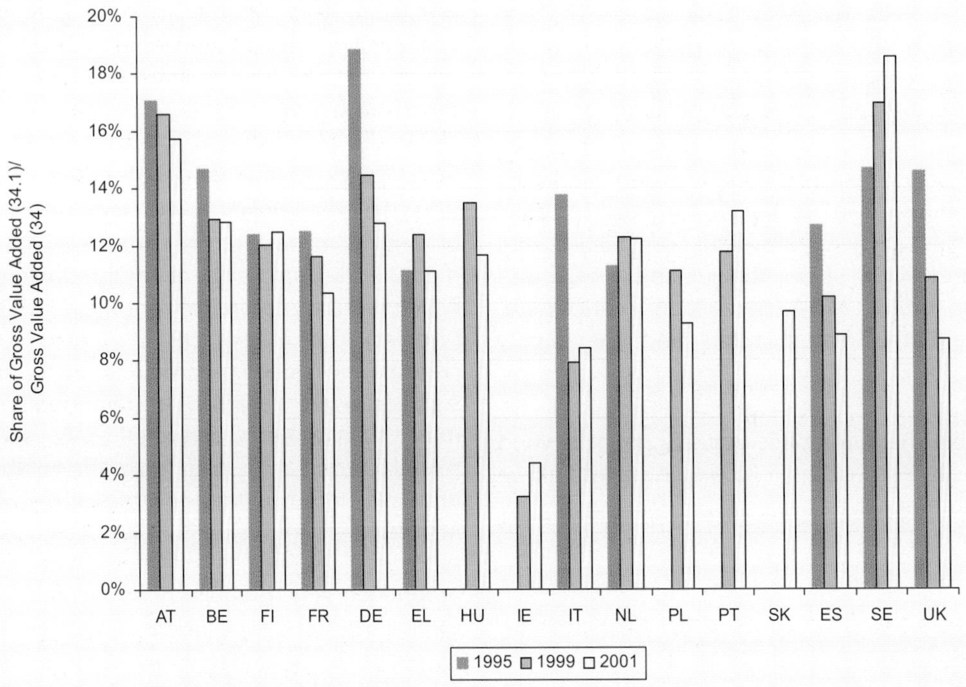

Source: Eurostat and the German Association of the Automotive Industry (VDA): International Auto Statistics Edition 2003, Frankfurt 2003.

suppliers. Manufacturers retain the highest control only in the areas of engine and car body.[128] First tier suppliers are thus becoming a close partner in the innovation and production process of vehicle manufacturers.

The trend to take on new responsibilities and the pressures for additional cost cutting are expected to result in a further consolidation and internationalisation of the supply segment, including down to second tier suppliers.

A comparison of the developments in Europe, North America and Japan reveals that European vehicle manufacturers lead on the trend of modular production and downstream integration. The European industry has at its disposal a large structure of specialised firms for shared product development and production tasks. 'If the future lies in the increased specialisation of actors in the value chain, the European automotive industry seems to be particularly well positioned in terms of structures and capabilities'.[129]

The American companies – (but also PSA and Fiat in Europe) – reduce in-house production via spin-off activities (Jürgens, 2003). However, the share of vehicle manufacturers in the total value added of the American automobile industry still lies around 55 %, way above that in Europe. Japanese vehicle manufacturers account for 15.4 percent of the value added in the automotive sector in Japan, which is more than in most car producing EU countries (Graph 4.10). The modularization of production in Japan has taken place in-house as Toyota and Honda see a strategic advantage in the total control of the value chain and avoid the handover of responsibilities to the supplier industry (Jürgens, 2003).

The interface between suppliers and vehicle manufacturers is expected to change further. The management consultant Roland Berger & Partners expects a world-wide decline in the number of suppliers from 5,600 at present to 3,500 by the end of the decade. In this period the number of first tier suppliers per modules/system is expected to fall from today's 7-8 to 5-3, with a simultaneous decrease in the number of modules/systems per vehicle from 20-18 today to circa 10 in the year 2010 (Berger & Partners, 2000). PricewaterhouseC-

---

[128] See Larsson (2002) and McKinsey&Company (2003).
[129] Jürgens (2003).

oopers – using a different definition of tier 1 and tier 2 suppliers – expects a decrease in the number of first tier suppliers from 800 to 35 and a reduction of second tier suppliers from 10,000 to 800 in the same time period (PricewaterhouseCoopers, 2003).

In any case, the upcoming innovations in the field of automobile manufacturing are likely to lead to a further transfer of R&D and other value generating activities, which are beyond the core competencies of the vehicle manufacturers, to the suppliers. McKinsey and Company (2003) expects a 10 percentage-point decrease in the value added share of vehicle manufacturers between now and 2015 (Graph 4.11). This will reflect mainly the externalisation of tasks in the area of chassis technology (18 percentage points) and engine technology (15 percentage points) to the suppliers. Even in the core competencies – the vehicle body – the value added shares of vehicle manufacturers are expected to decrease by 6 percentage points to 66 %.

4.2.4 Capacity utilisation and structural overcapacity

There is a close link between capacity utilisation and profitability. As a rule, car makers break even when capacity utilisation rates reaches 80 %, with some variation between plants.

In a world-wide perspective, the current output levels in the car industry are well below the production potential. On the one hand, there is transitional overcapacity which relates mainly to the cyclical variation of demand for cars. On the other hand, overcapacity is often seen as a more permanent feature in the automotive industry. Short-run fluctuations and long-run under-utilisation of existing capacities are quite distinct phenomena and highlight different aspects of car markets. Several features of competition in automotive markets contribute to overcapacity.

Car sales are cyclical, and a downturn in the car market induces a temporary under-utilisation of capacity. During the last fifteen years, movements in capacity utilisation rates in the car industry have been quite similar in the different EU-15 countries - see Graph 4.12. Capacity utilisation rates declined dramatically in the first half of the nineties and recovered until 2000. Since 2000, capacity utilisation has declined gradually to pick up again in some countries in 2003.

Even in boom periods capacity utilisation rates have remained clearly below 100 %. National data reveal that, as a rule, capacity utilisation rates in the final assembly of cars are significantly lower than in the manufacturing of parts (1st, 2nd and 3rd tier suppliers). Hence, over-capacity is primarily a problem of car manufacturers. Accordingly, over-

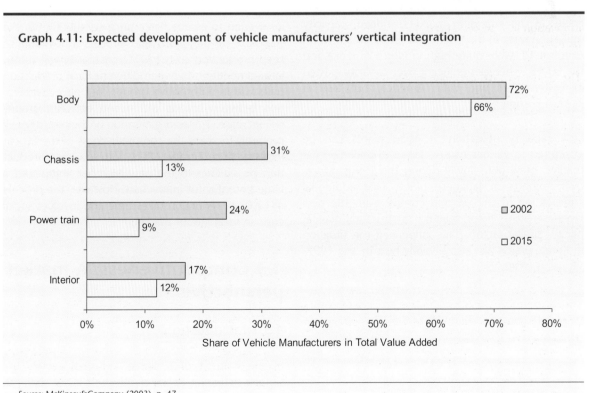

Graph 4.11: Expected development of vehicle manufacturers' vertical integration

Share of Vehicle Manufacturers in Total Value Added

- Body: 72% (2002), 66% (2015)
- Chassis: 31% (2002), 13% (2015)
- Power train: 24% (2002), 9% (2015)
- Interior: 17% (2002), 12% (2015)

□ 2002
□ 2015

Source: McKinsey&Company (2003), p. 47.

capacity can be linked to the market strategies of car manufacturers and the idiosyncrasies of the final assembly of cars. Three main factors explain the structural overcapacity:

- When setting up a final assembly plant, car makers must assess the market potential for the model(s) that will be produced in this assembly several years ahead. Since the marginal cost of an ex-post capacity increase is much higher than the cost of building the capacity at the start,[130] it may be preferable to err on the optimistic side;

- In addition, the cost of extended delivery times which are the result of lower capacity is especially high in market segments which are fiercely competitive and where the possibilities of product differentiation between companies are relatively low. Also in this case, companies may choose to build new plants on the basis of the more optimistic variants of sales forecasts;[131]

- Finally, car manufacturers may seek first mover advantages in new or emerging markets by being the first to produce locally and reaching a significant market share very early. As a consequence, the overall capacity of new plants in emerging markets often exceeds current and near-future market potential quite dramatically.[132] Presently, this seems to be the case in the expansion plans of automotive producers in China.

Hence, one should expect more significant overcapacity in the emerging markets. Indeed, capacity utilisation rates in the boom year 2000, as shown in Graph 4.13, were quite high in North America and the EU-15, whereas significant over-capacity existed in Eastern Asia and Latin America, but also in Eastern Europe.

Low capacity utilisation in Asian plants can be attributed to various causes. Japan, the leading car market, grew only slowly during the 1990s. Moreover, exports of Japanese plants face additional competition in the US and Europe from the new Japanese plants there, leading to structural overcapacity. Similar factors have influenced the situation in Korea, which was also severely hurt by the 1997-98 Asian crises.

Eastern Europe faced a rapid expansion of production capacities in the last decade. Capacity utilisation in the standard car segment in Eastern Europe is far below that in the EU-15. A recent study by PWC autofacts (2004) estimates capacity utilisation for car plants in Poland at about 50 % and in Slovakia at 40 % in 2004. The study forecasts the average capacity utilisation rate to remain at the present level in Poland, while a strong increase is expected in Slovakia (to 70 %). Even in the long run, capacity utilisation rates in the new Member States are expected to remain below those of most of the EU-15 countries. The excess capacity will put traditional car producing locations in the EU-15 under pressure as well.

More recently, capacity utilisation rates in major assembly facilities seem to be on the rise again. PWC autofacts (2004) projects a slight increase in capacity utilisation for car assembly plants in the EU: on average, capacity utilisation is expected to rise to around 78 % in 2004 (77 % in 2003; 76 % in 2002). However, this is the result of capacity reductions, not of an increase in demand, and new capacity is being built up in the new Member States.

In summary, sluggish growth in major car markets, together with a rapid expansion of production capacities in emerging markets, will fuel overcapacity. This will lead to stronger competition, especially in the traditional segments of the car market, and increase the pressure on production costs. This should stimulate the search for product innovation to escape fierce price competition in the standard car segment, and process innovation to keep production costs low. Overcapacity will stimulate competition between different local production units within automotive groups, but also co-operation between brands within and between groups will increase. The re-organisation of the industry will probably increase the competitiveness of the EU car industry since Europe offers both low cost production possibilities in the new Member States and a large potential for innovation. However, the process of capacity reduction takes time and involves social costs in local labour markets.

4.3 Competitiveness: A market perspective

4.3.1 Introduction

In the context of a single industrial sector, the simpler definition of competitiveness is the ability to defend and/or gain market share in open, interna-

---

[130] Admittedly, there is the possibility to change from a two-shift to a three-shift and vice a versa, which gives some ex-post flexibility. However, changing the number of shifts also induces different unit labour costs.

[131] Therefore one should expect lower capacity utilisation rates for plants producing standard cars than for those producing for the luxury or the SUV segment of the market.

[132] See Sturgeon (1997) for a more detailed discussion of this argument; as a striking example Sturgeon and Florida (2000) report an average capacity utilisation rate in transplants in Vietnam of around 10 %.

Graph 4.12: Capacity utilisation in the EU-15 car industry – 1988:Q1- 2003:Q4

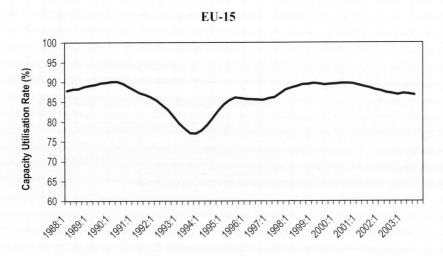

EU-15

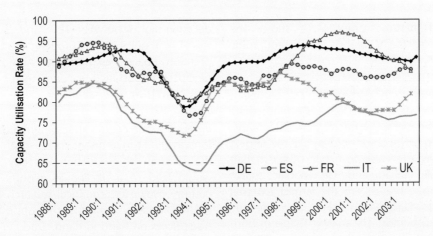

Large car producing countries

Note: The original quarterly capacity utilisation rate is smoothed by a moving average filter using 3-quarter lags and leads. The original data do not show any evidence of seasonal variation.

Source: European Commission, DG ECFIN, Business and consumers surveys, May 2004.

tional markets by relying on price and/or the quality of goods. This ability is affected by a wide range of factors and conditions.

The Section begins with examining the performance of the European automotive industry in export markets. It then reviews foreign direct investment (FDI) developments. In automotive industry, FDI is a major instrument in the internationalisation strategies at both country and firm level. Subsequently, the section reviews prospects in two emerging markets, China and Russia, in more detail. Finally, the section turns to the European home market to identify sources of competitiveness and concludes with an assessment of the impact of enlargement on the European automotive industry.

4.3.2 International markets

The automotive sector is characterised by a relatively low trade/sales ratio. As a consequence, market-oriented FDI is the dominant feature of globalisation. However, trade and FDI are not always substitutes, and the automotive industry illustrates this. In order to determine how competitive the European automotive industry is, it is necessary to examine performance at both country and company level. A brand-and-unit-based approach offers some useful initial insights.

While the production of most automotive producers in the world is spread over various countries in the value chain, the brands are still considered to reflect

Graph 4.13: Capacity utilisation rates in car assembly plants by major region during the 2000 boom

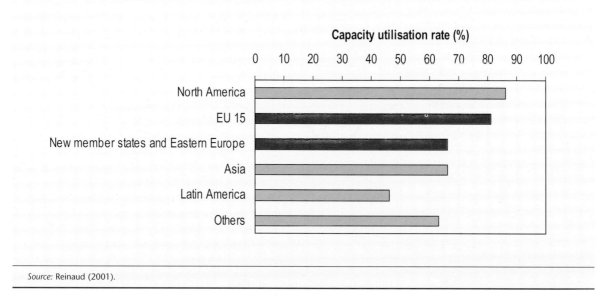

Source: Reinaud (2001).

some national identity. Graph 4.14 shows the market shares of major brands in a geographic context.[133]

The EU-15 market is dominated by European brands. Between 1998 and 2002, only minor shifts took place in the market shares of different brands. German and French brands hold by far the largest shares, and were even able to expand their market presence, while Italian and UK market shares declined. Japanese brands are the largest external players on the European markets, considerably ahead of Korean brands. The market shares of both Asian brand groups remained changed little between 1998 and 2002. Large American manufacturers serve the European markets mostly through their European branches and hence brands (e.g. Opel). Therefore, while traditional American brands might be absent from the European markets, the US manufacturers are not.

The Japanese brands control almost completely the Japanese market. Only some German brands have made recognisable inroads into the Japanese market, but they were not able to increase their market share between 1998 and 2002. In the US market, American brands hold the largest shares and even expanded further between 1998 and 2002. Japanese brands hold a sizeable, but declining stake. In contrast, Korean brands gained considerably in the US between 1998 and 2002. German brands hold the third largest share of the US market; their share

declined slightly between 1998 and 2002. Nonetheless, for a number of European manufacturers of premium quality cars the North American market is of crucial importance, accounting for a substantial portion of their total sales.

Intuitively, one could expect international trade and foreign direct investment to be substitutes, so that the creation of production capacity in a country would lead to a decline in exports towards this country. However, empirical research for the automotive industry suggests the opposite: FDI and trade flows go hand in hand. Trade in intermediate inputs as well as exports from supplying firms facilitate this connection.

Internationalisation strategies may change over the lifecycle of the product. Vernon (1966) argues that the uncertainty associated with new products requires closer customer interaction in production, which could best be accomplished by on-site operations and hence foreign direct investment. Once the product becomes more mature and standardised, cost considerations become the central driver of production decisions and therefore markets will best be served through exports from the most cost effective production sites. The following sections review the international performance of the European automotive industry with regard to both trade and FDI.

4.3.2.1 International trade

Exposure to international competition invariably forces domestic companies into a virtuous circle of demanding customer feedback, peer pressure from

---

[133] It is worth noting that market shares in terms of car registrations do not reveal possible price differences across different brands and may thus differ from market shares expressed in terms of pecuniary sales volumes.

global competitors and growing domestic excellence in operations. In addition, trade generates jobs, economic opportunities and growth as well as tax revenues. Trade performance is an important indicator of competitiveness.

In 2001, the combined worldwide exports of automotive products (SITC 78) from all the OECD countries were worth almost USD 523 billion (total merchandise exports were almost USD 4 trillion). Of the automotive exports, 58 % were exports of passenger cars (SITC 781), 10 % trucks (SITC 782), 3 % buses (SITC 783) and 25 % parts (SITC 784).[134] EU-15 accounted for almost USD 270 billion of these exports but only USD 85 billion were exports outside EU-15. Poland, the Czech Republic, the Slovak Republic and Hungary exported a combined total of USD 13.6 billion to the world. The US exported automotive products worth USD 56.7 billion and Japan USD 80.8 billion. However, the first largest export country in that field is Germany with USD 105 billion exports. Canada is ranked fourth (USD 52.7 billion), France is fifth (USD 38.9 billion). In terms of export growth, automotive products as a

whole grew by the same rate as total merchandise exports by OECD countries. Graph 4.15 shows that the EU increased its share in total OECD exports between 1991 and 2001 while Japan and, to a much lesser proportion, the US lost market share.

In 2001, OECD countries imported automotive products worth almost USD 486 billion. The division among the automotive segments is almost identical to the export segmentation mentioned above. EU-15 imported roughly USD 231 billion in automotive products while only USD 46 billion originated outside EU-15; Poland, the Czech Republic, the Slovak Republic and Hungary imported almost USD 11 billion in automotive products. Automotive product imports in the US account for almost USD 159 billion whereas Japan imported only USD 9.6 billion. This makes the US by far the largest import country for automotive products followed by Germany (USD 44.5 billion), the UK (USD 38.8 billion), Canada (USD 37.3 billion) and France (USD 30.7 billion).

The volume of trade in absolute terms gives a good idea of the importance and the size of the sector for the global economy. The performance of a particular country, though, is best assessed in comparison

---

[134] All numbers based on data from OECD: ITCS – International Trade by Commodity Statistics, Rev. 3, 2001, 2002.

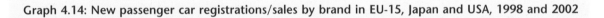

Graph 4.14: New passenger car registrations/sales by brand in EU-15, Japan and USA, 1998 and 2002

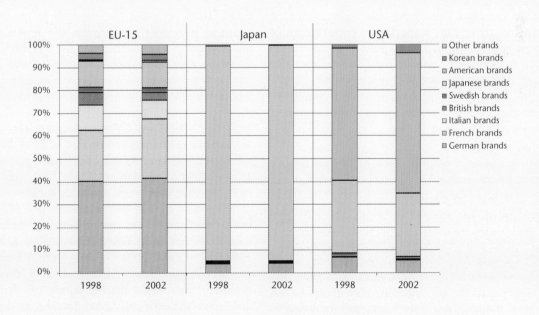

Note: German brands (Audi, BMW, Ford, Mercedes, Opel, Porsche, Smart, Volkswagen); French brands (Citroen, Peugeot, Renault); Italian brands (Alfa Romeo, Ferrari, Fiat, Lamborghini, Lancia, Maserati); British brands (Ford, Jaguar, Land Rover, Lotus, Morgan, Rolls Royce, Rover, Vauxhall); Swedish brands (Saab, Volvo); Japanese brands (Daihatsu, Honda, Isuzu, Mazda, Mitsubishi, Nissan, Subaru, Suzuki, Toyota); American brands (Chrysler, Ford, General Motors); Korean brands (Asia, Daewoo, Hyundai, Hyundai Prec., Kia, Ssangyong); Other European brands (Seat, Skoda).

Source: ZEW calculation using data from the German Association of the Automotive Industry (VDA); no comparable data were available for the new Member States.

Graph 4.15: Shares of EU-15, Japan and US in total OECD exports (in percent)

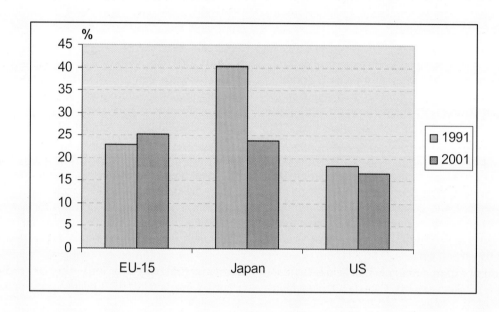

Source: European Commission calculation using data from OECD: ITCS – International Trade By Commodity Statistics, Rev. 3, 2001, 2002. Intra-EU trade excluded.

with major competitors on the global markets. Graph 4.16 shows the shares for major exporting countries in total OECD exports in the main market segments.

From a European perspective, the most prominent feature of these data is the strong performance of Germany across all market segments. It commands world market shares well above 20 % for cars and buses, with a significant lead in each segment. For trucks and parts Germany is second. However, Germany's world market shares have remained virtually identical as in 1991.

Japan occupies a second place in the **passenger cars** segment. Even if 17.6 % is a high market share, it is also significantly lower than the 27 % Japan enjoyed in 1991 - see Annex Tables A4.1 and A4.2 for export market share developments, by country and market segment). Canada follows in third place. Both Canada and Mexico increased their world market shares over the last ten years, most likely due to NAFTA and the consequent easier access to the large US market. The US itself accounts for only 6 % of world car exports which is lower than France and Belgium/Luxembourg, the European countries in car exports behind Germany. On the downside, while being among the major car producing countries in Europe, Italy's share in the world trade markets declined from 3.5 % in 1991 to 2.3 % in 2001. It is now also below the South Korean world

market share of 4 % which is South Korea's only significant showing in international markets apart from the bus segment. South Korea's car export share is expanding slowly, from 3.2 % in 1995.

In the **truck** segment the strength of the NAFTA countries is evident. Canada has the largest world market share, Mexico is third and the US fourth. Only Germany appears between them in second place. Still, a fair amount of trade in trucks takes place among the NAFTA countries. Canada and Mexico are the most important trading partners for US truck exports. While US and Canadian world market shares are virtually unchanged compared to 1991, Mexico remarkably increased its share from half a percentage point in 1991 to more than 12 % in 2001. This trend indicates that new truck assembly facilities in the NAFTA region were largely built in Mexico to supply the whole market. On the other hand, Japan lost more than half of its world market share between 1991 (24 %) and 2001 (10 %). From a European perspective the major truck producing countries defended their world market during this ten year time span. In particular, Spain doubled its share in world exports from 2.2 % in 1991 to 5.2 % in 2001. Apparently, Spain increased its competitiveness as an operation site for truck assembly with the goal of supplying foreign markets.

In the small and declining **bus** exports, Germany has a dominant market position. What is more,

Germany expanded its world market share from an already high level of 20.8 % in 1991. Canada and Belgium/Luxembourg follow as distant second and third. While the former increased its world market share significantly since 1991, the latter fell during that time from 13.4 % to 9.2 %. The loss of world market shares is more extreme for Japan whose 2001 share (6.9 %) is almost half of what it was in 1991 (13.5 %). This decline might be due to strongly increased bus production in other Asian markets that traditionally relied on imports from Japan but benefit now from lower labour costs at home. South Korea was able to expand its share in bus exports from 2.3 % in 1995 to 3.7 % in 2001. Italy held a bus world market share of 4.6 % in 1991 which has almost completely disappeared by 2001.

As automotive value chains become more internationally dispersed, exports of **intermediate automotive products, parts and accessories** have gained more importance. In this segment the US is the undisputed world market leader. Some of this remarkable lead might be due to the strategy of major American car producers to supply foreign markets through local subsidiaries. This would necessarily appear in weaker export shares for cars from the USA but would still open up export channels for intermediate products and parts from US-based supplying firms. Mexico's world market share in the parts segment rose from 0.7 % in 1991 to 4.4 % in 2001 while Canada's share remained relatively stable during that time at 7.8 %. The continuing lead of US parts export firms in direct competition with local competition at the international

Graph 4.16: Shares of major exporting countries in total OECD exports of automotive products, 2001 (in percent)

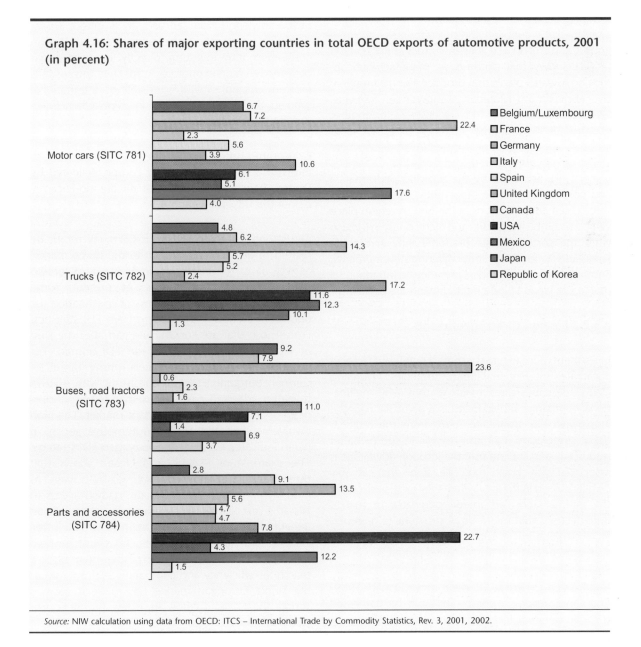

Source: NIW calculation using data from OECD: ITCS – International Trade by Commodity Statistics, Rev. 3, 2001, 2002.

assembly sites underscores the extraordinary performance of the US in this field. The global number two in world market shares for parts is Germany which largely kept its 13.5 % share consistently from 1991 till 2001. Japan as the third largest player in international parts exports comes close with 12.2 %. Still, compared with its share of 17.1 % in 1991 the loss is significant. The UK (1991: 8.1 %; 2001: 4.7 %) and France (1991: 12 %; 2001: 9 %) lost market share, too.

Thus, the European automotive industry shows mixed signs. First, the performance of the German and French industry is strong; their success in international markets is substantial and sustained. Spanish firms are also growing successful while Italy and the UK have lost market shares. The majority of trade of European automotive companies happens within the EU. The single market facilitates production concentration in few sites from which subsequently the whole European market is supplied and this translates into more import and export activities. A current study by ECG (2004) shows that automotive manufacturers are moving towards plants that produce a single model or two, at maximum. Moreover, it shows that 75 % of all vehicles produced in EU-15 are destined for another country, 58 % for another Member State. The same rationale appears to apply to the NAFTA areas where stable or diminishing trends in Canada and the US, respectively, are offset by the growing performance and potential of Mexico. Apparently, the automotive value chain configurations in the NAFTA region place vehicle assembly in Canada and increasingly in Mexico while the parts originate predominantly in the US. Japan and South Korea show differing developments. South Korea is expanding its presence on international markets as Japan's world market shares are declining.

4.3.2.2 Foreign Direct Investment

Investments abroad have become a significant factor in corporate internationalisation strategies. Dunning (1981) describes three major reasons why multinational companies should invest in a particular country: The ownership advantage stems from the multinational corporation itself and may lie in size or better resource capability and use; the location advantage is associated with certain immobile factors that can only be fully utilised in the area where they exist; and, finally, the internalisation advantage originates in market imperfections that might be of structural (e.g. imperfect competition) or cognitive nature (e.g. costly or scarce information on the marketed products).

In the same context, Bartlett and Goshal (1989) find three 'leverage points' that can be harnessed through different forms of internationalisation:

- Efficiency (global economies of scale, comparative advantage of location);

- knowledge leverage (use people and ideas globally); and,

- responsiveness (adapt to local customer demands).

The European automotive industry could potentially benefit from all those leverage points. For this, FDI appears an especially appropriate mechanism since production expertise and customer preferences are sticky, i.e. they can not be extracted and codified to be transferred from one country to another without substantial loss or at high costs. Investing in especially influential regions, be it for R&D, production or distribution reasons, opens up a more efficient channel for companies to harness these forms of tacit knowledge from abroad. In addition, trade-distorting measures may also pressure foreign companies into investing directly in a particular country. From an economic perspective this result is far from efficient. Still, it is a reality on international markets and should be born in mind when interpreting the results.

Concerning outgoing FDI, the German automotive industry is the most active in Europe, followed by France, Italy and the UK; but all are significantly below the US - see Graph 4.17.

The strong outgoing FDI from Germany might be related to decelerating growth in the home market as well as to the increasing importance of foreign markets for German brands. At present, some important partners (countries of destination or origin of FDI flows) are missing from FDI statistics. From those that are known, one can infer the kind of leverage sought by European FDI abroad. For instance, flows into the US, a prime target of German outgoing FDI, are consistent with a strive to better adapt to customer demands (responsiveness) of an increasingly important market. The high involvement of the French automotive sector in Japan indicates a knowledge-leveraged FDI strategy. The example of Renault and Nissan shows that these transfers of knowledge can go both ways. As industry experts indicate, Renault gained access to Nissan's excellence in production while Nissan benefited from Renault's abilities in streamlining the value chain. At the same time, EU countries hold substantial FDI positions in each other, pointing to a search for efficiency and comparative advantages as the single European market has made it easy to supply the EU as a whole from few production or distribution sites.

Graph 4.17: Outgoing FDI (stocks abroad) from major automotive producing countries, € million (NACE 34)

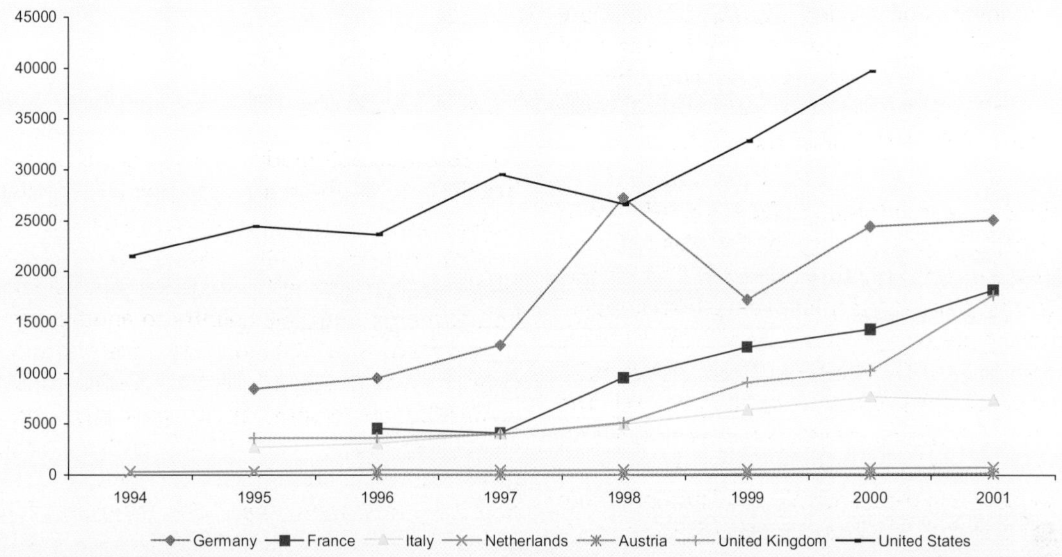

Source: Eurostat (2003), NewCronos database.

Evidence of corporate strategies towards internationalisation beyond exports can also be found at the company level. Graph 4.18 shows that not only do motor vehicle producers realise sizeable, if not dominant (Volvo), shares of their sales abroad but they also hold significant assets there.[135] This is especially so for Honda, BMW and Volvo. In terms of employment, Toyota, Volvo and Ford show the strongest tendency for operating outside the home market. On the contrary, DaimlerChrysler, BMW, Nissan and Renault rely mostly on employees in their home market. However, DaimlerChrysler should be interpreted carefully here since it is considered the only company with two home economies (Germany and the US).

Large sales abroad appear to require also a strategic shift in assets towards foreign countries. Those investments abroad should generate the crucial information from the target markets for the multinational company as a whole both in terms of a knowledge (e.g. R&D infrastructure, access to clusters of expertise) and a responsiveness (e.g. market trends, customer needs) leverage. This must not necessarily imply a massive shift of employment out of the domestic country (BMW case). Still, most

manufacturers (Volvo, Toyota, Honda, Volkswagen, Fiat) accompany their international market orientation in sales not only with investing in assets abroad but also with transferring employment out of the home market. These companies likely utilise all leverage points (efficiency, knowledge and responsiveness) in their internationalisation strategies. On the other hand, those enterprises with relatively low shares of sales abroad (General Motors, Ford, Mitsubishi) and high shares of employment abroad appear to be following primarily an efficiency leverage internationalisation strategy by utilising comparative advantages especially in labour costs in foreign countries.

The data in Graph 4.18 provide a perspective of developments among global EU, US and Japanese players that complements the discussion of export in the previous section (see Graph 4.15. If one considers Nissan as controlled by Renault, Volvo by Ford and DaimlerChrysler as a German company, it becomes apparent (see Graph 4.19) that the share of EU and US companies in total sales increased slightly while the share of Japanese companies declined between 1995 and 2001.

These developments have been brought about primarily through acquisitions, as several medium-sized manufacturers became vulnerable to takeovers in the last decade. In any case, and notwithstanding

---

[135] All data provided by UNCTAD relies on company annual reports or revised data based on company survey. The numbers should be interpreted as proxies since precise asset classification and valuation (e.g. financial assets, depreciation) can hardly be achieved at a cross-country comparison level.

Graph 4.18:   Share of foreign assets, sales and employment for major motor vehicle producing companies, 2001 (home economies in brackets)

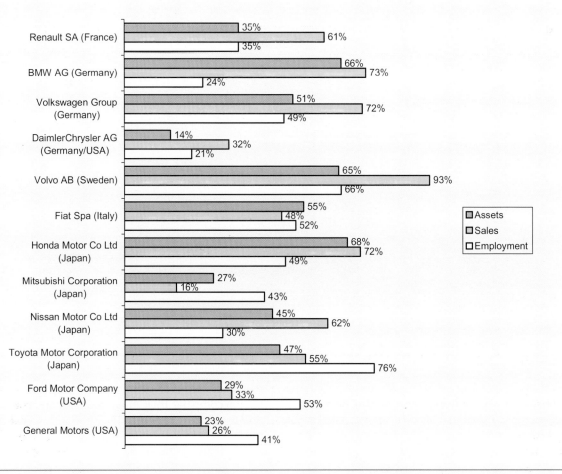

Source: ZEW calculation using UNCTAD World Investment Report 2003; No comparable data available for PSA Citroen.

Graph 4.19: Total sales shares by region of origin of manufacturer

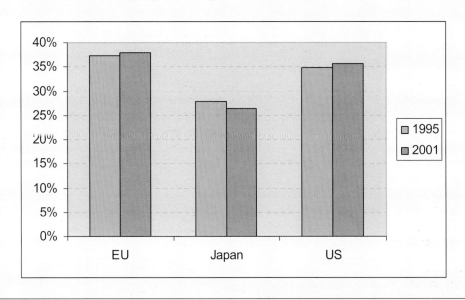

Source: European Commission calculation using UNCTAD World Investment Report 2003; PSA Citroen excluded.

its completeness, the data support the suggestion that the European automotive industry is defending its competitive position with success.

4.3.2.3 Emerging markets

With the Triad markets saturated to a large extent, further growth of the automotive industry is expected to depend on the development of new markets in the emerging and developing economies. Two markets will be reviewed in more detail here, China which is regarded as the market with the highest overall potential, and Russia, because of its size and proximity to the EU.

4.3.2.3.1 China

The Chinese automotive market

As can be seen in Graph 4.20, the Chinese automotive market is growing very rapidly. In the first nine months of 2003 sales increased by 69 % reaching up to 1.45 million cars (Automotive Resources Asia, 2003). Sales of commercial vehicles increased by about 30 percent between 1999 and 2002 while sales of buses doubled in the same time. According to forecasts, China will be the third largest market for automobiles by the end of the decade (the

German Association of the Automotive Industry (VDA): World Auto Statistics, 2003).

Contrary to developments until recently, the crucial market segment in the future will be private demand, fuelled by the emergence of a middle class. In spite of the persistence of negative factors such as high import tariffs, high government-determined prices for imported and locally produced cars by foreign companies, luxury, license number plates and street taxes as well as expensive parking lots, private demand is expected to grow further and even accelerate.

Production conditions for the Chinese automotive industry

The Chinese automotive industry is still burdened with highly inefficient structural characteristics. The number of independent enterprises is far too high to allow for economies of scale. The bulk of the enterprises is far below the critical size that allows for cost effective production and sensible R&D activities. But protected by local governments the majority of these enterprises has been allowed to exist in artificial niches up to now. Taking auto manufacturing as an example, currently there are 117 whole-car manufactures – more than the

Graph 4.20: Index of new registrations or sales of passenger cars 1999-2002 (1999=100)

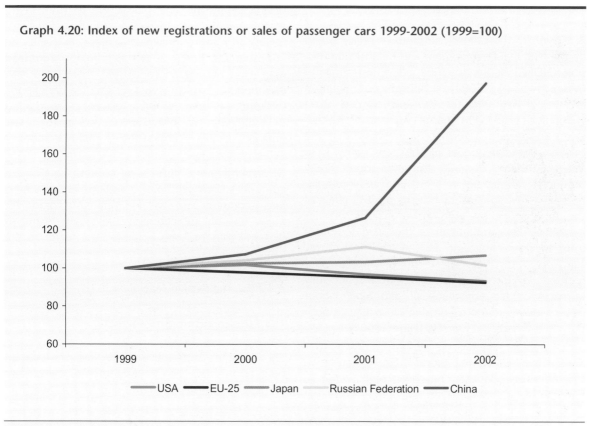

Source: ZEW calculation using data from the German Association of the Automotive Industry (VDA).

amount for Europe, the US and Japan combined. Out of these, only two OEM manufacturers had a production volume of more than 250,000 units in 2003, while nearly 100 of them had an output of less than 10,000 units.

Since 1994, China's government has been following an explicit industrial policy for the automotive sector. The objective is to set up an own and independent automotive industry. To ensure international competitiveness, the government's strategy is to involve international automobile corporations in minority joint ventures with local firms. By doing so China gains access to capital and technologies from other countries, but also valuable know-how for the domestic automotive industry. It also dictates the rules for international companies: imports are constricted, earnings have to be reinvested and component suppliers and their prices are predetermined, too (Hoon-Halbauer, 1999). In addition, by getting into parallel agreements with more than one foreign partners, Chinese companies can safeguard their independence. As can be seen from Table A4.6 in the annex, for instance, the Shangai Automotive Industry Association (SAIC) is involved with both GM and Volkswagen; First Automotive Works (FAW) is involved with Toyota, Daihatsu, Mazda and Volkswagen etc. China's policy is to reduce drastically the number of manufacturers and component suppliers and organise the remaining ones around a few 'national champions'.

A revision of the Chinese automotive policy issued by the National Development and Reform Commission (NDRC) in Spring 2004 addressed some of these issues (Yu, 2004): It introduced minimum investment thresholds for new auto projects (2 bn yuan) and production permit withdrawal mechanisms to prevent a further fragmentation of the market. The stated goal of the new policy is to satisfy Chinese demand through domestically produced vehicles before 2010 and enter international markets significantly but the positive effect of the new policy on automotive exports remains doubtful. The combination of the need to source from local less efficient and hence more costly suppliers with the capital intensive production methods of foreign producers that do not fully leverage China's advantage of affordable labour puts Chinese automotive products in a difficult position on international markets (Farrel, 2004).

Since China joined the World Trade Organisation the automotive industry has been opening up to international competition. Import quotas for foreign automotive manufacturers will be increased by 20 % per year until 2006, starting from 30.000

units; the quota will be eliminated by 2006. Furthermore, import duties will decrease from 80-100 % to 25 % following 2006 (10 % on components) (Weidner, 2004; Zhang, Taylor, 2001). Technical barriers, however, are expected to remain a problem.

Table 4.3 shows current and planned production capacities and the current (2002) exposure rate of major car manufacturers in China. Planned capacity and the elimination of import barriers point towards increased rivalry and, hence, diminishing profit margins. Although labour costs in China are low, it remains to be seen whether Chinese plants will be able to produce efficiently enough to turn potential domestic excess capacity into exports.

There is no special pattern in the way European companies enter the market compared to major international rivals. Some manufacturers in the premium segment (BMW, DaimlerChrysler) are moving cautiously which might be due to fact that the protection of intellectual property rights (e.g. technology, design) is still difficult in China and there are obstacles for the manufacturers in controlling the quality of there value chain in services and repair.

Nearly all investment activities of foreign car manufacturers in China have been oriented towards serving the local market, with the exception of Honda,[136] and national players are far from being able to meet international standards in quality, technology and prices. Individual Chinese companies do not have the potential to tap into the European market, at present. In conclusion, there is no realistic medium term prospect for Chinese car exports to Europe. Besides, all major players are increasing their engagement in Eastern Europe at the same time as they are enlarging their China-operations.

Oil dependency is an issue of concern for Chinese authorities. Fuel efficiency standards for cars have been adopted and will be phased-in gradually. Know-how on implementing fuel-saving technologies will thus become a competitive factor in the Chinese market.

4.3.2.3.2 The Russian Federation

The Russian automotive market

The Russian automotive fleet has more than doubled over the last ten years from 10 million cars in 1992 to 22 million at the end of 2002 with an

---

[136] Honda is setting up a plant with a final production capacity of 300,000 units exclusively for export.

Table 4.3: Rated auto manufacturers exposure to mainland China market

Company	Exposure to China market (2002)	Units
Heavy existing or planned exposure		
Hyundai Motor Co./Kia Motors Corp.	3 % of total unit sales	Current: 100,000; By 2007: 650,000 (incl. Kia)
Nissan Motor Co. Ltd.	Some import activity	Current: 0; By 2010: 900,000 (passenger cars and commercial vehicles)
Volkswagen AG	10.3 % of total unit sales	Current: 600,000; By 2006: 1.6 million
Medium existing or planned exposure		
Fiat SpA	1.5 % of total unit sales	Current: 70,000; By 2007: 150,000
General Motors Corp.	3.3 % of total unit sales	Current: 380,000; By 2006: 766,000
Mitsubishi Motors Corp.	5.8 % of total unit sales	Current: 120,000; By 2010: 300,000
Peugeot S.A.	3.0 % of total unit sales	Current: 150,000; By 2006: 300,000
Toyota Motor Corp.	3.8 % of unit sales (total Asia excl. Japan)	Current: 180,000; By 2010: 650,000 (incl. Daihatsu)
Limited existing or planned activities		
BMW AG	1.7 % of total unit sales	Current: 0; By 2005: 30,000
DaimlerChrysler AG	4.4 % of revenues (total Asia)	Production capacity expansion from 80,000 to 100,000 units
Ford Motor Co.	3.3 % of revenues (total Asia-Pacific)	Current: 20,000; Future: 150,000
Honda Motor Co. Ltd.	1.2 % of total unit sales	Current: 150,000; By 2004: 290,000
Renault S.A.	0	0
Suzuki Motor Corp.	n/a	Current: 250,000; Expansion plans: 0

Source: ACEA and Standard&Poor's (2004).

average annual growth rate of 8 %, reaching 152 cars per 1000 inhabitants – see Graph 4.21. This rate of growth is stronger than in the EU and this trend is likely to continue. The Russian government estimates that car ownership in Russia will reach 230 cars per 1000 inhabitants within the next ten years which means an additional growth by 12 million cars (Ashrafian, Richet, 2001; Pricewater-houseCoopers, 2002).

About 70 percent of the market demand in 2,000 is for passenger cars priced below USD 5,000. In the near future demand is expected to shift to passenger cars in the USD 5,000 – 10,000 price range and to a lesser degree to USD 10,000 – 15,000 priced cars. The segment for more expensive cars is expected to remain stable. These changes will be the result of price increases for locally produced cars and the introduction of import tariffs on used foreign cars in the segment below USD 5,000 (Ashrafian, Richet, 2001).

Replacement sales are a big factor. The average age of cars is 10.8 years. Older vehicles will become more expensive to operate as auto insurance becomes compulsory by about mid 2004. Ernst & Young expects these factors to push many people into newer vehicles, including imported used vehi-

cles. Demand for new cars has been growing at an overall rate of more than 10 percent annually and there is great potential for even stronger growth (Ernst & Young, 2003).

The automotive industry in the Russian Federation

Like China, Russian automotive manufacturers are still organised as huge industrial complexes that include auxiliary and component-producing facilities. They supply 80 % of the market demand in Russia. The biggest companies are AvtoVAZ, GAZ, IzhMash-Auto and UAZ. The large manufacturers still produce up to 70 % of their components on their own, which prevents them from operating efficiently (Kansky, 2000). Furthermore most of Russian manufacturers use outdated and inefficient technologies which hamper improvements in product quality and labour productivity. The models the plants produce are 15 to 20 years out of date by world standards. Still, this is the main reason why high production volumes have been possible. There has been a lack of investment to develop new models, although that situation has changed with new Russian strategic investors (Ashrafian and Richet, 2001).

Russian car manufacturers have to cope with the new competitive environment, like the presence of

Graph 4.21: Index of car ownership per 1000 inhabitants for selected markets (1999=100)

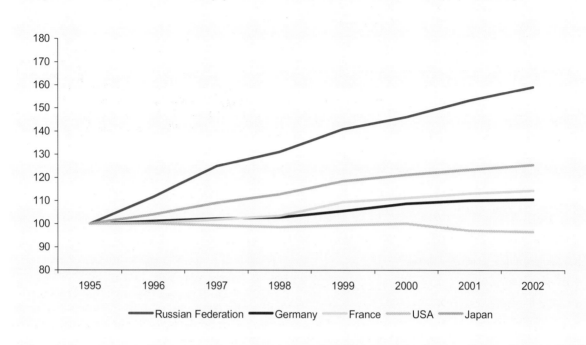

Source: ZEW calculation using data from the German Association of the Automotive Industry (VDA).

foreign car makers in the country, the lowering of tariffs and the new constraints coming from the WTO regulation when Russia will join the WTO. Recently, some companies began implementing restructuring programmes which include shifting component production to independent companies. It seems likely that efficiency will increase. But that also means that some companies might vanish from the market.

Russian manufacturers have begun exploring ways of cooperating with Western car and component makers, mainly through joint ventures (PricewaterhouseCoopers, 2002). BMW and Kia assemble their cars (BMW 2,200; Kia 3,500 cars in 2002) at the Avtotor facility in Kalingrad based on imported assembly kits. Ford has chosen a green field investment near St. Petersburg. The current capacity is 25,000 cars a year but could be boosted up to 100,000 if demand remains increasing (WardsAuto.com, 2003). Volkswagen, the most successful foreign brand in Russia, has not announced any intentions to produce in Russia so far while Toyota signalled plans to produce their Land Cruiser model there in 2006 (PricewaterhouseCoopers, 2002).

In contrast with most other emerging automotive markets, Russia and the EU are direct neighbours with a shared land border. Hence, the potential trade channels are broader and more flexible. Not surprisingly, car exports from EU-15 to Russia have sharply increased since 1993 – see Graph 4.22. At the moment, this demand is covered through used cars but these exports should give European producers an edge in brand recognition once incomes in Russia increase and customers begin shifting their attention to new cars.

In summary, Russia may soon follow China as the next big new market in this sector (Ernst & Young, 2003). Demand for vehicles is rising quickly but manufacturers and suppliers face unique challenges. The forthcoming entry to the WTO will spark exposure to intense international competition.

4.3.3 The home market

4.3.3.1 Market size

A large home market enables domestic firms to achieve economies of scale and scope. Hence, they benefit early in the product life cycle from learning curve effects and an increasing expertise in production. In turn this leads to diminishing unit costs that make the domestic products more competitive on foreign markets. Furthermore, a large domestic customer base provides invaluable feedback for innovative products. A significant home market for primary products also opens up new opportunities for secondary products and services that might not reach the necessary critical mass to evolve elsewhere. Therefore, a comprehensive assessment on home market size as a possible source of competitiveness includes both the market in total numbers but also its segmentation.

4.3.3.1.1 Passenger cars

With 209 million passenger cars in use in 2002 the European Union (EU-25) is by far the largest single market for cars in the world. It accounts for roughly 38 % of all cars on major international markets, followed by the US and Japan – see Graph 4.23.

Size becomes more important in relative terms. Car ownership in Europe varies widely indicating the relative importance of cars for citizens of different countries. On average, four out of ten EU inhabitants own a car which is in line with Japan and the US – see Graph 4.24. Luxembourg, Italy and Germany post the highest values here among the Member States.

Why would the population in some countries buy more cars than in others?

Obviously, there is the mere need for transportation. This factor should be especially important in countries with low population densities, since the citizens of those countries need to travel longer distances on average for every aspect of social interaction. Clearly, there are generally other options available as well but transport by car has some unique advantages that make it the dominant

mode of transportation:[137] it is essentially the only one that enables the user to choose his/her travel time and exact destination individually and the only option that allows direct door to door trips.

On the other hand, cars and the relationship of owners towards them appear to run much deeper than their practical value in use. Today's car manufacturers offer a startling variety of different models to satisfy the needs of their customers. Those needs include rational deliberations like the wish for spacious family vans. However, cars have become also an element of style through which their owners can express their individuality. The choice in car models reflects this clearly as does the wide variety of supplementary interior and exterior car equipment.[138] Cars have a social signalling function, proving that one can afford a special car or even more than one. This fact certainly reflects a country's wealth but also its general tendency to treat cars as a status symbol. Graph 4.25 shows the relationship between car density and GDP per capita and population density as proxy variables for wealth and the need for transportation, respectively.

An accompanying multivariate regression analysis[139]

---

[137] Passenger cars accounted for 80.4 % of all passenger kilometres in EU-15 2001 (European Commission, 2003).

[138] Econometric analysis can disentangle to a certain extent the various functionalities of a modern car and the values that consumers attribute to them. Thus, in Germany higher price margins can best be achieved through features that improve driving performance and convenience or make the vehicle more exclusive or individual. At the same time, German customers recognise quality through the car brand and are willing to pay for it accordingly, accepting an up to 100 % price mark-up for an equally equipped car, depending on its brand (see background study).

[139] See background study.

Graph 4.22: Index of new and used car exports value from EU-15 to Russia, 1993-2002

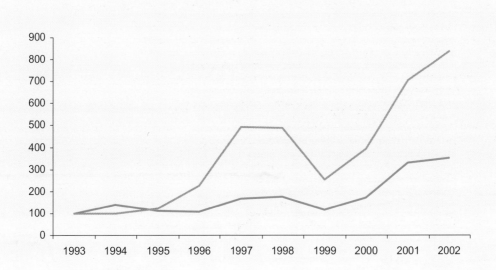

Source: ZEW calculations using Eurostat Intra- and extra-EU trade 2003 data. Base year 1993 = 100.

Graph 4.23: Passenger cars in use in major international markets, 2002

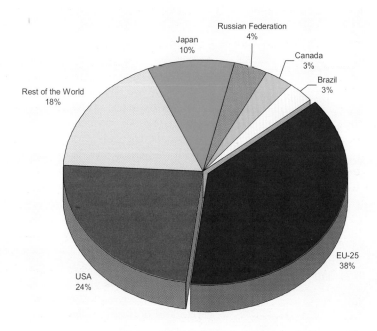

Source: ZEW calculation using data from ACEA, the German Association of the Automotive Industry (VDA) and Eurostat; data for Cyprus, Estonia, Latvia, Lithuania and Malta are for 2001.

Graph 4.24: Cars per 1000 inhabitants, 2002

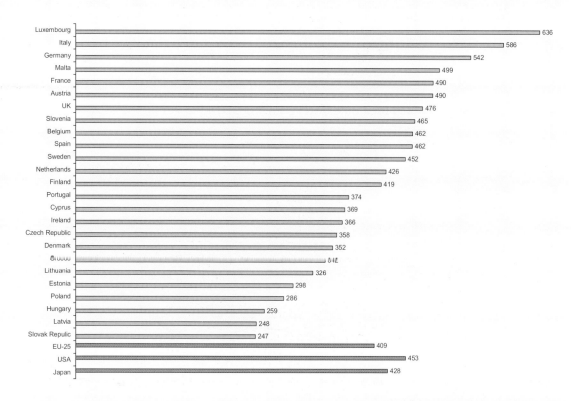

Country	Value
Luxembourg	636
Italy	586
Germany	542
Malta	499
France	490
Austria	490
UK	476
Slovenia	465
Belgium	462
Spain	462
Sweden	452
Netherlands	426
Finland	419
Portugal	374
Cyprus	369
Ireland	366
Czech Republic	358
Denmark	352
Greece	342
Lithuania	326
Estonia	298
Poland	286
Hungary	259
Latvia	248
Slovak Repulic	247
EU-25	409
USA	453
Japan	428

Source: ZEW calculation using data from ACEA, the German Association of the Automotive Industry (VDA), and Eurostat; for Cyprus, Estonia, Latvia, Lithuania and Malta, the data are for 2001.

shows that GDP per capita has a highly significant positive impact on car density whereas population density shows only a positive influence at an 80 % significance level. In major European markets (Netherlands, Belgium, Germany, Italy, UK) high car density ratios can hardly be explained by the need for transportation among sparsely populated areas. Instead, these countries appear to support the argument of an affinity for cars beyond mere practical use. The same is true for Japan. For the US, Australia, Canada, Spain, Sweden and France affordability as well as the transportation motive appear in more congruence. Especially in the new Member States high car densities appear to be mostly stipulated by the requirement to own a car as the primary source of mobility and less as a status symbol.

Consequently, the Member States of the European Union extend over all customer segments in this relatively broad classification which appears reasonable for country comparisons. The mix of consumers with a primary interest in affordable passenger transportation and better-off car-enthusiasts should prevent the industry from myopic, idiosyncratic product designs. This demand advantage is an attribute of the market not the industry. It can become a competitive advantage for those manufacturers that have complete

access to the relevant market and customer information. The question remains whether European automotive manufacturers benefit predominantly from the size of their home market.

It is appropriate to consider a brand perspective since the brands are the primary channels through which customers recognise manufacturers. Graph 4.26 shows the market shares of major brands in selected markets. It suggests a strong affiliation of French and German car buyers towards brands that originated in their respective home market. This suggests an atmosphere of trust into cars that were domestically built and designed. For Italian, Swedish and British brands this link is weaker. Customers there appear to be less focused on domestic brands but keep a strong interest in other European brands. Combined European brand shares command more than 80 % of the market in the five selected European markets. Korean and Japanese brands exhibit significantly smaller shares but are slightly better positioned in European countries without a strong home market brand affiliation.

Japanese brands enjoy an enormous popularity in their home market where all other brands are of minor importance. In sharp contrast, American

Graph 4.25: Population density, GDP per capita and cars per 1000 inhabitants in 38 major car markets in 2001

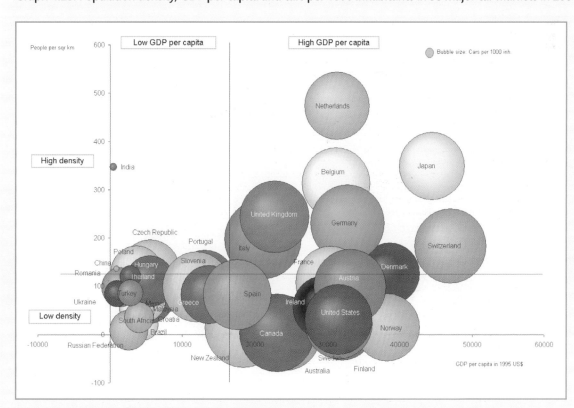

Source: ZEW calculation using data from ACEA, the German Association of the Automotive Industry (VDA), and World Bank World Development Indicators.

Graph 4.26: Brand segmentation in first registration cars for selected markets, 2002

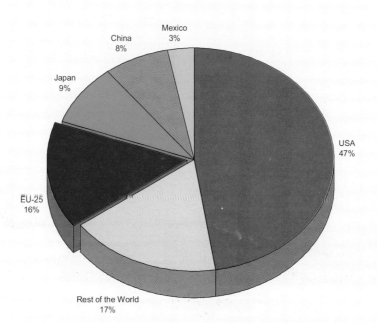

Note: German brands (Audi, BMW, Ford, Mercedes, Opel, Porsche, Smart, Volkswagen), French brands (Citroen, Peugeot, Renault), Italian brands (Alfa Romeo, Ferrari, Fiat, Lamborghini, Lancia, Maserati), British brands (Ford, Jaguar, Land Rover, Lotus, Morgan, Rolls Royce, Rover, Vauxhall), Swedish brands (Saab, Volvo), Japanese brands (Daihatsu, Honda, Isuzu, Mazda, Mitsubishi, Nissan, Subaru, Suzuki, Toyota), American brands (Chrysler, Ford, General Motors), Korean brands (Asia, Daewoo, Hyundai, Hyundai Prec., Kia, Ssangyong); other European brands (Seat, Skoda).

Graph 4.27: Commercial vehicles in use in major international markets, 2002

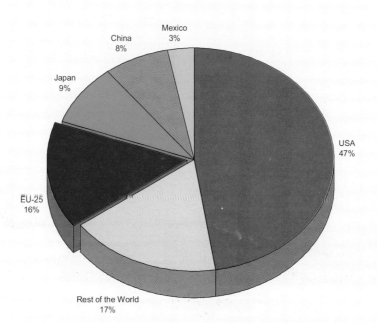

Source: ZEW calculation using data from ACEA, the German Association of the Automotive Industry (VDA) and Eurostat; data for Cyprus, Estonia, Latvia, Lithuania and Malta are for 2001.

Graph 4.28 Percentage share of goods transport ton-kilometres on the road on total goods transport, 2001

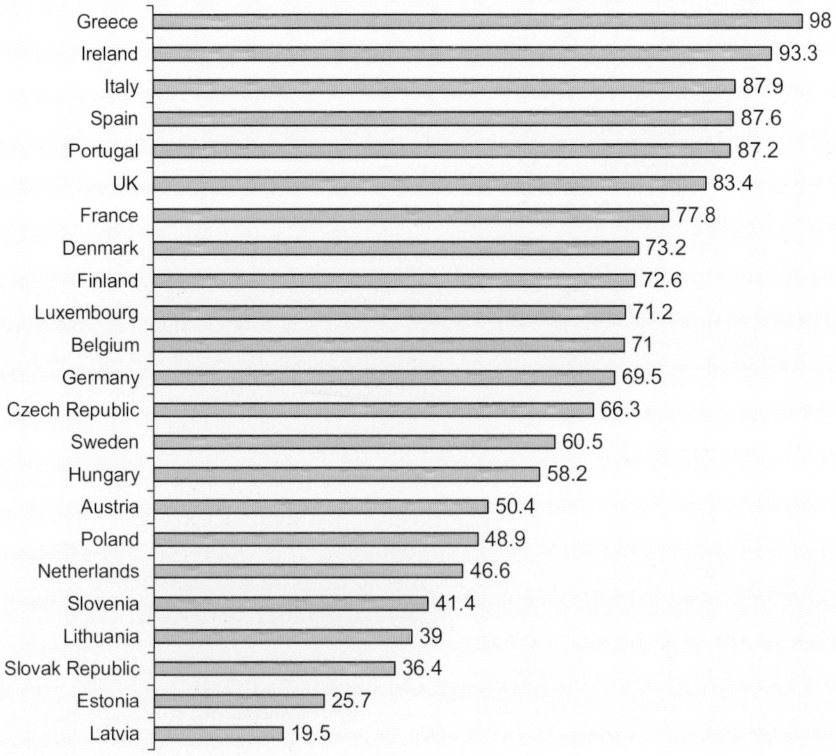

Country	Value
Greece	98
Ireland	93.3
Italy	87.9
Spain	87.6
Portugal	87.2
UK	83.4
France	77.8
Denmark	73.2
Finland	72.6
Luxembourg	71.2
Belgium	71
Germany	69.5
Czech Republic	66.3
Sweden	60.5
Hungary	58.2
Austria	50.4
Poland	48.9
Netherlands	46.6
Slovenia	41.4
Lithuania	39
Slovak Republic	36.4
Estonia	25.7
Latvia	19.5

Source: EU Energy and Transport in Figures 2003; for new Member States 2000 data were used; no data available for Cyprus, and Malta.

brands command only about 60 % of first car registrations. At least in terms of units sold, Japanese brands control a large portion of the US market for new cars.

There is evidence that this demand advantage in the home market has already translated into success abroad. The average buyer of European brand cars in the US has a far higher median household income (USD 115,492) than the customers of Asian (USD 70,353) or American brands (USD 58,154).[140] This indicates that the demand for premium cars at home and the subsequent customer feedback help to shape products that are attractive to wealthy customers abroad.

4.3.3.1.2 Commercial vehicles

The EU is the second largest market in the world for commercial vehicles with slightly more than 30 million in use in 2002, followed by Japan and China; still, the US's 92 million commercial vehicles make it a distant second – see Graph 4.27. Signifi-

cant parts of that gap might be due to the fact that light trucks have made remarkable inroads in the US market for passenger cars. In 2002, 8.1 million passenger cars were newly registered in the US compared to 8.7 million light trucks.[141] There is currently no meaningful distinction between light trucks that replace passenger cars in the private use segment and those that go into traditional commercial use. Accordingly, this gap should be interpreted carefully.

Demand for commercial vehicles reflects the importance of freight road transportation. This degree of reliance on commercial vehicles is influenced significantly by an adequate infrastructure and the opportunity costs of alternative modes of transportation which include not only price differences but also availability and flexibility in use. In Greece and Ireland road transportation appears to be the almost indisputably dominant form of transportation (Graph 4.28). This trend is also strong in Italy, Portugal, Spain and the UK. On the contrary, only 40 % or less of goods' transport in ton-kilometres in

---

[140] See Ward's Automotive Yearbook 2003.

[141] See THE GERMAN ASSOCIATION OF THE AUTOMOTIVE INDUSTRY (VDA): International Auto Statistics 2003.

Lithuania, the Slovak Republic, Estonia and Latvia is by road. Although the intermodal split of goods' transportation is not uniform among Member States, road transportation is a strong if not dominant pillar in most EU countries transportation. Accordingly, demand for commercial vehicles should remain substantial.

By combining transported goods and kilometres travelled, Graph 4.28 disguises the primary fields of use for commercial vehicles in the EU. Graph 4.29 draws a clearer picture in this regard. Most goods in the EU are transported over rather short distances. Especially in Ireland, Germany, Finland and Austria the majority of transport happens over distances below 150 kilometres. In other Member States this relationship is weaker (Belgium, Italy, Luxembourg) but the share of short distance transportation volume is still above 60 %. The emphasis on shorter distance road transportation in the European Union should give rise to commercial vehicle concepts that address this specific need.

In conclusion, despite the special impact of light trucks for private use in the US, the EU is still an attractive volume market for commercial vehicles. Most European countries rely heavily on road transportation. This fact reflects heavy investments in a suitable infrastructure both from the private (e.g. value chain configurations) and the public sector. These sunk costs discourage the development of alternative modes of transportation and ensure a stable demand for commercial vehicles in the foreseeable future. Transport over short distances is a particularity of most road freight in the EU.

4.3.3.2 Market growth

A large market size can generate significant sources of competitive advantage. Market growth is another critical factor in this respect. Slow growth in large markets can still represent high volumes but it becomes increasingly difficult for them to provide growth in relative terms. It is this type of new sales opportunities that helps automotive companies to continue growing and benefiting from up-to-date trends in a dynamic market. As a result, market growth is as much a prerequisite for competitive advantage internationally as market size.

4.3.3.2.1 Passenger cars

Some measurement concepts of growth find it difficult to cover cyclical fluctuations of demand or are highly sensitive to the choice of the base year. To avoid those pitfalls an alternative concept was developed, distinguishing between a long term trend and a short term movement based on the last four years – see Graph 4.30. This concept aims at covering basic multi-year market trends that can easily be compared among countries. This approach was developed for that specific purpose and should be treated as complementary not a substitute of traditional market analysis.

The long term trend in car sales is driven by more fundamental elements such as customer preferences, infrastructure, demographic development and wealth. For car passenger transportation as well as all other modes of transportation, infrastructure upgrades (e.g. railway tracks, motorways) take years to be planned and implemented. On the other hand, short-term trends might be more influenced by the overall economic outlook or changes in consumer confidence. Since most new car sales today are for replacing an older car, the majority of these sales can be easily postponed. Hence, customers can easily control their time of purchase which could severely influence short term movements while the long term trend should not be materially affected.

Graph 4.29: Share of million tons transported on the road by distance, 2001

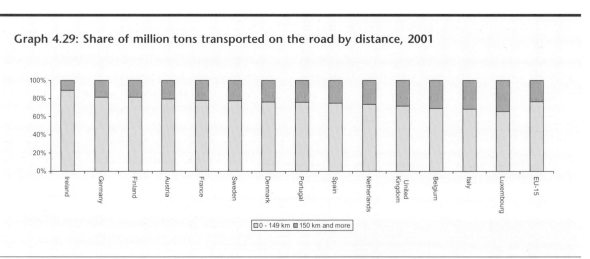

Source: EU Energy and Transport in Figures 2003; no data available for Greece and the new Member States.

Graph 4.30: Illustration on slopes of short and long term trends

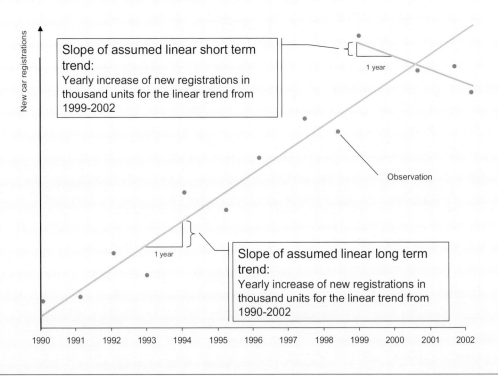

Slope of assumed linear short term trend:
Yearly increase of new registrations in thousand units for the linear trend from 1999-2002

Slope of assumed linear long term trend:
Yearly increase of new registrations in thousand units for the linear trend from 1990-2002

Source: ZEW.

Individual countries can be classified according to a combination of long and short term developments[142] (Graph 4.31). For instance, the long term for most of Members States is positive, promising a continuing growth. At the same time, short term (most recent four year observation period) developments were negative in a majority of Member States indicating that growth might be decelerating.

Developments outside the EU place these numbers into perspective. The countries under consideration with the strongest long term growth trend are Brazil, India, Mexico, South Korea and Australia. On a long term downward trend are Romania, Turkey, US and Japan. However, the numbers for passenger cars in the US might be somewhat misleading since demand for light trucks in private use has significantly affected the sales of traditional passenger cars.

Over the short term, there was a massive increase in demand for cars in China, followed by South Korea, Japan, Mexico and Brazil, that made these countries the most promising markets for growth in passenger cars. For Japan, this upward short term trend indicates that the negative long term trend may have been overcome.

4.3.3.2.2 Commercial vehicles

Graph 4.32 shows the results of the same approach applied to the case of commercial vehicles. The long term trend here is positive for almost all EU Member States with the large markets of Italy, Spain, France and the UK in lead. A notable downward trend is only evident in the case of Poland. Over the shorter (four year) period Italy, the UK and France perform the best. Germany, Spain and Portugal exhibit the strongest movement which indicates that their positive long term trends might come to an end. The EU-25 would lose 24 000 new registrations annually if the short term trends continue. EU-15, for which a long term trend is available, adds more than 50 000 new registrations in commercial vehicles a year according to the long term trend while the short term trend is negative, implying a decline of almost 10 000 new registrations annually.

In the US long and short term growth trends are strong which, again, should be interpreted carefully since a significant number of light trucks in that segment substitute for passenger cars instead of going into traditional commercial use. Canada, Australia, Brazil and Mexico show the best long term growth trends. However, South Korea and notably Japan are on a highly negative trend. Over the last four years a number of countries have

---

[142]   See the Annex of the background study for the long and short term trend values (slopes of linear trends expressed as thousands of units) for individual countries.

Graph 4.31: Combinations of short and long term growth trends for passenger cars

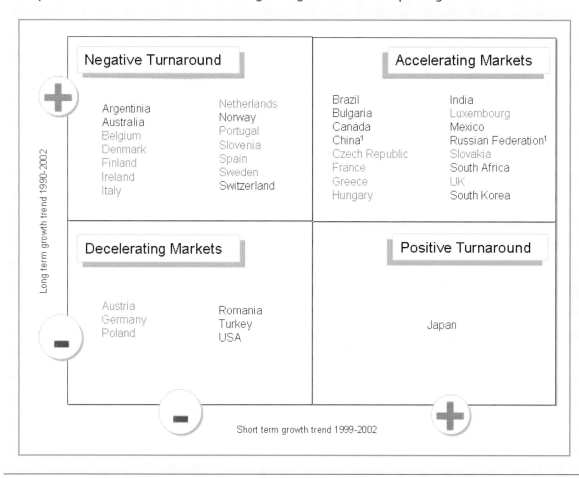

Negative Turnaround	**Accelerating Markets**
Argentinia / Netherlands / Australia / Norway / Belgium / Portugal / Denmark / Slovenia / Finland / Spain / Ireland / Sweden / Italy / Switzerland	Brazil / India / Bulgaria / Luxembourg / Canada / Mexico / China[1] / Russian Federation[1] / Czech Republic / Slovakia / France / South Africa / Greece / UK / Hungary / South Korea
Decelerating Markets	**Positive Turnaround**
Austria / Romania / Germany / Turkey / Poland / USA	Japan

Long term growth trend 1990-2002

Short term growth trend 1999-2002

[1] Due to data availability long term trend was only estimated for 1995-2002.

Source: ZEW.

entered a significant positive demand trend for commercial vehicles. On top of the list is China which would, if its four year trend continues, add more than a quarter million new commercial vehicles registrations to its fleet. Excluding the US, Indonesia, Australia and Thailand are also on strong short term growth trends. Declining demand for commercial vehicles is evident in Turkey and Argentina but primarily in Japan where the long term downward trend appears to have accelerated in recent years.

4.3.3.3 Enlargement and the European automotive industry

Inward foreign direct investment plays a far bigger role for the automotive sector in the new Member States rather than in EU-15.[143] Many global vehicle producers and suppliers have established them-

selves in the region and the development of the automotive industry in the individual countries is closely linked to the location decisions of these international producers. The countries which have attracted most FDI in the automotive sector are the same which show a strong specialisation in this industry, namely the Czech Republic, Hungary, Poland and, more recently, Slovakia. Slovenia is the only country with a significant automotive industry, but relatively little foreign direct investment. At the end of 2002, the Hungarian automotive industry showed the biggest stock of foreign direct investment, followed by the Czech Republic and Poland (see Table 4.4).[144]

Taking into account the size of the economies, FDI stock *per employee* is a preferred indicator of the

[143] Outward direct investment on the other hand does not play any role in these countries.

[144] For Hungary and Poland FDI data were available at the level of the transport equipment industry (DM) only, including motor vehicles (34) and other transport equipment (45). But as this industry is a minor target for FDI in the new Member States, the data are fairly comparable.

Table 4.4: FDI stocks in the new Member States, 2002, €mio

	Czech Rep.	Hungary	Poland	Slovak Rep.	Slovenia	Estonia	Latvia	Lithuania
Manufacturing (D)	11,539.7	13,522.7	16,378.7	2,713.1	1,696.2	759.0	407.5	1,119.0
Motor vehicles (34)	1,933.3	3,235.7	2,280.3	147.9	53.2	23.5	1.7	43.2

Source: WIIW FDI database.

relative attractiveness of individual countries for FDI in the automotive industry. As shown in Graph 4.33, Hungary is still at the top position. Notably, the FDI stock per employee is higher than the average for manufacturing in all these nations.

The disproportionate attractiveness of the automotive industry for foreign direct investment is confirmed by data on foreign invested enterprises (FIEs). These data also demonstrate the dominant role of foreign investors in the automotive industry in new Member States – see Table 4.5.

In 2001 (the latest year available), FIEs owned 83 % of the *equity capital* in the Czech automotive industry, accounted for 94 % of all *investment,* sold 91 % of all vehicles and had a share of 94 % in the industry's exports. These shares were even higher in Hungary and the lowest in Slovenia (equity: 76.7 %, sales 82.7 %, exports: 86.2 %). In all countries, foreign penetration has increased over time; notably, FIEs are more export oriented as shown by their higher share in export sales than in total sales.

*T*The bulk of foreign direct investment in the new

Graph 4.32: Algebraic signs of short and long term growth trends for commercial vehicles

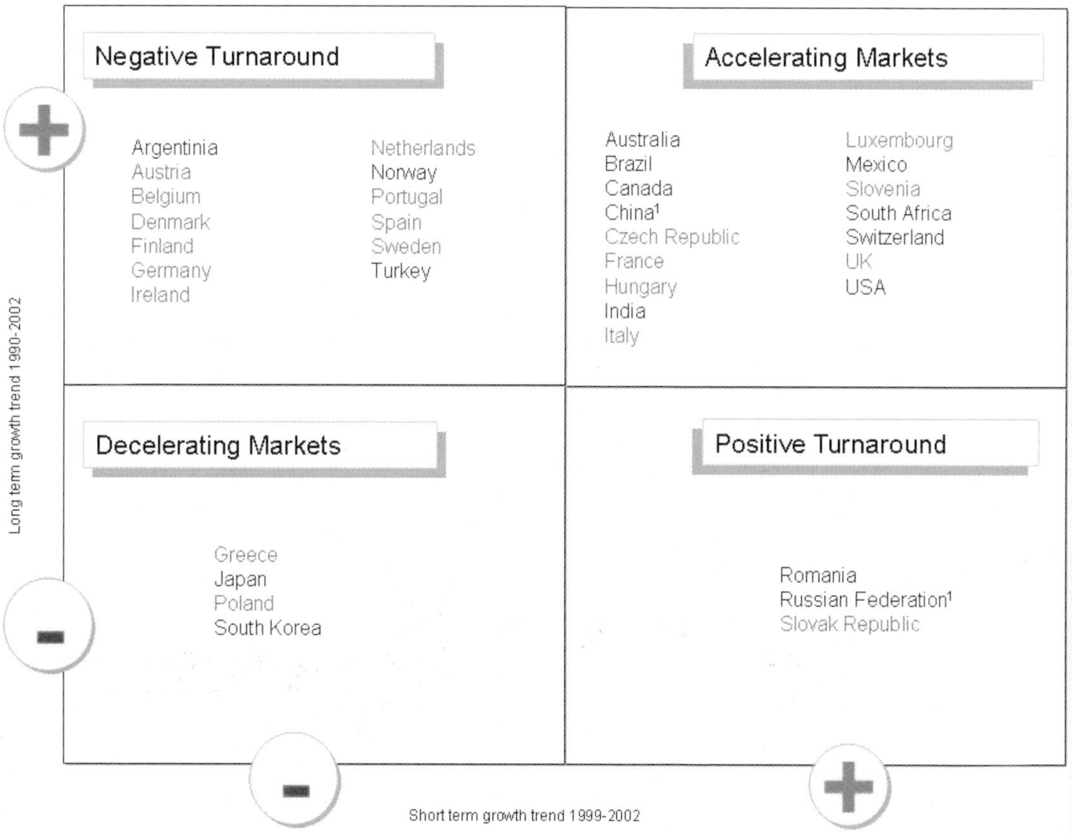

Long term growth trend 1990-2002

Negative Turnaround

Argentinia	Netherlands
Austria	Norway
Belgium	Portugal
Denmark	Spain
Finland	Sweden
Germany	Turkey
Ireland	

Accelerating Markets

Australia	Luxembourg
Brazil	Mexico
Canada	Slovenia
China[1]	South Africa
Czech Republic	Switzerland
France	UK
Hungary	USA
India	
Italy	

Decelerating Markets

Greece
Japan
Poland
South Korea

Positive Turnaround

Romania
Russian Federation[1]
Slovak Republic

Short term growth trend 1999-2002

1 Due to data availability long term trend was only estimated for 1995-2002.

Source: ZEW.

Graph 4.33: Inward FDI stock per employee 2002/2001

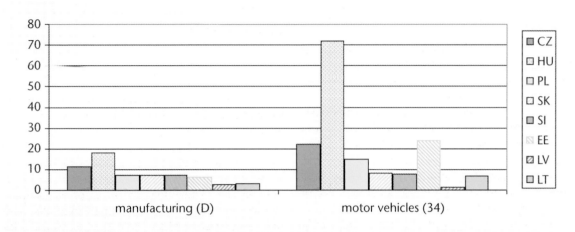

Source: WIIW FDI database

Table 4.5: Foreign penetration of the automotive industry in the new Member States (NACE 34, 1995 and 2001, in percent)

Country	Equity		Sales		Export sales		Investment	
	1995	2001	1995	2001	1995	2001	1995	2001
Czech Republic [1]	61.4	83.1	61.3	91.0	n.a.	94.0	70.0	94.0
Hungary [2]	73.7	99.6	88.1	93.9	94.1	96.6	94.4	97.5
Poland	62.5	83.3	55.4	93.2	88.4	98.4	52.9	95.3
Slovak Republic [3]	36.8	78.6	56.6[4]	95.1	n.a.	n.a.	85.0	97.8
Slovenia	74.3	76.7	72.3	82.7	80.8	86.2	n.a.	n.a.

Notes: [1] 1995, 1996 own capital. [2] 1995-1999 nominal capital. [3] 1995, 1996 DM (=NACE 34+35). [4] Output.

Source: WIIW FIE database.

Member States originates in manufacturers of European origin - see Annex Table A4.7. But with enlargement, overseas investors have become more interested in the region, attracted by growing markets but also using the new Member States as a location for their all-European exports as well. This has been stated, for example, by the Hyundai company, which decided in March 2004 to establish its first European assembly plant in Slovakia, with a capacity of 200 000 to 300 000 cars per year. If the other two big investment plans already announced materialize (namely, PSA Peugeot Citroen (Slovakia) and a consortium of Toyota and PSA Peugeot Citroen (Czech Republic) the production capacity in the new Member States will rise to over 2 millions passenger cars in 2006, roughly double the production of 2002; this will undoubtedly be more than can be sold in the region.

These developments refer only to assembly plants. Large component suppliers tend to follow manufac-

turers in their foreign locations and benefiting from local cost advantages is an additional incentive for establishing plants in the new Member States. Graph 4.34 presents a site map of important manufacturers and suppliers there.

As a conclusion, enlargement is highly important for the European automotive industry. First, a very dynamic manufacturing cluster with high output and export potential is developing in the new Member States; second, investment in these locations reinforces the European value chain by adding to it lower cost locations and permitting more options in combining existing components and intermediary parts; and, third, the European home market is extended to include a high-growth potential customer base which displays a variety of preferences in comparison to the EU-15 Member States.[145] However, increased capacity in the new

---

[145] See Section 4.3.3.

Member States - be it from European or overseas owned plants - will exacerbate competition and price pressures for existing locations.

4.3.4 Conclusion

Taking as a criterion performance on the global market, one can conclude that the European automotive industry is without any doubt competitive. It has expanded its export shares, and has maintained or improved slightly its share in global sales. Its position in emerging markets such as China and the Russian Federation is strong and offers prospects for further growth. This success of the European automotive industry in international competition is primarily based on its dominance of a large, loyal, sophisticated and diversified home market. Moreover, enlargement has been beneficial to the industry through its productive base and market effects.

However, not all is positive. If the performance of the German, French and Spanish industry is strong, Italy and the UK have lost market shares. The new production locations in Eastern Europe will increase pressures on existing locations. Finally, if the home market is indeed the largest in the World, it relies mostly on the replacement of existing cars and its growth potential (at least for EU-15 countries) has peaked.

4.4 Innovation and competitiveness

4.4.1 Introduction

Innovation and R&D activities are central to competitiveness. The Chapter begins with a review of productivity developments and then moves on to skilled labour, R&D expenditures, innovation patterns and technological trends, with emphasis on the concept of lead market.

The ability of firms to compete in foreign and home markets depends crucially on innovative products that can be produced and sold at attractive prices. In the short run, productivity and labour costs are important competitiveness factors. In the long run, the ability of firms to innovate and invest in R&D take over as crucial determinants of competitiveness. This section reviews these factors driving competitiveness more closely. The analysis begins with examining labour cost and labour productivity developments and then moves on to skilled labour, R&D expenditures and innovation patterns and trends in the automotive sector.

The Section reviews the position of Member States relative to the most important car producing countries. Hence, the approach focuses on countries and not firms and the interpretations of the data might

differ from a company-based view which is independent of where the production takes place.

4.4.2 Labour costs, labour productivity and unit labour costs

4.4.2.1 Labour costs

Low production costs are one of the main sources of international competitiveness of an industry. High cost countries can only compete against low cost countries if their products are of superior quality. Given increased openness and global presence of suppliers, standardised intermediate products will be increasingly similar in price. Likewise, the international presence of major manufacturers and large scale suppliers will tend to equalise the costs of capital. Hence, international differences in labour costs are a major source of differences in production costs. In order to compare the level of labour costs across nations it is necessary to convert all data into the same currency. Here, purchasing power parity (PPP) rates calculated by the OECD to convert national currency to US dollars are used. In addition to wages and salaries the comparison

---

Graph 4.34: A new regional cluster of automotive production

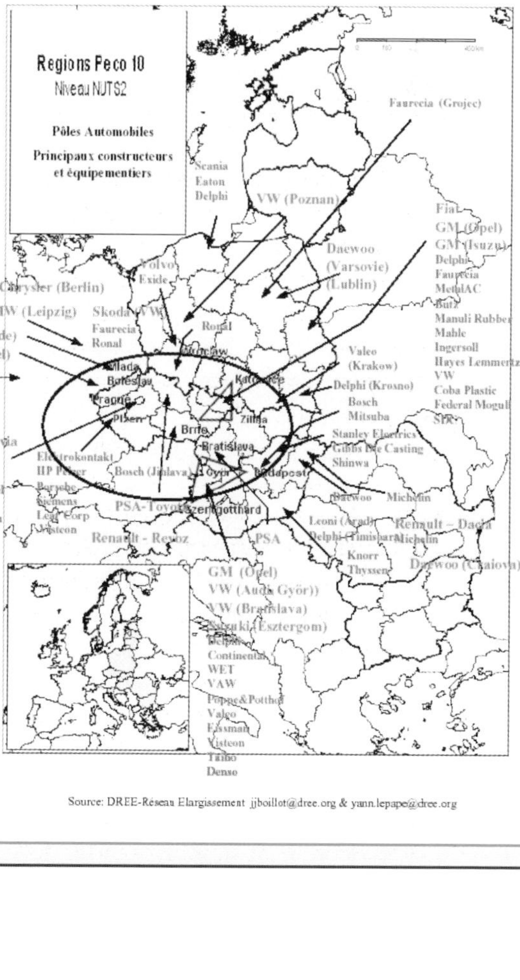

Source: DREE-Reseau Elargissement jjboillot@dree.org & yann.lepape@dree.org

includes other elements of labour costs such as employer's contribution to social security.

Table 4.6 provides data on total labour compensation per hour, in US dollars. In the short run, movements in exchange rates might also affect the ability of a country to sell products internationally, therefore, information for the dollar values of labour compensation based on current exchange rates is also reported.[146] The data refer to 1990, 1995 and 2001, the most recent year for which data is available.

The most impressive result of this comparison is that the EU-15 automotive industry has caught up with the US in terms of hourly labour compensation (based on PPP values). Now, the three most important production regions for automotive products (Japan, US, EU) are more similar with regard to labour cost than before. Another feature of the table is the stagnation of US hour labour costs during 1995-2001, even in current values.

The high valuation of US dollar in 2001 resulted in lower nominal hour labour costs in the EU and Japan. This illustrates the influence of exchange rates on the price competitiveness of the sector and one can conclude that the current Euro/US dollar

exchange rate puts under pressure the competitiveness of the EU industry. However, it is also clear that European producers will try to absorb the impact of exchange rate fluctuations also by the international distribution of production locations and the internationalisation of the supply chain.

Within Europe there are striking differences.[147] Germany is the most expensive country with labour costs per hour in the German automotive industry 8 % above the US in 2001. Labour compensation per hour worked is below US and Japan in all other Member States - labour costs in Portugal are only 54 % of the US level, for example. The high labour costs in Germany endanger its competitiveness unless they are matched by an above average labour productivity. In addition, given the currently low value of the US dollar, labour costs in the EU are above US labour costs. This currently puts the cost competitiveness of EU-produced cars against the US locations at a disadvantage.[148]

The data in Table 4.6 suggest that over the 1990s an initial and significant cost advantage of Europe

---

[146] Average yearly exchange rates and PPP-values are based on OECD data and are taken directly from MSTI 2003-2.

[147] Labour cost differences also reflect differences in skill composition of the labour force and also the composition of the automotive industry. Typically, labour costs per hour worked are lower in the automotive parts (suppliers) industry than in car assembly.

[148] Using the average €/USD exchange rate, in 2001 labour costs in EU-15 amounts to 76 % of the US level. The average €/USD exchange rate in 2001 was about 1.12, the PPP value 0.88 €/USD.

Table 4.6: International comparison of hourly labour costs in the automotive industry

	Conversion to US $ based on PPPs			Conversion to US $ based on exchange rates		
	1990	1995	2001	1990	1995	2001
Korea	5.4	8.4	12.9	4.3	8.0	7.3
Japan	17.8	24.1	29.0	24.0	43.5	35.7
USA	25.4	34.3	33.8	25.4	34.3	33.8
EU-15	19.1	26.3	32.7	23.1	31.6	25.7
Austria	13.4	21.0	23.8	16.6	28.6	19.7
Belgium	20.7	27.9	31.5	24.4	34.7	25.2
Denmark	12.8	17.0	21.4	26.4	40.8	31.5
Finland	12.5	18.3	21.0	19.4	25.5	21.7
France	17.4	22.2	25.6	19.2	19.0	15.8
Germany	20.5	29.0	36.8	20.8	24.5	18.6
Greece	7.4	10.6	12.2	21.1	28.7	21.1
Ireland	9.5	13.1	17.5	6.5	9.3	8.0
Italy	17.0	21.4	23.9	10.9	13.3	15.6
Luxembourg	13.0	14.8	19.2	20.2	20.4	17.2
Netherlands	13.2	17.2	24.1	15.5	19.5	17.2
Portugal	8.1	14.7	18.3	15.7	21.8	19.7
Spain	17.9	19.4	23.3	5.9	11.7	11.1
Sweden	15.8	18.5	19.4	24.9	25.3	18.3
UK	17.9	22.3	26.2	19.2	23.0	24.2

Source: See text.

Table 4.7: Unit labour costs in the automotive industry

	Total Labour Costs per Gross Production (%)			Total Labour Costs per Value Added (%)		
	1990	1995	2001	1990	1995	2001
Korea	14.4	16.7	12.2**	41.0	46.2	42.1
Japan	12.9	15.2	15.1*	52.0	60.2	55.6
USA	19.0	21.1	18.7	88.1	70.7	59.7
EU-15	n.a.	n.a.	n.a.	75.0	73.2	78.9
Austria	20.8	18.1	15.9	74.6	64.9	53.1
Belgium	n.a.	13.4	12.5*	76.3	70.1	73.2
Denmark	21.2	28.3	26.5	56.2	71.9	63.7
Finland	21.6	28.0	28.6	64.5	76.2	76.2
France	14.9	14.2	10.0	63.8	65.2	46.4
Germany	26.3	25.6	21.7	74.8	75.3	79.7
Greece	n.a.	27.5	25.8	94.6	102.1	86.0
Ireland	19.6	17.5	14.1	98.0	95.3	n.a.
Italy	n.a.	n.a.	n.a.	70.9	74.1	69.6
Luxembourg	n.a.	n.a.	n.a.	58.3	72.8	86.5
Netherlands	14.8	14.7	13.7*	74.9	74.0	73.9
Portugal	n.a.	n.a.	n.a.	98.5	75.5	50.8
Spain	22.9	14.9	13.5*	88.9	62.6	70.9
Sweden	21.1	15.9	n.a.	73.7	59.2	56.9
UK	24.0	21.8	20.1*	75.2	77.6	81.5

*: 2000; **: based on employees only.

Source: OECD Stan Database, Internet Version March 2004

against the US has been diminishing. The catch-up in labour cost occurred not only in the high-wage Member States but even more in the low-wage ones where hourly labour costs increased sharper - see for example the case of Portugal and Greece. During this period, labour cost differentials within EU-15 decreased and the wage increases became increasingly more uniform.

Unit labour costs relate labour costs to the value of production. Unit labour costs crucially depend on the composition of automotive industry; usually, they are higher in the supplier industry than in car assembly. They are also affected by the degree of outsourcing. Table 4.7 shows a wide variation of unit labour costs between countries. Unit labour costs have been traditionally low in France and also in Korea, Ireland, Netherlands, Belgium and Spain. However, the reasons for this are different. In Belgium, unit labour costs are low despite of high labour cost per hour because of a high labour productivity and an above average use of interme- diate inputs from outside the automotive industry. Also, in the Netherlands, France, and Spain high labour productivity helps to keep unit labour costs below average. Germany has seen a strong decline in labour unit costs which is primarily caused by

increased outsourcing. This is reflected in the increase of the share of labour costs in value added.

The ratio of total labour costs to value added informs on the relative importance of labour costs in comparison to capital cost and capital remunera- tion. Table 4.7 shows no clear trend within the EU. However, there are remarkable differences between EU, US, Japan and Korea that point to a deteriora- tion of EU labour cost competitiveness.

One of the important factors causing high labour costs in the EU is the low range of effective working hours per employee in automotive industry – see Table 4.8).

Different trends prevail in the last decade in the major automotive producing regions. Average yearly working hours in the USA increased by about 1 % p.a. in the last 15 years. In Japan, Korea and EU-15 there is a downward trend in annual working hours in the last two decades amounting to about –0.5 % per year. Japan and the US show a quite similar yearly working time amounting to around 2000 hours per employee. Despite some recent shortening of working time, the Korean automotive industry still shows the largest working time. The

Table 4.8: Average yearly working hours in the automotive industry, by country

	Hours worked per employee per year relative to US US = 100					Average working hours per year per employee
	1981	1985	1991	1995	2001	2001
Korea	140.8	130.0	129.8	121.7	121.1	2460
Japan	114.8	112.3	115.6	98.4	99.6	2023
USA	100.0	100.0	100.0	100.0	100.0	2032
EU-15	90.9	84.0	84.6	79.7	77.9	1583
Austria	97.6	91.1	92.9	81.5	80.0	1626
Belgium	92.5	86.1	87.7	80.2	77.2	1569
Germany	82.5	78.5	78.0	73.8	71.2	1447
Denmark	92.1	85.0	84.8	80.7	79.2	1609
Spain	102.8	92.3	94.2	88.6	89.3	1815
Finland	90.0	86.3	84.4	76.9	80.8	1641
France	101.1	87.3	84.6	79.1	77.4	1572
Greece	104.4	96.8	98.7	93.9	94.9	1929
Ireland	103.7	94.8	99.2	89.6	82.8	1682
Italy	87.4	80.7	84.2	77.8	80.3	1631
Luxembourg	89.6	82.1	84.6	76.5	76.8	1560
Netherlands	92.1	84.3	93.9	77.9	76.4	1552
Portugal	100.1	93.1	97.2	89.0	84.4	1714
Sweden	77.6	75.0	79.1	83.1	83.5	1697
UK	96.7	94.3	98.0	91.5	88.9	1806

Source: Groningen Growth Development Centre Industry Data Base, OECD/STAN.

EU-15 reaches only about 75 % of the US labour time. Again, there are significant differences within the EU. German workers face the lowest working hours amounting to only 70 % of the US level. The strongest decline in working time in the last two decades can be observed in France where it reached about 1.1 % p.a. However, in some EU-15 Member States the downward trend to shorter working time stopped in the last 10 years. Some countries like Spain, Finland, Italy and Greece even follow the US trend of increased working time.

4.4.2.2 Labour productivity[149]

Labour costs represent only one side of the story. Their impact on price competitiveness will depend crucially on developments regarding labour productivity.

The EU-15 automotive industry shows a significant labour productivity[150] gap compared to the US and Japan. However, it has recorded higher cumulative growth rates in labour productivity during the

1990s than either the US or Japan when labour productivity levels are compared with the help of automotive unit value ratios (UVRs or, else, automotive industry-specific purchasing power parities). However, as can be seen from Table 4.9, the catch up process has been slow. Using UVRs to convert national currencies to US dollars, the data show that Japan's automotive industry is losing its competitive edge compared to the US. Not surprisingly, there has been a steep increase in the labour productivity in Korea although there is still a considerable productivity gap between Korea and the other leading automotive producing regions.

The table shows that the picture of international productivity trends strongly depends on the way we convert national currencies to US dollar. Based on automotive unit values, Japan is losing its leading position. When we convert Yen to US dollar using expenditure purchasing power parities relating to the GDP (PPPs), we find a lower labour productivity level in Japan in the 80s and a catching-up with the US later. This difference rests on an upwards trend in the Yen/$ relation in the automotive unit value ratio and a decreasing one in the PPP conversion factors.

Within Europe, the picture is mixed with France showing high productivity growth while Germany

---

[149] We omit multi-factor productivity for two reasons: Data are only available for some EU countries. International productivity differences as well as productivity growth differentials in the automotive sector reflect primarily developments in labour productivity itself (see e.g. MGI 2002, 2003).

[150] Labour productivity is defined as value added per hour worked.

had a disappointing performance, albeit coming from a high level. Recently, France is leading in labour productivity not only in Europe but even against the US and Japan. This reflects a variety of reasons. First, lead French manufacturers produce more standardised cars than the German industry which increasingly relies on product differentiation and offer a highly diverse set of automobiles; the French strategy makes it easier to exploit economies of scale. Second, the French industry seems to have some strategic advantage with regard to outsourcing (see MGI 2002). Finally, the German automotive industry invests more heavily in R&D than the French industry. A recent study of MGI (2002) argues that there is significant potential in the German automotive industry to increase the efficiency of R&D investment.

Graph 4.35 shows the ranking of the Member States according to labour productivity in the automotive industry in 2001. France and Belgium show a significant lead. The Dutch, German and Swedish automotive sectors are slightly above EU-15 average while Greece and Ireland show the lowest labour productivity.

Graphs 4.36 and 4.37 present trend values of labour productivity as well as trends in labour productivity growth. The main messages are as follows:

- The speed of the catching-up process of EU-15 against the US and Japan is slow. This is especially true against the US since 1995. More recently, the catching-up process of EU-15 against Japan nearly came to a halt. This could be a attributed to the sluggish European car market in the 1990s;

- The most remarkable development in EU-15 is the French productivity upswing of the 1990s. However, since the end of the 1990s trend productivity growth in France is declining and the German trend productivity growth is recovering;

- Similar to France, labour productivity in the Dutch, Belgian, Austrian and Swedish automotive industries has also developed strongly but lost momentum in recent years;

- Labour productivity developments in smaller automotive producing countries are more volatile than in countries with a significant automotive industry.

4.4.2.3 Special focus on the new Member States

4.4.2.3.1 Labour productivity

Labour productivity, defined as gross output per employee,[151] in the automotive industry in the new Member States is very high compared to the manufacturing industry as a whole, reflecting the importance of significant foreign direct investment and technology transfer. Regarding the major vehicle producers in the new Member States, gross output per employee relative to manufacturing reached, in 2001, 471 % in Slovakia, 222 % in the Czech Republic, 325 % in Hungary, 187 % in Poland and 319 % in Slovenia, which is a small producer but with a relatively high specialisation. The productivity lead of the automotive industry is far larger in the new Member States than in EU-15 where gross output per employee was around 150 % of manufacturing productivity on average – although France and Spain were recording a ratio of 195 % in 2000.

Nevertheless, because of the much lower overall level of productivity in the new Member States, productivity in the automotive industry is still lower than in EU-15 in most countries – although to a far lesser extent than in most other industries. However, the exact size of this productivity gap is difficult to measure, because of lack of adequate data.

---

[151] Value added and hours worked by sector are not available for all new Member States.

Table 4.9: Labour productivity relative to the US (levels, US=100)

	Based on Automotive Unit Values			Based on expenditure PPPs		
	1990	1995	2001	1990	1995	2001
EU-15	59.6	65.9	75.2	71.7	69.0	75.3
Korea	19.4	32.3	33.7	36.4	37.6	46.0
Japan	131.8	110.8	108.8	78.4	82.4	101.7
USA	100.0	100.0	100.0	100.0	100.0	100.0

Source: ZEW calculations.

Graph 4.35: Labour productivity of Member States relative to EU-15 average, 2001

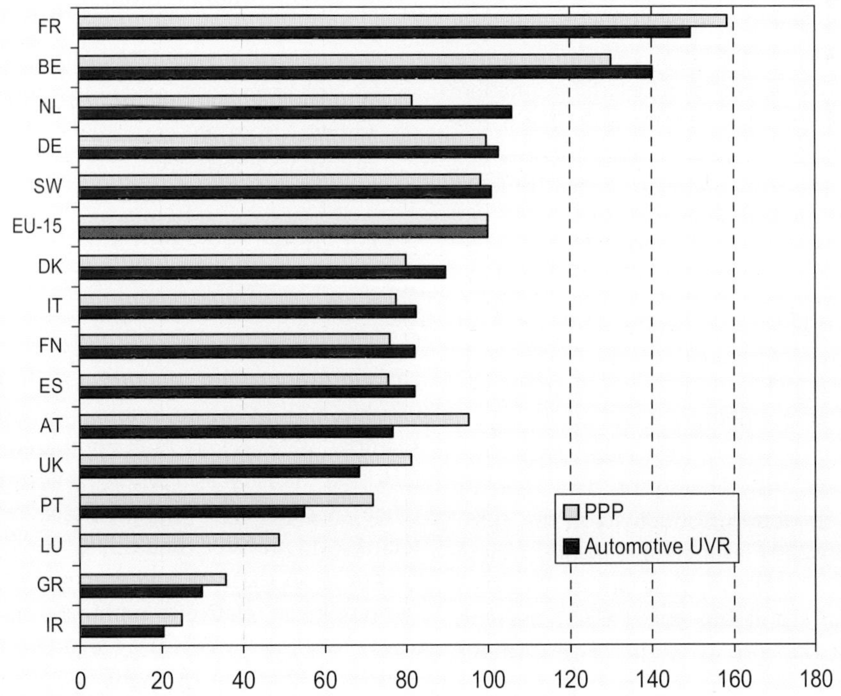

Source: ZEW calculations.

Table 4.10 presents two measures of PPP-based (1999 weights) estimates of productivity differences across the new Member States, PPPs for the *whole gross domestic product* (PPPGDP 99) and PPPs for *gross fixed capital formation* (PPPCAP 99). The latter estimates for productivity are lower because prices for investment goods in the new Member States are higher in relative terms (higher share of imports). For the rare cases where UVRs were available for comparison,[152] they showed a closer correspondence to the latter measure and thus productivity levels expressed at PPPCAP 99 are probably closer to reality. However, PPP for GDP are more frequently used by researchers.[153]

According to these estimates, labour productivity in the automotive industry ranked highest in the Slovak Republic (101.1 % – 172.3 %) and Hungary(100 % - 149.1 %), probably even surpassing the average productivity level of the automotive industry in the EU-15, followed by Slovenia, the Czech Republic and Poland, reaching between 58 % and 97 % (PPPGDP) and 43 %-83 %

(PPPCAP) of the respective EU-15 level. Even on the basis of the lower measure, Slovakia and Hungary ranked among the top productivity performers in Western Europe, just behind France and Belgium, but ahead of Germany, Italy, the UK and Spain. In Slovenia, productivity (measured at PPPCAP) is only slightly lower than in neighbouring Italy. However, the Czech Republic and Poland belong more towards the lower end of the Western car producers in terms of productivity.

4.4.2.3.2 Unit labour costs

High productivity in the automotive industry combined with low wages gives the new Member States a clear competitive cost advantage, reflected in low unit labour costs (ULC).[154] Using GDP PPPs as a conversion factor, ULCs ranged between 9 % of EU-15 average in Slovakia and 65 % in Latvia, in 2001. Using PPPs for fixed investment, the range was between 15 % and 107 % of EU-15 average. As

---

[152] UVR estimates for the year 1996 are available for the Czech Republic, Hungary and Poland relative to Germany from a joint research project by WIIW and the University of Groningen (Monnikhof and van Ark (2000)).

[153] See, for instance, Dollar and Wolff (1993).

[154] Unit labour costs are defined as labour costs (LC) per unit of output (OUT). ULC = LC/OUT. Labour costs were calculated as gross wages (W) multiplied by the number of employees (EMP; W: gross wages). As labour productivity (LP) is defined as output per employed person (LP =OUT/EMP), ULC may be rewritten as wages divided by productivity (W/LP): ULC = (W*EMP)/OUT = W/(OUT/EMP) = W/LP. Total labour costs would be more suitable than gross wages for international comparisons. However, these data exist for some new Member States only and, even there, they do not change the picture significantly.

shown in Table 4.11, apart from Slovakia, Hungary shows a particularly high relative cost advantage - reflecting high productivity and relatively low wages - followed by Lithuania - very low wages compensating for low productivity - and the Czech Republic - with a relatively high productivity but higher wages than for instance Slovakia; Slovenia ranked 6th because of its high wages and Poland ranked 7th, showing a relatively lower productivity and relatively higher wages than the other new Member States.

Given the existing very large cost advantage of most new Member States in the automotive sector, even substantial wage increases will not threaten their competitive advantage compared to the EU-15 in the foreseeable future. However, different wage developments in the individual new Member States may, among other things, influence foreign investors' location decisions within the region.[155]

4.4.3 Human resources in science and technology

Well-trained workers and scientists are key actors in the generation, rapid dissemination and utilisation

of know-how. In most Member States employees classified as Human Resource in Science and Technology (HRST)[156] count for about 25 % of all employees in services and manufacturing and in almost every Member State this share is increasing.

In the EU-15 medium high technology manufacturing sector – which includes the automotive industry – almost one quarter of all employees (25-64 years old) can be classified as HRST. More precisely, in Germany, France, Spain, Sweden, and the UK the share of HRST in the motor industry is at some 30 %.

The structural and organisational changes of recent years have had implications for human resource management and have led to dividing the labour force in the automotive industry. The share of low skilled occupations has been reduced to a minimum, resulting in a considerable decline in this category of jobs. Low-skilled labour in car factories was replaced or outsourced to other companies. High-skilled labour became more valuable and an

---

155   As ULCs are expressed in Euros for international comparison, exchange rate developments play a certain role as well.

156   HRST is defined as a person fulfilling one of the following conditions: successfully completed education at the third level in an S&T field of study; or, not formally qualified as above, but employed in an S&T occupation where the above qualifications are normally required.

Graph 4.36: Trend labour productivity by country, 1981-2001 (in US dollars; automotive UVR)

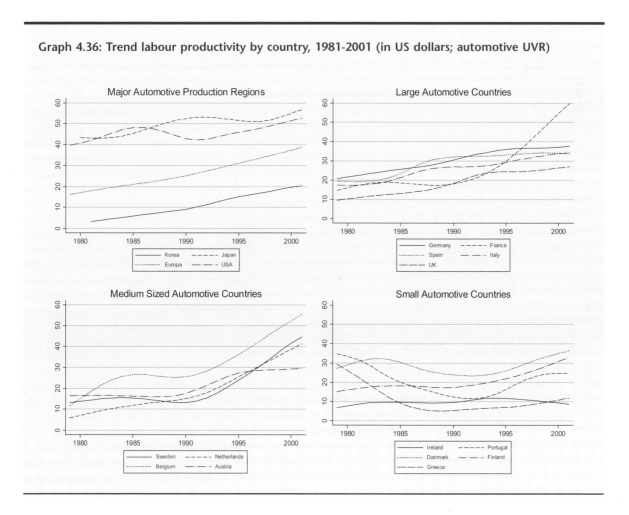

Graph 4.37: Trend labour productivity growth by country, 1981-2001 (in US dollars; automotive UVR)

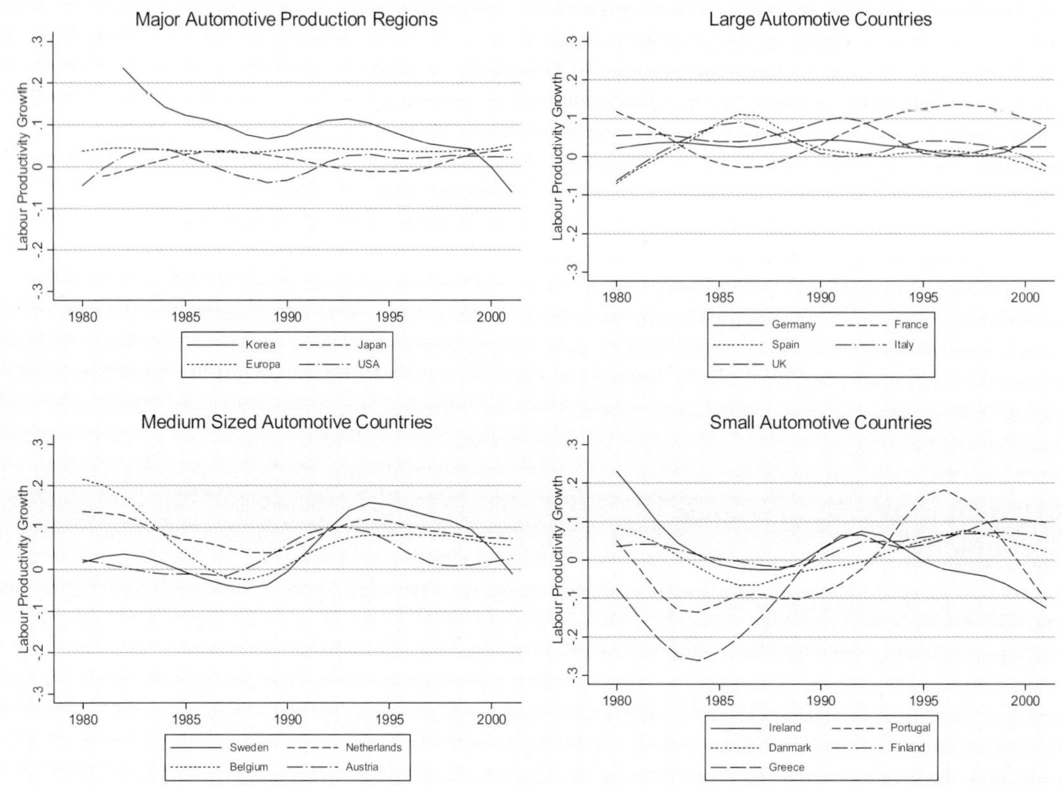

Table 4.10: Motor vehicles, trailers and semi-trailers (NACE 34) Productivity in percent of EU-15, 2001

Country	PPPGDP 99	PPPCAP 99
Czech Republic	83.6	58.0
Estonia	34.7	20.3
Hungary	149.1	100.0
Latvia	12.8	7.8
Lithuania	34.3	19.5
Poland	58.1	43.4
Slovak Republic	172.3	101.1
Slovenia	97.5	82.8

Source: WIIW Industrial Database; Panorama of Czech industries, Eurostat, New Cronos, SBS.

asset for the enterprises. That is especially the case for R&D, engineering, industrial design and other knowledge-intensive tasks. A similar development took place on the supply side. Suppliers of high quality products and services, based on high-skilled workers, stabilised their market position and studies predict that their importance will increase.[157] Suppliers providing ubiquitous products and services lost their market position and were substituted by global sourcing.

During the 1990s, the European automotive industry was able to recover from the slump at the beginning of the decade and the number of people employed has remained more or less constant. In the supply sector the workforce even expanded as a result of taking on additional tasks in the value chain. But the division of labour in the work force increased even more. The general labour qualification level in the EU motor vehicle industry is relatively low ('low skilled'), although a dynamic use of highly qualified people in R&D and knowledge-intensive occupations is taking place along with a high and growing information technology (IT)-

---

[157] See Dudenhöfer (2003).

Table 4.11: Unit labour costs as percentage of EU-15, 2001 (calculated with gross wages, NACE 34)

Country	PPSGDP 99	PPSCAP 99
Czech Republic	20.5	29.6
Estonia	36.3	62.2
Hungary	11.9	17.8
Latvia	65.3	107.2
Lithuania	18.7	33.0
Poland	33.8	45.2
Slovak Republic	8.8	15.1
Slovenia	30.2	35.5

Source: WIIW Industrial Database; Panorama of Czech industries, Eurostat, New Cronos, SBS.

Table 4.12: Skill structure in the German automotive industry

	Manufacturing of				
	Motor vehicles NACE 34	Motor vehicles and engines NACE 34.1	Vehicle bodies, trailers, caravans NACE 34.2	Parts and accessories NACE 34.3	For comparison: Manufacturing
Production-Intensity[1]	72.7	72.0	74.3	73.7	63.3
Skill-Intensity in production[2]	43.7	46.6	63.0	32.5	46.1
Service-Intensity[3]	27.3	28.0	25.7	26.3	36.7
Intensity of academics in services[4]	32.7	35.8	17.0	28.7	20.9
Intensity of academics[5]	8.9	10.0	4.4	7.5	7.7
Intensity of scientists[6]	6.0	6.9	2.2	4.8	4.4

[1] Share of blue-collar workers of all employees in %.
[2] Share of skilled (blue-collar) workers of blue-collar workers in %.
[3] Share of white-collar workers of all employees in %.
[4] Share of academics (graduates) of white-collar workers in %.
[5] Share of academics (graduates) of all employees in %.
[6] Share of engineers/natural scientists of all employees in %.

Source: German Statistical Office.

personnel intensity that is responsible for a relatively high percentage of high skilled labour.[158] Hence, a classification of the automotive sector as a 'low skilled' sector (see e.g. Robinson et al., 2003) is misleading because of the increasing division along qualifications.

The case of the German automotive industry offers a typical illustration of this qualification division (Table 4.12): in the sub-sector of motor vehicles and engines (NACE 34.1) a relatively larger proportion of low skilled jobs than in manufacturing (production intensity row in Table 4.12) coexists with a higher proportion of academics (graduates) and of engineers/natural scientists (two last rows) in the work force.[159]

4.4.4 R&D and Innovation

4.4.4.1 Expenditures on R&D

In the industrial sector, technological R&D is crucial for innovation activity and an important factor in determining technological performance and competitive advantages.

In Japan, the US and the EU-15 high-tech industries account for 40 % to 45 % of manufacturing business enterprise R&D (BERD), medium-high-tech industries for about 45 %, and medium-low-tech and low-tech industries for 10 % to 15 %.

Concerning the R&D expenditures of the motor industry in the three major car producing regions, it can be seen that EU's share increased between 1995 and 2000, from 34 % to 38 %. - see Graph 4.38.

---

[158] See European Communities (2003).
[159] These figures on the skill structure in the German automotive industry rest on different definitions than those in use in the HRST calculation. HRST also include third level vocational training like the German 'Masters' degree and technicians.

Graph 4.38: R&D expenditures in the motor industry, 1995 and 2000 (in % of the sum of EU, US and Japanese R&D expenditures)

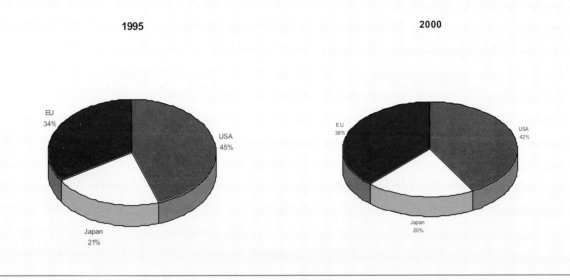

Source: OECD Research and Development Expenditure in Industry database, 1987-2001.

At the company level, relating the annual growth rate of R&D expenditure of the top 300 international companies to absolute R&D expenditure levels suggests interesting insights about the competitiveness of the automotive industry. In particular, 'IT hardware', 'automobiles & parts' and 'pharmaceuticals & biotechnology' constitute the top three sectors in terms of absolute R&D expenditure levels in 2002 but 'IT hardware' has grown hardly at all in recent years and the other two, especially 'automobiles & parts', have experienced rapid growth.

A sector-by-sector comparison of business R&D expenditure between EU-15 and US companies from the top 300 international firms shows that EU-15 companies spend substantially less than their US counterparts in 'pharmaceuticals & biotechnology', 'IT hardware' and 'software & computer services', but maintain a substantial lead in 'automobiles & parts' and 'electronics' – see Graph 4.39. The data suggests that the automotive sector is one of the few sectors where EU-based multinationals have a competitive edge compared to the other triad regions.

4.4.4.2 Innovation patterns

Technical progress, competitiveness and innovation are based on research and development. But even in R&D-intensive industries, R&D is only one but essential core of all innovation activities. Innovation means in this context the development and

economic exploitation of new or improved products and services, and the optimisation of business processes. Innovation continuously redefines markets and opens up new sectors of economic activity. It concerns every industrial sector, especially the automotive industry. Discussions in this section are based on data from the second Community Innovation Survey of 1996 (CIS II).

As can be seen from Table 4.13, about 50 percent of the companies of the manufacturing sector introduced new or significantly improved products or processes, and are categorised as innovating enterprises. In the manufacturing of transport equipment[160] the share of innovators was slightly higher at nearly 60 %. Germany accounted for the largest share of innovators where more than 70 % of the car manufacturers introduced innovations, 72 % developed product innovations, and 30 % are innovators with new products also new to the market. Compared to Germany, the other European car producing enterprises in France and Italy are less innovative. The EU-15 manufacturers of transport equipment account on average as 52 % product innovators, and 24 % are innovating companies with products also new to the market. In total, the results for EU-15 are influenced significantly by Germany – and to

---

[160] Data are only available at the level of transport equipment (NACE 34-35). Given the relative size of the automotive sector in terms of the number of enterprises (NACE 34) results presented mainly reflect the data of automotive sector. In addition, data from CIS III referring to the year 2000 are not available at the two digit level. For selected countries we obtained some information of trends between 1996 and 2000 calculated in the Commission funded IEEF project. We will mention trends between 1996 and 2000 in the text where appropriate.

some extent by France, Sweden, and UK – based on its weight in the European automotive industry.

A comparison of CIS II (1996) and CIS III (2000) results shows declining shares of innovative active firms in the leading car producing countries in the EU; this may suggest that the contribution to technological progress has become more concentrated.

However, technological innovation in the automotive industry is still above the average of the manufacturing sector. This shows that even second- and – to a lesser extend – third-tier suppliers need to innovate to stay in the market. At the same time, however, cost pressures in small supplier companies have increased and some companies have had to stop their innovating activities for financial reasons.

Table 4.13: Share of NACE DM enterprises with innovation activity 1996 (in percent)

	Innovation active enterprises	Process innovators	Product innovators	Innovators with products new to the market	Share of innovation active firms performing R&D
EU-15	60	42	52	24	69
Benchmark:					
EU-15 manufacturing	54	39	44	21	68

Note: NACE DM: Manufacture of transport equipment.

Source: Results of the second Community Innovation Survey (CIS2) © Eurostat.

Graph 4.39: R&D expenditure by top EU-15 and top US business R&D spenders in selected sectors, 2002

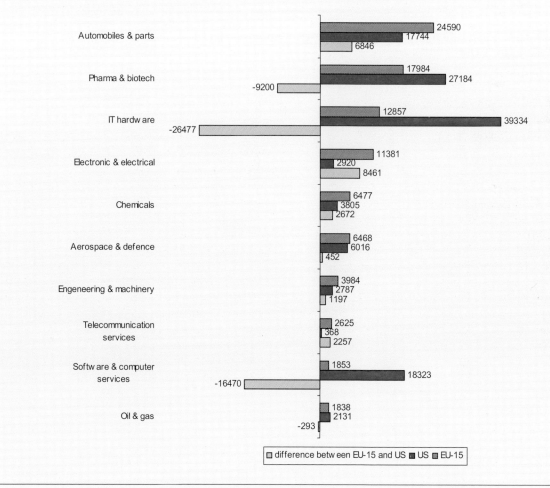

Source: European Commission (2004); Towards a European Research Area; Science, Technology and Innovation, Key Figures 2003-2004.

Enterprises have their own innovation strategies and follow different paths. One strategy is to develop in-house R&D and to combine in-house activities with additional R&D undertaken by external partners. Another strategy is technology transfer through the purchase of new equipment and machinery. For companies with less internal and/or external R&D the purchase of equipment, imitation and learning by doing seem to be valuable innovation strategies. Therefore, these firms invest in trial production, training and tooling-up in combination with industrial design and product design.

In general, EU-15 innovators spend most of their innovation expenditures on R&D and invest in intra-mural and extramural research projects – see Table 4.14. Especially German companies are following this path of innovation. Here, 53 % of the innovation budget goes into in-house R&D and 24 % is dedicated to joint projects with external R&D partners. The behaviour of firms in France and Sweden is comparable to those in Germany. Firms in Italy and the UK opt for other innovation processes, using various channels of technology transfer and

innovating via R&D that is embodied in new equipment. Here, the companies purchase new machinery and equipment and integrate these installations into the in-house production and innovation processes. In Italy, industrial design is of some importance in the innovation process and an Italian strength.

The structure of innovation expenditure underlines the importance of suppliers and their specific contribution even during the R&D stage. The share of external R&D in the automotive sector is considerably larger than in manufacturing as a whole; this is especially the case in those countries where automotive R&D is particularly strong (Finland seems to be an exception).

The combination of mass production with the complexity of specific goods such as cars and other transport equipment makes the risks of failure related to radical innovations very high. Therefore, processes and products are developed incrementally. In-house R&D activities and product engineering are the main sources of technical progress.

Table 4.14: Composition of total innovation expenditures (in % of total innovation expenditures) 1996, by NACE DM

Country	Industrial design (manufacturing sector)	Machinery and equipment acquisition	Market introduction of innovation	External technology acquisition	Extramural R&D	Intramural R&D	Training directly linked to technological innovation
Belgium	8	33	5	1	4	47	2
Denmark	3	11	1	11	2	72	-
Germany	6	11	3	1	24	53	1
Spain	10	19	2	2	7	60	1
France	4	12	17	-	11	53	3
Ireland	4	28	6	5	3	52	2
Italy	16	41	5	3	4	29	2
Netherlands	3	10	?	1	13	60	3
Austria	6	20	6	1	7	55	3
Portugal	10	32	1	28	1	28	-
Finland	2	14	3	6	15	58	2
Sweden	13	15	7	5	9	49	3
United Kingdom	2	33	5	4	-	53	3
EU-15	7	17	5	2	16	51	2
EU-15 manufacturing	6	22	4	4	9	53	2

Note: NACE DM: Manufacture of transport equipment.
Source: Results of the second community innovation survey (CIS2) © Eurostat.

Graph 4.40: Technological Innovations

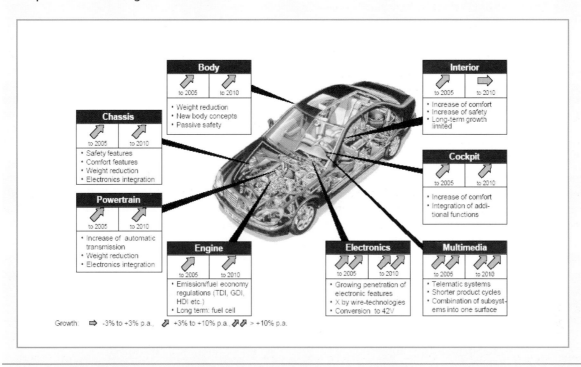

Source: Roland Berger & Partners-Automotives supplier trend study, March 2000.

Additionally, the work of specialised suppliers – sometimes research facilities – is integrated into the value chain.

4.4.5 Trends in innovation activities

Many studies reflect on 'the car and the future'. After euphoric forecasts on the introduction of technologies for 'automated guided driving' or alternative propulsion technology, like the fuel cell, more recent studies take a more sceptical view as concerns the time horizon for the implementation of such technologies. This change can be explained by a number of factors such as the degree of maturity of these technologies, legal problems of product liability or high opportunity costs in comparison with other technologies. Hence, one should expect the basic features of vehicles to be the same for some time to come. Automated-guided-vehicle-technologies for example will not take place in the near future; innovations will be incremental rather than radical and will be hidden to the end customer or revealed only at second sight.

A study accomplished by Roland Berger & Partners (2000) suggest the illustration of Graph 4.40 for the expected growth in value added for different car components induced by innovations.

This illustration highlights especially the importance of incorporating IT into automotive innovation; it is expected that 90 % of all future innovation will be driven by IT [Electronics Engineer (Centaur Communications), 2002]. This affects both the electronics-dominated spheres of multimedia and the traditional mechanical components as the chassis, body or engine. For instance, the fraction of electronics in the chassis will increase from 12 % to 40 %. Similar developments are expected for safety features e.g. pedestrians' protection, traction control, backward driving cameras, night-view display in windshield, sensor controlled brakes or fuel economy regulation. Even product differentiation will take place more and more through electronics: engines constructed in the same way could be adjusted to different performances. The value of electronic components in vehicle would rise from 20 % today to 40 % in 2015. This development will undoubtedly have an impact on vehicle manufacturers and their component suppliers. It appears likely that component suppliers specialised on electronic interfaces could occupy this growth segment (McKinsey&Company, 2003).

When and where technologies will be accepted depends, first of all, on the characteristics of final markets. Apart from differences in consumer's preferences with regard to mobility, technical performance, taste, costs, product reliability, environmental performance etc, the availability (and costs) of fuels play a major role. In theory one might expect that due to

203

globalisation the same products are being consumed and similar processes are being applied worldwide. However, in reality significant regional, national and even local differences can be observed in applied technologies and product designs. In the US, for example, other automobile designs are preferred than in Europe or Japan. This may be rooted in differences with regard to the fit of local frameworks and technical specifications which then lead to county-specific innovation designs. Road conditions, infrastructure, fuel prices and customer preferences differ across nations. Even within a region the markets differ. Some European consumers, for example, seem to pay more attention than others to the variable costs of ownership; for others car safety may be of greater importance. As consumers are increasingly more affected by the variable costs of a motor vehicle (for example, fuel prices), a large increase in the share of diesel-fuelled passenger cars in first registrations can be noted – see Graph 4.41.

In contrast, diesel cars are not present in the American market because the incentive to buy is much weaker due to the low fuel prices and due to the fact that diesel cars have difficulties to meet the environmental standards. This applies as well to Japan. Accordingly, the European and Japanese manufacturers are leading in the production of diesel technologies and in related innovations. Japanese manufacturers produce diesel cars mainly for the European and the 'third world' market. When and to what extent the diesel technology will be used outside Europe will depend on future developments regarding fuel availability and fuel price but also environmental performance.

The **Lead Market** concept (Beise, 2001) suggests that for many innovations lead markets exist that initiate the international diffusion of a specific design of an innovation. Once a specific innovation design has been adopted by users in the lead market subsequent adoption by users in other countries is more likely. One can define lead markets as regional markets with specific attributes that increase the probability that a locally-preferred innovation design becomes internationally successful as well (Beise and Cleff, 2003). In addition, based on first mover advantages, producers supplying these markets early on will have permanent advantages when the technology spills over to other countries. Several European countries show the characteristics of a lead market concerning the automobile branch. Porter (1990) describes the demand conditions in Germany as one of the factors explaining the success in export of German firms. French companies seem to have an advantage in designing cars as well due to the responsiveness of their local customers.

According to Beise and Cleff the lead market for automobiles in Germany is characterised by a combination of several factors:

- The high propensity to consume the automobile leads to a comparatively high valuation of

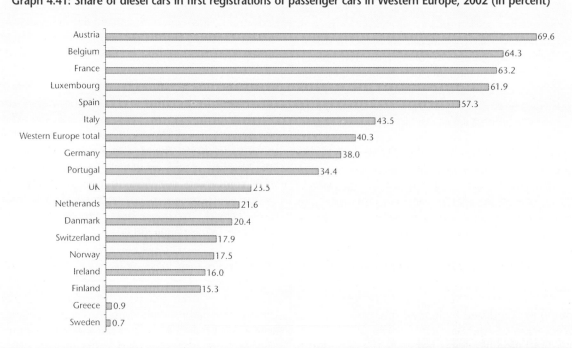

Graph 4.41: Share of diesel cars in first registrations of passenger cars in Western Europe, 2002 (in percent)

Austria	69.6
Belgium	64.3
France	63.2
Luxembourg	61.9
Spain	57.3
Italy	43.5
Western Europe total	40.3
Germany	38.0
Portugal	34.4
UK	23.5
Netherands	21.6
Danmark	20.4
Switzerland	17.9
Norway	17.5
Ireland	16.0
Finland	15.3
Greece	0.9
Sweden	0.7

Source: Eurostat and the German Association of the Automotive Industry (VDA): International Auto Statistics Edition 2003, Frankfurt 2003.

this good which goes together with a willingness to search, examine and select new products; this fosters the perception of product innovations by the consumer;

- High fuel prices have stimulated the diffusion of new engines with high fuel efficiency early on; this may result in a price advantage due the manufacturing experience of large lot sizes for corresponding product innovations;

- The German automotive industry also benefits from a transfer advantage,[161] which is maintained through the strong presence of its firms abroad and the established image of the German automotive industry as high-quality suppliers; the transfer advantage reduces possible hesitations of foreign consumers concerning a new innovation, hence leading to an export advantage;

- The German automobile market is open and overall intensely competitive especially between local manufacturers. In addition, the size of the German automotive industry leads to industry-structure advantages through a dense network of highly specialised and technologically competent component supplier firms from all industrial sectors. Those are – opposed to the industry-structures in the US and Japan – not bound to certain manufacturers but deliver mostly to several manufacturers; therefore, innovations in the area of parts and components diffuse especially rapidly between the companies and foster competition further;

- Finally, the lead market role is also strengthened by infrastructure and legal framework (dense motorway network, no speed limits, taxation) and this reinforces customers' demand for driving qualities at high speed and safety features.

ABS offers an example of the importance of the market in the case of complex products and it is discussed in the accompanying box.[162]

Lead markets do have an impact on the value chain. Companies of a lead market convert the specific demand to a demand of components and intermediary products, thus passing lead market impulses upstream along the value chain. On the other hand, **idiosyncratic product innovation**, which is

adopted locally but does not spread to other countries, limits the competitiveness of firms acting within this country. A firm responding to idiosyncratic markets can achieve a temporary local innovation success but is later pushed to switch to the dominant design. A consideration of the lead market aspect in the national innovation policies generally means the following:

(1) To support the competition between innovation designs;[163] the high competition between the European automotive manufacturers and between suppliers is particularly characteristic for the European market;

(2) To be amenable to the diffusion of new technologies from other countries/regions and an early adopter, or adapter, of new technological trends; the case of ABS brakes is a good example. Diffusion is further facilitated when manufacturers and suppliers are global players, which is particularly true for the European suppliers and automotive industry;

(3) To operate an open markets policy, especially by supporting the diffusion of international standards.

Graph 4.43 lists innovations in vehicle manufacturing that are expected at different dates of introduction in different regions of the triad. Europe and Japan may be called a lead market for innovations in the field of driving security (chassis and body). Customers have a high interest in those aspects, even if their willingness to pay for particular features remains uncertain. Due to high fuel costs, the main thrust of innovation on the Japanese market will be in the field of power train technologies. Innovations in driving assistance systems are also expected in Japan and Europe. In North America many innovations are expected to be introduced with a lag of three to five years due to the legislation of product liability and cost pressure. In addition, the organisation of the value chain and the limited role of suppliers in innovation may hinder further an early introduction by US firms.

The interest of society to protect the environment and reduce accidents, shared throughout the world, became a major driver for innovations. Key issues are here the reduction of gaseous emissions, safety, material recycling and noise. Since the overall trend in the last 30 years is towards cleaner, safer, quieter and waste-free vehicles, manufactures which invested

---

[161] A country has a transfer advantage if customer acceptance of innovations in this country is indicative of acceptance in other countries' markets as well.
[162] For details, see M. Beise et al. (2002).

[163] For example, the different power train technologies (petrol-operated engine, diesel engine, liquid gas engines, electric motor, fuel cell) represent different innovation designs.

early into appropriate technologies have an advantage. Many of the innovations shown in graph 4.43 are driven by environmental concerns, e.g. power train improvements and light weight materials.

Comparing the customer requirements for commercial vehicles with those for passenger cars, there seem to be differences that one may assume would result in differences in innovation priorities, too. For a buyer of a passenger car the cost of purchase is most important, while a buyer of commercial vehicles aims at minimising the 'total cost of ownership'. Innovations for minimising repair time through self and remote diagnostics and for

The ABS

After the Second World War, ABS systems were at first developed by American and British companies, particularly for aeroplanes and racing cars. The first development steps of German companies consisted of testing the existing (foreign) ABS systems in the sixties (Bingmann, 1993). Due to insufficient technological maturity, it took until the late 70's that a – now electronic- system was introduced at the market as special equipment for luxury class vehicles Graph 4.42 shows the estimated process of the diffusion of ABS in passenger cars in Germany, Western Europe, US and Japan.

Graph 4.42: International diffusion of ABS

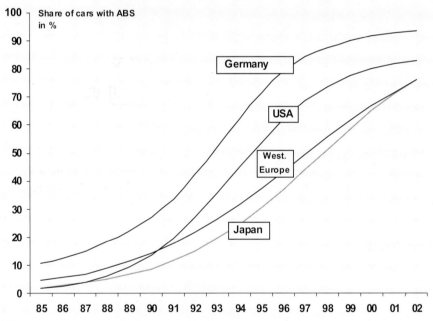

Source: Beise (2001).

At first, the additional costs for the ABS equipment were not fully reflected in the sale price in order to establish the ABS at the German market. The prices could be cut even further through the realisation of economies of scale, the automatisation of the production and the rapid entry of new suppliers in the market, as the ABS could not be patented. In the US the market for ABS developed with a delay of approximately two years. Because the US lower speed limit and drier climate made ABS less usefull, its penetration of the market succeeded only when cost advantages of mass production made possible lower prices. In addition, the US market is generally subject to a strict manufacturer's liability which makes US automotive manufacturers reluctant to introduce security innovations. Each novel electronic component in the vehicle could lead to additional accidents by malfunction or faulty operation and even few accidents can lead to extremely high compensation payments. For this reason, US automotive manufacturers normally wait until they observe the experiences in Europe before offering innovations in vehicles on their own. The reason for the sluggish diffusion in Japan was the additional price for ABS in proportion to the basic price of the vehicle (Bingman, 1993).

Due to the first-mover effect, German companies have a significant world market share in passenger car anti-lock braking systems up to now. This national advantage has been extended to further developments of electronic brake control systems (e.g. ESP, Sensotronic, ASR). Although the technical know-how was already well-known, German companies have acquired lead function which is due to early adoption of this technology in Germany (Beise et al, 2002).

lowering insurance rates through higher driving safety (e.g. electronic driving assistance like night-view display) do not vary from the needs of a passenger car customer (McKinsey&Company, 2003).

For both passenger cars and commercial vehicles, customer requirements go in some instances in the same direction as regulation; for instance, lighter car body materials can reduce the costs of utilisation but also contribute to lower emissions This applies also to environmental concerns and it can be expected that it will, in the medium term, lead to innovations in fuel-injection technology and in emissions-after-treatment systems which will affect both sectors.

Graph 4.43:   Innovation road map for different functional themes in the EU, US and Japan

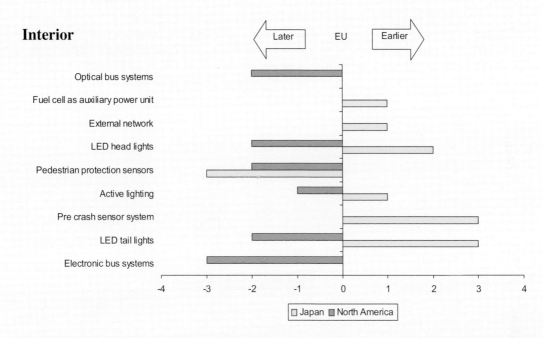

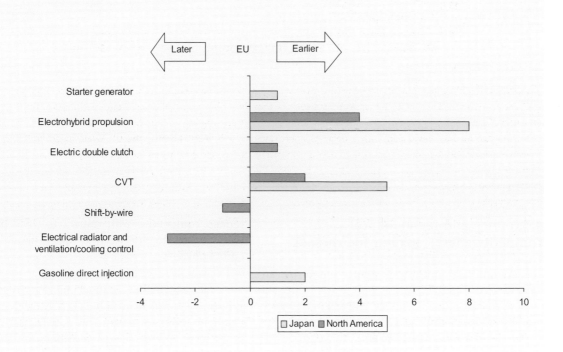

Chassis

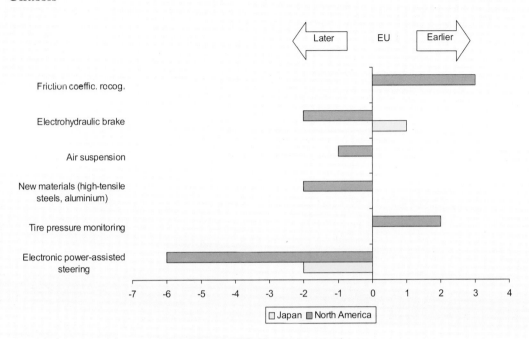

Body

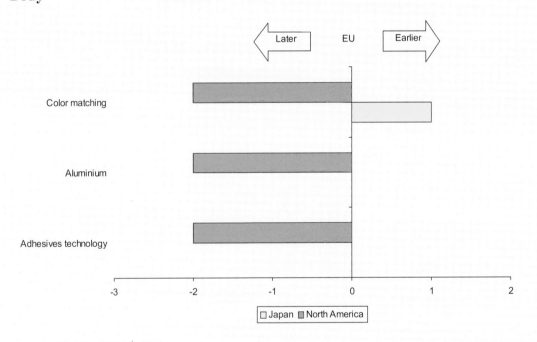

Source: McKinsey&Company HAWK 2015 – Knowledge-based changes in the automotive value chain, Frankfurt 2003, pp. 20. ZEW calculations.

4.4.6 Price and technological competitiveness – joining the threads

The automotive industry is characterised by an increasing competition on a world-wide scale. All leading manufacturers produce and sell in all major regions of the world and customers are able to choose from a wide variety of automotive products. In order to be in the market manufacturers need to remain competitive with respect to price but also with regard to the technological dimension of competitiveness.

A key factor is certainly productivity, and as explained previously, productivity in the EU is lower than in, for example, the US or Japan. This puts pressure on the profit rates. The exchange rates between the main currencies play also an important role in this respect.

In recent years the EU-15 automotive industry has been gradually catching-up in terms of labour productivity which is contributing to improving price competitiveness. However, the catching-up in the area of labour costs has been slow. Taken together, the EU automotive industry is since some years under severe pressure with regard to price competitiveness. This is especially true relative to the US which has gained price advantages due to decreasing labour costs relative to productivity growth.

Enlargement has added to the EU regions with extremely low labour costs. This will help the automotive industry to regain price competitiveness. However, traditional locations of car or car-parts production in the EU-15 will face an increasing pressure resulting from the need of improving their price competitiveness in world markets and from competition by low cost production in the new Member States. In summary, enlargement will help the EU automotive industry to stay competitive and to restructure the value chain.

Given the problems in the area of price competitiveness EU automotive industry invests heavily in R&D in order to foster product and process innovation. The technological competitiveness of the European automotive industry rests not only on the presence of leading car makers but also on widespread innovation activities within the supplier part of the industry. There are several indications that this investment has already improved the technological competitiveness of the industry, especially in the area of construction of car bodies and chassis. In some other areas of technological innovation (e.g. active safety features and engine technology) the EU lags behind Japan.

4.5 The regulatory environment

4.5.1 Introduction

In general, regulations address legitimate concerns of general interest. However, they sometimes put importers at a disadvantage because their obligation to comply is not accompanied by the benefits of scale economies. In addition, regulatory requirements in many cases absorb R&D spending and increase the costs of certain products. More generally, by affecting almost all aspects of doing business, the regulatory environment is one of the major determinants of competitiveness.

However, the impact of individual regulations on competitiveness is far from being straightforward; it can be positive if they lead to strengthened competition or to innovations that the market wants, or negative, if they misdirect the course of innovation towards areas where demand prospects may not be promising. New regulations, at least in the short run, are also generally associated with additional costs. This section presents the major elements of recent regulatory initiatives which affect the automotive industry and reviews some specific regulations, such as the block exemption or the end of life vehicle directive, as well as the efforts of the industry to take on the environmental challenges. Moreover, it should be mentioned that the automotive industry is affected not only by regulations that are specific to it (e.g. End-of-Life vehicle regulation) but also by numerous regulations of broader scope (e.g. industrial design protection).

The following list is indicative. It contains measures that either were recently adopted or are in (sometimes early) discussion. Some of them are presented more in detail later in this section. The list draws a rough distinction between measures and procedures that are supply-side oriented, and measures with a focus on the demand side.

On the supply side, regulations have an impact on various parts of the value chain such as procurement, construction, production, distribution or services; their influence on the cost structure of the automotive industry is very likely. Among these measures are:

- Block exemption: regulating the distribution of cars and vehicle services;

- Industrial design protection and design patents;

- Registration, Evaluation, Authorisation and Restriction of Chemicals (REACH);

- End-of-Life vehicle directive;

- CO_2 voluntary commitment;

- Mobile Air Conditioning (MAC): work on possible options to reduce emissions of fluorinated greenhouse gases from air conditioning systems fitted to or designed for vehicles;

- EURO 5: setting new limits for particle emissions and other gaseous pollutants for light duty vehicles for the medium term;

- Pedestrian protection directive: a measure to reduce injuries to pedestrians and other vulnerable road user who are hit by frontal surfaces of vehicles.

The EU type-approval system sets out the technical requirements for motor vehicles. With the United Nations Economic Commission for Europe Agreements of 1958 and 1998 a regulatory mechanism was established to adopt global technical regulations for motor vehicles. Some of the measures listed above are part of the type-approval system.

On the demand side, regulation measures affect consumer behaviour and the use of motor vehicles. The intervention will probably have an impact on business-to-business as well as business-to-consumer interactions. The selection hereafter gives an overview of some policy measures that are being envisaged:

- Charging for external costs of transportation: Encouraging competition between alternative modes of transportation by charging for infrastructure and social costs;

- Taxation: harmonisation of fuel taxes and restrictions which currently differ widely across the EU by fuel category (petrol versus diesel), customer segment (industrial versus private use), and purpose (heating etc.);[164]

- Fostering bio-fuels: a new directive will allow tax breaks for hydrogen and bio fuels;

- Harmonisation of rules and penalties, i.e. disregarding road signs, laws on drink-driving or speed limits;

- Setting common limits on lorry drivers' working hours;

- Harmonisation of weekend bans for lorries;

- Driver certificate: to enable inspectors from a Member State to check whether a driver from another Member State is lawfully employed;

- Proposals for the initial training for 'new' drivers in the transport of goods and passengers and ongoing training for all drivers.

Some of these measures are aimed directly at the automotive sector while others affect it indirectly by changing consumer preferences and demand attitudes. Regulations with an impact on the level and structure of costs will rapidly affect the competitiveness of manufactures and force them to react. Compared with supply-side measures, those on the demand side may take some time before they are effective. When consumers change their buying behaviour or postpone their purchase following higher taxes or increased fuel prices a decline, perhaps temporary, in market demand can be expected. The same result may occur when transportation businesses become less profitable due to raising taxes, infrastructure tolls, new restrictions on working hours, weekend bans etc.

4.5.2 Measures affecting the supply side

Given the oligopolistic structure of the final-producers segment and the ongoing M&A activities the automotive sector is tightly watched by competition authorities. One of the concerns about market power which has an impact on European consumers is related to the price differentials in the European car market which prevails despite the internal market. Recent regulation initiatives aim at stimulating competition by putting restraints on vertical relations between the vehicle manufacturer and the car dealer. Special attention will be paid here to the impact of Block Exemption Regulation and the current discussion about the harmonisation of industrial design for spare parts.

Another field of regulation addresses the environmental impacts of transportation and the automotive industry. The section will review the end-of-life directive, the new chemical legislation, and actions to reduce CO_2 emission.

4.5.2.1 Block Exemption Regulation

The sectors downstream of the vehicle manufacturer comprise all motor vehicle retail enterprises (NACE 50.1), all motor vehicle maintenance and repair enterprises (NACE 50.2) the sale of motor vehicle parts and accessories enterprises (NACE 50.3), the sale of motor bikes, motor bike maintenance and accessories enterprises (NACE 50.4) and the retail sale of automotive fuel (NACE 50.5). The sector consists mainly of small-scale enterprises. In 2000, 42.5 % of all employees in the sector worked in enterprises with less than 10 employees. Only sectors between NACE 50.1 and NACE 50.3 will be discussed here (the retail and maintenance of motorbikes is not covered by the block exception regulation).

Since October 2002 motor vehicle distribution and servicing agreements within the EU have come under the new Block Exemption Regulation - Regu-

---

[164]   It should be mentioned that fuel accounts for around 20% of the operating costs of road haulage companies.

lation no. 1400/2002, replacing Regulation 1475/95 which expired on 30.09.2002. The new Block Exemption Regulation strives to foster competition between dealers of the same brand and in the after-sales market, for example, by facilitating cross-border sales.

Vehicle manufacturers have to choose between two models of distribution (i.e. they cannot accumulate both) (European Commission, 2002):

(4) In the 'Selective Distribution Model' no dealer has an allocated sales territory. They can sell to any customers in the EU except to other dealers outside the manufacturers' network. Sales to supermarkets or internet-dealers are not possible. Starting October 1, 2005 dealers are allowed to open up other branches in optional locations in addition to their original location.

(5) In the 'Exclusive Distribution Model' every dealer has an allocated sales territory. Dealers are permitted to sell outside their sales territory only passively and they are also free to sell to operators outside the manufacturers' network.

In both models the sales and service processes will be unbundled. Vehicle manufacturer cannot insist on a mandatory link between sales and after-sales services. 'Any person who can fulfil the quality criteria set by the manufacturer can become an authorised repairer and carry out all servicing, warranty and recall work on vehicles of the brand for which they are authorised, without incurring an obligation to sell vehicles' (Emanuel, 2002). Furthermore, an authorised retailer will not need permission to take over another authorised retailer. This is also true for a repairer. However, the acquisition of a sales business by a repairer (or vice versa) requires the consent of the vehicle manufacturer.

As in the previous block exception regulation, the repairer cannot be forced to use original spare parts anymore. Only if repair costs arise which are covered by the vehicle manufacturer, for example warranty work, free servicing and vehicle recall work, the vehicle manufacturer can insist on the use of original spare parts. Other than that, matching quality spare parts of the manufacturers or of independent suppliers can be used. A warranty, which is guaranteed beyond the legal limit, may oblige vehicle repairers to use original spare parts (European Commission, 2002).

Furthermore, the prohibition of multi-brand distribution will be abolished, even though vehicle manufacturers can still demand their brand to represent at least 30 % of the dealer's turnover. However, even though multi-brand dealers are not obliged to employ separate sales forces, manufacturers can impose requirements regarding the display of brands and Corporate Identity (for example the appropriate equipment of a showroom) (European Commission, 2002).

Trends in retail of motor vehicles and parts

In the past, licensed dealers operated as legally independent companies acting locally, selling the producer's vehicles on their own behalf and expense. Exclusive agreements governed, among other things, the size of the sales and exhibition area, the scale of the new cars stock, quantity of demonstration cars, placement of the spare parts storage and the amount of marketing expenditure (Terporten, 1999).

Since the mid nineties the margins of licensed distributors have been increasingly under pressure as, on one hand, a maturing market and sales from unlicensed outlets tended to reduce prices while, on the other hand, manufacturers' requirements regarding quality of service to the customers tended to increase costs. Whereas it was possible in the seventies to earn high margins in automobile retail, nowadays this business has to be subsidised with funds earned in the after sales, service and accessories business. Graph 4.44 shows that the gross operating rate in automobile retail (NACE 50.1) is well below corresponding values in automobile parts and accessories (NACE 50.3) and considerably lower than in automobile repair (NACE 50.2).

The new Block Exception regime is expected to reinforce competition further both at the sales level, through improved access of hitherto 'outsiders' to a brand's retail business, and at the after sales level. One possible outcome is increased concentration as dealerships seek to balance out decreasing margins with economies of scale. This will not necessarily lead to a marked reduction of the number of sales outlets but, more likely, to their absorption into larger retail groups. For the vehicle manufacturer the distribution costs will be lower with fewer access points (Cap Gemini Ernst & Young, 2003).

It is also possible that dealers seek economies of scope by including additional brands into their sales range. Particularly those brands that were as yet unable to assert themselves against large dealer networks are expected to benefit from the higher density of multi franchise dealers. Particularly Asian vehicle manufacturer will win over dealers who

Graph 4.44: Gross operating rate of different downstream sectors, 1998 (NACE 50)

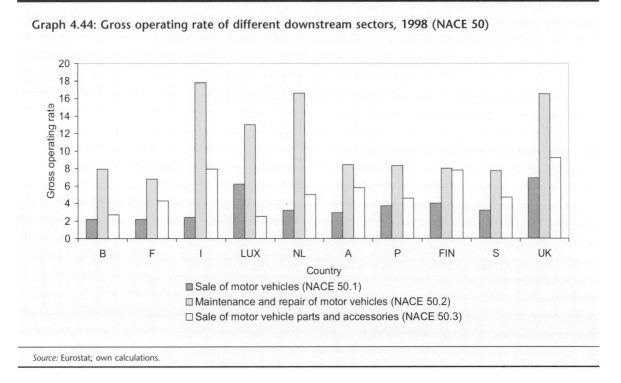

Source: Eurostat; own calculations.

already sell an upper-end car line (Cap Gemini Ernst & Young, 2003). European vehicle manufacturers are aware of this risk. Therefore, they are intensifying brand specific investments. Downstream integration activities of the vehicle manufacturers establishing their own sales outlets can be observed. Especially some 'prestige manufacturers have been buying up certain of their key dealerships in order to retain control of those outlets' (Emanuel, 2002).

For years, vehicle manufacturers have supported concentration of the dealer network because of efficiency aspects. This process would have continued even without the Block Exemption, because new distribution structures alongside the licensed dealers would have been created, leading to stiffer competition and increasing consolidation pressure on dealers. The new distribution structures are, among others, car broker/online agents, internet,[165] new players in the industry, like supermarkets and international mega dealers, as well as smaller non-authorized dealers. In the case of EU re-imports to Germany, for example, every fifth new car is sold by a non-authorized dealer.

Simulation studies (Dr. Lademann & Partner, 2001) estimate the market share loss of franchised dealers induced by the Block Exemption at around 35 %.

---

[165] Even if the internet was used by some vehicle producers for distributing new cars – e.g. Fiat offered a special edition of its Barchetta in Italy exclusively via the internet and Vauxhall (UK) offered substantial reductions on list prices for internet purchasers (PricewaterhouseCoopers, 2000) – the internet is more often used for used cars than as distribution channel for new cars. As regards new car purchases it is primarily used to increase the customer's knowledge and to make consumers more demanding about benefits such as price and warranty coverage (Cap Gemini Ernst & Young, 2003).

Trends in automotive repair and maintenance

Another problem for the dealers arises by the unbundling of sales and service. As yet, the bulk of the retailers' margins were earned in service, to some extent sales outlets were subsidised by after sales service. These earnings threaten to decrease when new competitors access the market. This effect is amplified by the fact that the service needs of vehicles are declining, and the loyalty of customers having their service carried out by the dealer has decreased and will continue to do so in future (Dudenhöffer, 1997).

Unlike in Europe, the US service and sales sector is remarkably independent. Franchise dealers in the USA retain only 20 % of the overall maintenance market. Even with respect to vehicles not older than one year they hold no more than 40 % (autopolis, 2000). The amount of cars in use per establishment in automotive repair and maintenance, however, corresponds to that of Japan or to the European average.

The technology development of cars themselves and corresponding repair technologies will determine the degree to which competition in the repair segment increases. Due to the increasing complexity of vehicle technology, repair services can only be carried out by those companies who can afford the infrastructure required for diagnostic systems and special tools. These are investments that can hardly be generated by smaller companies.

Either they simply disappear from the sector or they will have to content themselves with repairs with lower value added.

Due to increased capital requirements, traditional repair companies must generate further earnings from other areas. This might include providing service for other brands as well as using cheaper 'matching quality' spare parts (Emanuel, 2002). As vehicle manufacturers continue to pursue their platform and parts sharing policies, repair companies are likely to benefit from synergy effects too (Cap Gemini Ernst & Young, 2003). Smaller companies, however, are less likely to profit from these opportunities.

4.5.2.2 Harmonisation of Industrial Design Regulation on Spare Parts

At the time when the Community Directive 98/71/EC on industrial design protection was adopted no agreement could be reached with regard to the spare parts for complex products. Presently, in some Member States (for example, France, Austria, Denmark, Sweden) spare parts can be protected by industrial design registration whereas in others (for example, UK, Italy, Belgium, the Netherlands) they cannot.

In order to complete the Single Market in this area the Commission has ordered an impact assessment of possible options (Technopolis, 2003). The impact assessment concludes that a modification will increase competition in the repair market. However, the concrete impact will vary in different market segments of the spare parts industry (glass vs. body parts). Despite the increase of competition it is less obvious whether the final consumer will see lower repair prices. It may well be the case that the reduction of the market power of the vehicle manufacturers and, hence, the reduction in their profits will be reaped by other actors down the value chain (e.g. repair shops, producers of spare parts). In addition, there are concerns about the impact of the liberalisation of the aftermarket on the quality of spare parts and hence on car safety.

Vehicle manufacturers (see ACEA, 2004) claim that industrial design protection on 'must match' spare parts is needed to recoup their initial investment in the design of certain parts of cars; for instance, the envisaged modification would endanger the viability of the investment (e.g. extended testing of bumpers) needed to fulfil the recent pedestrian safety regulation. They also contest that dropping the protection would result in any significant consumer benefits.

Increased competition will put EU vehicle manufacturers and existing suppliers under pressure which will likely induce innovation and foster competitiveness. Furthermore, new entrants in the spare part markets will be primarily based outside the EU and, hence, some of the rents currently earned by EU industry will be lost. In any event, it will be necessary to have a mechanism to ensure that spare parts and original parts meet the same safety standards.

4.5.2.3 End-of-Life Vehicle (ELV) Directive 2000/53/EC

About twelve million vehicles reach their end-of-life each year in Europe, around 25 percent of which go to landfills as eight million tonnes of waste (PriceWaterhouseCoopers, 2002b). After three years of debate, the European Parliament and the Council adopted on 18.09.2000 Directive 2000/53/EC according to which vehicle manufacturers are obliged to take back old vehicles, substitute certain specific hazardous substances and, together with other economic operators, such as dismantlers and recyclers, increase the level of material re-use and recovery up to 85 percent by 2006 and up to 95 percent by 2015.

The ELV Directive obliges the vehicle producer to pay for the costs related to the collection and further treatment of the end-of-life vehicle from the delivery to an authorised treatment facility onwards. Additional compliance costs stemming from the ELV Directive have been estimated at €20 to €150 (PriceWaterhouseCoopers, 2002b) and €6 to €17 (Umweltbundesamt, 2003).

In addition to the impact on costs, the Directive might also affect the value chain of the vehicle manufacturer. For instance, in product development vehicle manufacturers will have to avoid using materials that reduce the share of recyclability. The automobile industry criticises the fact that a high recycling ratio collides with other environmental protection measures, such as fuel consumption. According to the automobile industry 'Light-weight construction, one way of fulfilling this objective, is significantly hampered by the enforced recycling ratio, since the cost of plastic parts and composites would be particularly affected by a high material recycling ratio.' (Lucas, Schwartze, 2001). The Commission services, addressing this question, could not at this stage identify any negative repercussions of the ELV Directive on the CO_2 emissions of passenger cars.

Economic operators are responsible for the observance of recycling ratios. Because tier 1 suppliers take more responsibility for R&D but are not obliged to withdraw products, the ELV Directive requires a close co-operation among operators along the value chain.

Since the end-of-life vehicle directive concerns all cars sold in Europe no cost disadvantage will arise for European manufacturers compared to non-European ones. In fact, the proximity of the European automotive industry with car-recycling firms constitutes an advantage, considering that Asian manufacturers have not established as dense a network of dealers up to now. In addition, Asian manufacturers will have to invest in the general use of recyclable materials as well.

4.5.2.4 Implications of the New EU Chemicals Legislation (REACH)

On 29 October 2003 the European Commission adopted the REACH proposal (**R**egistration, **E**valuation and **A**uthorisation of **Ch**emicals) for a new EU regulatory framework for chemicals. Enterprises which manufacture or import one ton or more per year and per manufacturer/importer of a specific chemical substance would be required to register it in a European-wide central database, managed by the new European Chemicals Agency. The registration would include information on properties, uses and safe ways of handling the products. This safety information will be passed down the supply chain. Some groups of substances would not have to be registered because they are subject to a different EU legislation.

REACH is meant to provide for coherence on a European level in the different national and sometimes inconsistent rules and regulations on the treatment of old and new materials throughout the whole 'life' of a specific substance. Old materials and new materials should be subjected to a standardised regulation replacing as many as 40 existing European directives and regulations.

While a wide agreement exists on the goals of the proposal, there is disagreement with regard to its effects on the capacity for innovation and the competitiveness of the chemical industry and downstream industries. The argument is basically about the expenses resulting from additional administrative expenditure and about the time delay due to the procedure for the introduction of new products and processes. The European Commission doubts whether - compared to the already existing directives and the different national admittance regulations - significant additional cost will arise at all while industry representatives

produced estimates that put such costs at a very high level.

The chemical regulation has – through the application of chemical products in components and intermediate products and the typical supply of hundreds of chemical parts to the aftermarket - a high relevance for the automotive industry, because all actors in the supply chain will be obliged to ensure the safety of any chemical substance they handle. Where a chemical is not used according to the original registration, the new uses or risk-reduction measures will have to be reported to the European Chemicals Agency if the volume is higher than 1 ton. Downstream users will have the right to demand from their suppliers that they register substances for all their uses, or the downstream user can choose, for reasons of commercial confidentiality, to do their own Chemical Safety Assessment and Report.

These registration and testing requirements may involve additional costs, most probably by component suppliers. At this stage, however, there is no generally accepted estimation of the overall additional burden and its distribution within the European industry.

4.5.2.5 The Kyoto targets: CO2 Emission Reduction – the Manufacturers' Contribution

Containing the threat of climate change is one of the greatest challenges facing the international community. According to the Kyoto protocol[166] the European Union must reduce greenhouse gas emissions by 8 % compared to 1990 levels in the period of 2008–2012; countries like Germany must reduce emissions by 21 %.

Many countries throughout the world take measures to reduce the specific emissions for vehicles. In particular, the traditional car producing countries and regions have implemented legislation or have set targets in order to increase the fuel efficiency of cars, e.g. the US, Japan, China, Korea etc. At this stage the targets set in the EU are more severe than in these other countries.

The EU strategy to reduce CO2 emissions from passenger established early a framework for measures to improve the fuel efficiency of cars. A cornerstone of this strategy is the voluntary commitments

---

[166] The Kyoto Conference took place in 1997. The protocol will enter into force if it is ratified by at least 55 of the 160 signatory countries provided that these countries account in total for at least 55 % of the emissions of the industrialised countries. By the end of 2003 more than 100 countries, including the EU and its member states have deposited their instruments of ratification. However, some large countries have so far not ratified the protocol.

of the car industry. The European Automobile Manufacturers Association (ACEA)[167] negotiated a voluntary commitment with the European Commission in 1998 to undertake every effort to reduce average CO_2 emissions of newly registered cars to 140 grams per kilometre (140gCO_2/km) by 2008. At the time, the average specific emissions of the ACEA's car fleet registered in the European Union were 165 g/km (see Annex Table A4.8). Between 1995 and 2002, the overall reduction achieved in the car fleet was 12.1 %. CO_2 emissions and fuel consumption go hand in hand so that the average consumption (petrol and diesel) fell from 7.6 litres per kilometre (7.6 l/km) to 6.5 l/km. Another positive sign is the increasing share of passenger cars which emit 140 g/km CO_2 or less. ACEA stated that some manufacturers plan to include more models which fulfil the 120 g/km criterion in their product range. The share of these cars in new registrations was 5 % in 2002 compared to 0.7 % in 1999. Besides the many positive signs, the industry considers that the targets remain extremely ambitious.

The members of the Japan Automobile Manufacturers Association[168] (JAMA) made a commitment to fulfil the 140 g/km level by 2009. The car fleet of JAMA registered in Europe has an average CO_2 emission of 174 g/km which is slightly more than the European manufacturers'. They managed to reduce average fuel consumption from 8.0 l/km to 7.3 l/km.

A different picture is drawn by the Korean Automobile Association[169] (KAMA) which reduced emissions from 197 g/km in 1995 to 183 g/km in 2002. The monitoring of their achievements indicates that KAMA will have difficulties in achieving their indicative target range for 2004 which lies between 165 and 170 g/km. KAMA has nevertheless reaffirmed its commitment of a reduction to 140 g/km by 2009.

All manufacturers have to undertake dedicated research work, involving themselves, suppliers, research institutes and universities, in order to develop promising technologies for the reduction of CO_2 emissions. Funding for this work is sought from the EU Framework Programme for Research and Development (European Commission, 2003).

There is a large number technologies used by manufactures to reduce CO_2 emissions from passenger cars. In the past the improvement of diesel engine power trains turned out to be most efficient for the EU market. In future improvements of the gasoline power train, the application of hybrid technology and the usage of alternative fuels look most promising.

Hybrid Engines

Given present limitations in technologies such as batteries and fuel cells, the most viable powertrain alternatives are hybrid configurations that include a relatively small internal combustion engine and an electric motor. In 1997, Honda Insight and Toyota Prius became the first commercially available hybrid models.

The commitments have contributed to technology developments that may be even more relevant in the context of the recent increases of fuel prices and the interest of many countries to secure their energy supply.

In its strategy to reduce CO_2 emissions, the EU relies only in part on the commitment of the industry. Consumers also need to be informed about the importance of CO_2 emissions and fuel economy. Fiscal measures will be part of the strategy to provide incentives for consumers to buy cars that fulfil the requirements of low CO_2 emissions and fuel consumption (European Commission, 2004). National taxes should establish a more direct relation between tax level and the CO_2 performance of new cars. Such measures will also help to develop a strong home market for fuel efficient cars.

4.5.3 Measures affecting the demand side

While investment in infrastructure and the mobility of people, goods and services will boost productivity, economic growth and employment, external (social) costs, especially pollution are more likely to consume resources and affect the economy adversely. Higher living standards in Europe have given rise to demands for environmental protection, quality of work, corporate social responsibility and health protection. While transportation by car enhances the standard of living, it also generates undesired environmental impacts that can lead to human health problems and ecological damage. In many ways, the demand for sustainability is an enormous challenge and leads to developments such as charging for infrastructure and social cost, taxation of motor vehicles in general, and CO_2 taxes.

4.5.3.1 Charging for infrastructure and social costs of transportation

The automotive industry depends on a highly developed and functioning transportation infrastructure

---

167   BMW, DaimlerChrysler, Fiat, Ford, General Motors, Renault, Volkswagen, Volvo, DAF TRUCKS NV, MAN NUTZFAHRZEUGE AG, Dr. Ing. h.c. F. PORSCHE AG, PSA PEUGEOT CITROEN, SCANIA AB.
168   The members are: Nissan, Honda, Mitsubishi, Suzuki, Mazda, Toyota, Daihatsu, Yamaha, Kawasaki, Isuzu, UD, Fuji Heavy Industries.
169   The members are: KIA, GM Daewoo, Renault Samsung, Hyundai, Ssangyong.

(e.g. uninterrupted road traffic) to assure that their customers can turn their automotive investments into economic profits. The capacity of the roads is already too small even for today's traffic. In its 2001 White Paper, the European Commission notes that not only roads in major agglomerations but also large sections of the trans-European transport network are chronically congested. There are daily traffic jams on 7,500 kilometres of Europe's roads – that is, on 10 per cent of the trans-European trunk roads and motorways. Users' preferences for transport by road seem to rely on flexibility, convenience, and independence. Other modes of transport are not able to carry freight from door to door, as road transport can.[170]

Many parts of the motorway and trunk road network in Europe no longer comply with the requirements of modern traffic. Maintenance claims an increasing proportion of infrastructure funding. Congestion seriously jeopardises the competitiveness of the economy. The external costs of congestion on the roads alone amount to some 0.5 per cent of the European Union's GDP. Taking into account further growth in transport, the Commission fears that the costs of traffic jams could rise by 142 per cent to € 80 billion per year, which would be equivalent to 1 per cent of EU GDP.[171]

The European Commission has recently started a debate about the true cost of transportation.[172] CO_2 emissions from road transportation account for 19 % of total greenhouse gas emissions in the EC.[173] Further, there are roughly 41,000 deaths on the road every year and 1.7 million injured. The direct costs of road accidents are estimated at € 45 billion plus € 160 billion of indirect costs, almost 2 % of European GDP.

A large number of studies have been undertaken in recent years to find a way to internalise social costs.[174] Work has been done on the definition of different cost categories, the identification of cost drivers and with a certain focus on the appropriate method for monetary quantification. Although there is agreement on the ultimate objective - that social costs should be internalised - the strategies and instruments put forward to achieve this differ widely.

In the 2001 White Paper the cost levels generated by a heavy goods vehicle covering 100 km on a motorway in open country at off-peak times are specified in an interval ranging from € 8 to € 36 of which a little more than € 8 correspond to infrastructure charges. Broken down by different cost categories there are the following average ranges: costs of air pollution (cost of health and damaged crops) from € 2.3 to € 15, climate change (floods and damaged crops) from € 0.2 to € 1.5, infrastructure from € 2.1 to € 3.3, noise (cost on health) from € 0.7 to € 4, accidents (medical costs) from € 0.2 to € 2.6 and congestion (loss of time) from € 2.7 to € 9.3 (White Paper, European Commission, 2001).

In the recent RECORDIT study[175] internal and external costs were estimated for 16 EU countries. On a weighted average basis, the study found that an amount of € 0.21 of extra charge per kilometre was necessary to offset the net external cost for a 40t vehicle for road transportation. The latter consists of the sum of (marginal) infrastructure[176] costs and external costs (i.e. air pollution, noise, accidents, and congestion) minus already paid taxes.[177] The comparable costs for rail transportation are quantified at € 0.09/vkm. In order to compensate for the difference between road and rail a tax increase or extra charge on road transportation of € 0.12/vkm would therefore be necessary.

The variance of price or extra charges for the use of different modes of transportation is wide - a sign of understandable uncertainty – reflecting the analytical method, assumptions and data sources used. The outcome of additional charging[178] for road transport is critically dependent on the response of the users. By changing the relative price of road

---

[170] Trends in the character of transported goods as well as the enlargement of the EU will further stimulate road transport as flexibility and speed will became even more important in the future. And enlargement will foster road transport as it provides additional possibilities for reengineering value chains in manufacturing to profit from EU wide costs and competence differentials.

[171] This does not even take into account the massive development needs of the new member states for their transport networks. The Commission estimates that in these states, 20,000 kilometres of roads and 30,000 kilometres of rail tracks need either building or expanding, which would mean additional costs approaching 100 billion euros.

[172] In 2002 the EU proposed a framework directive setting out the principles and structure of an infrastructure charging system and a common methodology for setting charging levels, offset by for the removal of existing taxes, and allowing cross financing. The planned actions are meant to make the tax system more consistent by proposing uniform taxation for commercial road transport fuel by 2003 to complete the single market. See European Commission White Paper (2001), and the earlier Green Paper (1995) of the European Commission.

[173] European Environment Agency, Annual European Gas Inventory, 1990-2002 and Inventory Report 2004.

[174] RECORDIT, 2003; Link et al., 1999; Maibach et al., 2000; Prognos, 2001; Quinet, 1997; Verhoef, 1994; European Commission, 1999; For the U.S. Murphy and Delucchi, 1998.

[175] RECORDIT stands for real cost reduction of door-to-door intermodal transport; see RECORDIT (2003).

[176] The calculation of (marginal) infrastructure costs is based on the costs for maintenance and operation by a vehicle movement. The capital costs of infrastructure are regarded as fixed and not included in the analyses. The problem of an adequate charging of full (variable and fix) infrastructure costs for different modes is not solved yet. Therefore, price decisions or new charging systems should be introduced with care. Unless all cost categories are correctly quantified, prices are biased, and do not lead to an optimal solution.

[177] Some of these external and infrastructure costs are already covered by the charges imposed on the transport vehicle itself, comprising fuel and vehicle taxes and infrastructure charges. The different tax categories contain circulation tax, registration tax, road tolls and charges, fuel tax.

[178] The application in the charging system of price differentiation is suggested. There are a number of differentiation criteria such as category of infrastructure, time of the day, distance, size and weight of the vehicle etc. that could be taken into account.

traffic other modes of transport should become more attractive. But the demand for transportation services does not depend exclusively on the price. Quality and accessibility are further important determinants of demand.

4.5.3.2 Taxation of passenger cars

Vehicle taxation systems implemented in the Member States reflect a variety of influences beyond the obvious need to raise revenue. At the moment the approach to regulation of the automobile varies among European countries, reflecting different social priorities.[179] The operation of 15 different vehicle tax systems within the EU has resulted in tax obstacles, distortions and inefficiencies. In this respect, the car market in the EU is still a long way from a true single market.

Taxes on passenger cars vary widely in terms of structure and levels. They are based on one or a mix of elements such as fiscal horsepower, engine capacity, weight, kW, price of the car, fuel consumption, or CO2 emissions. There are:

- taxes payable at the time of acquisition, or first putting into service, of a passenger car, defined in most cases as Registration Tax (RT);

- periodic taxes payable in connection with the ownership of the passenger car, defined in most cases as Annual Circulation Tax (ACT);

- taxes on fuel (FT);

- any other taxes and charges, such as insurance taxes, registration fees, road user charges, road tolls etc.[180]

Member States having a large car industry tend not to apply a Registration Tax, or they apply a lower registration tax, while car importing Member States tend to levy higher Registration Tax. Tax levels range, in extreme cases, between zero and 180 % of pre-tax car price. In absolute terms average Registration Tax ranged, in 1999, between € 15 659 in Denmark and € 267 in Italy. All Member States apart from France apply Annual Circulation Tax at national level. Very different objective factors are used as tax bases (e.g. cm3, kW, CO2, weight).

The average Annual Circulation Tax paid in 1999 ranged from € 30/vehicle in Italy, to € 463/vehicle in Denmark.

Excise duties on motor fuels are seen as an effective fiscal instrument to influence the level of car use, or for internalising environmental and social costs linked to the use of passenger cars, such as infrastructure costs, accident costs, and air pollution costs. Usually, Member States applying no, or low Registration Tax, compensate revenue losses by higher fuel tax levels.[181] Motor vehicle taxation levels in the EU - measured as a tax percentage of the net price of the car - vary from 16 % in Germany up to 198 % in Denmark.[182]

The wide differences in tax systems have a negative impact on the ability of the car industry - and European consumers - to reap the benefits of operating within a single market. Car market fragmentation prevents industry from exploiting economies of scale, or to produce motor vehicles for the entire Internal Market, applying the same specifications and does not prevent pre-tax prices from varying significantly within the internal market. Different taxation levels can explain about 20 % of the European car price differentials.[183] Industry is often obliged to produce a specific car model, with different specifications, in order to soften the pre-tax prices, in particular when the vehicle is destined to high taxing Member States. This generates additional costs that undermine the competitiveness of the European car industry.[184] On the other hand, precisely because of the differences in tax levels, the car industry adapts its pre-tax prices taking into consideration the level of taxation in Member States. Pre-tax prices are much higher in those Member States applying no, or a low, Registration Tax.

4.5.3.3 Fiscal measures in order to reduce CO2 emission – CO2 taxes

Policies and options for future action in the field of passenger car taxation are being envisaged and the priority is to ensure the smooth functioning of the Internal Market.[185] That means a modernised and

---

[179] COM(2002)431 final, Taxation of passengers cars in the European Union - options for action at national and Community levels. See also the table in the annex 'Summary of tax, environment, transport and emission policy in 2003/4 by country' taken from ACEA (2004), EU-15 Economic Report.

[180] Value added taxes (VAT) for motor vehicles are generally subjected to the standard rate of VAT. Value added taxes range from 15 % in Luxembourg, 16 % in Germany, up to 25 % in Denmark and Sweden.

[181] With the only exception of the UK, they all apply lower tax levels on diesel, traditionally used by commercial vehicles. Diesel is taxed on average about 140 EUR/1000 litres lower than unleaded petrol.

[182] See ACEA (2003), Annual Tax Guide 2003.

[183] TIS Study (2002), Study on vehicle taxation in the Member States of the EU, TIS/PT.

[184] In parallel, as tax requirements differ, cars marketed in one Member State with specifications designed to meet national requirements and 'tax influenced' demand (e.g. brackets of fiscal horsepower, tax policy regarding diesel), are imperfect substitutes of and may not effectively compete with cars sold in a different Member State, thereby undermining the benefits which EU consumers should derive from a competitive and integrated market.

[185] In an earlier communication the Commission sets out its views on the fundamental priorities for tax policy in the European Union. See COM(2001)260 final, Tax Policy in the European Union - Priorities for the Years ahead.

simplified vehicle taxation system, and in particular an introduction of new parameters in the bases of taxes related to passenger cars in order to make them partially, or totally, CO2 based. The process should lead to better co-ordination, and an approximation of passenger car taxation systems within the Internal Market.

The use of fiscal measures is one of the pillars of the European Union's Sustainable Development Strategy. In the Commission's opinion vehicle taxation is an important complementary instrument to support the realisation of the EU-target of 120 g CO2/km for new cars by 2008-2010, and to contribute to the accomplishment of the EU engagements under the Kyoto Protocol.[186] This would imply establishing a more direct relation between tax level and the CO2 performance of each new passenger car, for instance, by replacing existing vehicle taxes by taxes fully based on CO2 emissions or, alternatively, by adding a CO2 sensitive element to existing Registration and Annual Circulation Tax. Add-on elements would also allow taking into account other national environmental objectives, e.g. the early introduction of EURO IV or the forthcoming EURO V standards.[187]

Taxation should take into account the increasing importance of company cars, and provide a clear and strong incentive to companies to use more CO2 efficient cars. In most Member States, existing corporate or income tax structures do not include such an incentive.

The Commission is aware of the potential conflict between the revenue objective of vehicle taxation and other policy objectives. If Registration Tax and Annual Circulation Tax were restructured in an environmentally friendly direction, revenues from these taxes could show a downward trend as a result of a successful environmental policy. However, this very much depends on the design of the restructured taxes, and on the way car buyers, and car drivers, react on new tax incentives. In order to ensure stable revenue, and to maintain the incentive function of these taxes, it may be necessary to amend the design, and the levels, of these taxes. Such amendments would also take into account the potential for revenue losses, due the expected higher fuel efficiency of future passenger car generations.

4.5.4 Assessment and implications

The impact of a new regulation on the automotive industry is difficult to evaluate. It can vary with time and introduce dynamic effects that are difficult to assess accurately. Measures like new pollution standards can have a negative effect on the performance and cost structure of carmakers, challenging the competitive strength of the industry. At the same time, dealing with the measures can be the first step towards new markets and achieving technology or quality leadership.

The world-wide demands for safer and more environment-friendly vehicles will continue. These demands will drive research and innovation in powertrains, fuels, electric vehicles and lightweight materials. For manufacturers, finding low-cost ways to meet these requirements is at least as important as adding customer-desired features to vehicles. Of crucial importance is to identify and implement innovative solutions that will become global, thus giving European industry a first mover advantage.

The key technological problem facing the automobile industry today in all markets is the complexity of the demands from society. The need to address several issues at the same time can make the development of technical solutions more demanding as the underlying physical and technical characteristics can give rise to trade-offs.

Things can be even more complex when conflicting objectives from different policies must be taken into account at the same time; for instance, passenger safety requirements may tend to increase the weight of the vehicle, which neutralises efforts to reduce fuel consumption. Efforts to reduce pollutant emissions may also tend to increase CO_2 emissions.

In practice, however, these effects are low compared to the technological potential for further CO_2 emissions improvements. Thus, the challenge is more an economic one since several issues have to be addressed at the same time, which puts pressure on the R&D budgets. Therefore the regulatory measures discussed previously may in the short term lead to a greater administrative burden and higher costs for companies. The extent to which it will be possible to pass on these costs to consumers will depend on the individual vehicle manufacturer and on the vehicle class. The fact that price elasticity is smaller on European markets compared to the US market should facilitate the transfer of at least part of the costs.

On the other hand, measures that manage to reduce the wide differences in tax systems should have a

---

[186] COWI (2001), Study on fiscal measures to reduce CO2 emissions from new passenger cars, Consulting Engineers and Planners AS, November 2001.
[187] Com(2002)431 final.

positive impact on the ability of the car industry - and European consumers - to reap the benefits of operating within a single market. Car market fragmentation prevents industry from exploiting economies of scale, or to produce motor vehicles for the entire Internal Market, applying the same specifications, and contributes to significant variations of pre-tax prices within the internal market.

The competitiveness of the automotive industry, and of the European economy, depends also on a stable, coherent, cost-effective regulatory framework which correctly reflects the demands of society and anticipates trends in the world markets. This drove the Commission to assess the repercussions of its legislation carefully, applying the tools of 'Better Regulation', such as impact assessment techniques with full involvement of all stakeholders. Nevertheless, there is still progress to be made as concerns reducing regulatory complexity and taking into account possible conflicts between regulations and their cumulative impact, while improving the regulatory process itself through better consultation and coordination, so as to come to a predictable and stable regulatory environment.

4.6 Challenges and opportunities for the European automotive industry

The European automotive industry has been defending its international position successfully, both in terms of exports and worldwide sales. Enlargement proved an opportunity to restore the efficiency and cost effectiveness of its value chain. Its positions in emerging markets are strong and promising further growth and its innovation potential remains strong. However, the many challenges facing the industry should not be underestimated.

This section provides a systematic overview of strengths (S), weaknesses (W), opportunities (O) and threats (T) - a **SWOT Analysis**. It is a well established and straightforward concept which is helpful in matching an industry's resources and capabilities to the competitive environment in which it operates. To extend this analysis into the future an additional scenario analysis was conducted to highlight major connections and interactions among SWOT-factors in a best and worst case scenario. These steps lay the groundwork for the formulation of implications and policy issues.

4.6.1 A summary of strengths and weakness, opportunities and threats

4.6.1.1 Strengths

Large home market: The EU is the largest single market for passenger cars and the second largest for commercial vehicles. It is best positioned to leverage economies of scale and scope.

Loyal European customers: European producers profit the most from positive demand factors in domestic markets since European customers predominantly prefer European brands.

Sophisticated demand: EU customers enjoy their cars beyond practical use. Many treat it as a status symbol or a hobby. Advanced feedback from sophisticated customers propels product quality.

Modular value chain: The value chain configuration of the European automotive industry supports flexibility and risk sharing. European producers have achieved excellence in value chain management, system standardisation and quality control.

Qualified labour: This industry is labour intensive and needs qualified personnel to produce highly complex, high-performance, quality products. Today, the automotive products are more complex and sophisticated than ever requiring a strong know-how base for technological innovation and flexibility to make possible organisation innovation in the value chain.

High innovation capacity: High expenditures for innovation and especially R&D indicate the confidence and commitment of the European automotive industry in the competition for innovative products and services.

Strong position in trade: Europe holds dominant world market shares in most automotive product categories.

Responsiveness for foreign demand: The European automotive industry is highly active in leveraging knowledge, customer and market information from abroad. Those benefits can only be fully exploited by operating on site. This engagement opens up new trade opportunities for intermediate products and parts originating in the European home base.

Promising position in China: With China's membership in the World Trade Organisation, it is expected that the automotive industry will be one of China's largest and most powerful industries in the next twenty years. All the major car manufacturers have already established different assembly plant and are still planning to build up new production capacities. The Volkswagen Group is still a step ahead according to their first mover advantage.

Affordable labour in new Member States: The privatisation of state-owned enterprises allowed international companies to acquire existing production plants and to employ their qualified labour force.

New Member States as efficient production locations in known European regulatory framework: New chances and possibilities arrive by the enlargement process of the EU. The ten new Member States offer profitable production circumstances based on their labour cost and tax policy together with the already known regulatory framework of the European Union.

Road transportation as major component of value chains: Road transportation is the backbone of the European transportation system. It is deeply embedded in the value chains of almost all industries. This fact translates into investments, learning curve effects and sunk costs that generate significant barriers to entry for alternative modes of transportation and subsequently stable demand for vehicles. In addition, the demand for mobility of European citizens is steadily increasing which also stimulates demand for affordable cars.

4.6.1.2 Weaknesses

Productivity: EU still lags behind the US and Japan in term of labour productivity despite a significant catch-up in recent times and despite the slowdown of the speed of catching-up during the 1990s. Also, this productivity disadvantage is not outweighed by lower labour costs. On the contrary, the catch-up in labour cost compared to the US is almost complete and hourly labour costs in EU-15 are higher than in Japan and Korea.

High labour costs and inflexible labour market regulation: Modern automotive production relies on high levels of flexibility and quality. To achieve these ambitious goals highly qualified employees are a prerequisite. This manpower is expensive and automotive companies want to utilise it as productive as possible. Stringent arrangements make it difficult to synchronise the use of the input factor labour with the dynamics of the automotive markets. Since other production locations catch up

in educated labour forces with less regulation, the European competitive position is eroding.

Knowledge loss due to forced joint ventures: In some countries (for example, China) the automotive industry must face the challenge of a loss of knowledge in return for market access. Some legal requirements force manufacturers to hold a minority stake of local companies. An insecure legal position concerning intellectual property rights leads not only to a loss of knowledge but also to a loss of a competitive advantage. The framework of FDI and IPR has improved in the major emerging markets but uncertainties, affecting predominantly internationally active supplier companies, remain.

Slow growth in the home market: The growth of the European automotive markets has been flat in recent years compared to promising markets especially in South America and Asia. In addition, some advanced automotive markets (e.g. US in the nineties) show more positive sales trends than EU markets. As other markets continue to grow the demand advantages from the large European market diminish over time.

Fragmentation of the single market: the EU market is not yet uniform, not least due to differing vehicle taxation in the Member States.

Political influence on value chain decisions: Success stories in automotive production have become the synonyms for economic success in many industrialised European countries. The European Union hosts many famous automotive production sites that are politically difficult to give up in favour of modern and more efficient facilities. This can undermine the future success of the industry.

Myopic demand feedback for premium segment in the home market: While demand in the home market is a strong competitive advantage, European customers might not be the best proxy for demand in emerging markets. The latter might emphasise affordability and robustness over de-luxe models incorporating high-tech and comfort. Only recently EU car manufacturers start to address the challenge of mass motorization in low income, emerging economies.

4.6.1.3 Opportunities

Strong position in world markets: While success in trade certainly indicates excellence in production it also generates valuable know-how in terms of assessing, opening and servicing foreign markets. This expertise can hardly be obtained without actually operating *in situ*. As a major player in international markets, Europe has established stable channels that constitute a competitive advantage.

Engagement in China: The Chinese automotive market is growing very rapidly. Among other things, the country benefits from FDI equal to around USD 60 billion per year. Market size, terms of investment and an improving infrastructure provide the basis for foreign automotive companies. The potential of the Chinese market attracts not only manufacturers but also the whole supplier industry.

Trend towards free trade: As the world trade organisation expands its membership and activities are under way for a new round of trade liberalisation, Europe as a major player in automotive trade should be among the prime beneficiaries from the opening of new markets and the strengthening of existing relationships.

New technologies and fuels: The technology of fuel cells presents new opportunities for business and the environment, beyond transportation. Due to the dominant part of motor vehicles in air pollution, manufacturers must develop products which could reduce CO_2 emission and energy consumption. In addition, European automotive firms are leading in some transitional drive-train and fuel technologies which can become profitable before the fuel cell technology is ripe for the mass market. Since the security of fuel supply is an issue for many markets, the large experience of European manufacturers with different types of fuels can be of crucial importance for the future.

4.6.1.4 Threats

Idiosyncratic innovation: It could be a danger for the European automotive industry that in some cases regulation might push innovation into dead end streets.

Impact of regulation on value chain flexibility: While changes in taste and technology require constant re-configurations in the automotive value chain, the regulatory framework may make this task more difficult and costly. Should these regulations strain European domestic producers more than importing competitors they could become the cause of a competitive disadvantage.

Deficits in road infrastructure: Obviously, rising levels of road congestion and lacking road maintenance in combination with increasing traffic volumes make road transportation and hence vehicle demand less attractive. Additionally, the shortcomings in road transportation links make the

geographically widespread automotive production system of Europe less competitive.

Over-capacities: In recent years European, North American and Japanese markets see a sluggish development in demand. In Europe and Japan the sluggish market now continues for nearly a decade. On the other hand, a rapid capacity build-up in emerging Asian markets and Eastern European markets is taking place. Both developments may induce world over-capacity and stimulate price competition. Due to high labour costs and lagging labour productivity EU producers are not very well equipped for price competition in the standard car segment. This may induce additional pressures for consolidation of the industry e.g. via mergers. However it remains to be seen whether the current slump in most established markets will continue. There are examples (e.g. UK, US in the 1990s) of revitalising established markets when the macroeconomic conditions become more favourable.

Macroeconomic trend in Europe: The recent economic downturn in most of Europe has also affected the demand for automotive products. Producers have largely stimulated demand through extensive sales tactics (e.g. rebates). Still, a prolonged economic downturn at home would threaten the global competitiveness of the European automotive industry.

Groundbreaking innovations challenge existing excellence in production: The European manufacturers distinguish themselves with an excellent position in different markets. However, the threat of missing groundbreaking innovations is still on the agenda. Success can breed failure, as manufacturers are in danger of being locked in traditional products and technologies and ignore revolutionising developments outside their traditional field of expertise. Some of those major breakthroughs are on the horizon in the automotive sector. They have the potential to make conventional value chain configurations obsolete and subsequently open up opportunities for new competitors.

Major innovation competition from Japanese producers: The Japanese automotive manufacturers have a very competitive position in global vehicle production and they are strong competitors of European and American companies. In some fields like hybrid engine they lead the market significantly ahead of other manufacturers.

4.6.2 Forward vision: A scenario approach

The previous SWOT analysis outlined the major driving forces in the competitiveness of the European automotive industry. While those items were presented separately they will obviously interact dynamically.

Even if it s not feasible to define all possible combinations of future outcomes it is useful to define at least the range of possible developments. Hence, two hypothetical scenarios were developed, a best and a worst case. Both scenarios attempt to review developments over the next 10 to 15 years based on the discussion of previous sections. Note though that undoubtedly new issues influencing competitiveness that have not been considered yet will emerge. Nevertheless, the scenarios stress key mechanisms and cross dependencies with a view to stimulate discussion.

4.6.2.1 The worst case: Killing the engine

The worst case scenario begins by assuming that the gap in productivity can not be closed, resulting in higher car prices and lower profit margins. Moreover, energy consumption outstrips supplies and drives up fuel prices. There is a consensus that eventually hydrogen will be the fuel of the future but the time of its arrival in the mass market has been postponed by another ten years. European manufacturers bet heavily on diesel technology while US manufacturers license hybrid technology from Japanese competitors. The deep gap between diesel technology demand in the home market and in their largest export market would make it difficult for European manufacturers to realise economies of scale while, in this scenario, Japanese manufacturers have a first mover advantage in the hybrid technology. Japanese manufacturers receive royalty incomes from licenses in the US market which combined with a strong diesel expertise for the European market makes them the dominant player. European hopes of exporting the diesel trend to other parts of the world, e.g. the US, China or Japan fade, too, as officials in these countries advocate hybrid technology because of the learning effects when the hydrogen engine eventually arrives and because of its environmental advantage in congested cities. By 2015 European manufacturers would have lost their position in world trade and focus primarily on the home market.

In the meantime, on the back of the large and steadily growing home market and without a viable alternative due to massive over-capacities and sunk investments, China has become the world's third largest automotive exporter since 2010. Chinese manufacturers have emerged as highly productive producers who have transferred know-how and competitive resources out of joint ventures into companies which are completely under Chinese control. While most trade tariffs are gone by now, Chinese standards and regulations make it difficult for European automotive producers to generate additional growth through exports. On the contrary, low-priced imports from China could threaten their home market and export markets in Eastern Europe.

Under the worst case scenario, European producers find it difficult to compete as concerns production. Innovation intensity and investment remains strong but most of these activities are spurred by regulatory requirements not by the market. Accordingly, they generate costs but rarely sales. Design – the traditional mainstay of European cars – would be not only limited by the dominant platform production concept but also by regulatory requirements. Product differentiation strategies become less feasible; as European customers are offered less design options, price would become the crucial sales argument. Customer loyalty towards home brands could suffer as a result. Hence, with the exception of a few niche players, all manufacturers would turn towards cost cutting. In a reverse of the previous small and flexible production trend, European manufacturers would then rely again on economies of scale. High costs for transportation, especially through fuel prices, and chronically congested roads could make it difficult to sustain elaborate multi-plant multi-location value chains. European manufacturers would refocus their production system, leaving only marketing and R&D facilities in Western Europe. Labour intensive production operations are at first shifted towards the new Member States and, as labour costs start rising there too, they might move further east.

Naturally, some Member States would be hit harder than others. The burden would weigh especially heavily on the largest ones. Keeping production and jobs there would become an issue of intense political debate, possibly leading to mounting union activism and pressures to subsidise and further consolidate production. By 2019 only three European producers might remain, serving primarily their home market, together with some smaller players serving niches in the domestic and foreign luxury car segments. They account for roughly 60 per cent of the home market; 25 per cent is held by Japanese brands, the rest is covered by low-priced imports from South Korea and China.

Under these hypotheses, the world market for automotive products would be dominated by Japanese and Chinese manufacturers, while NAFTA and European producers would have hardly any export success stories to tell. The vast majority of automotive production would be performed on the eastern border of the EU. EU employment in the sector could be down to 350,000 jobs while the race is on for the new hydrogen engine that will define automotive competitiveness anew.

4.6.2.2 European automotive industry: Taking the pole position

Under the best case scenario, the European manufacturers succeed quickly in their efforts to improve productivity, taking full advantage of the enlargement. Moreover, the joint ventures in China allow them to keep a high market share on the Chinese market and to produce competitive vehicle models for the Asian and US market. Own R&D efforts to develop hybrid technologies, are successful and complement technical breakthroughs in gasoline technology and alternative fuel technology. Diesel would become a viable option in the Chinese, Japanese and US markets for passenger cars, permitting the European automotive industry to benefit fully from its competitive edge in efficient and clear diesel technologies.

The groundbreaking innovation in commercialising fuel cell technology is not that far away. An optimistic perspective might see European governments calling for zero emission cars by 2015 and the European industry benefiting from previous R&D projects. By 2015, the fuel cell would not only one of the standardised products offered by European manufacturers but also the beginning of new age of technology.

In such a case, the European automotive industry would gain high returns for its R&D investments and make high profits thanks to increased productivity. It would be able to develop product differentiation even further and create tailor-made cars for new consumer groups. Passenger cars would also offer different features to meet the needs of older people as ageing advances.

The European automotive industry would, in this case, take advantage of an already familiar regulatory framework in the new Member States and relatively low wages. New clusters would emerge which make possible serving the Russian market after Russia's accession to the WTO. Living standards in China and Russia improve markedly and luxury goods become accessible to larger consumer groups.

In this view, by 2020 2.5 million people would work in the automotive industry in Europe. The three main players in global car markets remain Europe, Japan and the US but their respective weights would shift. Europe would control 55 % of the world automotive output followed by Japan and the US. The fuel cell would be part of almost every modern car by now. Pollution would no longer be an issue nor would traffic related deaths and injuries, due to the development of active and passive safety features. The automotive sector would still be one of the backbones of Europe's economy and other sectors would prosper in its shadow.

4.6.3 Policy issues

While the European automotive industry is currently in a strong position compared to its major rivals there are major challenges and opportunities ahead. The fate of the industry will primarily depend on the excellence and expertise of the individual companies. There is also an important role for policy to play as an enabler and facilitator and, more importantly, by setting framework conditions that are conducive to growth and innovation. Which are the policy areas that are the most relevant to the competitiveness of the automotive industry?

Increase labour productivity. The labour productivity gaps described in section 4.4.2 need to be addressed. This is primarily the task of manufacturers; it would become easier if a well functioning social partnership exists. Human capital investment needs to be commensurate to the increasing need for skilled and adaptable workers.

Technical innovation. The innovative capacity of the European automotive industry depends primarily on its own efforts; however, the effectiveness and efficiency of the European and national innovation systems play an important role also. In particular, given the structural shifts in the automotive industry, the need for R&D investment for small and medium sized suppliers has increased markedly. As cars will still be one of the most popular means of conveyance, **R&D** objectives in the automotive industry should be directed towards developing **environmental friendly vehicles**. This includes in particular finding **adequate technology/fuel solutions** which ensure a long-term security of supply at acceptable costs. Among others, one should aim at developing fuel cells as standardised products within the next twenty or so years.

Regulation. The importance of the car in the economy and in everyday life places it necessarily at the centre of many, sometimes divergent, regulatory requirements. The industry has an interest in the continuation and fruition of efforts to better regulate with a view to achieving a predictable and stable regulatory environment and to develop lead market advantages. In order to support the productivity catching-up process regulators have to continue to assess carefully the impact of future regulations on the competitiveness of the automotive industry. Regulations have to anticipate technology trends and take into account that EU automotive companies, in order to exploit economies of scale and scope, must be able to sell similar products in Europe and on the world market. International regulatory harmonisation for motor vehicles through the 1958 and 1998 Agreement in the framework of the United Nations Economic Commission for Europe becomes, therefore, crucial.

The automotive industry recognises the importance of environmental concerns and of demands for safer vehicles and has already taken, and will continue to take, action to contribute to long-term solutions. In the past, tax policies proved important to set incentives for consumers to buy advanced technologies and such a strategy could also prove successful again in the future. Such tax policies should also be used to further align the Member States' **vehicle tax systems**, so as to allow industry to reap the full benefits from operating within a single market.

Strong **competition** in the home market is necessary to succeed in international markets. An efficient merger and acquisition (M&A) framework and the rejection of possible attempts to adopt distortive protective measures should contribute towards preserving the competitiveness of the European automotive industry. In this context, social partnership, collective agreements and information and consultation will be instrumental in smoothing the social consequences of restructuring.

The European automotive industry is competitive in international markets. Still, this strength can only be fully utilised if barriers to **free trade** are removed. While these include traditional tariffs and quotas, major non-tariff barriers (for example, the lack of international standards or an IPR framework) should also be addressed. Moving further in trade liberalization, especially in major emerging markets and as concerns foreign investment, would certainly foster the competitiveness of the automotive industry.

While a discussion of **macroeconomic conditions** belongs elsewhere, it is important to note that despite reform steps taken in recent years there is still room for more flexible labour markets, improvements in existing company taxation systems, etc.

For the automotive industry a functioning **road infrastructure** is the necessary base for automotive demand. More generally, road transport is the backbone of the European transportation system. Neglecting Europe's road transport could jeopardise its competitiveness as a whole. Future transport needs, fuelled by new logistics, more intense division of labour and new characteristics of products, will require flexible modes of transport. Given the insufficiency of current transport infrastructure and in view of the additional demands associated with enlargement there is a strong need for additional transport investment.

4.7 Summary and Conclusions

The European automotive industry provides jobs for more than 2 million Europeans. One out of ten European automotive workers lives in the new Member States. The industry produced 17 million cars in 2002 (42 % of global production) and 14 % of all trucks produced world-wide. In EU-15, the industry invested more than € 30 billion in 2001 and accounted for 38 % of R&D expenses of the three leading automotive regions (Japan, USA and EU).

Some of the best known global automotive players have their roots in Europe. German and French companies hold four positions in the global production top ten. Additionally, Europe has some strong niche players especially in the premium segment. Not surprisingly, a strong European network of sophisticated suppliers has developed. The role of suppliers in the production process is increasing because of technological innovation and especially through consolidation and the restructuration of the value chain.

Recent trends in automotive production show a shift away from large standardised fleets towards differentiated products that follow customer tastes and needs more closely. Value-chain operations have adapted to this trend. The importance of economies of scale in production has diminished in favour of modular flexible production techniques. Large scale production is still a major instrument in achieving cost efficiency but this no longer applies to the complete car but to the basic platform instead. Therefore, high potential car factories are smaller and more flexible production sites that operate at the centre of an optimised supply and distribution network. This development stands in sharp contrast to gigantic production sites of the past. The modern production facilities are designed to operate profitably at almost all levels of capacity utilisation, no matter whether fluctuations are triggered by macroeconomic shocks or by changes in tastes.

The role of suppliers has been changing too. Suppliers have traditionally been responsible for achieving primarily cost efficiency in the automotive value chain while vehicle manufacturers focused on customer responsiveness. As suppliers are moving towards manufacturing whole modules the line between suppliers and manufacturers blurs, especially since the former are becoming also responsible for module innovation and development. This suggests increasing strategic power for first-tier suppliers. However, customers buy a product (a car) not an assembly of components and vehicle manufacturers control the prime element of this customer focus, the brand. Hence, vehicle manufacturers will ultimately keep the lead role in automotive production.

Europeans are avid car buyers. They used a total of 209 million cars in 2002 (38 % of all cars globally), making it the largest single market in the world. Apart from cars, the truck sector has also a considerable size of more than 30 million vehicles in use in 2002. However, due to low economic growth the demand for cars and trucks was sluggish in Europe and Japan in the last decade. Presently, there is no convincing sign for a sustained turnaround.

Europe's vehicle manufacturers have established a strong bond with domestic customers. These loyal customers in the largest car market in the world are a strong competitive advantage that can hardly be copied or assailed by foreign competitors. Developing and introducing a new car model requires considerable resources (time, finances and human capital) and involves substantial risks as to whether the investments can be recouped by future sales. Hence, developing a new automotive product isolated from its prospective market appears to be not a feasible option. Customer feedback and interaction is necessary for a successful product. It is also true that European automotive producers need to invest abroad to generate access to tacit customer and market information in order to be successful in foreign markets. As long as these foreign engagements are driven by the search for knowledge and customer responsiveness abroad they make the European automotive industry stronger, not weaker.

Based on its home market and its investments abroad, the European automotive industry has maintained a traditionally strong position in exports and global sales. This supports the suggestion that its automotive industry is competitive. Its presence in emerging markets, such as China and the Russian Federation, is a promising source of future growth and profits.

EU enlargement facilitates this development by combining affordable labour with the proximity to traditional European automotive clusters. The new Member States have emerged as great production opportunity for the European automotive industry. Especially Poland, the Czech Republic, the Slovak Republic and Hungary show a promising combination of a traditional expertise in the sector, affordable labour and the proximity to the large European markets.

However, EU automotive industry still lags behind the US and Japan in terms of productivity. The catching-up process of the EU automotive industry has slowed down in the last decade despite steep increases in some Member States.

The level of labour costs presents an increasingly serious problem for the automotive industry in some Member States. Still, labour cost per hour worked in the EU is somewhat below the US but significantly higher than in Japan and especially in Korea. In addition, Germany's labour costs are even higher than in the US. The US automotive industry contained the growth of real product labour costs in the last decade. The reverse is true for EU and Japan. Given the current level of labour productivity, this is clearly an adverse development than endangers jobs. In this context, EU enlargement has and will continue to provide automotive firms in high wage countries with new opportunities to profit from low labour costs by via restructuring and relocating significant parts of their value chain. This will help the EU-15 automotive industry to stay competitive albeit jobs prospects are less promising than in the past.

Relatively high labour costs and their negative impact on price competitiveness are a special threat in light of structural overcapacity in the global automotive industry. Seen in a global context, capacity utilisation rates are still high in the EU and there have been some signs of recovery in recent months. However, despite overcapacity in global automotive production, new capacity will enter the market soon from emerging countries like China but also from the new Member States. This will inevitably fuel price competition globally especially in the mass market segments of the automotive industry.

Based on performance on the global automotive market one can conclude that the European automotive industry is competitive. However, success in the future is clearly not guaranteed. Japanese manufacturers are equally strong in investing in automotive innovations and US producers are taking advantage not only the large home market but have also pursued internationalisation strategies for years. There are major technological challenges ahead, most prominently the development of new technology/fuel combinations, including fuel cells. Competition and innovation will continue to be central determinants of the viability and strength of Europe's automobile industry.

World-wide demands to make vehicles safer and more environment-friendly will continue. These demands will drive research and innovation; it is of crucial importance to identify and implement innovative technical solutions that will become global, thus giving European industry a first mover advantage.

The competitiveness of the automotive industry, and of the European economy, depends on a coherent and cost-effective regulatory framework. This drove the Commission to use increasingly the tools of 'Better Regulation', such as *Impact Assessment* techniques. Nevertheless, there is still progress to be made as concerns reducing regulatory complexity and designing regulations so as to meet their goals while taking into account possible conflicts between regulations, their cumulative impact and their external aspects.

References

ACEA (2004): 'ACEA Comments Regarding The Proposed Modification of Directive 98/71 On The Legal Protection Of Designs – Executive Summary', Brussels.

Automotive Resources Asia (2003): 'China Passenger Vehicle Market Sets Monthly Sales Record in September', online document: www.auto-resources-asia.com/Mas_CASR_09_2003.pdf.

Autopolis (2000): 'The Natural Link between Sales and Service. An Investigation for the Competition Directorate-General of the European Commission', November.

Bartlett, C. and Goshal, S. (1989): 'Managing Across Borders: The Transnational Solution', Harvard Business School Press.

Beise, M. (2001): 'Lead Markets: Country-specific success factors of the global diffusion of innovations', ZEW Economic Studies, 14, Heidelberg.

Beise, M. and Cleff, T. (2003): 'Assessing the Lead Market Potential of Countries for Innovation Projects', Discussion Paper Series, No. 142, Research Institute for Economics and Business Administration, September, Kobe University.

Bingmann, H. (1993): 'Antiblockiersystem und Benzineinspritzung', in: Albach, H. (ed.), *Culture and Technical Innovation: A Cross-Cultural Analysis and Policy Recommendations*, Berlin, New York.

Cap Gemini Ernst & Young (2003): 'Unlocking Hidden Value. A Cross-Channel Analysis of the Automotive Industry – From Consumer Demand through the Aftermarket', Cars Online 2003.

COWI (2001): *Fiscal measures to reduce CO2 emissions from new passenger cars*, Consulting Engineers and Planners AS, November.

Dollar, D. and Wolff E.N. (1993): 'Competitiveness, Convergence, and International Specialisation', Cambridge, MIT Press.

Dr. Lademann & Partner (2001): 'Customer Preferences for existing and potential Sales and Servicing Alternatives in Automobile Distribution', Hamburg.

Dunning, J.H. (1981): 'International Production and the Multinational Enterprise', London.

ECG (2004): 'Maintaining the Competitiveness of the European Automotive Industry by Supporting the Finished Vehicle Logistics Sector', European Car-Transport Group of Interest, January, www.eurocartrans.org.

Electronics Engineer (Centaur Communications) (2002): Driving force for innovation, 11/8/2002 Supplement, 291, iss. 7615.

Emanuel, I. (2002): 'The European Motor Vehicle Block Exemption: An Update', Pricewaterhouse-Coopers Global Automotive Financial Review 2002.

European Commission (2001): White Paper, 'European transport policy for 2010: time to decide', COM(2001)370 final.

European Commission (2001): 'Tax Policy in the European Union - Priorities for the Years ahead', COM(2001)260 final.

European Commission (2002): 'Distribution and Servicing of Motor Vehicles in the European Union', Directorate General for Competition, Commission Regulation (EC) No. 1400/2002 of 31 July 2002, Explanatory Brochure.

European Commission (2002): 'Taxation of Passengers Cars in the European Union - Options for Action at National and Community levels', COM(2002)431 final.

European Commission (2003): Directorate-General for Energy and Transport, 'Energy and Transport in Figures 2003'.

European Commission (forthcoming): Enterprise Directorate-General, *Pocketbook of EU Sectoral Indicators*.

Farrell, D. (2004), 'Making foreign investment work for China', Business Times Online McKinsey Quarterly, http://business-times.asia1.com. sg/sub/ mckinsey/ 0,5318,00.html.

Fieten, R. (1995): 'Automobilzulieferer im Verdrängungswettbewerb', Arbeitgebe, 15/16-47.

Freeman, Ch. (1994): 'The Economics of Technical Change'.

German Association of the Automotive Industry VDA (2004): *Annual Report 2003*.

Hoon-Halbauer, S.K. (1999): 'Managing Relationships Within Sino-Foreign Joint Ventures', Journal of World Business, 34(4), Winter.

Jürgens, U. (2003): 'Characteristics of the European Automotive System. Is There a Distinctive European Approach?', Discussion Paper SP III 2003-301, WZB 2003.

Kansky, A. (2000): 'Opportunities for U.S. Firms in the Russian Automotive Market', http://www.bisnis.doc.gov/bisnis/country/001026AutoISA.htm.

Larsson, A. (2002): 'The development and regional significance of the automotive industry: supplier parks in Western Europe', International Journal of Urban & Regional Research, 26(4), December.

Maibach, M. et al. (2000): 'External costs of transport: accidents, environmental and congestion costs in Western Europe', INFRAS and IWW, University of Karlsruhe, International Union of Railways (UIC), Zürich/Karlsruhe.

McKinsey&Company (2003): HAWK 2015 – 'Knowledge-based changes in the automotive value chain', Frankfurt.

Monnikhof, E. and van Ark, B. (2000): 'New estimates of labour productivity in the manufacturing sectors of the Czech Republic, Hungary and Poland, 1996', Groningen Growth and Development Centre, University of Groningen 6, The Conference Board, Second Report for the WIIW Countdown Project, June.

Murphy, J.J. and Delucchi, M.A. (1998): 'A review of the literature on the social cost of vehicle use in the United States', Journal of Transportation and Statistics, January.

Porter, M. E. (1990): 'The Competitive Advantage of Nations', New York, Free Press.

PricewaterhouseCoopers (2002a): 'Prospects for the Russian passenger car industry', Automobile Financial Review 2003.

PricewaterhouseCoopers (2002b): 'End of Life Vehicle Directive', September.

PricewaterhouseCoopers (2003): 'Supplier Survival. Survival in the modern automotive supply chain'.

PWC (2004): Wissen, Erfahrung, Innovation, May.

Quinet, E. (1997): 'Full social costs of transportation in Europe. Measuring the full social costs and benefits of transportation'.

Recordit (2003): Final report, 'Actions to promote intermodal transport'.

Reinaud, G. (2001): 'Hard Times for the Automotive Industry? Overcapacity and Downturn in the Markets', BNP Parisbas, Conjoncture, June.

Robinson, C., Stokes, L., Stuivenwold, E. and van Ark, B. (2003): 'Industry Structure and Taxonomies', in: O'Mahony, M. and van Ark, B. (eds.), *EU productivity and competitiveness: An industry perspective. Can Europe resume the catching-up process?*, European Commission, Brussels.

Roland Berger & Partners (2000): *Automotives supplier trend* study, March.

Standard&Poor's (2004): 'Mainland China's Auto Industry Prepares for More Competition', Publication date: 12-Feb-04, www.standardandpoors.com.

Sturgeon, T. (1997): 'Globalisation and the Threat of Overcapacity in the Automotive Industry', Research Note 1, Globalisation and Jobs in the Automotive Industry, MIT.

Sturgeon, T. and Florida, R. (2000): *Globalization and Jobs in the Automotive Industry*, a study by Carnegie Mellon University and the Massachusetts Institute of Technology, Final Report to the Alfred P. Sloan Foundation.

Technopolis (2003): 'Impact Assessment of Possible Options to Liberalise the Aftermarket in Spare Parts', final report to DG Internal Market, Paris.

Terporten, M. (1999): 'Wettbewerb in der Automobilindustrie', Duisburg.

TIS Study (2002): Study on *Vehicle Taxation in the Member States of the EU*, TIS/PT.

Verhoef, E. (1994): 'External effects and social costs of road transport', Transportation Research, 28A, No. 4.

Vernon, R. (1966): 'International Investment and International Trade in the Product Cycle', Quarterly Journal of Economics; 80(2), May.

Walsh, M. (2000): Vehicle Emission Trends, EUROPEAN CONFERENCE OF MINISTERS OF TRANSPORT.

WardsAuto.com (2003): 'Automobil Produktion – Begleitheft zu: Internationale Verflechtungen der Automobilhersteller'.

Weidner, M. (2004): 'China – Automobilmarkt der Zukunft?', in: WZB Discussion Paper SP III 2004-105.

Womack, J.P. and Jones, D.T. (1991): 'Die zweite Revolution in der Automobilindustrie. Konsequenzen aus der weltweiten', Studie aus dem Massachusetts Institute of Technology, Frankfurt/Main and New York.

Yu, W. (2004): 'New auto policy big leap forward', CHINAdaily, http://www.chinadaily.com. cn/ english/doc/2004-06/09/content_337978.htm.

Zhang, W. and Taylor, R. (2001): 'EU Technology Transfer to China - The automotive industry as a case study', Journal of the Asia Pacific Economy, 6, June.

Appendix

Table A.4.1: Ranking of suppliers in the automotive industry by turnover in 2001

	Company	Country	Turnover. € 2001bn
1	Delphi	USA	28.7
2	Bosch	D	23.2
3	Visteon	USA	19.6
4	Denso	J	17.9
5	Lear	USA	15.0
6	Johnson Controls	USA	15.0
7	Magna Int.	CDA	11.6
8	Continental	D	11.2
9	TRW	USA	11.1
10	Faurecia	F	9.6
11	Aisins Seiki	J	9.3
12	Dana	USA	8.5
13	Valeo	F	8.1
14	ZF Friedrichshafen	D	7.8
15	Yazaki	J	6.8
16	Arvin Meritor	USA	6.4
17	Thyssen Krupp Automotive	D	6.2
18	DuPont	USA	5.7
19	Siemens VDO Automotive	D	5.7
20	Michelin	F	5.1

Source: AP.

Table A.4.2: M&A transactions 2002 – manufacturer

Target	Target Nation	Buyer	Buyer's Nation	Deal value ($m)	% Acquired
Daewoo Motor Co - Certain Assets	KOR	General Motors (& affiliates)/Daewoo Creditors	INT	2,627	100
Renault SA	FRA	Nissan Motor Co Ltd	JPN	1,959	15
Nissan Motor Co Ltd	JPN	Renault SA	FRA	1,620	7.6
Ferrari SpA	IT	Mediobanca (net 24 %)/Commerzbank (net 10 %)	IT/D	760	34
Dmax - diesel engines	USA	General Motors Corp	USA	422	20
Maruti Udyog Ltd	IND	Suzuki Motor Corporation	JPN	285	4.2
Tianjin Automotive Xiali Co Ltd	CHN	First Automotive Works	CHN	171	51
Aixam	FRA	Norbert Dentressangle SA	FRA	129	100
Yantai Bodyshop Corp	CHN	General Motors/Shanghai Auto	US/CHN	109	100

Source: PriceWaterhouseCoopers.

Table A.4.3: M&A transactions 2002 – supplier

Target	Target Nation	Buyer	Buyer's Nation	Deal value ($m)	% Acquired
TRW Inc	USA	Northrop Grumman Corp	USA	11.7	100
Edscha AG	D	Carlyle Management Group/Edscha Management	USA	605	98
Teksid SpA	IT	Questor/JP Morgan PE/PE Partners/AIG	USA	453	100
Donnelly Corp	USA	Magna International Inc	CAN	389	100
Varta AG (Auto Batteries Div)	D	Johnson Controls Inc	USA	308	100
FTE Automotive GmbH	D	Hg Capital Ltd	UK	198	100
Conti Temic Microelectronic GmbH	D	Continental AG	D	188	40
Unisia Jecs Corp	JPN	Hitachi Ltd	JPN	184	83.3
Cie Financiere Michelin	CHN	Michelin SA	FRA	175	6.3
Aetna Industries & Zenith Inc.	USA	Questor Management Co	USA	145	100

Source: PriceWaterhouseCoopers.

Table A.4.4: World market share in automotive of OECD-countries in 1991[1]

Country	78 Automotive products	781 Motor cars	782 Trucks	783 Buses, road tractors	784 Parts and accessories	Other road vehicles	Total merchandise
Germany	20.7	21.6	14.8	20.8	12.9	47.0	17.1
France	8.5	8.0	5.8	8.9	11.9	5.4	8.8
UK	5.0	4.3	2.5	1.9	8.0	6.3	7.1
Italy	4.6	3.5	6.0	4.6	6.1	5.9	7.2
Belgium/ Luxembourg	6.1	8.1	4.7	13.4	2.7	2.1	4.9
Netherlands	1.7	0.9	3.0	14.5	1.4	2.9	5.0
Denmark	0.3	0.1	0.4	0.5	0.4	0.9	1.4
Ireland	0.1	0.0	0.1	0.0	0.1	0.1	1.0
Greece	0.0	0.0	0.0	0.0	0.0	0.0	0.3
Spain	4.4	5.8	2.2	2.0	3.6	0.6	2.3
Portugal	0.3	0.1	1.1	0.5	0.4	0.2	0.7
Sweden	2.0	1.8	2.2	1.4	3.0	0.6	2.2
Finland	0.3	0.4	0.3	0.8	0.2	0.3	1.0
Austria	0.8	0.3	2.2	0.9	1.1	1.0	1.8
Switzerland	0.2	0.1	0.6	0.3	0.4	0.4	2.6
Norway	0.1	0.0	0.1	0.1	0.3	0.3	0.7
Iceland	0.0	0.0	0.0	0.0	0.0	0.0	0.1
Turkey	0.1	0.0	0.0	0.4	0.1	0.0	0.5
Poland							
Czech Republic							
Slovak Republic							
Hungary							
Canada	8.8	8.7	17.8	7.5	7.7	0.3	4.3
USA	10.7	6.8	11.5	8.1	21.5	3.8	15.5
Mexico	1.4	2.2	0.5	0.1	0.7	0.1	0.7
Japan	23.6	27.0	24.2	13.5	17.1	19.8	13.6
South Korea							
Australia	0.2	0.2	0.1	0.0	0.3	0.1	0.9
New Zealand	0.0	0.0	0.0	0.0	0.0	0.0	0.3
EU-15 excluding intra EU-15 trade	22.9	22.3	16.3	38.0	20.6	45.1	34.7

World market share: Share of national exports on total OECD exports.
[1]) OECD without Poland, Czech Republic, Slovac Republic, Hungary and Korea.
Source: OECD: ITCS - International Trade By Commodity Statistics, Rev. 3, 2001, 2002. - NIW calculation.

Table A.4.5: World shares in vehicles automotive of OECD-countries in 2001

Country	78 Automotive products	781 Motor cars	782 Trucks	783 Buses, road tractors	784 Parts and accessories	Other road vehicles	Total merchandise
Germany	20.1	22.4	14.3	23.6	13.5	34.7	13.9
France	7.4	7.2	6.2	7.9	9.1	4.0	7.3
UK	3.8	3.9	2.4	1.6	4.7	2.9	6.4
Italy	3.7	2.3	5.7	0.6	5.6	7.9	6.1
Belgium/ Luxembourg	5.4	6.7	4.8	9.2	2.8	3.2	4.6
Netherlands	1.7	1.2	2.4	13.2	1.1	3.7	4.1
Denmark	0.2	0.1	0.2	0.3	0.3	0.9	1.1
Ireland	0.1	0.1	0.2	0.1	0.1	0.2	1.9
Greece	0.0	0.0	0.0	0.0	0.0	0.1	0.2
Spain	5.1	5.6	5.2	2.3	4.7	2.4	2.7
Portugal	0.7	0.9	0.6	0.2	0.5	0.3	0.6
Sweden	1.6	1.4	0.7	3.4	2.4	0.8	1.8
Finland	0.3	0.3	0.3	0.5	0.2	0.4	1.1
Austria	1.3	0.9	2.0	2.0	1.5	1.7	1.6
Switzerland	0.2	0.0	0.4	0.2	0.4	0.3	2.0
Norway	0.1	0.0	0.2	0.1	0.3	0.2	0.5
Iceland	0.0	0.0	0.0	0.0	0.0	0.0	0.0
Turkey	0.4	0.3	0.7	2.4	0.4	0.2	0.7
Poland	0.6	0.5	0.7	0.8	0.8	0.9	0.9
Czech Republic	1.0	1.0	0.2	0.6	1.6	0.7	0.8
Slovak Republic	0.4	0.6	0.0	0.0	0.4	0.3	0.3
Hungary	0.5	0.5	0.0	0.9	0.7	0.7	0.7
Canada	10.1	10.6	17.2	11.0	7.8	1.3	5.2
USA	10.8	6.1	11.6	7.1	22.7	7.7	16.9
Mexico	5.3	5.1	12.3	1.4	4.3	1.3	3.6
Japan	15.5	17.6	10.1	6.9	12.2	22.2	9.8
South Korea	2.9	4.0	1.3	3.7	1.5	0.8	3.8
Australia	0.4	0.5	0.1	0.2	0.4	0.2	0.8
New Zealand	0.0	0.0	0.0	0.0	0.1	0.0	0.3
EU-15 excluding intra EU-15 trade	25.3	26.5	17.9	36.8	21.4	41.0	31.5

World market share: Share of national exports on total OECD exports
Source: OECD: ITCS - International Trade By Commodity Statistics, Rev. 3, 2001, 2002. - NIW calculation

Table A.4.6: Joint ventures in China

Foreign Company	Chinese Ventures
GM	1. GM: Shanghai GM, Jinbei GM, SAIC-GM Wuling, Shanghai-GM Dongyue 2. Suzuki: Chang'an Suzuki, Changhe Suzuki 3. Isuzu: Qingling Motor (Isuzu), Jiangling (Isuzu), Guangzhou Isuzu Bus 4. Fiat: Nanjing Fiat 5. Fujiheavy: Guiyang Yunque
Ford	1. Ford: Chang'an Ford, Jiangling (Ford) Motors Group 2. Mazada: Hainan Mazada, FAW Car (technology cooperation)
Toyota	1. Toyota: Tianjin FAW Toyota, Sichuan Toyota, FAW Xiali (technology cooperation), Brillance Auto (technology cooperation, FAW Toyota Sales) 2. Daihatsu: FAW Xiali (technology cooperation), FAW Huali (technology cooperation) 3. Hino: Shenfei Hino
Volkswagen	1. VW: FAW-VW, Shanghai-VW, SAIC-VW Sales 2. Audi: FAW-VW (10 %)
Daimler-Chrysler	1. Daimler-Chrysler: Beijing Jeep, Yaxing Benz, Beijing Benz Truck (under negotiation), South East Motor Benz (under negotiation) 2. Mitsubishi: Hunan Changfeng, Beijing Jeep (technology cooperation), South East Auto (technology cooperation), Harbin Hafei Motor (technology cooperation) 3. Hyundai: Beijing Hyundai, Dongfeng Yueda-Kia, Jianghuai Auto (technology cooperation), Rongcheng Huatai (technology cooperation)
Renault-Nissan	1. Renault: Sanjiang Renault 2. Nissan: Zhengzhou Nissan, Dongfeng Motor Co. Ltd. 3. Nissan: Fengshen Motor (Nissan Motor).
PSA	1. Peugeot – Citroen: DPCA – Dongfeng Peugeot Citroen Co. Ltd.
Honda	1. Honda: Guangzhou Honda, Honda China Co. Ltd. (Guangzhou), Dongfeng Honda Wuhan) Co. Ltd.
BMW	1. Brillance - BMW
FIAT	1. Fiat Auto: Nianjing Fiat 2. Iveco: Naveco (Iveco-Yuejin Group) 3. Iveco: Haveco (Iveco-Yuejin Group-Hanghzou Group) 4. Iveco: Iveco-Changzhou Bus Company (CBC)

Source: China Automotive Technology & Research Center.

Table A.4.7: Assembly plants in Central and Eastern Europe

Manufacturer	Country (country of mother company)	Plant Site/Name	Products
Andoria-Mot Sp. z.o.o.	Poland	Andrychów	Honker Suv, Lublin
Audi Hungaria Motor Kft.	Hungary (VW Germany)	Györ	Audi TTCoupé/Roadster
Automobile Dacia S.A.	Romania (Renault France)	Pitesti	Dacia Berlina/Break, pick up, Supernova
Daewoo Automobile Romania, S.A.	Romania (Rep. Korea)	Craiova	Daewoo Cielo, Matiz, Nubiera, Lanos, Takuma (CKD)
Daewoo Avia	Czech Republic (Rep. Korea)	Prague	Avia small trucks
Daewoo-FSO Motor	Poland (Rep. Korea)	Warsaw	Daewoo Matiz, Nubria, Lanos
Fiat	Czech Republic (Italy)	Vysoké Myto	Karosa buses
Fiat Auto	Poland (Italy)	Tychy	Fiat Palio Weekend, Seicento, Nuova Panda
Magyar Suzuki	Hungary (Japan)	Esztergom	Suzuki: Wagon R+, Ignis
MAN	Poland (DaimlerChrysler Germany)	Starachowice Tarnowo	STAR trucks, NEOPLAN
NABI	Hungary	Kaposvar	Compobus vehs.
OpelPolska Sp.z.o.o.	Poland (GM USA)	Gliwice	Opel Agila
Revoz	Slovenia (Renault France)	Novo Mesto	Renault Clio
Scania	Poland (Sweden)	Slupsk	Scania buses
Skoda Auto a.s.	Czech Republic (VW Germany)	Kvasiny Mlada Boleslav Vrchlabi	Superb Fabia, Octavia Octavia
Volkswagen Poznan Sp.z.o.o.	Poland (Germany)	Poznañ	Skoda, Fabia, VW: T5
Volkswagen Slovakia	Slovakia (Germany)	Bratislava	VW: Bora, Polo A04, Golf R32, Golf A4, Touareg, Porsche Cayenne bodies, SEAT Ibiza
Volvo Trucks	Poland (Sweden, Scania?)	Wroclaw	Volvo trucks

Source: Ward's Automotive Yearbook 2003, p. 18 f.

Table A.4.8: CO2 Emissions and Fuel Consumption, 1995-2002

ACEA	1995 CO2 (g/km)	1998 CO2 (g/km)	1999 CO2 (g/km)	2000 CO2 (g/km)	2001 (3) CO2 (g/km)	2002 (3) CO2 (g/km)	Change 95/02 [%] (4)
Petrol-fuelled vehicles	188	182	180	177	172	172/171	-8.5/9.0 % (6)
Diesel-fuelled vehicles	176	167	161	157	153	155/152	-11.9/13.6 % (6)
All fuels (1)	185	178	174	169	165	165/163 (5)	-10.8/12.1 % (6)
JAMA (2)	1995 CO2 (g/km)	1998 CO2 (g/km)	1999 CO2 (g/km)	2000 CO2 (g/km)	2001 (3) CO2 (g/km)	2002 (3) CO2 (g/km)	Change 95/02 [%] (4)
Petrol-fuelled vehicles	191	184	181	177	174	172	-9.9 %
Diesel-fuelled vehicles	239	221	221	213	198	180	-24.7 %
All fuels (1)	196	189	187	183	178	174	-11.2 %
KAMA (2)	1995 CO2 (g/km)	1998 CO2 (g/km)	1999 CO2 (g/km)	2000 CO2 (g/km)	2001 (3) CO2 (g/km)	2002 (3) CO2 (g/km)	Change 95/02 [%] (4)
Petrol-fuelled vehicles	195	198	189	185	179	178	-8.7 %
Diesel-fuelled vehicles	309	248	253	245	234	203	-34.3 %
All fuels (1)	197	202	194	191	187	183	-7.1 %
EU-15 (2)	1995 CO2 (g/km)	1998 CO2 (g/km)	1999 CO2 (g/km)	2000 CO2 (g/km)	2001 (3) CO2 (g/km)	2002 (3) CO2 (g/km)	Change 95/02 [%] (4)
Petrol-fuelled vehicles	189	182	180	178	173	172	-9.0 %
Diesel-fuelled vehicles	179	171	165	163	156	157	-12.3 %
All fuels (1)	186	180	176	172	167	166	-10.8 %

(1) Petrol and diesel-fuelled vehicles only, other fuels and statistically not identified vehicles are not expected to affect these averages significantly.

(2) Data from Member States are taken for 2002. For the 'change 95/02', 95 data are taken from the associations and 2002 data originate from the Member States. New passenger cars put on the EU market by manufacturers not covered by the Commitments would not influence the EU average significantly.

(3) The figures for 2001 and 2002 are corrected by 0.7 % for the change in the driving cycle.

(4) Percentages are calculated from unrounded CO2 figures; for 2002 data is taken from Member States.

(5) The first figure is based one data from Member States; the second figure is based on data from ACEA.

(6) The first figure is based on 2002 data from Member States and 1995 data from ACEA; the second figure is based solely on data from ACEA.

Source: European Commission (2004).

## Chapter 5

The Challenge to the EU
of a Rising Chinese Economy

5.1 Introduction

In the course of the last quarter century China has become a major presence in the international economy and today seems to be on a trajectory towards even greater prominence. The market-oriented transformations initiated in the late seventies have created conditions supportive of economic growth and for China's progressive integration in the international economy. The gradual establishment of market-based conditions has opened up possibilities for economic actors to exploit comparative advantages resulting in a more rational division of labour that previously.

Economic relations between China and Europe are entering a new era.[188] Two major events have contributed to this. First, China's accession to the WTO in December 2001 and the subsequent implementation of the accession protocol is changing its position in the global economy. Secondly, enlargement and the integration of ten new Member States in May 2004 will alter economic structures in Europe. As a consequence, a large number of institutional barriers to trade and investment are being dismantled and, as a result, new trade and investment possibilities are emerging. It is likely that these changes will lead to new patterns in the international division of labour and significant pressure for structural change will be exerted on virtually all EU economies.

Whereas a rising Chinese economy offers great trading potential and investment opportunities for European business, this Chapter mainly considers the challenges it will pose to the EU and especially to the new Member States and the candidate countries.[189] The economic structures and factor endowments of the new Member States, and even more so of the candidate countries, would appear to make them more susceptible to China's competitive pressure than the more industrialized EU-15 economies.[190] The chapter is divided into three parts, followed by some concluding remarks. Section 5.2 discusses China's economy and the forces that are determining China's recent advance in the global economy; Section 5.3 discusses China's role in the global division of labour and the China-EU economic relations in particular, including trade patterns and foreign direct investment flows; Section 5.4 addresses the impact a rising Chinese economy might have on various industries in the EU and especially in the new Member States; finally, Section 5.5 concludes.

5.2 Growth factors and risks in China's economic development

China's economic transformation during the last 25 years has been spectacular. GDP has been growing at an annual average of 9.0 % between 1979 and 2002 and parts of the economy have become highly integrated in the global production system.[191] In the process, China has narrowed significantly the large developmental gap separating it from the industrialized economies only two decades ago.

---

[188] Throughout the Report 'China' refers to 'People's Republic of China', 'Hong Kong' to 'People's Republic of China – Hong Kong Special Administrative Region', and 'Taiwan' to 'Taiwan Province of China'. All statistical data presented are based on customs territories. Data for China are therefore constrained to 'Mainland China'. Statistical data for Hong Kong and Taiwan are provided separately.

[189] Unless otherwise indicated, candidate countries are Bulgaria, Romania, and Turkey.

[190] See the Competitiveness Report 2003 for a detailed analysis of the competitiveness of manufacturing in the accession and candidate countries.

[191] The validity of China's statistics has been often questioned (see e.g. Rawski 2001, 2002). It would be mistaken, however, to deny the extraordinary growth performance of the Chinese economy during the last quarter century and dismiss it as a statistical mirage. Alternative, independent, efforts to measure economic activity in China indicate that at least in recent years the growth performance of China's economy might be understated by the official data (see especially the Goldman Sachs China Activity Index and Goldman Sachs, 2003).

Nevertheless, large segments of China's economy are still underdeveloped and, especially in the Western provinces, notably poor. There remains a long way to go and it is anything but certain that China will be able to uphold the dynamics of its recent development process.

5.2.1 Determinants of Economic Development in China

China has traditionally been endowed with favourable conditions for economic development and growth. Abundant natural resources, a very high savings rate, a huge supply of low-cost labour, a (potentially) large domestic market as well as a sophisticated administrative system bode well for economic development. But, as China's experiences during three decades of central planning have shown, the existence of these ingredients alone is not enough.

The abandonment of the economically inefficient ideological foundations and institutional arrange-

ments of the Maoist era in the late 1970s has laid the foundations for a higher growth path.[192] Ideological changes adopted by the ruling elite have facilitated a reorganisation of industry and the creation of a new set of institutions and performance enhancing property rights structures. These ideological breakthroughs together with the establishment of an increasingly performance oriented institutional set-up have created the foundation of China's contemporary economic successes through increasing incentives to respect market signals about scarcity and profits. But although the Chinese economic system has been gradually transformed, it is still far from being a full market economy and further progress is needed concerning, for example, the widespread

---

[192] Two watershed-events may be distinguished (Bell 1993, Qian 2000): 1. At the third plenary session of the Central Committee in 1978 the main contradiction in Chinese society is defined to be the insufficient performance of the economic system with respect to the material needs of the population. 2. In 1992 Deng Xiaoping proclaims the 'socialist market economy' as China's new economic system of order. It is declared that the market mechanism is nothing but a means to achieve economic development and growth.

Box 5.1: China's Low Labour Cost Advantage

The Chinese economy is endowed with a huge and growing labour force (see Graph B.1). Today close to 900 million people are in the age group 15-64 but this will rise to 1 billion in the year 2015. The majority of these people have been brought up in the countryside with little or no knowledge of industrial production. However, bereft of sufficient job opportunities in the rural areas a large and growing number is migrating to the industrial centres in the coastal belt area. This army of unskilled labour, approximately 150 to 200 million strong, has been the backbone of China's 'economic miracle' of the past two decades. The perpetual inflow of new labourers has been keeping wages low, although production facilities had been expanding rapidly.

Graph B.1: Intertemporal Development of China's Labour Force Population aged 15-64, in million (forecasts)

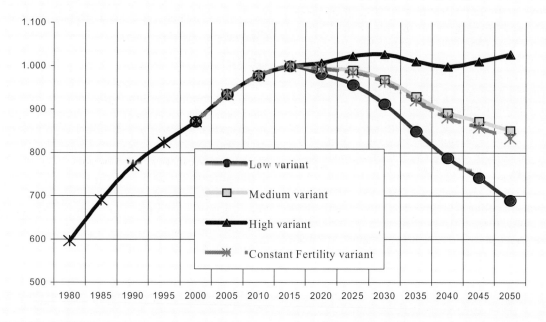

Source: Graph based on United Nations World Population Prospects: The 2002 Revision Population Database.

influence of the state and the lagging implementation of private property rights.[193]

Opening up to the outside world has allowed a highly productive combination of China's most abundant factor of production, unskilled labour (see Box 5.1), with the capital as well as the technological and organisational knowledge of the world economy.

Foreign trade has been the lever to adjust prices in the Chinese economy and indicate relative scarcities of goods and factors of production. Foreign Direct Investment (FDI) has also been a catalyst to bring China to the global economy. It was foreign investors, initially overseas Chinese from Hong Kong and South East Asia, that provided the knowledge of what products China could manufacture for the global market and how to penetrate the markets of the industrialized world. In later stages China has been successfully trading domestic market shares for technological and organizational know how introduced to the economy by foreign investors from the industrialised world.

China's economic policy makers, however, are not content with China being the global centre for labour intensive manufacturing. While industries establishing labour intensive production capacities in China will be promoted in order to create jobs for China's growing population, the real focus of China's industrial policy lies on the promotion and establishment of higher value added, technology intensive industries. From the beginning, foreign investors have been courted to transfer technology intensive production facilities to China.[194] Foreign investors introducing new technologies or establishing R&D facilities in China have been able to receive the greatest benefits in form of tax exemptions, special import/exports rights, access to the domestic market, etc.

China's industrial policy does not stop with the selective promotion of FDI projects. Rather, the domestic enterprise sector is the most important target of these policies. Enterprises thought to posses the potential to become global players have been promoted by a number of preferential policies. These 'national champions' have enjoyed a wide range of special policies and direct support measures (Nolan, 2001, Nolan and Zhang, 2002).

From this heavy handed industrial policy approach, China has upgraded its industrial capacities much faster than if market forces alone would have been at play. Any positive short-term effects of this policy, however, are endangered by long-term repercussions resulting from such 'growth engineering'.

5.2.2 Downside Risks to China's Economic Development

How sound are the foundations of China's remarkable growth process? Four areas of concern stand out.

(a) The Dismal Banking Sector – State Owned Enterprise Sector Nexus

The greatest risk to the development process is probably the poor performance of the banking sector and its dismal relationship with the state owned enterprise sector. The banking sector is highly successful in attracting savings but the allocation of these savings to investment projects undertaken by state-owned enterprises is not always the more efficient one.[195] The banks are still pushed to finance projects that are deemed socially necessary but yield no commercial rates of return. As long as such projects are financed by the banking sector the problem of soft budget constraints persists – enterprises are not concerned with the profitability of their business activities and banks have no incentive to diligently monitor and restrict their credit outlays. As a result, a large share of credit allocated by the banking sector has turned into non-performing loans and is not recoverable. Estimates of the costs of bailing out the Chinese banking sector range from 30-58 % of China's 2000 GDP (OECD, 2002) to 41 % of the 2003 GDP (Goldman Sachs, 2003).[196]

Bailing out the banking sector and establishing a firewall separating policy loans from commercial banking activities can be only one, albeit inefficient, measure to solve this problem. Further efforts addressing the reform of the banking system include the need for banks to run on a commercial basis, meet prudential requirements, establish risk control procedures, etc. It is also necessary to transform the state-owned enterprises – which are not only the main recipients of bank credit but also the main source of non-performing-loans – into commercial entities. These enterprises must be

---

[193] According to a recent European Commission report (European Commission, 2004) some of the areas of concern include: state interference, corporate governance, property rights and bankruptcy regime, and the financial sector.

[194] Li (1988), and Hiemenz and Li (1988) show that relative factor prices have been manipulated in favour of capital, resulting in a higher capital intensity of foreign invested enterprises production than would comply with local factor endowments.

[195] In the last two decades China's savings rate has been in the range of 35-43 % of GDP.

[196] Although substantial progress has been made in recent years many challenges remain. No real breakthrough can be expected while the nexus between the banking sector and a not really accountable state-owned enterprise sector remains in existence.

confronted with a threat of dissolution if they become insolvent. Such a threat, however, cannot be credible if these enterprises are not freed from the implementation of tasks that belong to the domain of government.

(b) An Irreconcilable Gap between Labour Supply and Demand

China's abundant (unskilled) labour supply is the key to its successful transformation into the world's manufacturing power. At the same time it constitutes a threat to sustainable socio-economic development for as long as the supply of labour exceeds the demand for low-cost labour by such a wide margin as today. At the moment, China is barely able to contain the excess supply of unskilled labour at a level acceptable to society.

According to some estimations the rural sector could be sheltering a high unemployment number (around 150 million people).[197] The state-owned enterprise sector could also be harbouring a large reservoir of hidden unemployment. To raise enterprise competitiveness, these employees must enter the open labour market. Due to the restructuring process speeded up by China's accession to WTO up to 5 million people may be shed by China's state-owned enterprise sector annually over the near term while the demand for labour in the agricultural sector is falling dramatically.[198] China is also facing a demographic shock which will lead to an increase of its population aged 15-64 years at least until the year 2015 (see Box 5.1). This shock alone amounts to a net enlargement of the Chinese labour market by three times the equivalent of the total German labour market during the next 10 years.

The political task to create an environment in which such an enormous number of new jobs can be created year by year is momentous. The promotion of private initiative (domestic as well as foreign) will be of decisive importance if the phenomenon of open unemployment is kept in dimensions that are still socially accepted. The recent ideological upgrading of private property as well as the continued encouragement of FDI indicates the political will to strengthen such private initiatives. The concept of a heavy handed discretionary industrial policy and the idea to create 'national champions', however, raises doubts in how far the funda-

mental elements of competition-driven economic development are in place.

A pertinent question concerns the market where the products manufactured by the Chinese workforce will be made available. Domestic demand is the main destination and with growing affluence of the population it will expand in coming years. An export to GDP ratio of 31 % in the year 2003, however, indicates that the world economy is also a very important net indirect employer of Chinese labour. Without the enormous international demand for Chinese goods the economic miracle could give way to severe unemployment and poverty. Given the insufficient state of China's social security net serious social unrest could become a likely scenario.

(c) Regional Disparity: How much is too much?

The policy of regional differentiation has been an important factor in economic developments in China. It has freed entrepreneurial acumen, concentrated scarce resources in those regions able to put them to best use and established a new form of inter-regional competition. After 25 years of economic transformation and policies of openness, however, it becomes obvious that these positive effects have been purchased at a high price. There is no significant intra-China pattern according to which booming coastal provinces would transfer industries and value chain segments no longer profitable in their locations to the less developed hinterland. Instead the development gap is widening and the distribution of income is becoming increasingly more inequitable. The Gini coefficient has been estimated at 0.45 for 2002, up from 0.4 in 1998. In 2002 the level of per-capita income in the richest province was more than ten times that in the poorest one (Prasad, 2004).

The key to these developments relates to self-enforcing effects that have improved further the location advantages of those regions first to enter the present growth path. Net-capital flows have been moving from the West to the East, where the rate of return is higher (Zweig, 2002); the Western regions suffer a substantial brain drain as the most skilled and entrepreneurial youth migrate to the East Coast, lured by higher salaries and better living conditions; and an enormous flow of unqualified labour from the poor Westerns regions has been migrating towards the coastal belt too.[199] The

---

[197] Prasad (2004).
[198] See the background paper 'The Challenge to the EU by a Rising Chinese Economy,' prepared for the 2004 edition of the *European Competitiveness Report*.

[199] While per capita income seems to be converging within each region, the two regions show a diverging development pattern (see Aziz and Duenwald, 2001). Besides income disparities, the delivery of public services also favours the richest provinces. Local governments –particularly in the poor provinces- experience difficulties in financing basic services thus contributing to perpetuating regional disparities. This situation is partly a reflection of the system of intergovernmental fiscal relations introduced in 1994. The transfer system, designed to compensate local governments for revenue lost to the center and promote equalization across provinces, clearly is in need of reform (see Prasad, 2004).

'Great Western Development Strategy' launched in 2001 is one of the policy initiatives designed to address the problem of regional disparity.

(d) State Capitalism and Corruption: Learning from the Asian Crisis?

China's policy of creating 'national champions' by means of selective support measures and an accommodating regulatory policy as well as institution building recalls memories of unsustainable industrial policies in Korea and South East Asia, which eventually led to the dramatic events of the 'Asian crisis' in 1997-1998. China's 'national champions' policy coexists with a highly underdeveloped competitive system. The allocation of resources and the resulting industrial structures are to a considerable extent not the outcome of market processes but rather of political fiat. This has inevitably led to corruption.

During the transformation process numerous functions in the administrative apparatus have become superfluous and the structures of personal influence and power have been altered considerably. Many of those having lost discretionary power and influence now occupy management positions in the corporate sector, thus becoming a new bridge between the corporate sector and the government. This interface threatens the long-term performance of China's economic system in so far as it becomes a gateway for corruption and strengthens the political leverage on the corporate sector. In recent years reports of corrupt behaviour have become a regular feature of the Chinese media, revealing the omnipresence of corruption which has already been permeating all areas of social and economic life in China.

Besides the imbalances discussed above, there are other important risks affecting the Chinese economy. In particular, the rapid economic development of the last decades has come at a steep cost to China's environment. And with economic development, population growth and higher living standards, the amount of primary energy consumed will increase in the future (despite technological improvements and reductions in energy intensity). The authorities are beginning to take seriously the need of environmental regulation. But the efforts are being partly countered by weak law enforcement and by the low levels of central government funding for environmental protection (well under the level that Chinese experts claim is necessary to prevent further deterioration).

5.2.3 Development Prospects

Prospects for continued robust economic growth in China appear to be very favourable. The key determinants of growth will continue to be in place over the foreseeable future and the institutional setting is characterized by increasing incentives for performance and entrepreneurial initiative.

Cheap unskilled labour will remain the foremost asset. The steady influx of unskilled labour from the rural areas of Western China will allow China to uphold its competitive advantage in the field of labour-intensive manufacturing. However, skilled labour (in the fields of engineering as well as management) continues to be a scarce resource. Skilled labour already commands prices similar to those in the industrialized world. Skilled workers' bottlenecks could hamper China's economic expansion in coming years even as domestic demand takes the leading role in the growth process.

Although significant, it is likely that the risks to China's economic future will be at least in the short term contained. A stronger and better structured economy will eventually contribute to correcting distortions accumulated during years of sectorally and regionally unbalanced development. But even though high economic growth would make possible the reduction of various imbalances (non-performing-loans, arrears in the financing of the social security system), structural reforms in the banking sector and in the pension system, among others, need to be addressed in order to secure the way towards sustainable economic growth.

Though short-term risks appear to be manageable, there is a danger of setting up structures that might impede longer term economic performance. The lack of a workable competitive system combined with a heavy-handed industrial policy and widespread corruption bode ill for the creation of industrial structures that are to guide China's economic prospects in the coming decades. The danger of a new substantial misallocation of capital is high. Foreign investors may exercise influence but in view of distorted incentive structures FDI will also contribute to a sub-optimal allocation capital.

5.3 China in the global division of labour and China's economic relations with the EU

The ascendancy of China in the global economy amounts to a formidable challenge to established patterns of specialisation and division of labour. China has increasingly become a destination for foreign direct investment in the developing world and has turned into a manufacturing centre for a wide range of products. As a consequence, China is absorbing large quantities of intermediate products that are inputs for its export production. As China will likely upgrade its industrial structures in the foreseeable future it will inevitably further strengthen its position in global trade.

Economic links between China and Europe have intensified in recent years, in part to take advantage of China's favourable production facilities and growing domestic markets.[200] However, China's broadening competence in industrial manufacturing is exerting significant competitive pressures on EU industrial economies and especially on those of the new Member States and candidate countries.

In the EU during a quarter century since the beginning of China's transformation process key events bringing about a significant reorganization of the European economies' structure have been (i) the single European market and (ii) the transformation of the Central and Eastern European economies into market economies. Both have provided business opportunities for European enterprises allowing them to take advantage of cost differentials and easy access to markets. This has contributed to rationalization and concentration of business activities across a wider Europe. Nevertheless, European enterprises have also expanded their activities in China and China-EU economic links have intensified. This has led to China becoming the most important non-European trading partner of the EU second only to the US and the most important one in Asia in 2002.[201]

5.3.1 China's Position in Global Trade

General Features of China's Foreign Trade[202]

At the onset of China's reform era its foreign trade was determined by the amount of goods available for export; i.e. exports basically constituted the residual item between domestic production and consumption. Since then China has converted its export structure into one determined by a price system based on relative scarcities.[203] China' exports integration in international trade has

increased significantly in recent years, gaining market shares in most of the broad product groups and enjoying the highest growth rates in IT products (Table 5.1). Exports have soared, making China globally the fourth largest exporter (see Table 5.2) and third in terms of merchandise imports. Strong demand from China has contributed to raising prices for commodities and raw materials and has stimulated global growth.[204]

China's high share of exports in GDP of 31 % in 2003, remarkable in itself for a large country, is partly a reflection of China's extensive export processing activities which correspond to about half of China's foreign trade. China is importing unfinished products which are then processed in labour-intensive processes and subsequently exported as finished or further processed products, thus generating high import and export volumes. The contribution of these processing activities to GDP is, however, comparatively low.

European Trade Relations with China

Trade between China and the EU has expanded at great speed since China's re-orientation of policy in mid 1970s (see Graph 5.1). China's importance for Western Europe is primarily as a market to source imports more than as an export market. While the share of China in extra-EU15 imports was 7.4% in 2001 up from 2.6% in 1990, the share in extra-EU15 exports was 3% in 2001 up from 1.5% in 1990. This unbalanced trade structure has led to the emergence of deficits in the China-EU trade. While exports from the EU to China have grown annually at 9 % over the period 1995-2002, West European imports from China have grown faster, at an annual rate of 14.4 %.

More detailed data by product groups suggest that the trade balance of EU-15 with China worsened between 1996 and 2002 in nearly all of the broad product groups. The only exception to this among the biggest industries is trade in chemicals where improvement was caused primarily by the soaring Chinese demand for intermediary goods - see Table 5.3.

There are several reasons for the import surge and the worsening of the EU-China trade balance:

1. China is implementing a vigorous export-oriented strategy and, in terms of trade balance movements, this has contributed to offsetting imports from the EU with its own exports.

[200] Detailed accounts of the developments in Chinese-European economic relations can be found in Taube (2002), and van den Bulcke et al. (2003).

[201] According to Eurostat, the Chinese dominance is based on the large EU import volume from China. In terms of exports Japan is still the most important European partner in Asia.

[202] Different trade statistical sources are used knowing that they are often not directly comparable (for example, regarding trade volume Chinese Customs Statistics measure direct trade only, while Eurostat includes the flow of goods via third countries as well). The additional information gained by accessing different sources justifies such a procedure.

[203] China abstained from foreign borrowing during the Maoist era and was virtually (foreign) debt free in the early 1980s. See Kamm (1989) for an account of China's foreign trade reform in this period.

[204] China accounts for around 24% of world growth during the period 2001-2003 (Prasad, 2004).

Table 5.1: China's Share in World Merchandise Trade by Product Groups 2001

Product groups (NACE)	2001			Annual average growth of exports	
	OECD exports*	China's exports		1996 - 2001 in %	
	€ billion	€ billion	Share of OECD trade in %	OECD	China
Total trade	3,806.17	297.2	9.2	4.1	10.2
Of which:					
Food products, beverages and tobacco	195.42	14.6	8.8	1.3	3.0
Textiles and textile products	199.86	60.6	35.7	3.0	5.8
Leather and leather products	46.85	17.1	43.0	4.8	7.3
Wood and wood products	39.38	2.6	7.7	1.6	8.6
Pulp, paper and paper products; publishing and printing	72.88	1.6	2.6	-1.2	7.5
Coke, refined petroleum products and nuclear fuel	118.48	8.4	8.4	6.3	7.3
Chemicals, chemical products and man-made fibres	337.86	14.9	5.2	5.4	6.3
Rubber and plastic products	111.06	3.0	3.2	4.0	10.2
Other non-metallic mineral products	76.76	5.4	8.3	4.3	6.0
Basic metals and fabricated metal products	226.89	18.1	9.4	1.0	5.1
Machinery and equipment	503.91	14.9	3.5	2.5	15.8
Office machinery and computers	138.49	26.3	22.4	5.1	30.4
Electrical machinery and apparatus n.e.c.	264.59	28.2	12.5	5.0	19.0
Radio, television and communication equipment and apparatus	109.65	26.5	28.5	7.8	18.9
Medical, precision and optical instruments, watches and clocks	118.64	7.6	7.5	5.8	9.0
Transport equipment	433.48	10.1	2.7	5.2	15.6

*Exports include OECD plus China and Hong Kong exports and exclude intra-EU exports.

Source: UN World Trade Database; WIFO; own calculations.

Table 5.2: Share in World Merchandise Trade by Region, 2003

	Export				Import		
	Rank	US$ billion	%		Rank	US$ billion	%
Germany	1	748.4	10.0	United States	1	1305.6	16.8
United States	2	724.0	9.7	Germany	2	601.7	7.7
Japan	3	471.9	6.3	China	3	412.8	5.3
China	4	438.4	5.9	France	4	388.4	5.0
France	5	384.7	5.1	United Kingdom	5	388.3	5.0
UK	6	303.9	4.1	Japan	6	383.0	4.9
Netherlands	7	293.4	3.9	Italy	7	289.0	3.7
Italy	8	290.2	3.9	Netherlands	8	261.1	3.4
Canada	9	272.1	3.6	Canada	9	245.6	3.2
Belgium	10	254.6	3.4	Hong Kong	10	232.6	3.0

Source: WTO; own calculations.

Graph 5.1: Development of EU-China Trade, 1980-2002

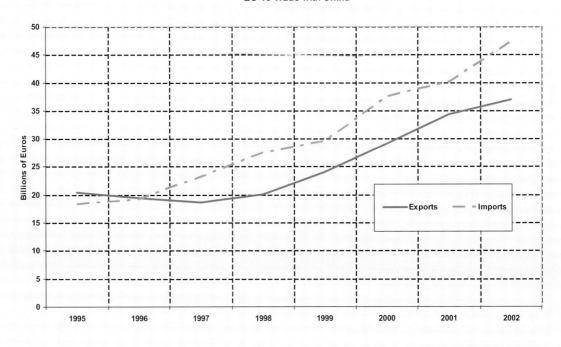

EU-15 Trade with China

Source: UN World Trade Database; WIFO; own calculations.

2. Growth of European investment projects in China. As more and more enterprise ventures entered into production in the 1990s, they not only became important suppliers for European imports but also increasingly substituted European exports as firms gradually entered the local market. At the same time, foreign enterprises in China are also major buyers of European capital goods, and this makes it nearly impossible to ascertain the net effects on the bilateral trade balances of economies like the UK and Germany.

3. The rise of export processing business in China has led to a redirection of European import flows in China's favour as production facilities have moved from Hong Kong, Taiwan and South East Asia to China. Imports which until then had been classified as originating from those countries now originate in China.

4. The surge of imports from China to the EU has to a considerable extent been boosted by EU assistance measures. China was included in the EC's System of Generalized Tariff Preferences (GSP) in 1980 and has since become one of its greatest beneficiaries.[205] The value of imports to EU member countries from China that fell under the GSP in 1995 amounted to 53.6 % of total EU imports from China. Since then the EU has been phasing out GSP preferences towards China. According to recent data China is still the main beneficiary with a share of more than 30 % of all EU imports eligible for GSP preferential rates. In addition, export subsidies and a distorted price structure, at least until the middle of the 1990s, had enhanced the price competitiveness of some Chinese exporters in a way that seemed to warrant the label 'dumping' and made China the target of numerous anti-dumping measures by the EU.[206]

5. China has a long tradition of protecting domestic industries thought to be unfit for international competition (Fukasaku and Lecomte 1998, Shirk 1994). These measures have constrained European sales to China and have adversely affected bilateral trade balances. However, under its WTO commitments China has been reducing the level and dispersion of its average tariff and its non-tariff barriers. Satisfactory compliance will minimize the impact of protected domestic industries on EU exports to China.

---

[205] The GSP scheme has been designed in order to strengthen the export activities of developing countries in the markets of the developed industrialized countries.

[206] For a detailed discussion of the role of anti-dumping measures in the Sino-European trade relations see Strange (1998), Carzaniga (1997), Fu Donghui (1997).

Table 5.3: EU-15 Trade with China by Broad Product Groups

Product groups	Exports		Imports		Trade balances		
	2002	Growth[a] 1996-2002	2002	Growth[a] 1996-2002	2002	1996	Changes 1996-2002
	€ million	in %	€ million	in %	€ million	€ million	€ million
Total manufactured products	37,016	8.9	47,389	14.5	-10,373	1,992	-12,366
Of which:							
Food products, beverages and tobacco	546	-2.8	1,097	2.2	-551	-277	-274
Textiles and textile products	696	10.0	6,810	8.6	-6,114	-3,455	-2,658
Leather and leather products	452	13.7	2,537	9.0	-2,085	-1,201	-884
Wood and wood products	251	38.8	587	4.5	-336	-405	69
Pulp, paper and paper products; publishing and printing	1,101	20.3	248	17.7	853	223	630
Coke, refined petroleum products and nuclear fuel	59	25.6	338	3.4	-279	-256	-24
Chemicals, chemical products and man-made fibres	4,867	15.9	2,955	5.5	1,912	-297	2,209
Rubber and plastic products	513	23.0	1,517	14.7	-1,005	-460	-545
Other non-metallic mineral products	358	6.1	755	9.8	-397	-155	-242
Basic metals and fabricated metal products	2,938	12.4	3,019	8.4	-81	-426	345
Machinery and equipment	11,450	4.1	4,379	21.7	7,072	7,542	-471
Office machinery and computers	942	33.6	6,556	31.3	-5,614	-1,313	-4,301
Electrical machinery and apparatus n.e.c.	2,961	13.0	2,826	22.0	135	382	-246
Radio, television and communication equipment and apparatus	3,088	4.8	5,988	23.4	-2,900	289	-3,190
Medical, precision and optical instruments, watches and clocks	2,236	17.5	1,293	14.6	943	34	909
Transport equipment	4,308	8.8	1,938	30.9	2,369	2,092	277

[a] Average annual growth rate.

Source: UN World Trade Database; WIFO; own calculations.

Regarding China's relations with the former COMECON countries and Turkey, the absolute volumes of bilateral trade are markedly smaller than those with Western Europe. Furthermore, developing a trading relation with these countries met obstacles in the form of structural rigidities, political dependencies and ideological principles in the COMECON group. Only a decade after the dissolution of the eastern block was it possible for these nations to embrace a systematic development of economic relations with China. On the export side, the intensity of interaction with China is even smaller than on the import side.

5.3.2 The Role of FDI Inflows in China's Economic Development

FDI is one of the most important mechanisms for transferring technology and knowledge internationally. Such inflows have been playing a central role in China's economic development during the last two decades. Foreign invested enterprises (FIE) have been the driving force in the modernization of China's industry, providing it with new technological and organizational know how as well as access to new markets.[207]

China has been extremely successful in attracting FDI, becoming since the early 1990s the prime destination in the developing world (See Graph 5.2).[208] China has been absorbing 20-25 % of all FDI directed towards developing countries and a multiple of the FDI the whole African continent has been able to attract. In comparison to the East European economies China has also been attracting by far more FDI - see Graphs 5.3 and 5.4.

---

[207] For earlier discussion on this topic see Lemoine (2000) and Development Bank of Japan (2003).

[208] It should be noted that this upswing of FDI inflows to China coincides with a general increase in global FDI flows to developing countries. According to UNCTAD data average annual flows directed towards developing countries in 1990-1993 were double those of 1987-1989.

Box 5.2:   The Institutional Foundations of the Chinese – European Economic Relations

The institutional foundations of modern Chinese-European economic relations have already been laid in 1975 when the EC and China established diplomatic relations and recognized the People's Republic of China as the only government of China. Since then relations have improved and the institutional framework has been continuously evolving and improving.

Milestones in EU-China Relations

1975	May	Diplomatic relations established
1978	April	EC and China sign Trade Agreement
1980	January	EC includes China in its Generalized System of Preferences (GSP)
1980	November	First meeting of the EC-China Joint Committee for Trade
1983		Launch of first EC-China Scientific Programme
1984		Launch of first EC cooperation project in China (business management training and rural development)
1985	May	EC and China sign Agreement on Trade and Economic Cooperation
1988	October	Delegation of the European Commission opens in Beijing
1989	June	Tian'anmen Square incident. EC freezes relations with China. A number of sanctions are imposed
1992		Most EC-China relations are normalized. Embargo on arms trade remains in force
1993	October	European Commission opens office in Hong Kong
1994	June	New bilateral political dialogue opens between EU and China
1995	July	Strategy paper 'A Long Term Policy for China-Europe Relations'
1995		First project of European Investment Bank in China
1996	March	First Asia-Europe Meeting (ASEM) with participation of EU and China
1998	March	Policy paper 'Building a Comprehensive Partnership with China'
1998	April	First EU-China Summit
1998		EU classifies China as 'non non-market economy'
2000	May	Conclusion of bilateral negotiations on China's accession to the World Trade Organisation
2000		European Chamber of Commerce in China established
2001	June	Communication 'EU Strategy Towards China: Implementation of the 1998 Communication and Future Steps for a More Effective EU Policy'
2003	October	Policy paper 'A Maturing Partnership – shared interests and challenges in EU-China relations'
2003	October	Chinese government releases its first policy paper towards the EU

Source: European Commission.

Two thousand has been an important year in the history of bilateral economic relations with the establishment of the European Chamber of Commerce in China and the conclusion of the bilateral negotiations on China's accession to the World Trade Organisation. Since then, bilateral institution building has gathered speed. Following an evaluation of the 1998 policy paper, the EU published in 2001 a Communication in which the EU's China-strategy was discussed. The European concept of a 'constructive engagement' of China was further strengthened in a policy paper published in 2003. In direct response to this paper China published its first policy paper on its relation with the EU.

The economic dimension of bilateral relations is central to political developments and lays the foundation for improvements in bilateral relations in other policy fields. At the same time the political process has provided a very strong institutional basis for economic exchange in all areas and at the beginning of the 21st century has consolidated the respective importance of China and the EU as key partners (Algieri, 2002).

China's success in the attraction of FDI is mirrored by the important role Foreign Invested Enterprises (FIE) are commanding in terms of industrial production. The share of FIE in China's industrial output has risen dramatically in recent years and today they produce about one third of China's gross industrial value. The distribution of China's FDI inflows to various sectors, however, does not follow market parameters alone, but has been and still is rather heavily regulated by the Chinese government. The 'Foreign Investment Industrial Guidance Catalogue' outlines in which industries foreign investors are welcome, restricted or not permitted. FIE have an especially strong impact on the production of electronic and telecommunication equipment (73 % share of industrial output), office machinery (62 % share), leather and sports goods (both over 53 % share of industrial output), furniture (47 % share), as well as garments and plastic products (both with a share over 42 %).

European FDI in China and Europe's trade with FIE in China

The bulk of China's FDI inflows has been undertaken by the overseas Chinese community. Hong Kong, Taiwan and South-East Asia have been the most important investors in China. The Triad economies of the EU, Japan and the USA each have accounted for only about 10 % of all China-bound FDI.

During the five year period 1998-2002 only about 1 % of Europe's FDI flows have been directed towards China.[209] Even if potential distortions in the data related to investments executed by affiliates of European companies registered in Hong Kong, Singapore, etc., are taken into consideration, European FDI in China is very moderate especially in view of the total size of European economies.

The comparatively weak presence of the European economies in China can, to a large extent, be explained by historical developments in Europe itself. European integration, German re-unification

and emerging possibilities to access the East European markets, has absorbed substantial amounts of capital and management capacities that otherwise might have been allocated to ventures in China. Nevertheless, the absolute volumes of China-bound FDI flows have multiplied in recent years. For example, British enterprises' FDI in China amounted to only US$ 71.6 million in 1985 but rose to US$ 895.8 million in 2002. In the same period German FDI flows rose from US$ 24.1 to US$ 928.0 million, while French enterprises committed US$ 32.5 million in 1985 but US$ 575.6 million in 2002 to activities in China – see Table 5.4.

The growth of European investment in China mirrors the path of China's market transformation and its opening to the world economy. The 1980s, characterized by a wait-and-see attitude, reflected institutional obstacles in China's FDI regulations (Taube, 1997). A change occurred towards 1992, when it was clear that the party leadership was strongly committed to China's integration in world markets, and global and European FDI flows to China increased markedly. Since then the institutional environment has continued to improve while China's entry to the WTO has, generally, provided further stimulus to European FDI. However, a reduction in European FDI flows occurred in 2002, reflecting various economic factors but also a preoccupation with the prospective enlargement.

---

[209] European investment projects, however, are on average more technology intensive than those from Hong Kong, Taiwan and South East Asia in general. As such they are making a larger contribution to China's industrial upgrading than the latter. A detailed discussion of European FDI in China can be found in van den Bulcke et al. (2003).

Graph 5.2: FDI Inflows to China 1978-2003 (US$ billion)

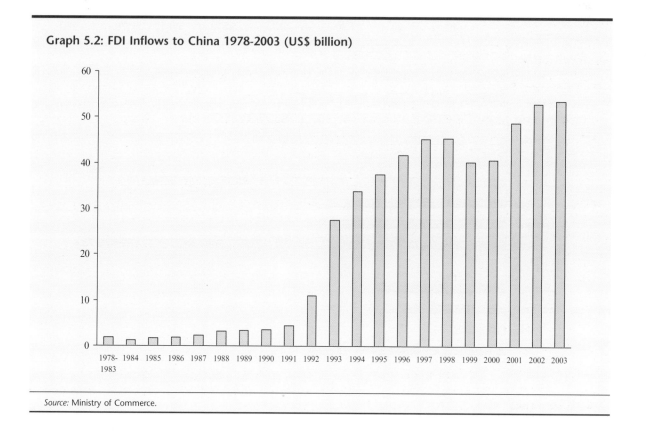

Source: Ministry of Commerce.

Graph 5.3: Foreign Direct Investment Attraction by Selected Economies, (FDI Inflows 2002, US$ million)

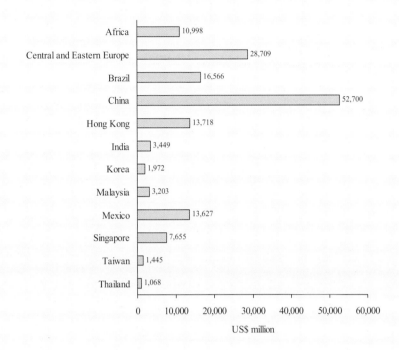

Source: UNCTAD (2003); own calculations.

Graph 5.4: Foreign Direct Investment Attraction (FDI Stock to GDP, 2002)

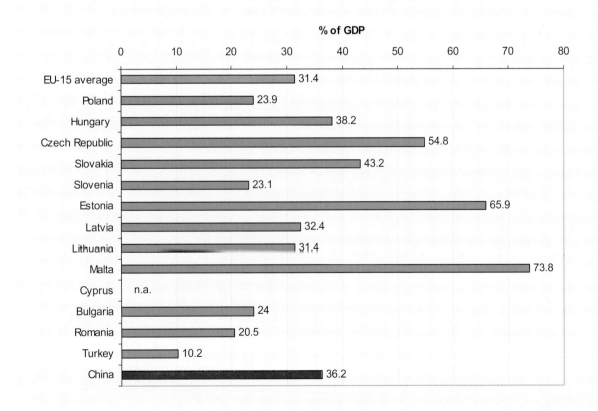

Source: UNCTAD data.

Table 5.4: European FDI Flows to China, 1994-2002, (US$ million)

	1994	1995	1996	1997	1998	1999	2000	2001	2002
Austria	10.10	18.65	16.75	74.61	21.13	23.17	22.59	57.78	67.27
Belgium	31.83	54.07	45.49	33.26	28.04	83.22	56.16	20.02	124.28
Denmark	1.65	35.35	28.85	16.81	62.66	84.91	49.46	56.38	71.09
Finland	1.18	4.86	7.10	4.95	39.30	67.65	59.83	73.71	64.65
France	192.04	287.02	423.75	474.65	714.89	884.29	853.16	532.46	575.60
Germany	258.99	386.35	518.31	992.63	736.73	1,373.26	1,041.49	1,212.92	927.96
Greece	0.05	1.02	-	-	0.30	0.03	12.89	7.31	6.17
Ireland	-	0.90	10.03	0.30	-	3.05	0.76	1.29	13.22
Italy	206.16	263.31	166.94	215.04	274.57	187.44	209.51	219.98	176.74
Luxembourg	1.44	10.29	10.26	1.00	11.51	4.22	23.44	28.78	13.53
Netherlands	111.05	114.11	125.11	413.80	718.82	541.68	789.48	776.11	571.75
Portugal		1.36	6.32	4.89	8.67	8.31	3.40	26.02	9.76
Spain	10.18	26.32	20.73	38.81	53.83	17.54	34.00	33.89	92.24
Sweden	24.18	13.56	56.69	42.81	133.42	155.80	159.24	84.39	99.80
United Kingdom	688.84	914.14	1,300.73	1,857.56	1,174.86	1,044.49	1,164.05	1,051.66	895.76
EU-12	1,415.28								
EU-15		2,131.31	2,737.06	4,171.15	3,978.73	4,506.51	4,479.46	4,182.70	3,709.82
Czech Rep.	3.32	7.29	10.42	4.98	5.07	14.07	9.75	4.87	15.69
Hungary	3.71	3.06	3.93	5.67	10.73	12.04	10.65	21.53	20.73
Poland	1.86	1.57	3.38	0.94	0.94	3.54	4.64	3.67	3.67
Norway	2.31	1.53	26.79	6.46	25.92	18.59	24.10	6.22	28.99
Switzerland	70.54	63.53	187.61	215.67	228.82	247.09	194.03	205.44	199.80
World	33,766.5	37,520.5	41,725.5	45,257.0	45,462.7	40,318.7	40,714.8	46,877.6	52,742.9

Source: National Bureau of Statistics, Ministry of Commerce.

Early European FDI to China has been motivated primarily by low costs and less by the size and potential of China's market. Consequently, a considerable share of FIE production has been exported. However, more liberal FDI regulations resulting in better access to the Chinese market (especially in the service sector), and rising incomes are gradually changing the character of European FDI as new investment opportunities are exploited. Market seeking FDI is becoming more important and is expected to gain a further impetus following the WTO accession.

Reflecting the resource-oriented character of many investment projects, a considerable share of the EU trade with China is conducted with FIE located in China amounting to around 50 % of the EU-15 trade with China – see Tables 5.5 and 5.6. For the FIE sector, however, the EU represents no more than about one seventh of total FIE trade. The share of FIE exports to the EU in total Chinese exports to EU has continuously risen and from 1998 on FIE exports have become larger than imports – see Graph 5.5. Today, exports by Chinese FIE to the EU surpass FIE imports from the EU by a wide margin, reflecting growth rates differentials in FIE absorption of European capital goods and machinery and in EU imports of light industrial products from China.

EU exports to China are largely dominated by capital goods, especially machinery imported by local enterprises to establish or upgrade production facilities. While such exports have been directed to customers in China irrespective of their ownership structures (state, collective, domestic private or foreign) and therefore have been able to evolve in an early stage, most EU imports from Chinese FIE are founded in complex, long-term business relationships. A considerable share of these imports concerns intra-firm trade, according to which EU enterprises are sourcing inputs or final products from their Chinese affiliates. Another part concerns (European or third-country) Original Equipment Manufacturers (OEMs) which have relocated their manufacturing plants from a third country (e.g. South East Asia or Eastern Europe) to China in order to benefit from lower production costs and continue to supply their European customers from this new production base. Accordingly, the marked increase in FIE exports to the EU mirrors the establishment of large production capacities by resource seeking FIE beginning in 1992 and likely to continue further following the 2001 accession to WTO.

Table 5.5: Imports by FIE from the EU to China, 1991-2003

	FIE imports from the EU, US$ million	Total FIE imports, US$ million	FIE imports from EU in % of total FIE imports	Total Chinese imports from EU, US$ million	FIE imports from EU in % of total Chinese imports from EU
1991	2,347	16,908	13.88	8,402	27.93
1992	3,229	26,387	12.24	9,802	32.94
1993	6,399	41,833	15.30	14,108	45.36
1994	7,875	52,934	14.88	16,939	46.49
1995	14,913	62,943	23.69	21,254	70.17
1996	11,381	75,604	15.05	19,868	57.28
1997	10,615	77,720	13.66	19,192	55.31
1998	11,220	76,717	14.63	20,715	54.16
1999	12,496	85,884	14.55	25,465	49.07
2000	16,623	117,273	14.17	30,845	53.89
2001	18,577	125,863	14.80	35,723	52.00
2002	18,943	160,272	11.82	38,543	49.15
2003	26,041	231,914	11.23	53,062	49.08

Source: Ministry of Commerce, Chinese Customs Statistics.

Table 5.6: Exports by FIE from China to the EU, 1991-2003

	FIE exports to EU, US$ million	Total FIE exports, US$ million	FIE exports to EU in % of total FIE exports	Total Chinese exports to EU, US$ million	FIE exports to EU in % of total Chinese exports to EU
1991	457	12,047	3.79	6,739	6.78
1992	713	17,360	4.11	7,601	9.38
1993	2,894	25,237	11.47	11,692	24.75
1994	3,714	34,713	10.70	14,580	25.47
1995	4,821	46,876	10.28	19,090	25.25
1996	7,030	61,506	11.43	19,831	35.45
1997	9,136	74,900	12.20	23,811	38.37
1998	11,523	80,962	14.23	28,148	40.94
1999	12,660	88,628	14.28	30,211	41.91
2000	17,300	119,441	14.48	38,193	45.30
2001	19,277	133,235	14.50	40,904	47.13
2002	23,946	169,936	14.09	48,210	49.67
2003	39,514	240,338	16.44	72,155	54.76

Source: Ministry of Commerce, Chinese Customs Statistics.

5.3.3 Assessing China's Competitiveness

The Competitive Edge of China's Export Industry

China's reform process and rapid economic development have gone in parallel with a notable shift in China's revealed comparative advantages (RCA).[210]

While resource-intensive, low-tech and labour-intensive products were core exports during the 1980s, by 1995 China's export structure had already changed significantly, notwithstanding strong and even growing competitiveness in traditional Chinese products such as textiles, clothing and leather.

Foreign trade developments indicate that China's competitiveness has improved more widely since the mid-1990s. RCA indices for selected industries suggest that positive RCA values are not restricted

[210] In this section, the RCA index is used as a proxy of a country's unobserved comparative advantage and thus as a proxy of a country's international competitiveness. To the extent that the index is sensitive to government strategies and policy actions it might not be a good proxy for competitiveness. Still, it is a widely used index and that justifies its use here.

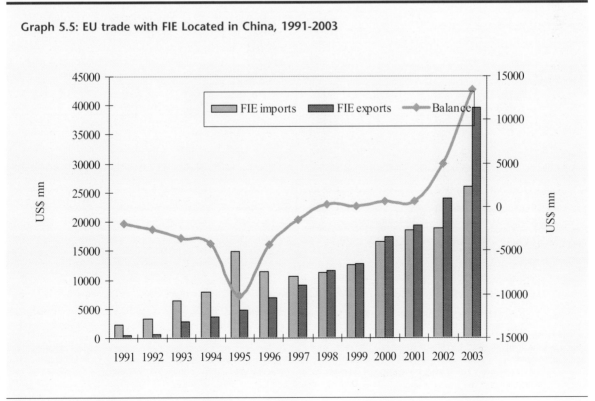

to agricultural and labour-intensive products only but also apply to some medium-tech and more capital intensive products. Also, there have been RCA (competitiveness) improvements in industries supplying more complex products, such as information and communication technologies (See Graph 5.6, upper panel). Even in machinery and equipment products where China has been strongly dependent on foreign technology negative RCA values are improving.[211]

Some of the sectors showing a strong trade performance are sectors where output from FIE represents a high share of the total sector's production (e.g. telecommunication equipment 73%, office machinery 62%). As mentioned, European FDI flows to China have traditionally been resource oriented, and presumably some of these flows respond to multinationals' strategy of splitting up production processes and reallocating them across countries in order to benefit from international labor arbitrage.[212] It is thus probable that China's RCA evolution in modern sectors is partly driven by vertical FDI; i.e. by multinationals-linked plants specializing in those parts of the production processes intensives in low-medium skill labor. In order to adequately illustrate this fact a more disaggregated data analysis would be needed.

---

[211] In transport equipment the improvement is driven by efficiency seeking subcontractors to the major brands of the automotive industry.
[212] Therefore contributing to improve EU firms' competitiveness.

Box 5.3: Revealed Comparative Advantage

The Revealed Comparative Advantage (RCA) index measures the relative export performance by country and industry. It is defined as the share of a country's exports of a certain product in the total exports of this country divided by the share of the exports of this product by the world in the world's total exports. The result is transformed in a natural logarithm and multiplied by 100. The index takes a positive (negative) value if the first ratio is higher (smaller) than the second. A positive value indicates a revealed comparative advantage, i.e. relative strong export performance, of a country in the said good.

The RCA index takes the form:

$$RCA = 100* \ln\left(\frac{x_{i,j}}{X_i} : \frac{x_{i,w}}{X_w} \right)$$

with: $x_{i,j}$ denoting exports of product i by country j
$x_{i,w}$ denoting exports of product i by world
X_i denoting total exports of country i
W_w denoting total exports world

Raw materials and intermediary goods are among the product groups characterized by declines in RCA values (Graph 5.6, lower chart). The negative RCA values for pulp and paper, coke and refinery products appear to reflect primarily the increased internal demand which has contributed to diverting production away from exports. It is also a reflection

Graph 5.5: EU trade with FIE Located in China, 1991-2003

Source: Ministry of Commerce, Chinese Customs Statistics; own calculations.

249

Graph 5.6: Dynamic Development of China's RCA (NACE 2-digit level)

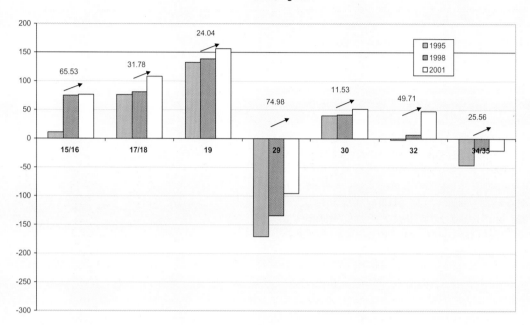

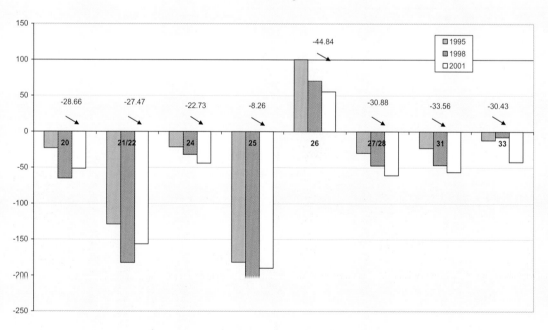

Description of the NACE categories:
15/16 Food and beverages - 17/18 Textiles, apparel - 19 Leather products - 20 Wood products - 21/22 Pulp, paper, media products - 24 Chemicals - 25 Rubber and plastics - 26 Non-metallic minerals - 27/28 Basic metals and metal products - 29 Mechanical engineering - 30 Computers - 31 Electrical engineering - 32 Electronic components, IT-consumer goods - 33 Optical instruments, measurement-, process control equipment - 34/35 Transport equipment.

Source: ECD, UN World Trade Database, WIFO; own calculations.

Graph 5.7: Dynamic Development of EU-15's RCA (NACE 2-digit level)

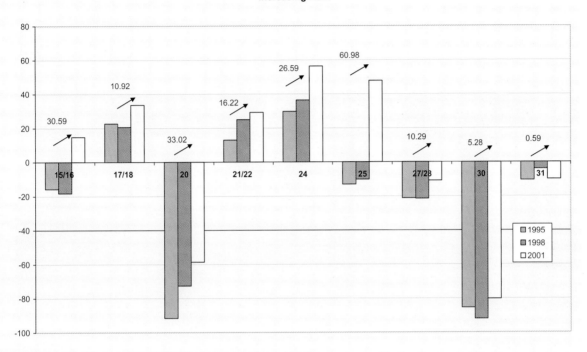

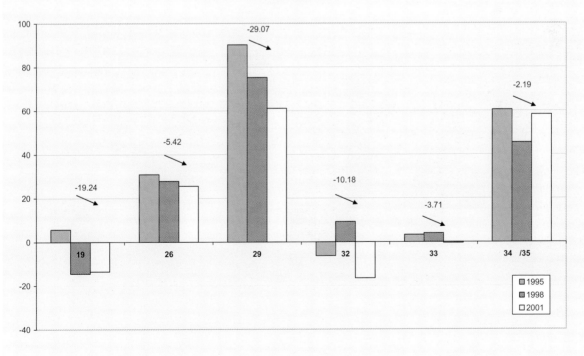

Source: OECD, UN World Trade Database, WIFO; own calculations.

Graph 5.8: Dynamic Development of the new Member States' RCA (NACE 2-digit level)

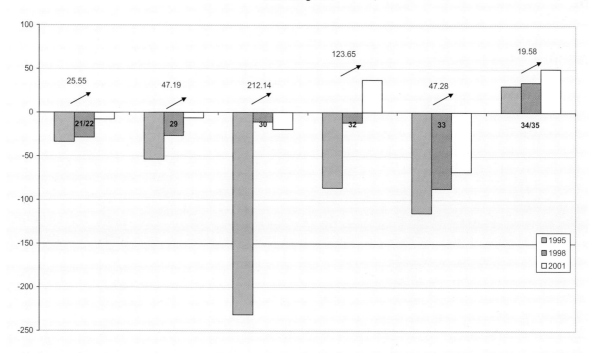

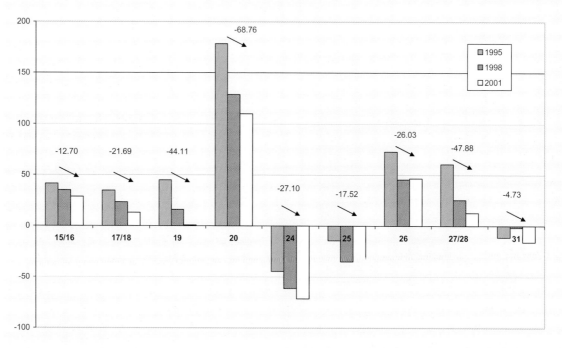

Source: OECD, UN World Trade Database, WIFO, own calculations.

of growing downstream capacities which provide an opportunity to processing intermediary products thus gaining a higher proportion of the overall value added of final products.

There is a degree of complementarity between developments in China's and the EU-15's RCAs - compare Graphs 5.6 and 5.7. In most areas where China shows decreasing trade competitiveness the EU-15 shows gaining revealed advantages. One of the few exceptions is textile and clothing products. The improved situation for European producers in this market reflects the strength of high-end products and luxury brands. However, the data reveal weakness in areas in which Europe possesses an outstanding position in international markets, such as in the manufacture of transport equipment and machinery (see Graph 5.7, lower chart). This reflects to an extent growing imports of low value added intermediate goods but also the impact of the integration of the new Member States into the EU-15 manufacturing networks.

Since the mid-1990s the new Member States have improved their trade performance in machinery and transport equipment (see Graph 5.8). Among those sectors with declining RCAs are textile, clothing and leather products, branches in which the new Member States had performed strongly in earlier times but currently are unable to compete against low-wage countries in Asia.

The Competitive Challenge to the new Member States

The challenge posed by Chinese industrialization is of particular importance for the new Member States. The similarity of trade structures could be a good indicator of the market competition they are facing (see Box 5.4 for the definition of the similarity index). The underlying assumption is that the EU-15 is the most important market for exports of the Czech Republic, Poland, Hungary and Turkey and they face competition from China in this market.

The structures of trade to the EU-15 of the three largest new Member States are quite homogenous. At the 3-digit level the similarity of trade indices range between 55 and 59 and at the 2-digit level the range is somewhat higher between 62 and 67 - see Table 5.7. In contrast, EU trade with China greatly differs from EU trade with any of the new Member States. Exports from Hungary and China to the EU show the greatest similarity while Turkey's export pattern to the EU differs the most from that of China's.

Hungary's exposure to China's challenge is partly a reflection of its success in attracting FDI in the

---

Box 5.4: Similarity Index

The Similarity Index takes the form:

$$S = \sum \min (S_i^{ad}, S_i^{bd}) \, 100$$

with i	denotes	products group i
$a, b, d,$		country $a, b, d,$
S_i^{sd}		percentage share of product i in exports of country a to d

The Similarity Index measures the similarity of country a's exports to country d with that of country b's exports to country d. Here, 'country d' is the EU-15. The index may take values running from 0 to 100. A complete identity of export structures would be equivalent to an index value of 100. The index values are dependent on the level of aggregation, usually recording smaller values the more disaggregated the sectors or products are.

---

manufacture of IT equipment, investment which led to large exports of these products. While initially IT was not important in Hungary's exports, these products accounted to 13 % of its exports to the EU by 2001. This is the highest IT share among exports from the new Member States and compares well with the share of 15 % of IT equipment in China's exports to the EU in 2001.

A comparison of trade shares for the period 1996-2001 shows that product groups which gained in Chinese exports also gained shares in exports from the new Member States, in particular, of the Czech Republic and Hungary - see Table 5.8. This might be a typical pattern in industrialization and market growth, but it also indicates that there is a growing competition in markets for more sophisticated products.

For Poland and Turkey the opposite has occurred, with both experiencing declines in the share of competing products. In the case of Poland this has been caused by strongly growing exports of internal combustion engines which do not play an important role in Chinese exports. Moreover Poland is a leading exporter of furniture, a peculiarity among new Member States that has increased over time. The low similarity index in the case of Turkey is to a large extent caused by a poor regulatory environment which inhibits foreign direct investment, especially efficiency seeking FDI. This suggests that Turkey's declining exposure to Chinese competition is primarily a reflection of a lagging industrialization process.

Table 5.7: Similarity of Trade Structures of Selected Economies (Exports to EU-15 in 2001: SITC 2-digit and SITC 3-digit Level)

2-digit	3-digit	China	Czech Republic	Hungary	Poland	Turkey
China		x	41.69	49.96	38.65	30.37
Czech Republic	57.62		x	58.00	58.97	36.13
Hungary	60.51	62.71		x	55.37	34.10
Poland	54.70	67.29	62.39		x	43.71
Turkey	44.77	44.05	40.22	50.05		x

Source: Own calculations based on OECD data.

Table 5.8: Selected Economies' Direct Competition with Chinese Exports into EU-15 in the Ten Most Important Product Groups

	Share in 1996*	Share in 2001*	2001-1996 change in percentage points
Czech Republic	1.92	9.04	+7.12
Hungary	16.17	21.05	+4.88
Poland	10.13	4.36	-5.77
Turkey	29.42	11.77	-17.65

* Percentage share of competing product groups in percent of respective economies' total exports to EU-15.

Source: OECD; own calculations.

Factor endowment and trade patterns

Mature industrialized countries face a challenge from emerging economies which have especially a labour cost advantage. Therefore technological progress and investment in human capital are key strategies for industrialized countries.

Graph 5.9 shows exports to the EU by quality of labour inputs for 1995 and 2002.[213] Across the three sub-regions (new Member States, candidate countries and China) there is a notable improvement in the quality of labour input between the two dates. For China, the share of products which require high-skill labour has grown by around 70 % between 1995 and 2002 to a share of 20 % of exports in 2002 while the share of products of low-skill industries fell by ten percent-points to less than 30 %. These developments point at growing competitive pressure for human-capital intensive industries which used to be less exposed to competition from low-wage countries. One example of growing import penetration in the EU-15 by China concerns IT products.

Exports of the new Member States and candidate countries to the EU-15 are considerably different from those of China. Although the share of high-skill industries in total exports has grown during this period it has still remained much lower compared to China's. In 2002, for example, such exports from the more advanced new Member States reached 12 %, which is about half of that of China. Instead, industries employing medium-skilled blue-collar workers advanced reaching more than 30 % of total exports from new Member States to the EU. This reflects in part FDI in the new Member States especially in the automotive sector. The share of qualified blue-collar skill exports from China grew only proportional to their overall exports to the EU.

The share of low skill-labour industries shrank in all exports. And while the share of low-skill products in China's exports is comparable to that of the new Member States, in the case of the candidate countries this share is in excess of 60 %. Exports of textiles and apparel are of major importance in this skill category and most originate in Turkey.

Graph 5.10 presents another classification of exports of the same countries based on industry characteristics. Products are grouped according to (i) technology with high R&D content (ii) capital intensity (iii) labour intensity and (iv) marketing-

---

[213] For clustering industries by labour quality and by endowments factor inputs the WIFO categorization has been applied, see 2003 Competitiveness Report.

driven, mostly consumer goods. A fifth residual group comprises all other industries.

The data show a remarkable growth of exports in technology sectors. This group comprises computers and telecommunication equipment as well as life science products, measurement equipment and transport equipment (the latter category being accountable for much of the new Member States' technology driven exports). Furthermore, new Member States and candidate countries exports of computers and telecommunication equipment show strong growth but for the time being these shares are still small compared to China's.

Marketing driven exports from the three regions have generally lost some of their importance over the period under consideration, reflecting to some extent a flat consumer demand growth over much of the past decade. China's strength here reflects marketing-driven exports of articles such as games, toys, sports goods and the like.

Capital intensive industries are predominantly process industries which mostly manufacture intermediary goods. Pulp and paper production, man-made fibres, most of the chemical products, the manufacture of construction material and basic metals are within this category. Exports of these goods have generally lost some of their importance, reflecting flat demand in the EU and in part relocation of production of, for example, textiles fibres overseas.

As shown in Graph 5.10, the share of exports from labour intensive industries varies between one third and one fifth of total exports to the EU, being more important for candidate countries than for new Member States and China. The most important product group here is wearing apparel but also handicraft products and labour intensive assembled machinery and transport equipment.

Finally, the residual category groups most of the engineering industries and products of different

Graph 5.9: Exports to the EU by Labour Quality Indicators (% of manufacturing exports to the EU-15)

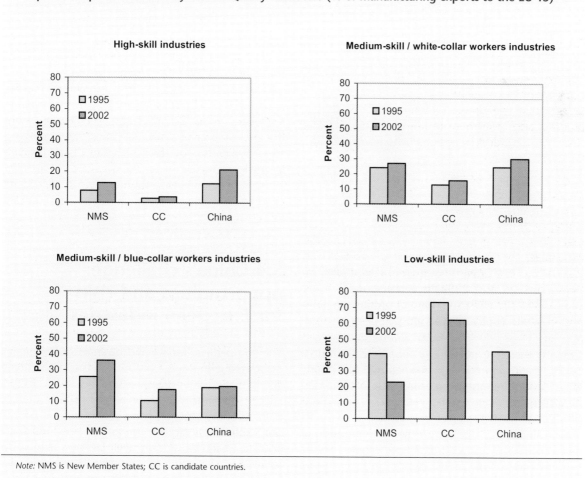

Note: NMS is New Member States; CC is candidate countries.

Source: WIFO; own calculations.

Graph 5.10: Exports to the EU by Input Endowment Indicators (% of manufacturing exports to the EU-15)

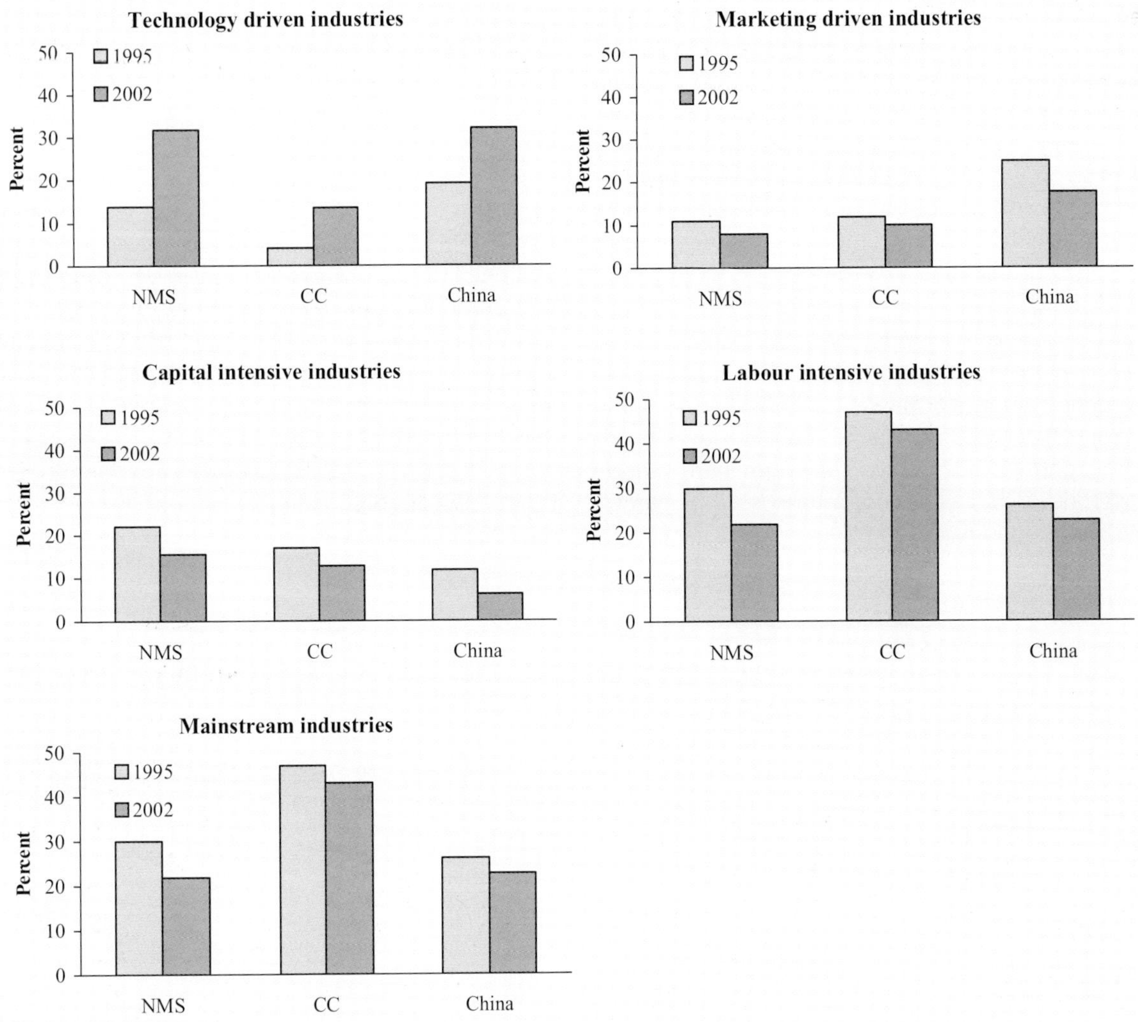

Note: NMS is New Member States; CC is candidate countries.

Source: WIFO; own calculations.

materials. These mainstream industries make up nearly half of the candidate countries' exports to the EU but the shares of the new Member States and of China have shrank to around 20 % in 2002.

China is therefore not only a supplier of industrial goods manufactured with inexpensive and poorly skilled labour but also of so-called technology-based high-tech products. Hence, China's competitive position in global market relates not only to its labour abundance but also to the modernization of its industrial structures. Thus, China's challenge has become increasingly more complex in recent years and its exports could adversely affect a broad range of industries in the EU.

5.4 China's challenge: opportunities and risks for European industries

The competitive impact and business opportunities associated with the rise of China in the international economy will differ greatly across industries. Sector-specific differences in protection of EU and China's markets against foreign competitors are only part of the explanation. Equally important are industries-specific characteristics as well as the degree to which the production process (the value chain) can be (is) divided across national boundaries; the latter being one indicator of how much local industry may be affected by developments in other regions of the world.[214]

China has entered the global markets with increasingly sophisticated products that require a certain level of labour qualifications and production technology. Beyond the textile and apparel industry, which has been at the forefront of China's success in exports markets, the present section reviews trends and developments in the area of high tech products, such as telecommunication equipment and computers; of electrical and non-electrical machinery such as the engineering industry;[215] and in the chemical industry, one of the most important in the EU and one that has seen an improvement of its trade balance with China during the latter half of the 1990s.

5.4.1 Information & Telecommunication Industry

This industry comprises a wide range of products which as a common denominator are based on an application of electricity.[216] Specifically, it includes: 1) office machinery and computers; 2) electronic parts and components necessary for the manufacture of the whole product range of information and telecommunication equipment, and products for the final demand;[217] and, 3) precision, medical, and optical instruments, measurement, testing and industrial process control equipment, watches and clocks.[218] With the exception of some product groups within the third category, the industry supplies information and telecommunication (IT) equipment.

The IT industry has been dominated by global competition in technology where a certain specialization among regions has occurred. The US has emerged as the predominant actor in computers and the Internet and it is leading in IT software development (not included in industrial output as defined above). Its industrial policy has been successful to ensure the US a lead in the manufacturing technology for the total value added chain in electronics. Europe is ahead in telecommunication technology, in digital fixed networks as well as in

mobile networks. Japan took over the lead in consumer electronics from Europe during the early 1970s. This was a success based on technological progress and the availability of cheap labour in the early years of Japan's industrial development. During the 1980s relocation of assembling operations of consumer electronics began and South-East Asia became a centre for this labour-intensive production.

The IT industry is still dominated by the industrialized economies. Technological leadership as well as the largest share of value added to the global industry' output is generated here. Only about one sixth of manufacturing value was created in the developing world in 2001. But it is this industry that is leading in the international division of labour. Most of the assembly of consumer goods including handsets has been carried out in low-wage countries. The area of gravity was in South-East Asia but during the latter half of the 1990s China has become increasingly important.

In the future, not only the assembly but also the upstream production of high-tech components is expected to expand at significantly higher rates in the developing than the industrialized world – with China playing a particularly important role. According to a recent World Bank study (IFC, BAH, 2003) China had a share of 8.1 % (51.7 %) of global (developing economies') IT production in 2001. Its share in newly added production value until 2005, however, is expected to amount to 33 % of the global total and 77 % of that of the developing world. Nearly half of all high-volume assembly is expected to be done in China in the year 2005. China is becoming the hub of electronics manufacturing in the developing world and is a key step in the value chain of many electronic products.

Development Trends in China

China's electronic industry as well as the domestic market for electronic goods has developed spectacularly in all segments since the 1990s. The build up of production facilities, however, has shown quite different patterns with productivity levels increasing much faster in mobile handsets and PCs and peripherals than in the field of consumer electronics.[219] The

---

[214] Taking the trade/sales ratio as a proxy for this phenomenon it may, for example, be argued that the automotive sector with a trade/sales ratio of 42 has much less global leverage than for example the consumer electronics industry with a ratio of 118 (McKinsey, 2003).

[215] Chapter 4 of this report analyzes the Chinese challenge for EU car industry.

[216] The sector includes products in NACE 30, 32 and 33.

[217] Such as valves, tubes, semiconductors, integrated circuits in the first group, and equipment for the investment in telecommunication networks needed by operators and the whole range of consumer electronics in the second group.

[218] Electrical engineering products (NACE 31) are mentioned below as part of the sector engineering industries since many of the products are closely related to mechanical engineering (NACE 29). Household appliances are also mentioned in the engineering section.

[219] The Chinese mobile phone market has become the largest worldwide, commanding a share of about one quarter of total global sales in 2003. FIE, which in the late 1990s were dominating the market to nearly 100 % are being squeezed out by domestic companies who are profiting from heavy handed government support. According to Chinese sources, the share of Chinese companies in the market for mobile handsets has raised from 5 % in 1998 to 43 % in 2002 and Chinese government plans this share shall rise up to 80 % in 2005. European companies who are key players in this market are most affected.

reason for this is the relative importance of FDI for the respective industries. Resource-seeking FDI designed to produce in China for the global markets have been highly welcome and have benefited from tax and other incentives. In contrast, market-seeking FDI, meant to produce for the domestic market have been largely discouraged. This pattern also relates with the strength of domestic industry at the beginning of China's opening. While there existed virtually no IT industry before the entry of foreign investors, China had its own (stated-owned) producers of brown and white goods.

Since government bodies and entrepreneurs are not content with a high dependence on foreign knowledge and marketing strategies, they have started to develop their own new systemic technologies[220] that provide, at the same time, an indirect means to protect domestic enterprises from foreign competition in the home market. The government's industrial policy has had a crucial impact on the development of the IT industry, an industrial policy aimed at supporting domestic chip manufacturing and offering tax and other incentives as well as pressing forward to introduce Chinese standards in key areas effectively increasing market access barriers to foreigners. Furthermore, global suppliers in the IT market have been required to reveal the source code of their software and submit their intellectual property to Chinese experts. Despite concerns by foreign firms, it is unlikely that the government will abandon its objective to create a strong national electronics industry with broad access to leading technology.[221]

Thus, China intends to reduce the strong dependence on foreign technology of this industry whose share is more than 18 % of all of the Chinese manufacturing industries in 2002 – see Table 5.9. The share of employment of the electronics industry in China's total manufacturing is comparable to that in the EU-15. As the share of electronics in China's manufacturing output is high this suggests that this industry is very efficient in comparison with other manufacturing industries. In fact, labour productivity is 50 % higher than the average Chinese manufacturing productivity.

Impact on Europe

Today, China's electronics production is already more than four times the size of that of Eastern Europe and these volume advantages occur in all segments of the value chain. The advantage is lesser in production equipment and semiconductors, two segments that are also less important in terms of production value for both regions. Production equipment and the related process technology are key technologies to gain technological leadership in semiconductors and their manufacture. This know-how is dominated by US enterprises and it is only in peripheral areas that there are significant suppliers from other countries.[222]

The manufacture of Dynamic Random Access Memories (DRAMs) is a capital-intensive process which usually is not the first step for an emerging country to engage in but it will follow after downstream production has developed. The construction of high capacities for the assembly of electronic components in an industrializing region will attract investment in upstream component manufacturing which means that the construction of plants for the production of memory chips will take place if a certain threshold is met. Currently, China has surpassed this level by far and attracts – supported also by political means – the production of semiconductors.[223]

It is likely that China will cease to be dependent on upstream deliveries for the assembly of electronics since the whole value added chain will be established in China, including the capital-intensive manufacture, to meet at least domestic demand (see EIU, 2003). China will remain dependent on foreign deliveries of production equipment for the manufacture of semiconductors. This suggests that there are only few opportunities for European exports to China. Most promising are those areas in which European companies are technological leaders and a demand for systems and engineering exists. This concerns primarily the installation and upgrading of infrastructure for telecommunication operators.

Already today Europe has a high trade deficit with China. EU-15 imports grew by an average annual rate of more than 25 % over the past seven years, dominated by three subgroups of the electronics industry: computer, telecommunication and consumer electronics – see Graph 5.11. In standardized volume products China has the advantage of

---

220 For example, the mobile phone protocol TD-SCDMA and the EDS system as a DVD standard.

221 Yet there are cases of successful political initiatives in this area. After concerns raised by the EU and the US both bilaterally and in the WTO, China announced the indefinite delayed of the implementation of authentication national standard regulations in the area of wireless local area networks, which were supposed to enter into force on June 2004.

222 Europe has a strong position in production technologies for small-batch manufacture and is on the leading edge in some other processes.

223 According to the EU services information, some EU Enterprises (STMicroelectronic, Infineon and Philips, respectively the 6th, 7th and 10th largest world largest semiconductor manufacturers), have established 7 development centres and manufacturing plants that supply the Chinese market. These are fully owned or are joint-ventures or other technology licensing partnerships.

Table 5.9: Key Data for the Electronics Industry

Indicator	Units	EU-15 2001	New Member States[a] 2001	Candidate countries[b] 2000	China 2002
Value added					
Value	Millions €	178,854	7,779	458	34,309
Share of GDP	in %	3.0	2.2	0.6	2.2
Share of manufacturing industries	in %	12.0	11.7	4.1	18.4
Average annual growth rate 1996 - 2002 [c]	in %	4.9	16.9	-6.2	10.9
Employment					
Numbers	1000	3,274	624	121	3,390
Share of total	in %	2.8	2.3	1.0	0.5
Share of manufacturing industries	in %	11.6	10.4	5.2	12.0
Average annual growth rate 1996 - 2002 [c]	in %	6.8	3.9	-8.6	-5.5
Labour productivity [d]					
Indicator	€ per employee	54,632	12,476	3,791	10,120
Average of manufacturing industries = 100	in %	102.8	107.0	78.7	153.2
Average annual growth rate 1996 - 2002 [c]	in %		12.5	2.6	17.3
Unit-labour costs					
Indicator	€ per €	0.58	0.47	0.76	0.21
Average of manufacturing industries = 100	in %	116.0	98.3	144.0	29.9

a) Czech Republic, Hungary, Poland, Slovak Republic, Slovenia; - b) Bulgaria, Romania; - c) 1997-2000 for candidate countries.

d) Value added per capita.

Source: National Bureau of Statistics, Ifo Institut.

an enormous labour force which will enable China to steadily expand the capacities in this kind of production without major difficulties. This will likely attract further relocation of large-batch production from Europe. The European electronics industry could shift towards a more knowledge-oriented industry exploiting advantages in system engineering and hence stay in the technology lead.

In the recent years, EU production in electronics, especially consumer goods, has become more involved in the final customisation of products and smoothing the impact of volatility in demand on output. This suggests a division in labour between Chinese and European plants along the value chain according to logistic needs. Imports of preassembled components will grow and product specification and final assembly will take place within Europe - close to final customer markets.

The extraordinary growth of Chinese electronics exports to the new Member States, at an annual average rate of more than 50 % between 1996 and 2002, indicates that adjustments to a new form of international division are taking place. In countries such as Hungary and Estonia, which have a stronghold in the manufacture of electronics, structural changes would follow very likely.

However, IT exports from new Member States to the EU-15, at growth rates of more than 25 %, suggest

that the production sites in these countries continue to sustain their importance. The high exposure of the new Member States to low-wage competition in this industry is indicated by the similarity index for exports to EU-15. Compared to China's deliveries to EU-15 the similarity index for total IT goods climbed to 81.5 (Table 5.10), indicating that there are opportunities for substitution of a considerable range of products from the new Member States by China's products. The new Member States and candidate countries will inevitably be obliged to develop alternative advantages in their competition with production locations in China to justify higher wages especially as convergence in real incomes towards EU-15 levels proceeds.

5.4.2 Textiles and Clothing

The textile and clothing sector has traditionally been one of the least liberalised and most highly protected industries in the international economy.[224] Treated as a special case, this sector was exempt from most trans-industry regulations developed under the auspices of the GATT/WTO. A final breakthrough was eventually reached in the

---

224 The industry is defined as including the NACE categories 17.1-17.7 and 18.

Graph 5.11: Chinese exports of electronics and electrical products to Europe

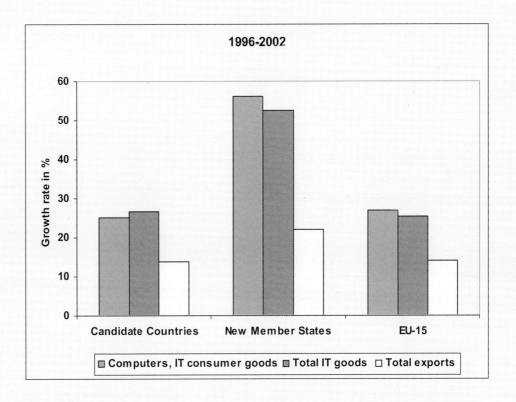

Source: UNIDO, WIFO, Ifo Institut.

Table 5.10: Comparison of Electronics and Electrical Products Exports to EU-15

Origin of products/industry & subgroups	2002 in € million	2002 Share of total exports	1996 - 2002 Average annual growth rate in percent	Similarity Index[a] 1995	Similarity Index[a] 2002
China					
Total IT goods	13837	28.7	25.3		
Computers, IT consumer goods	11927	24.7	26.9		
New Member States					
Total IT goods	15268	14.8	25.7	43.2	81.5
Computers, IT consumer goods	12449	12.1	42.9		
Candidate countries					
Total IT goods	1669	6.2	32.5	52.7	46.1
Computers, IT consumer goods	1549	5.8	34.3		

a) In this table the similarity index is calculated between exports of China and the new Member States to the EU-15 as well as between exports of China and the candidate countries to the EU15; see Box 5.4.

Source: UNIDO, WIFO, Ifo Institut.

Table 5.11: The MFA Phase-out

1993, December	'Agreement on Textiles and Clothing' (ATC) agreed upon in the Uruguay Round final draft act. All MFA and other quotas on textiles shall be phased out in a 10 year period, starting 1995
1995, January 1	1st ATC *tranche* liberalised by importing countries – 16 % of the 1990 import volume
1998, January 1	2nd ATC *tranche* liberalised by importing countries – further 17 % of the 1990 import volume
2002, January 1	3rd ATC *tranche* liberalised by importing countries – further 18 % of the 1990 import volume
2005, January 1	4th ATC *tranche* to be liberalised by importing countries – final 49 % of the 1990 import volume

Note: Quotas not lifted in the first three stages are to be increased on a yearly basis.

Source: Spinanger (1999).

Uruguay Round, when the elimination of the Multi-fiber Agreement and other quotas on textiles for WTO member countries was concluded.[225] This process started in 1995 and will be completed by January 1st, 2005, when 49 % of the quota volumes existing in 1990 are to be eliminated - see Table 5.11. It is also in the last liberalisation phase that the most sensitive products will finally be subjected to WTO principles (Spinanger, 1999). Although the market will be fully liberalized by the end of 2004, WTO members will still have a transitional option to impose quantitative restrictions on China as a result of the safeguard clauses that have been included in the protocol of accession of China to the WTO - until 2008 for the textile specific-clause and until 2013 for the general safeguard clause.

China became a member of the WTO in December of 2001. With the quota reductions under the Agreement on Textiles and Clothing (ATC) applying to WTO members only, China was not able to profit from these liberalization measures directly until the third phase in January 2002. At this moment however the liberalization effect for China had been substantial.

Development Trends in China

China's textile and clothing industry is one of the largest in the world. In recent years the industry has gone through drastic reorganisation designed to increase the productivity of the industry, improve quality standards and increase its global competitiveness. As a result, the number of enterprises as well as total employment declined dramatically while overall output increased substantially.

In recent years a multitude of studies have investigated the effects of China's accession to WTO on its economy,[226] and nearly all suggest that, at least in the short term, the main positive impact of China's WTO accession will result from the textile and clothing industry. Indeed, there is no other industry in which the difference between the level of protection against China's products before and after WTO accession is larger, and no industry in which China's factor endowments can create greater leverage effects in the global division of labour, than textiles and clothing. China does not only possess an abundant labour force, but has a competitive edge in the availability of basic materials for the textile industry. China is the world's largest cotton producer with a one quarter of global production and it accounts for 70 % of the world output of mulberry cocoons and silk materials, and 99 % of the global ramie fibre production (Bhalla and Qiu, 2004).

Impact on Europe

The textile and clothing industry has remained an important segment of EU-15 manufacturing. The industry represents about 7 % of employment in manufacturing and its share in total EU manufacturing value added is about 4 % but decreasing - see Table 5.12.

With the recent enlargement the European textile and clothing industry is experiencing a shock that will induce a substantial reshuffle of industrial and regional specialization. The impact on the European labour market may be large, with a net addition of about one third of the already employed 1,800,000 people in the textile and clothing industry of the EU-15.[227] The greatest challenge however will result from the elimina-

---

[225] The Multifiber Arrangement (MFA) is a trade agreement adopted in 1973 by industrialized countries that set quotas for the amount of textiles and apparel that other countries could export to these countries.

[226] OECD (2002) provides an overview of major studies that use computable general equilibrium models.

[227] According to data from the Viena based WIIW. In recent years, however, substantial relocations of production facilities from the EU-15 to the new Member States have already anticipated a good deal of the structural adaptations that become necessary with the enlargement. The enlargement may strengthen the textile and clothing industry of the EU-15 countries as well as in the new Member States as the business formalities between EU-15 enterprises and their affiliates, subcontractors etc. in the new Member States will become less burdened with transaction costs.

Table 5.12: Key Data for the Textile Industry

Indicator	Units	EU-15 2001	New Member States[a] 2001	Candidate countries[b] 2000	China 2002
Value added					
Value	€ million	59,333	2,764	761	10,799
Share of GDP	in %	1.0	0.8	1.1	0.7
Share of manufacturing industries	in %	4.0	4.1	6.8	5.8
Average annual growth rate 1996 - 2002 [c]	in %	1.8	0.0	-0.7	-4.8
Employment					
Numbers	1000	1,881	663	532	4,100
Share of total	in %	1.6	2.5	4.6	0.6
Share of manufacturing industries	in %	6.7	12.0	23.1	14.5
Average annual growth rate 1996 - 2002 [c]	in %	-3.4	-4.5	-1.0	-9.9
Labour productivity [d]					
Indicator	€ per employee	31,537	4,168	1,432	2634
Average of manufacturing industries = 100	in %	59.3	35.7	29.7	39.9
Average annual growth rate 1996 - 2002 [c]	in %		4.8	0.3	5.6
Unit-labour costs					
Indicator	€ per €	0.50	0.86	1.21	0.46
Average of manufacturing industries = 100	in %	101.0	181.3	231.2	63.9

a) Czech Republic, Hungary, Poland, Slovak Republic, Slovenia; - b) Bulgaria, Romania; - c) 1997-2000 for candidate countries.

d) Value added per capita.

Source: National Bureau of Statistics, Ifo Institut.

tion of import quotas on January 1, 2005 – and thus the competitive pressure arising from the expected greatest beneficiary of this liberalization, China.

The textile and clothing industries in the new Member States has yet to become adequately efficient. Although labour productivity has grown since the mid-1990s by nearly 5 % per annum, it still remains low compared to other manufacturing industries of the regions. Even though this industry laid off 4.5 % of their labour force per year labour productivity is only 36 % of the manufacturing industries and thus even lower than for the Chinese textile industry which is close to 40 %. For the candidate countries the situation appears to be even worse (there are no output and employment data for Turkey however).

After three ATC liberalisation rounds, imports from China to the EU are still subject to strict quota limits. In 2003 out of 42 product groups subject to import quotas 26 have utilized more than 90 % of the quota. This high utilization level indicates that quotas are actually binding and they are suppressing imports from China. Obviously, with the elimination of all import quotas it is certain that European imports from China will increase.

An increase in imports from China will probably not be accompanied by an equal increase in total textile and clothing imports in the EU. At least in the EU-15 markets for textiles and clothing seem to be saturated. In Germany, for example, overall imports of textiles are stagnant, while clothing imports are declining. Therefore, it is likely that imports from China will crowd out other textile producers and exporters with China taking over market shares from them. This process will probably accelerate by an increasing price competitiveness of Chinese exporters which will not only be able to make full use of labour abundance but, from January 1, 2005 onwards, will also save on costs that currently relate to the purchase of export licenses.[228]

---

[228] With these costs amounting to up to 20 % (Jungbauer, 2004) there exist scope for considerable price cuts.

A first glimpse of what might happen in 2005 was provided in 2002 when in the wake of its WTO accession and the 3rd ATC round China was able to increase its exports and expand its market share substantially. At the same time, very significant unit price reductions came into effect. For all product categories liberalised for China under the third ATC stage EU imports increased by 46 % in value and 192 % in volume while prices fell by 50 % on average.[229] Thus besides forcing (always painful) restructuring, the impact on Europe will also translate into lower prices for consumers and a more efficient, less-distorted global division of labour.

The impact of integration of China's textile and clothing industry on the new Member States is likely to be very significant. In 2002 more than 50 % of the total exports of the new Member States were accounted for by textile and clothing –about 90 % was exported to the EU. In 2003, in all but two of the sector's products exported by new Member States China's import quotas were utilized to or in excess of 90 %. The economy facing the greatest challenge could be Turkey notwithstanding its textile industry having a broad basis and good

upstream link. Turkey's most important export goods to the EU ('articles of apparel, of textile fabrics, n.e.c.') are also part of China's top ten exports to the EU-15.

China's exports of textile and clothing goods to EU-15 have grown moderately compared to other industries but imports by the new Member States have been growing strongly while exports to candidate countries have grown at annual rates of less than 5 % - see Graph 5.12. Two sub-groups within textiles and clothing exports – fabrics, knitted and crocheted articles representing around 15 % of EU-15 textile and clothing imports from China – grew markedly stronger than the average.

The three regions (new Member States, candidate countries and China) share a high similarity in trade structure. Already in 1995 the similarity index was above 80 and it further grew to a value above 90 indicating the potential for substitution and price competition between the three regions – see Table 5.13.

There is a possibility to contain the restructuring effect of the integration of China's textile and clothing industry on the EU based on specific safeguards

---

[229] See European Commission, 2003.

Graph 5.12: Chinese exports of textile and clothing products to Europe

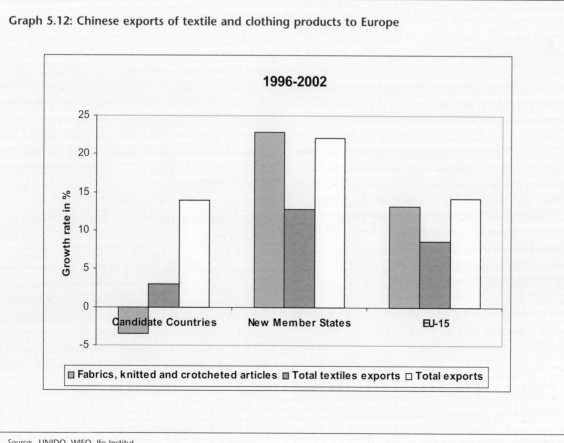

Source: UNIDO, WIFO, Ifo Institut.

Table 5.13: Comparison of Textile and Clothing Exports to the EU-15

Origin of products/industry & subgroups	2002		1996 - 2002	Similarity Index[a]	
	in € million	Share of total exports	Average annual growth rate in percent	1995	2002
China					
Textiles and clothing	6810	14.1	8.6		
Fabrics and knitted apparel	1012	2.1	13.2		
New Member States					
Textiles and clothing	7768	7.5	2.0	82.4	93.0
Fabrics and knitted apparel	1343	1.3	2.2		
Candidate countries					
Textiles and clothing	10927	40.7	6.9	80.2	80.9
Fabrics and knitted apparel	1967	7.3	4.9		

a)   In this table the similarity index is calculated between exports of China and the new Member States to the EU-15, as well as between exports of China and the candidate countries to EU-15; see Box 5.4.

Source: UNIDO, WIFO, Ifo Institut.

providing for limiting imports if an increase causes or threatens to cause domestic market disruptions or result in 'significant trade distortions'. Such safeguard provisions, which may take the form of customs duties or quantitative restrictions, are included in China's WTO accession protocol and were enshrined in Community law by the EU in early 2003. WTO-sanctioned safeguards designed especially for the textiles and clothing industry may be applied until the end of 2008. A further product-specific protection mechanism may be applied until the end of 2013.

China is not only a threat to the European textile and clothing industry but also an opportunity. As EU home markets are at least partly saturated, China is a potential target market for European manufacturers of high-quality products. In acceding to WTO China made substantial concessions about access to its domestic market. In 2005 average customs duties on textiles and clothing will be reduced to 13 %, while quantitative restrictions on the import of particular textile pre-products will be lifted. Growing affluence especially of China's young urban population can be expected to raise demand for high quality clothing and fashion items made in Europe.[230]

It may, however, be the knowledge as well as capital intensive area of technical textiles that will prove to be most interesting for European actors.[231]

European enterprises with their superior knowledge in the production of technical textiles may profit from a booming Chinese economy and its growing demand for technical textiles used in infrastructure and construction projects. Among others, a booming automotive sector can be expected to add further momentum.[232]

FDI must also play an important role to promote European interests in China's market. As such, European FDI in China's textile and clothing industry should not be confined to resource-seeking ventures that seek to exploit China's cheap labour resources. In particular, in the area of technical textiles, where innovation is driven by new technologies, opportunities exist to supply China with textiles important for a broad range of industrial applications and above all for infrastructure projects and construction.

5.4.3 Capital Goods and Engineering Industry

Engineering industries carry out the manufacture of capital goods. They comprise the manufacture of electrical engineering (NACE 31) and of mechanical engineering goods (NACE 29.1-5). These do not only manufacture capital goods for final demand but also intermediary goods, parts and components which are necessary for the assembly of capital

---

230   However, in order to make full use of this market potential both non tariff barriers and intellectual property rights protection issues will have to be thoroughly addressed.

231   This segment includes textiles for the health industries, textiles for chemical applications (barriers against viral infections, news materials such as carbon fibre fabrics, etc). One of the most important areas by volume is textiles for the automotive industry.

232   It is exactly the three product groups mentioned here (high quality products, fashion items, technical textiles) for which a study commissioned by the European Commission (IFM, 2004) suggests Europe as having particular competitive strength.

goods. Most of these intermediary goods, whose share is more than 50 % of the total production volume, are complex and sophisticated products.

Mechanical engineering industries are characterised by a large number of small and medium-sized companies, a size structure that reflects production requirements. Only in some sub-branches are mechanical engineering products suitable for large-scale production (such as roller bearings, earth moving machinery and tractors) and, hence, there are few opportunities for production in which economies of scale could be achieved and large players can gain advantage against smaller competitors.

The structure of the electrical engineering industry differs somewhat. Here, large industrial groups are more important. Some sub-branches have a predominant output of serial products, e.g. controls, primary cells, electric motors etc. Another area where large industrial groups are active in is plant engineering. In these markets large industrial groups do not exploit advantages in economies of scale but are in a better position to raise funds for financing large projects with high contract volumes compared to SMEs.

The engineering industries are part of the metal industry and highly dependent on upstream linkages and the supply of high quality and technologically advanced intermediary products to manufacture high performance products, plants and customized systems. Thus, close industrial linkages provide strategic advantages and support the evolution of regional clusters that enjoy comparative advantages through direct contact between the supplying and procuring plants. This relation even holds in the era of the Internet and e-business because of specific market conditions and product characteristics. Small-scale production requires high logistic efforts which cannot be distributed on a high volume output. The relatively high transport costs hamper long distance deliveries. Therefore, the trade-sales ratio for engineering industries of 30 % (EU-15, US and Japan) is low.

In 2002, two thirds of total EU-15 engineering output was mechanical engineering goods such as machine tools, steel works, precision tools, robotics, etc. (statistics of the German Mechanical Engineering Association). An analysis of major non-EU competitors reveals that the EU is globally in the lead with an output surpassing that of the US and also Japan. The EU is in an outstanding position in the global technology competition. Although some industrial revival has taken place in the US, it

remains well behind European suppliers' state-of-technology in most areas. Competitors from Japan have caught up in many areas and are eager to apply advanced technologies, for instance, new materials and components of IT industries. This area of activity has been identified as the most challenging task for European manufacturers.[233]

Development Trends in China[234]

The industries in question are of outstanding importance for emerging countries because they provide the necessary capital goods. The Chinese government has always had an interest in being, at least partly, self-sufficient and this, even after accession to WTO, has continued to be a factor in the design of industrial policies. Liberalization has led to some restructuring and reform resulting in the abolition of direct control but the agency in charge, the State Administration of Machine Building Industry (SAMB), developed other more complex instruments for the administrative guidance of the companies under its responsibility.

The objective of developing a national machinery industry and upgrading the state of technology has led to a set of regulations guiding the integration of foreign companies in joint-ventures and the execution of major industrial projects. These rules are stringent for large projects. In the case of power plants, foreign deliveries are not allowed for units below a certain threshold. Even beyond that threshold, government approval and a joint venture are necessary prerequisites before a contract will be signed. Further, there exist requirements for the share of local content (Nolan, 2001). Although such an explicit regulation is no longer adequate after the accession to the WTO, implicitly major projects will be handled in line with these or similar requirements. These restrictions will not pose major difficulties for most of the projects which are of interest to global enterprises in the power generating market given the usual size for a plant. The government's plan for the establishment of power plants until the end of the decade will provide many opportunities for foreign companies because China is lagging behind in this technology.

The engineering industries are highly diversified and plant engineering is only one area which has been dominated by specialized companies which pursue a global approach in sales. These compa-

---

[233] See, among others, Kriegbaum et al. (1997), and Vieweg et al. (2002).
[234] See the background study 'The Challenge to the EU by a Rising Chinese Economy' prepared for the 2004 edition of the *European Competitiveness Report* for further details.

Table 5.14: Key Data for the Engineering Industry

Indicator	Units	EU-15 2001	New Member States[a] 2001	Candidate countries[b] 2000	China 2002
Value added					
Value	€ million	182,485	4,126	552	11,933
Share of GDP	in %	2.9	1.2	0.8	0.8
Share of manufacturing industries	in %	11.3	6.2	5.0	6.4
Average annual growth rate 1996 - 2002 [c]	in %	2.8	2.6	-8.6	-2.0
Employment					
Numbers	1000	3,411	554	245	3,230
Share of total	in %	2.8	2.1	2.1	0.4
Share of manufacturing industries	in %	11.2	9.9	10.6	11.5
Average annual growth rate 1996 - 2002 [c]	in %	0.1	-4.7	-13.1	-10.6
Labour productivity [d]					
Indicator	€ per employee	53,499	7,448	2254	3,694
Average of manufacturing industries = 100	in %	101.2	63.9	46.9	55.9
Average annual growth rate 1996 - 2002 [c]	in %		7.7	5.2	9.7
Unit-labour costs					
Indicator	€ per €	0.74	0.78	1.25	0.48
Average of manufacturing industries = 100	in %	142.0	163.1	238.5	67.2

a) Czech Republic, Hungary, Poland, Slovak Republic, Slovenia; - b) Bulgaria, Romania; - c) 1997-2000 for candidate countries.

d) Value added per capita.

Source: National Bureau of Statistics, Ifo Institut.

nies are strongly involved in China but many sub-branches of the engineering industries are dominated by medium-sized enterprises which are specializing in market niches often on a single machining process, such as spinning or weaving, printing or metal cutting. For them it is more difficult to tap into the Chinese market. Although there are success stories of SMEs gaining export contracts for the delivery of manufacturing technology, only few of these companies have ventured on to start their own subsidiary or to become a partner in a joint-venture. In this area, joint-ventures and other associations have not yet become as important as in plant engineering, and domestic engineering industries are lagging behind overall economic trends in China.

Chinese authorities are enacting regulations that require mandatory compliance with national standards and a burdensome and costly conformity assessment procedure. Given the extensive information needed by Chinese laboratories for product testing purposes, concerns have been raised about the protection of intellectual property right of

foreign firms. Compliance with the system places a particularly heavy burden on SMEs.[235]

China's mechanical engineering industry has not gained the importance necessary for an emerging economy with soaring investment activities in new production capacities. Its share on total manufacturing value added is 6.5 %, around 5 percentage points lower than in EU-15 and more similar to the share in new Member States and candidate countries. On the basis of labour productivity, China's engineering industry is highly inefficient even in comparison with other manufacturing industries. Labour productivity in engineering amounts to only 56 % of the average labour productivity in manufacturing which is lower than the corresponding estimated for the new Member States – see Table 5.14.

---

[235] The European Commission has intensified co-operation with the competent Chinese authorities in the field of product certification with a view of obtaining a simplification of the system.

Impact on Europe

During the recent slowdown of global economic growth China has continued to be the only major market for engineering products, and has become one of the largest destinations for capital goods originated in EU-15. Most large European engineering companies are now involved in China. In 2002 the value of exports of engineering products reached € 14.4 billion and the trade surplus with China came to € 7.2 billion.

In some sub-branches of the industry characterized by a high intra-industry trade (machine tools, agricultural machinery, electric motors, insulated wires and cables),[236] intermediary products are procured from China for the manufacture of capital goods in Europe. Although close regional linkages and short-distance transport are an advantage for an industry with predominance of one-piece and small-batch production, there are clearly areas open to overseas procurement for intermediary parts.[237]

---

[236] The Grubel-Lloyd index values are higher than 0.9.
[237] While the intra-industrial trade between China and the EU-15 is high only in some sub-branches, the intra-industrial linkages between the EU-15 and the new Member States are strong in most sub-branches. For a decade, an intense division of labour for the exploitation of the regional comparative advantages has emerged between EU-15 and new Member States companies. A new cluster in the engineering industries has come into view.

The engineering industries as defined by the NACE nomenclature also contain some sub-branches, such as equipment for the distribution of electricity and accumulators, batteries etc. and domestic appliances. Most of these products are manufactured in large-batch and are not to be understood as capital goods. In these subgroups, the EU-15 trade with China shows high deficits, suggesting that the potential challenges for these European industries are above all in the production of serial, large-batch, products.

China's engineering exports have grown strongly since the mid-1990s but exports to the new Member States and candidate countries have grown even faster than to EU-15, in part reflecting the impact of the opening up of these economies to the international trade system – see Graph 5.13. Exports from the new Member States and candidate countries to the EU-15 have grown somewhat slower than those of China since the mid-1990s. Trade structures across the three regions show significant similarities suggesting that there are opportunities for substitution – see the estimates of the similarity index in Table 5.15. This means that price competition is likely to be strong especially in those segments dominated by serial products manufactured in large batches, such as domestic

Graph 5.13: Chinese exports of engineering products to Europe

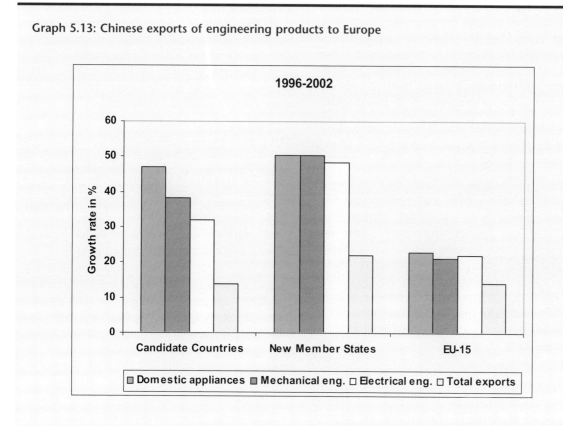

Source: UNIDO, WIFO, Ifo Institut.

Table 5.15: Comparison of engineering exports to the EU-15

Origin of products/industry & subgroups	2002		1996 - 2002	Similarity Index[a]	
	€ million	Share in total exports	Average annual growth rate in percent [a]	1995	2002
China					
Engineering industries	7204	14.9	21.8		
Domestic appliances	1785	3.7	22.8		
New Member States					
Engineering industries	17329	16.8	14.7	87.2	83.7
Domestic appliances	1474	1.4	22.8		
Candidate countries					
Engineering industries	2526	9.4	15.1	88.6	94.1
Domestic appliances	628	2.3	18.9		

a) The similarity index is calculated between exports of China and the new Member States to the EU-15, as well as between exports of China and the candidate countries to EU-15; see Box 5.4.

Source: UNIDO, WIFO, Ifo Institut.

appliances etc. The core of parts and components produced by engineering industries will be less contested.

Undoubtedly, it will be necessary to modernize the outdated and obsolete structures of China's engineering industry and this will inevitably require high investment growth. However, given the government's objective to raise the competitiveness of its domestic companies it will be necessary to depend and to import international technology and know-how. If not, domestic industries compelled to invest in indigenous technology would have to use poor quality and outdated machinery that would undermine their efficiency. This prospect provides interesting opportunities for European engineering firms both in the short- but even in the long-term.

The core of engineering industries is highly dependent on strong inter- and intra-sectoral linkages with companies on the leading edge of technology that can provide high-quality parts and components. These features and the predominant single-unit and small-batch production makes manufacturing production facilities less suited for relocation and thus provide opportunities to build on the advantages of the engineering cluster in the EU. The EU is technologically in the lead in these industries. These considerations suggest that European engineering industries can be attractive partners active in the industrialization of China. To further strengthen the already good position, continuous efforts in R&D and more involvement from medium-sized firms should be encouraged.

5.4.4 Chemical and Pharmaceutical Industry[238]

Most of this industry's products are intermediary goods delivered to a broad range of downstream industries and only in some sub-branches, such as pharmaceuticals and cosmetics, products are dedicated to the final demand. Standardization is very important - nearly all of the industry's output consists of serial products - and many products are commodities sold in international markets. Only in some segments, in particular in life sciences, there are opportunities to gain a unique market position on the basis of product innovation.

Basic chemicals, above all petrochemicals, count for around one third of the total industry output. Life science chemicals, dominated by pharmaceuticals and cosmetics, provide another quarter of the industry's output. This segment is driven by research and development and global technological competition. In particular, genetic engineering has become a driver for product innovation since the early 1990s.

More than 70 % of the chemical industries turnover is supplied by large industrial groups, although more than 90 % of the companies are SMEs. Even in the life science segment global enterprises play a central role.[239] Global competition has induced structural changes in the industry and, in particular,

---

238 The analysis and data refers to products under NACE 24. Other analysis also includes NACE 25 -Manufacture of rubber and plastic products- under the industry.
239 Most of the small companies in genetic engineering are affiliated with the large groups.

the large European groups are increasingly focusing on fewer market segments where they can maintain or gain a leading position.

Most of the global chemical production has been carried out in mature industrialized countries. The Triad economies constitute two thirds of the global supply, with the EU-15 and the USA producing around one quarter each. While the US has gained a strong position in genetic engineering, the European industry is characterized by its broad involvement in all areas.[240]

The trade-sales ratio of the chemical industry is only 35 % indicating that regional clusters are of importance and long-distance trade is hampered by a high weight-price ratio, particularly as it concerns basic commodities.

Development Trends in China[241]

China's chemicals industry is dominated by state-held groups, conglomerates that in spite of all

efforts have been unable to adjust in order to exploit economies-of-scale and scope similar to the large international producers. They command an unaccountably high number of small out-of-date plants. The government has announced plans to shut down these unproductive and environmentally hazardous operations, most of which are run by local authorities.

As a consequence, on average, the chemical industry has remained inefficient in spite of the establishment of efficient new capacities over a period of more than a decade. Data in Table 5.16 show that labour productivity in China's chemicals industry is only a fraction of that of the EU. This suggests that there are opportunities not only for growth but also for broad restructuring of the industry to improve the allocation of resources and ultimately to safeguard the environment.

China is strongly dependent on the imports of raw materials for the chemical industry. It has become a net importer of oil during the 1990s and analysts expect continued high growth until the end of the decade.[242] To sustain high rates of economic growth rates heavy investment in the chemical industry, among others, will be necessary. In partic-

---

[240] The Japanese chemical industry is on the leading edge of technology in the development of man-made fibres, a small segment as measured by its volume, but with strong downstream linkages to the Asian textile industry.

[241] See the background study 'The Challenge to the EU by a Rising Chinese Economy' prepared for the 2004 edition of the *European Competitiveness Report* for further details.

[242] ATKEARNEY (2003), and SRI (2003).

Table 5.16: Key Data for the Chemical Industry

Indicator	Units	EU-15 2001	New Member States[a] 2001	Candidate countries[b] 2000	China 2002
Value added					
Value	Millions €	160,379	4,729	996.9	22,191
Share of GDP	in %	2.7	0.4	1.4	1.4
Share of manufacturing industries	in %	10.7	7.1	8.9	11.9
Average annual growth rate 1996-2002 [c]	in %	11.7	2.6	-4.1	3.7
Employment					
Numbers	1000	1,685	250	115	3,250
Share of total	in %	1.4	0.9	1.0	0.4
Share of manufacturing industries	in %	6.0	4.5	5.0	11.5
Average annual growth rate 1996-2002 [c]	in %	-0.6	-4.6	-11.0	-7.5
Labour productivity [d]					
Indicator	€ per employee	95,194	18,927	8,687	6,828
Average of manufacturing industries = 100	in %	179.1	162.3	180.7	103.5
Average annual growth rate 1996-2002 [c]	in %		7.6	7.8	12.1
Unit-labour costs					
Indicator	€ per €	0.40	0.42	0.44	0.27
Average of manufacturing industries = 100	in %	80.8	89.0	83.6	37.5

a) Czech Republic, Hungary, Poland, Slovak Republic, Slovenia; - b) Bulgaria, Romania; - c) 1997-2000 for candidate countries.

d) Value added per capita.

Source: National Bureau of Statistics, Ifo Institute.

ular, production capacity in basic chemicals can emerge as a bottleneck for many manufacturing industries. Consequently, government plans include the establishment of new capacities and new projects are being developed favouring the growth of the chemical industry.[243]

Most of the newly established capacities are characterized by high capacity per manufacturing unit as compared to Europe or the US. This will enable the exploitation of economies of scale and will strengthen China's position as a location for the manufacture of chemicals. This suggests that the new capacities are not only established for the domestic market but to supply chemical products to other Asian countries (although this may not ultimately be as important in the basic chemicals industry that faces a strong demand from downstream industries). Foreign owned companies have been involved in the set up of new plants by funding investment or participating in joint ventures.

In pharmaceuticals, the Chinese market is characterized by certain peculiarities. There exists a broad market for traditional Chinese medicines but Western pharmaceuticals have taken over 80 % of the market. In volume terms, however, it is estimated that both segments command half of the total market. The traditional market is dominated by Chinese enterprises and about 1,000 of the total 3,300 Chinese pharmaceutical companies produce Chinese medicines.

The liberalization of the pharmaceutical industry has been lagging behind other industries. For the old-state-planned plants, run under control of the public administration, the situation changed only at the end of the 1990s. In contrast, the government has permitted multinational investment in the Chinese pharmaceuticals industry from early on in the reform process. By the mid-1990s, investment had increased to significant levels and all of the top companies had set up joint ventures by that time. Additional stimulus to the restructuring of the pharmaceutical industry was given by the liberalization of enterprise funding.

The Chinese pharmaceuticals market is one of the largest in the world, although expenditure per capita is on the low side. Demand has been dominated by health organizations under public administration subject to an outdated regulatory system. The state-controlled hospitals are run inefficiently and utilization is below 50 %. The government has planned to bring in professional management and shut down many of these facilities. Even more important for the pharmaceutical industry are initiatives to scrap the current distribution system directed by the central government, regional, and local authorities.

Impact on Europe

Most of Europe's international firms have invested in China and are well positioned to benefit from strong growth in that country. The size of the market and China's policy objective not to leave the industry to foreign companies necessitates the establishment of sales subsidiaries and of joint ventures with leading Chinese groups and indigenous production capacities.

In the area of basic chemicals it will be essential to run plants in China where the size of the market provides opportunities to benefit from economies-of-scale. Moreover, as mentioned earlier, production capacity in China can be used to supply other Asian countries. It is likely that an industrial cluster will ultimately emerge that will permit the exploitation of intra-industrial division of labour, with close linkages between plants along the value chain.

Europe has a surplus in its trade with China in these products which in 2002 was € 1.9 billion. Exports to China, which account for around 12 % of total European exports, grew at a double-digit rate between 1995 and 2002 in most sub-branches. Basic chemicals with a share of around 40 % were the dominant products, followed by pharmaceuticals. Exports of basic chemicals, induced by soaring Chinese demand and high economic growth, could weaken if new capacities in China start production. In pharmaceuticals the situation is somewhat different since these are not bulk export commodities but in many cases niche products which are not suited to be produced at different locations simultaneously.

In 2002, the value of China's exports was € 3 billion representing 6 % of total exports. Three small groups are registering high growth, each of them representing 1-2 % of chemical exports: paints and varnishes, soaps and detergents, and man-made fibres. Average growth of the deliveries to EU-15 for the period 1995-2002 was between 28 % and 35 % per annum - see Graph 5.14. Chinese exports to new Member States and candidate countries grew even faster.

Growth in the first group is mainly determined by exports of ink for PC printers; in the second group by intermediary chemicals necessary for life science

---

[243] The gradual loosening up of the financing restrictions, in particular overseas listing has provided opportunities for financing major projects, but it also provides opportunities for foreign players to tap into the Chinese market.

products; and in the third group by basic chemicals necessary for the manufacture of textiles. The three groups encompass above all intermediary goods delivered for further processing. With the exception of ink, these products are mass commodities and growing exports to the EU-15 might be a reflection of excess capacity in China and sales at marginal costs to European chemicals companies.

The chemicals industry in the new Member States and candidate countries represents a smaller share of GDP and employment than in the EU-15 – see Table 5.16. Countries in both regions are strongly dependent on chemicals imports and are recording high deficits in their chemicals trade with the EU-15. There is a trade deficit even for basic chemicals even though new Member States and candidate countries have important production capacities in this area, but the technology is outdated and plants, despite cheaper labour costs, can still not be competitive.

Thus, the chemicals industry in both the new Member States and in candidate countries is encountering difficulties. The industry is neither competitive in comparison with EU-15 production sites nor in comparison with China's plants which, at least as part of joint-ventures or due to FDI, incorporate latest technologies. Table 5.17 presents some basic data. The new Member States' and candidate countries' exports of two of the sub-branches characterized by the highest export growth from China to the EU-15 have shares of 9 % and 26 % in total chemicals exports to the EU-15. Although Chinese exports in these sub-branches are

still small, a continuation of past growth trends will imply further pressure to new Member States' and candidate countries' industries.

Most of the opportunities for the European chemicals industry from the integration of China in the world trade system and the access to the WTO will arise from direct involvement via FDI and own production facilities in the domestic market. Exports are less suited to obtain a strong and sustainable position in this market especially if its size has surpassed a certain threshold.

Despite problems related in particular to respecting of intellectual property rights all the big European chemical producers are already present in China's market. Investment projections suggest plans to benefit from the growth prospects of the economy. However, it will be necessary to strengthen R&D in order to stay on the leading edge of technology. Without state-of-the art technology and products China's bureaucracy will not see the need to invite foreign companies in the domestic market. This will be crucial especially in pharmaceuticals where Europe has a strong position, although the US is gaining the lead in technology with enormous efforts in R&D. In technical textiles European suppliers are on the leading edge and can benefit from China's growth, in particular the necessity to invest in infrastructure.

Finally, note that Europe's trade with Asia could slowdown or even decline if China's growth decelerates and new capacities come into operation. These new Chinese plants will be run at lower

Graph 5.14: Chinese exports of chemical products to Europe

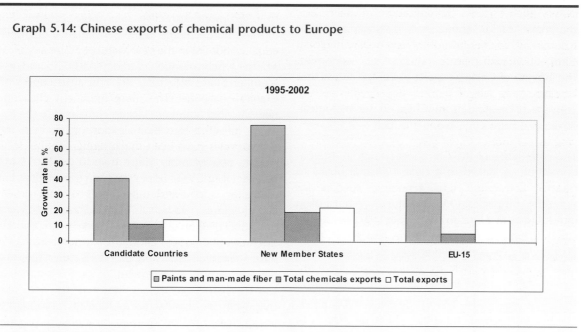

Source: UNIDO, WIFO, Ifo Institut.

Table 5.17: Comparison of Chemical Exports to the EU-15

Origin of products/industry & subgroups	2002 in € million	2002 Share of of total exports	1996 - 2002 Average annual growth rate	Similarity Index a) 1995	Similarity Index a) 2002
China					
Chemicals	2955	6.1	5.5		
Paints & man-made fibres	85	0.2	32.5		
New Member States					
Chemicals	4292	4.2	2.4	71.8	78.6
Paints & man-made fibres	379	0.4	3.2		
Candidate countries					
Chemicals	609	2.3	-2.7	72.6	74.8
Paints & man-made fibres	163	0.6	0.0		

a) In this table the similarity index is calculated between exports of China and the new Member States to the EU-15, as well as between exports of China and the candidate countries to the EU-15; see Box 5.4.

Source: UNIDO, WIFO, Ifo Institut.

marginal costs than older facilities in Europe, in particular in new Member States and candidate countries, making it possible for chemicals, especially intermediary chemicals, from Asia to be exported to Europe. The impact on the price level for chemicals on the international market of a slowdown in Chinese imports is potentially one of the biggest threats for the global chemical industry in the coming years.

5.5 Concluding remarks

Competition from low-wage locations is nothing new for the EU-15 industries which have adapted to ever changing environments, thereby learning that 'soft factors' such as time, customisation, reliability, etc. can make up for labour costs disadvantages. But emerging China has brought a new quality in global competition with mature industrialized economies. The analysis of China's exports to Europe shows that beyond cheap labour there is already competitive pressure originating from China in technological-driven and knowledge-based products.

The emergence of the China's economy in international trade is linked to a clear industrial policy to transfer knowledge into economic success for domestic companies. China has shown an outspoken interest to attract foreign companies to accelerate the catch-up process. However, it has also put in place instruments to prevent domestic companies from takeovers by foreigners by setting upper limits for foreign equity shares and stimulating joint ventures.

For the time being, the main challenge relates to China's advantageous factor, in particular labour,

endowments. This was originally exploited by Chinese companies that played the role of original equipment manufacturers (OEMs) for the world's leading brands and retail labels. The growth of Chinese brand name producers exploiting these advantages will become a major challenge to established multinationals and brand owners affecting to a large extent well positioned EU-15 companies. Driven by the desire to tap the high profit pools of branded products in the industrialized world and being pushed by an ambitious Chinese government, China's OEMs are devising strategies to sell their products under their own brand names.

Faced with China's competition, the new Member States and candidate countries have so far been able to offer more attractive near-shore centres. But further improvements in the performance of knowledge economies in the new Member States as well as a better synchronization of traditional EU-15 and new Member States structures are crucial to cope with China's challenge. The more imminent challenge new Member States are facing, compared to the EU-15, is reflected by China's exports to Europe: the growth rates have been much higher for the deliveries to new Member States than to the EU-15 not only for all industries under review in this chapter, but total exports to new Member States have also grown at higher rates. This reveals that their integration into the global division of labour has made much progress since the mid-1990s, although industrial structures have not yet fully adjusted. Jobs reallocation to China has led to some employment losses, for instance in the Hungarian electronics industry. This indicates that even the manufacture of high-tech products is being challenged by low-cost locations for production of serial products.

Value migration, i.e. the shift of the principal source of value added from one stage to another in a given commercial activity, may guarantee European actors the most profitable segments in the value-added chain if they can maintain the leading edge in R&D to stimulate innovation and exploit comparative advantages in organization, coordination, marketing, logistics etc. Value migration effects on the labour market, however, cannot be a priori determined. As jobs will be lost in traditional production activities, new jobs will have to be created in activities more decisive to meet the challenges from the newly industrializing countries. Such change has been taken place already during the 1990s and has led to an employment structure with a stronger focus in high-skill labour. The final outcome will very much depend on the institutional set up in the economies and their flexibility and capacity to accommodate structural changes. Recent jobs losses in the manufacturing industries is clearly not a promising development in spite of the creation of new jobs with higher qualification requirements in the service sectors. Employment has shrunk in both EU-15 industries and in those in the new Member States.

The opening up of China is not only a challenge; it also provides great opportunities for European companies. Many of the market access barriers have been dismantled during the process of market reforms and with China's access to the WTO the situation has further improved. EU businesses are already benefiting from the size of the Chinese market and its increasing appetite for imports (e.g. capital goods). Also, as European firms have been relocating activities to China in order to profit from its cost advantage (e.g. through vertical FDI carried out by multinationals) they have been improving their overall competitiveness vis-à-vis international competitors. And to the extent that FDI flows are now increasingly turning into market-seeking rather than resource-seeking flows, fears of job losses to a low wage destination as China should be minimized across Europe. Indeed, given China's large market potential, the long-term utilization of the opportunities ought to be exploited above all by indigenous production. Thus, it is not only in the interest of the Chinese administration but also of European companies to substitute part of their exports to China by FDI. The success in this market does not only generate growth but economies of scale which are even more important for large enterprises to protect their strategic position against their competitors in these markets.

Currently, institutional conditions favouring innovations are better in the EU-15 as well as in the new

Member States than in China. But the vast, inexpensive, work force, combined with the development of a knowledge economy provides an excellent basis for offshore centres for the manufacture of a broad range of products and services. The competitiveness of Europe, its capacity to cope with the challenges as well as its ability to make use of the opportunities brought forward by a rising Chinese economy will, to a great extent, be determined by its innovation performance.

References

Algieri, F. (2002): 'EU Economic Relations with China: An Institutionalist Perspective', The China Quarterly, 169, pp. 64-77.

ATKEARNEY (2003): 'Think global act local - Haben wir künftig alle unseren Schreibtisch in China?', Speech of Kreuz, W. at the 4th Handelsblatt Annual Meeting for the Chemical Industry, May, Frankfurt.

Aziz, J. and Duenwald, C. (2001): 'China's Provincial Growth Dynamics', IMF Working Paper WP/01/3, Washington D.C.

Bell, M.W., Khor, H.E., and Kochhar, K. (1993): 'China at the Threshold of a Market Economy', IMF Occasional Paper, No. 107, Washington DC.

Bhalla, A.S. and Qiu, S. (2004): The Employment Impact of China's WTO Accession, London/New York.

Carzaniga, A.G. (1997): The EU's Trade Relations with China: Anti-Dumping Policy and The New Generalized System of Preferences, Brussels.

Development Bank of Japan (2003): 'China's Economic Development and the Role of Foreign-Funded Enterprises', Development Bank of Japan Research Report No. 39, Tokyo.

EIU (2003): Leaping dragons, trailing tigers? Taiwan, Hong Kong, and the challenge of mainland China, London.

European Commission (2003): 'The future of the textiles and clothing sector in the enlarged European Union', COM(2003)649 final, Brussels.

European Commission (2004): 'China/Market Economic Status', SEC(2004)901, June, Brussels.

Donghui F. (1997): 'EC Anti-Dumping Law and Individual Treatment Policy in Cases involving Imports from China', Journal of World Trade, 31(1), pp. 73-105.

Fukasaku, K. and Lecomte, H.-B. (1998): 'Economic Transition and Trade Policy Reform: Lessons from China', in: Bouin, O., Coricelli, F. and Lemoine, F. (eds.), *Different Paths to a Market Economy: China and European Economies in Transition*, pp. 63-86, Paris.

Goldman Sachs (2003): *Six Big Questions About China At Home* (Parts 1-6), Hong Kong.

Hiemenz, U. and Li, B. (1988): 'Zur gesamtwirtschaftlichen Effizienz ausländischer Direktinvestitionen in den Küstenregionen der VR China', Institut für Weltwirtschaft, Arbeitspapier 335, Kiel.

IFC [International Finance Organisation] and BAH [Booze Allen Hamilton] (2003): *Electronics Manufacturing in Emerging Markets*, Washington DC/New York, June, (http://www2.ifc. org/news/ IFC_BAH _study.pdf).

Institut Français de la Mode (2004): *Implications of the 2005 Trade Liberalization in the Textile and Clothing Sector* (http://europa.eu.int/comm/ enterprise/textile/documents/ifm_final_report_2005.pdf).

Jungbauer, S. (2004): *Textile giant China – a challenge for the German textile and fashion industry*, March, (http://www.gesamttextil.de/englisch/Publication/Yearbook2003/E1356.htm).

Kamm, J. (1989): 'Reforming Foreign Trade', in: Vogel. E.F., *One Step Ahead in China. Guangdong Under Reform*, pp. 338-392, Cambridge, London.

Kriegbaum, H., Uhlig, A., and Vieweg, H.-G. (1997): 'The EU Mechanical Engineering Industry - Monitoring the evolution in the competitiveness', Ifo Studien zur Industriewirtschaft, 54, Munich.

Lemoine, F. (2000): 'FDI and the Opening Up of China's Economy', CEPII – Document de Travail No. 11, Paris.

Li, B. (1988): 'Wirtschaftspolitische Rahmenbedingungen und ausländische Direktinvestitionen in der VR China', Institut für Weltwirtschaft, Arbeitspapier 339, Kiel.

McKinsey (2003): *New Horizons: Multinational Company Investment in Developing Economies*, San Francisco.

Nolan, P. (2001): *China and the global business revolution*, Basingstoke.

Nolan, P. and Zhang, J. (2002): 'The Challenge of Globalization for Large Chinese Firms', World Development, 30, No. 12, pp. 2089-2107.

OECD (2002): *China in the World Economy: The Domestic Policy Challenges*, OECD, Paris.

Prasad, E. (2004): 'China's Growth and Integration into the World Economy. Prospects and Challenges', IMF Occasional Paper 232, Washington DC.

Qian, Y. (2000): 'The Process of China's Market Transition (1978-1998): The Evolutionary, Historical, and Comparative Perspectives', Journal of Institutional and Theoretical Economics, 156, pp. 151-171.

Rawski, T. (2001): 'What's Happening to China's GDP Statistics?', China Economic Review, 12/4.

Rawski, T. (2002): 'Measuring China's Recent GDP Growth: Where Do We Stand?', August, (http://www.pitt.edu/~tgrawski/papers2002/measuring.pdf).

Shirk, S.L. (1994): *How China Opened Its Door. The Political Success of the PRC's Foreign Trade and Investment Reforms*, New York.

Spinanger, D. (1999): 'Textiles Beyond the MFA Phase-Out', World Economy, 22/4, pp. 455-476.

SRI Consulting (2003): The Chemical Industry and Technology Opportunities in China, Speech of Intille, G.M. at the 9th Annual China Chemical Industry Conference, September, Shanghai.

Strange, R. (1998): 'EU trade policy towards China' in: Strange, R., Slater, J. and Liming, W. (eds.), *Trade and Investment in China: The European Perspective*, pp. 59-80, London/New York.

Taube, M. (1997): 'Ökonomische Integration zwischen Hongkong und der Provinz Guangdong, VR China: Der chinesische Transformationsprozess als Triebkraft grenzüberschreitender Arbeitsteilung', ifo Institute, Munich.

Taube, M. (2002): 'Economic Relations between the PR China and the States of Europe', The China Quarterly, 169, pp. 78-107, March.

UNCTAD (2003): Trade and Development Report: Capital Accumulation, Growth and Structural Change, Geneva.

Van den Bulcke, D., Zhang, H., and do Céu Esteves, M. (2003): *European Union Direct Investment in China: Characteristics, Challenges, and Perspectives*, London/New York.

Vieweg, H.-G., Dreher, C., Hofmann, H., Kinkel, S., Lay, G. and Schmoch, U. (2002): 'Der Maschinenbau im Zeitalter der Globalisierung und New Economy', Ifo Beiträge zur Wirtschaftsforschung, 9, Munich.

Zweig, D. (2002): *Internationalizing China: Domestic Interests and Global Linkages*, Ithaca-London.

Annex:
Background studies to the European competitiveness report 2004

The European competitiveness report 2004 is based on material prepared by a consortium led by WIFO, the Austrian Institute of Economic Research.

Handler H. and Koebel B. (2004): "Productivity growth and the public sector".

Czarnitzki D., Ebersberger B., Falk M., Fier A., Garcia A., Hussinger K., Mohnen P. and Muller E. (2004): "European productivity, innovation and public sector R&D".

O'Mahony M., Stevens P. and Stokes L. (2004): "Performance in the EU health sector".

Cleff T., Heneric O., Licht G., Lutz S., Sofka W., Spielkamp A. and Urban W. (2004): "The European automotive industry: competitiveness, challenges and future strategies".

Taube M. and Vieweg H. (2004): "The challenge to the EU by a rising Chinese economy".

European Commission

European competitiveness report 2004

Luxembourg: Office for Official Publications of the European Communities

2004 — 277 pp. — 21 x 29.7 cm

ISBN 92-894-8227-3

Price (excluding VAT) in Luxembourg: EUR 35